INDIGENOUS ASPIRATIONS AND STRUCTURAL REFORM IN AUSTRALIA

Can the Australian state be restructured to empower Aboriginal and Torres Strait Islander peoples and ensure that their distinct voices are heard in the processes of government?

This book provides an answer to that question for Australia and provides guidance for all states that claim jurisdiction and authority over the traditional lands of Indigenous peoples.

By engaging directly with Indigenous peoples' nuanced and complex aspirations, this book presents a viable model for structural reform. It does so by adopting a distinctive and innovative approach: drawing on Indigenous scholarship globally it presents a coherent and compelling account of Indigenous peoples' political aspirations through the concept of sovereignty.

It then articulates those themes into a set of criteria legible to Australia's system of governance. This original perspective produces a culturally informed metric to assess institutional mechanisms and processes designed to empower Indigenous peoples.

Reflecting the Uluru Statement from the Heart's call for a First Nations Voice, the book applies the criteria to one specific institutional mechanism – Indigenous representative bodies. It analyses in detail the Aboriginal and Torres Strait Islander Commission and the Swedish Sámi Parliament, a representative body for the Indigenous people of Sweden. In examining the Sámi Parliament the book draws on a rich source of primary and secondary untranslated Swedish-language sources, resulting in the most comprehensive English language exploration of this unique institution.

Highlighting the opportunities and challenges of Indigenous representative bodies, the book concludes by presenting a novel and informed model for structural reform in Australia that meets Indigenous aspirations.

Indigenous Aspirations and Structural Reform in Australia

Harry Hobbs

•HART•
OXFORD • LONDON • NEW YORK • NEW DELHI • SYDNEY

HART PUBLISHING
Bloomsbury Publishing Plc
Kemp House, Chawley Park, Cumnor Hill, Oxford, OX2 9PH, UK
1385 Broadway, New York, NY 10018, USA

HART PUBLISHING, the Hart/Stag logo, BLOOMSBURY and the Diana logo are trademarks of Bloomsbury Publishing Plc

First published in Great Britain 2020

A catalogue record for this book is available from the British Library.

Library of Congress Cataloging-in-Publication data

Names: Hobbs, Harry (Writer of Indigenous aspirations), author.

Title: Indigenous aspirations and structural reform in Australia / Harry Hobbs.

Description: Oxford, UK : New York, NY : Hart Publishing, an imprint of Bloomsbury Publishing, 2020. | Includes bibliographical references and index.

Identifiers: LCCN 2020038488 (print) | LCCN 2020038489 (ebook) | ISBN 9781509940141 (hardback) | ISBN 9781509944040 (paperback) | ISBN 9781509940165 (pdf) | ISBN 9781509940158 (Epub)

Subjects: LCSH: Indigenous peoples—Legal status, laws, etc—Australia. | Aboriginal Australians—Legal status, laws, etc. | Torres Strait Islanders—Legal status, laws, etc. | Law reform—Australia.

Classification: LCC KU519.I64 H63 2020 (print) | LCC KU519.I64 (ebook) | DDC 342.9408/72—dc23

LC record available at https://lccn.loc.gov/2020038488

LC ebook record available at https://lccn.loc.gov/2020038489

ISBN: HB: 978-1-50994-014-1
ePDF: 978-1-50994-016-5
ePub: 978-1-50994-015-8

Typeset by Compuscript Ltd, Shannon

To find out more about our authors and books visit www.hartpublishing.co.uk. Here you will find extracts, author information, details of forthcoming events and the option to sign up for our newsletters.

Foreword

THE DESTRUCTION OF a cave at Juukan Gorge that contained invaluable Indigenous treasures and knowledge on the eve of Reconciliation Week in 2020 highlighted the ongoing and inherent tension in the relationship between Indigenous people and the Australian state. While there has been an increasing awareness and engagement with Indigenous issues and culture, there remain colonial structures and power imbalances that keep Indigenous people in positions of vulnerability.

Australia can no longer turn away from its colonial origins and their ongoing legacy through our institutions today. After an era of reconciliation, the *Bringing them Home* report, the National Apology to the Stolen Generations in 2008, and the overturning of the concept of *terra nullius* in the Mabo case, there is no more silence. NAIDOC celebrations, acknowledgements of country and greater Indigenous visibility on the screen are examples of the many ways in which Australians have significantly shifted to start to include Indigenous perspectives in national narratives and everyday practices.

However, against this backdrop, fundamental challenges continue. The Black Lives Matter movement in the United States that energised around the death of an African-American man, George Floyd, in Minneapolis in 2020 put a spotlight on to the continual over-representation of Indigenous people in the criminal justice system. Indigenous child removal rates have increased since the National Apology. Heritage protection laws remain weak. There is still a gap to close on health, education, employment and housing indicators.

As Harry Hobbs rightly points out, there is a thread of resistance and activism by Aboriginal and Torres Strait Islander people weaving through colonial Australia that consistently speaks to a sovereignty never ceded and asserts the rights to self-determination, including voice and representation, land justice, connection to land and culture, rights to family and access to the means to provide for one's family. At its heart, it embraces the idea that Indigenous people demand the freedom to make their own decisions and determine what is right for them.

This challenges a system that has dispossessed and disempowered Indigenous people and has occasionally and begrudgingly recognised rights but never handed back any significant power. The questions for our modern Australian legal and governance institutions are: how do you recognise the rights of an historically marginalised, culturally distinct group within a democratic society? How can a colonial system decolonise?

A key step towards answering those questions is a deeper understanding of the complexity, scope and nuance of the aspirations of Indigenous people. Careful analysis is required to better understand what has worked and what has failed as vehicles for structural and meaningful change, as is an examination of what has facilitated and what has blocked the achievement of those aspirations.

This book offers much insight into those questions. Importantly, it probes the question of how much can be achieved through the structures of the state and interrogates what is possible in terms of real shifts in power. In reflecting on the lessons of the past, the ATSIC era and its bold experimentation in public administration is much overlooked and under-researched. The lessons gleaned from its history and fate, as Hobbs explores, provide much food for thought in reflecting on the best way to move forward.

Indigenous Australians have not waited. They have asserted rights and acted in sovereign ways without the permission of the state. But they have also sought to use the mechanisms of the state to achieve their own political aspirations. While it is clear that native title is not land justice, as Gary Foley has often said, that has not prevented traditional owners from claiming rights, challenging and extending the reach of native title through negotiation and litigation, using it as a foundation for economic self-sufficiency and using its institutions to create self-governing structures. Some might call it using the master's tools. Indigenous people are expert at it.

Indigenous Aspirations and Structural Reform in Australia is an important contribution to the debate and its clear and consistent finding. Meaningful structural change is possible but there needs to be the will.

Hobbs rightly places William Cooper as a significant voice of the early clear articulation of a rights agenda and a set of political aspirations that continue to this day. Cooper organised on 6 December 1938 what is said to be the only citizen-led protest against the treatment of the Jewish community in Germany during Kristallnacht several weeks earlier. It was an important moment which highlighted the solidarity that is essential in the aim to better protect human rights, including the right to self-determination. Improving institutions and structures to better protect the rights of the most marginalised and the most dispossessed improves the rights protections of everyone.

Larissa Behrendt
Distinguished Professor, University of Technology Sydney

Acknowledgements

THIS BOOK HAS had a long genesis and it bears the influence of many hands and minds. Perhaps it started in my family home in Canberra, on Ngunnawal country, where a striking bumper sticker plastered on the fridge challenged me to reflect on Australian law, society and governance, before I could even explain those terms: 'Don't Celebrate '88: Two Hundred Years of Genocide'. Maybe it started later, when my parents, Karina and Neil, took my sister Georgia and me out of primary school to protest the Howard government's amendments to the Native Title Act. Maybe there was no single event; more an inculturation of values drawn from conversations and stories only partially understood with Aboriginal activists like Gordon Briscoe, whom my parents were fortunate to call friends. I hope that this book repays some of the faith they – both Gordon and my family – have shown in me.

This political and intellectual background may inform the book, but its academic rigour would not have been possible without the generous support of colleagues. Most prominent are my doctoral supervisors, George Williams and Megan Davis. Equal parts critical and encouraging, discussion and dialogue with George and Megan during the course of my studies shaped the contours of my thinking and developed my ideas in both difficult and productive ways. I am delighted that these relationships have continued in ongoing collaborations.

My supervisors may have borne the primary burden, but colleagues at the University of New South Wales (UNSW), where I undertook my doctorate, and now at the University of Technology Sydney (UTS) where I teach, have also been unfailingly generous. At UNSW, particular thanks are due to Sean Brennan, Gabrielle Appleby, Rosalind Dixon, Lauren Butterly, Lynsey Blayden, Stephen Young, Zsofia Korosy, Shreeya Smith, Shipra Chorida and Tristan Harley, who all read and commented on draft chapters, as well as contributed to an engaging and welcoming environment. At UTS, conversations with Thalia Anthony, Genevieve Wilkinson, Laura Smith-Khan and Alison Whittaker have all improved the final product. I am also grateful for Claire Charters and Alexander Reilly, whom examined the thesis and offered perceptive comments.

A PhD takes time and costs money. Generous financial support has therefore been critical to the completion of this book. I thank the Lionel Murphy Foundation, the Canadian Government's Queen Elizabeth II Diamond Jubilee Scholarship, and the UNSW Faculty of Law via the Sir Anthony Mason Prize, the Garth Nettheim Doctoral Teaching Fellowship and an Australian Postgraduate

Award, for providing me with the freedom to focus on research and writing. I thank all involved in maintaining these endowments and prizes for the assistance they provide students. I know that they helped me.

Financial support enabled me to travel and learn from experts internationally. In 2017, I spent four weeks at Stockholm University's Department of Political Science with Ulf Mörkenstam and Ragnhild Nilsson. Ragnhild kindly invited me to her hometown of Kiruna in Sápmi, where I attended a plenary session of the Sámediggi, and introduced me to several members of the Parliament. Ulf and Ragnhild both read and assisted with translation queries in chapter six. I also visited the University of Toronto's Faculty of Law for the 2018 Spring Semester. While at Toronto, Douglas Sanderson graciously allowed me to audit his class on Indigenous Legal Traditions and the Imperial Response, while Patrick Macklem suggested useful resources and contacts. Both Douglas and Patrick also read and provided perceptive comments on draft chapters.

Turning the manuscript into a book has been a really lovely experience. For that, I thank Kate Whetter for believing in the project immediately, as well as Rosemarie Mearns, Linda Staniford and Richard Cox, whom all assisted at editorial and production stages. I am particularly indebted to Larissa Behrendt for agreeing to write a foreword and Michael Cook for allowing me to grace my cover with one of his stunning pieces.

It is only because of convention that I thank Annabel last. This book owes more to her patience and support – intellectual, emotional, financial, etc. – than anyone else. Annabel moved to Canberra to be with me when she could not have been sure that we would last. She then made a life for herself there while I studied overseas. When I returned, she agreed to move to Sydney so that I could commence the PhD. She is still here with me now, as we make a life together on the lands of the Gadigal people of the Eora Nation.

Table of Contents

About the Artist

Michael Cook is an award-winning photographer of Aboriginal descent who worked commercially in Australia and overseas for twenty-five years. In 2009, he began to make art photography, driven by an increasingly urgent desire to explore issues of identity. His photographic series are unique in their approach, evocatively recreating incidents that emerge from Australian colonial history. His images unite the historical with the imaginary, the political with the personal. Visually striking, technically complex and sensitively inventive, they occupy a new space in the Australian artistic imagination.

Artist Statement

An exploration of issues that surround identity are central to Cook's approach to creating artwork, yet the stories he develops have an equally universal application to humanity. He suggests, 'I create artwork about Indigenous issues, past and present, about how the past relates to the present and, eventually, moulds the future. I'm a person of mixed ancestry – some of which is Indigenous. I look at the big picture: I tell my stories to Australians of all races and also to those beyond our shores. I am a part of the human race'.

Louise Martin-Chew

Michael Cook is represented by Andrew Baker Art Dealer, Brisbane

Tables of Cases and Legislation

Cases

Legislation

Australia

International Materials

Bills and Ministerial Reports

1

Introduction

I. WILLIAM COOPER'S CHALLENGE

In September 1937, Yorta Yorta man William Cooper dispatched a petition to Prime Minister Joseph Lyons. Formally addressed to His Majesty King George V, the petition called for measures to 'prevent the extinction of the Aboriginal race', secure 'better conditions for all', and provide for 'Aboriginal representation in the Federal Parliament'.[1] In the face of government obstruction and fears of victimisation, the petition enjoyed considerable support, securing the signatures of 1,814 Aboriginal[2] people from across the country.[3] In a letter to Lyons sent the following month, Cooper, Secretary of the Australian Aborigines League, expanded on the signatories' motivations:

> We are persisting in our claim for one who can speak for us in Parliament, influencing legislation on our behalf and safeguarding us from administrational officers, who with notable exceptions, interpret their responsibilities to the aborigines in much the same way as a gaol governor does his criminal population.[4]

Cooper pressed the importance of parliamentary representation further, when, along with members of the Aborigines' Progressive Association, he met with Lyons, Lyons' wife Dame Enid, and the Minister for the Interior, John McEwen, on 31 January 1938.[5]

The petition never made it to the King. Just a week after that meeting – the first between a Prime Minister and an Aboriginal deputation – Cabinet decided

[1] The petition was signed during King George V's reign, but by the time it was presented to the Prime Minister, King George VI had ascended to the throne.

[2] Throughout the book I refer to the distinct political communities that possessed the Australian continent prior to British colonisation as 'Aboriginal and Torres Strait Islander peoples' and 'Indigenous Australians'. I also use the term 'Indigenous' to refer to similarly situated polities across the globe. Acknowledging that not all Aboriginal and Torres Strait Islander communities prefer this terminology, I identify the relevant nation or political community where possible.

[3] A Markus, 'William Cooper and the 1937 Petition to the King' (1983) 7 *Aboriginal History* 46, 50–51.

[4] Letter from William Cooper to Joseph Lyons, 26 October 1937. Cited in ibid 57.

[5] 'Future of Blacks, Governments to Confer, Prime Minister's Promise' *The Argus* (1 February 1938) 2; 'Our Ten Points' *Abo Call* (1 April 1938) 1.

that 'no action [should] be taken'.[6] The Cabinet minutes are silent as to their reasoning, but as Andrew Markus notes, 'public service records and the written submissions to Cabinet indicate the context in which [the petition] was considered'.[7] Within the Department of the Interior, concerns were raised over how many of the petitioners were 'full-blood aboriginals'[8] and whether they would 'have the ability to exercise a vote'.[9] Considering that no 'good purpose would be gained by submitting the petition to the King', McEwen remarked that as Minister for the Interior he was 'virtually a representative of the aboriginals of the Northern Territory'.[10] In discharging the responsibilities of this office, Indigenous peoples in the Northern Territory could be assured that he would have their best interests in mind. For Aboriginal and Torres Strait Islander peoples elsewhere, their interests were presumably already – and would continue to be – respected by and reflected in the positions taken by the relevant state officers. A letter informing Cooper of this decision was apparently sent, though it never reached him.[11]

William Cooper's petition was not the first effort by Aboriginal and Torres Strait Islander people to seek structural reform to the framework of Australian governance. Neither was it the first call for 'an aboriginal representative in parliament'.[12] In obtaining nearly 2,000 signatures, however,[13] Cooper's petition revealed the sense of powerlessness and alienation that Aboriginal and Torres Strait Islander people experienced in the land they and their ancestors had possessed for over 60,000 years; alienation undoubtedly amplified by Cabinet's casual dismissal of their aspirations. Denied the right to vote or effectively excluded from exercising it,[14] let alone stand for Parliament, Aboriginal and Torres Strait Islander people felt that, 'virtual representation' or not, their voices were not heard, and their interests were not considered in the processes of government. Cooper and those who signed his petition, 'desire[d] … a change of heart in the electorate, reflected in Parliament and leading to a policy which

[6] Minutes of meeting of the Cabinet, Canberra, 7 February 1938. Cited in Markus, 'William Cooper' (1983) 51.

[7] Markus (n 3) 51.

[8] Letter from Joseph Carrodus (Secretary, Department of Interior) to Frank Strahan (Secretary, Prime Minister's Department), 30 September 1937. Cited in Markus (n 3) 51.

[9] J Barranger, Department of the Interior Memorandum, 22 September 1937. Cited in Markus (n 3) 51.

[10] Memorandum from John McEwen, Minister for the Interior, to Cabinet, 1 February 1938. Cited in Markus (n 3) 58. Constitutional complications were also discussed: See ch 5.

[11] Markus (n 3) 58.

[12] Shadrach Livingstone James, a Yorta Yorta man and William Cooper's nephew, is reported as making this call at a conference discussing John Bleakley's report, 'The Aboriginal and Half-Castes of Central and Northern Australia': 'Native Problems: Aboriginal Representation in Federal Parliament' *The Recorder* (16 April 1929) 3.

[13] Cooper had hoped to obtain 600 signatures: 'M.H.R. for Natives: King to be Petitioned' *The Herald* (15 September 1933) 2.

[14] M Goot, 'The Aboriginal Franchise and its Consequences' (2006) 52 *Australian Journal of Politics and History* 517, 524.

will be different from that administered by our gaolers'.[15] They believed that dedicated parliamentary representation would help achieve this.[16]

More than 80 years after William Cooper's petition was summarily rejected by Cabinet, Aboriginal and Torres Strait Islander people still do not enjoy dedicated representation in the Federal Parliament, but considerable legal and social changes have transformed their position within Australia. Today, Indigenous peoples possess a broad and formally equal distribution of political resources. On the same basis as non-Indigenous citizens they may vote, stand for Parliament, freely discuss political and governmental matters, and assemble and associate for that purpose. And yet, as this book argues, institutional and structural barriers persist, inhibiting the capacity of a distinct, socio-economically marginalised community comprising just three per cent of the population to have their voices heard in the processes of government. Considerable legal and social change has not rectified William Cooper's central concern: Indigenous Australians are not always present in the forum where policies are debated and laws enacted; their voices are not always heard, and their interests are not always considered.

Aboriginal and Torres Strait Islander people have always known this, but in recent years the deficit that rests at the heart of Australia's system of governance has taken on heightened significance in mainstream political debate. In May 2017, around 250 Indigenous Australians 'from all points of the southern sky' gathered on the red dust of Mutitjulu to call for meaningful reform to the Australian state. Grounded in their inherent rights as the 'first sovereign Nations of the Australian continent', the delegates called for the establishment of a constitutionally enshrined Indigenous representative body that would advise Parliament on laws concerning Aboriginal and Torres Strait Islander people and a legislated Makarrata Commission to supervise a process of treaty-making and truth-telling.[17] The culmination of 18 months of deliberation and dialogue at regional forums held across the country, the Uluru Statement from the Heart echoed Cooper's petition, as Indigenous peoples laid bare the 'torment of our powerlessness'.[18] In another reverberation from that period the Australian Government derisively rejected the proposition. In a joint press release, the Prime Minister, Attorney-General and Minister for Indigenous Affairs declared that Cabinet '[did] not believe such an addition to our national representative institutions is either desirable or capable of winning acceptance

[15] Letter from William Cooper to Joseph Lyons (n 4).

[16] Cooper's petition was related to but distinct from the major currents of Indigenous activism, which focused on securing equal political and citizenship rights, a goal Cooper also shared. See N Peterson and W Sanders, 'Introduction' in N Peterson and W Sanders (eds), *Citizenship and Indigenous Australians: Changing Conceptions and Possibilities* (Cambridge, Cambridge University Press, 1998) 1, 9–17.

[17] Uluru Statement from the Heart, Uluru, 26 May 2017 ('Uluru Statement').

[18] ibid.

in a referendum'.[19] This time Indigenous leaders were informed of Cabinet's decision, but only by that press release.[20]

II. THE SCOPE OF THIS BOOK

This book takes William Cooper's challenge seriously. It explores whether and how Australia's governance system can be restructured to empower Aboriginal and Torres Strait Islander peoples with the capacity to have their voices heard and their interests considered in the processes of government at the Commonwealth level. The project is therefore grounded in the wealth of literature that exists on the 'unfinished business'[21] of constitutional reform, an ongoing struggle to 'effect a more just basic distribution of public power'.[22] Scholarship within this field is diverse and wide-ranging. It encompasses institutional measures to recognise Indigenous sovereignty or rights to self-determination,[23] land rights,[24] and customary law;[25] processes through which such recognition can be realised, such as treaty-making,[26] federalism,[27] a constitutional racial non-discrimination clause,[28] or dedicated parliamentary representation;[29] and the necessity of attitudinal or relational changes within and between non-Indigenous Australians to catalyse and embed such change.[30]

[19] Prime Minister, Attorney-General, Minister for Indigenous Affairs, 'Response to the Referendum Council's Report on Constitutional Recognition' (media release, 26 October 2017).

[20] N Pearson, 'Betrayal' *The Monthly* (No 140, December 2017) 24, 29.

[21] P Dodson, 'Beyond the Mourning Gate: Dealing with Unfinished Business' in R Tokinson (ed), *The Wentworth Lectures: Honouring Fifty Years of Australian Indigenous Studies* (Canberra, Aboriginal Studies Press, 2015) 192.

[22] D Lino, *Constitutional Recognition: First Peoples and the Australian Settler State* (Annandale, Federation Press, 2018) 88.

[23] Aboriginal and Torres Strait Islander Commission, 'Recognition, Rights and Reform: A Report to Government on Native Title Social Justice Measures' (Commonwealth of Australia, 1995); S Brennan, B Gunn and G Williams, '"Sovereignty" and its Relevance to Treaty-Making between Indigenous Peoples and Australian Governments' (2004) 26 *Sydney Law Review* 307; A Vivian, M Jorgensen, A Reilly, M McMillan, C McRae and J McMinn, 'Indigenous Self-Government in the Australian Federation' (2017) 20 *Australian Indigenous Law Review* 215.

[24] B Hawke, 'Statement of the Prime Minister: Barunga Festival' (1988) 2(6) *Land Rights News* 22.

[25] Australian Law Reform Commission, 'Recognition of Aboriginal Customary Law', Report No 31 (1986); Law Reform Commission of Western Australian, 'Aboriginal Customary Laws: The Interaction of Western Australian Law with Aboriginal Law', Report No 94 (2006).

[26] G Williams and H Hobbs, *Treaty*, 2nd edn (Alexandria, Federation Press, 2020); M Langton, O Mazel, L Palmer, K Shain and M Tehan, *Settling with Indigenous Peoples: Modern Treaty and Agreement Making* (Annandale, Federation Press, 2006).

[27] M Mansell, *Treaty and Statehood: Aboriginal Self-Determination* (Annandale, Federation Press, 2016); H Hobbs, 'Aboriginal and Torres Strait Islander Peoples and Multinational Federalism in Australia' (2018) 27 *Griffith Law Review* 307.

[28] G Williams, 'Race and the Australian Constitution: From Federation to Reconciliation' (2000) 38 *Osgoode Hall Law Journal* 643.

[29] J Chesterman, 'Chosen by the People? How Federal Parliamentary Seats might be Reserved for Indigenous Australians without Changing the Constitution' (2006) 34 *Federal Law Review* 261.

[30] A Kwaymullina, 'Recognition, Referendums and Relationships: Indigenous Worldviews, Constitutional Change, and the 'Spirit' of 1967' in S Young, J Nielsen and J Patrick (eds), *Constitutional*

The book shares with this literature the belief that non-Indigenous Australians are capable of embracing the aspirations of Aboriginal and Torres Strait Islander peoples. As contemporary proposals for constitutional reform have coalesced around the idea of a First Nations Voice to the Parliament, however, it explores only one aspect of that complex and multifaceted broader reform project. It examines whether and how an Indigenous representative body – a First Nations Voice – will be effective at meeting Indigenous aspirations.[31]

In adopting this approach, the book speaks to several debates occurring across the globe, for Indigenous aspirations for structural reform are not limited to Australia. All over the world, Indigenous peoples continue to agitate for a new relationship with the state(s) that claims their lands. Political action comes in many forms. At the time of writing in early 2020, hereditary chiefs of the Wet'suwet'en First Nation have erected blockades to prevent the construction of an oil pipeline across their unceded territory in British Columbia,[32] while in New Caledonia, Kanak leaders patiently plan for an independence referendum they hope will sever their connection with France and allow them to 'attain full sovereignty and become independent'.[33] Action is not always so direct or confrontational. In January 2020, Sámi reindeer herders successfully obtained declaratory relief in the Supreme Court of Sweden, which held for the first time that Sámi people possess exclusive rights to manage hunting and fishing within their traditional lands.[34] Similarly, language and cultural revitalisation projects, like those established in Aotearoa New Zealand[35] or underway in Ecuador,[36] empower Indigenous peoples and communities and speak to a particular relationship with the state no longer premised on subordination and domination.

Indigenous peoples may seek a restructured relationship with the state, but there exists a wide variety of political strategies and end goals to realise that new relationship. In some cases, it may involve secession. In other cases, it may encompass structural reform within the state. Notwithstanding these differences, however, a commonality persists. In almost all cases, Indigenous peoples

Recognition of First Peoples in Australia: Theories and Comparative Perspectives (Annandale, Federation Press, 2016) 29; H Hobbs, 'Constitutional Recognition and Reform: Developing an Inclusive Australian Citizenship through Treaty' (2018) 53 *Australian Journal of Political Science* 176.

[31] See also S Morris, *A First Nations Voice in the Australian Constitution* (Oxford, Hart Publishing, 2020) for an examination of the politics of constitutional reform in Australia as it relates to constitutional recognition of Aboriginal and Torres Strait Islander peoples.

[32] 'The Wet'suwet'en Conflict Disrupting Canada's Rail System' *BBC News* (20 February 2020), available at www.bbc.com/news/world-us-canada-51550821.

[33] XIXème Comité des Signataires de l'Accord de Nouméa, 'Relevé de Conclusions' (media release, 10 October 2019).

[34] *Staten genom Justitiekanslern v Girjas sameby* (Högsta Domstolen, Case No T 853-18, 23 January 2020).

[35] R Benton, 'Perfecting the Partnership: Revitalising the Māori Language in New Zealand Education and Society 1987–2014' (2015) 28 *Language, Culture and Curriculum* 99.

[36] K King, 'Language Revitalisation Processes and Prospects: Quichua in the Ecuadorian Andes' (1999) 13 *Language and Education* 17.

articulate their claims in the language of sovereignty. Drawing on a wide survey of Indigenous peoples' political thought, this book articulates an account of Indigenous peoples' political aspirations through that fundamental, yet complex idea.

Sovereignty, and the related notion of self-determination, are two of the major concepts in the vocabulary of Indigenous rights claims and political aspirations. For this reason, these terms are subject to a range of divergent and often competing views. One expression is now enshrined in the United Nations Declaration on the Rights of Indigenous Peoples,[37] but sovereignty and self-determination are deeper and broader than this legal standard. As Sámi scholar Rauna Kuokkanen explains, examining these concepts 'solely through international law' is 'extremely limiting' as it 'excludes a range of normative understandings … that have to do with Indigenous ontologies and philosophies'.[38] This book explores what Indigenous peoples mean when they speak in the language of sovereignty and considers how they intend that term to be understood.

It is hoped that this approach encourages new ways of meaningfully responding to those claims. Law is a valuable means of transformation and agent for political change, but it can also serve to derail potentially productive conversations. Sometimes it can be helpful to set aside contentious matters and focus on practical issues when seeking to restructure relations and fashion 'a mutually satisfactory and peaceful coexistence'.[39] By recentring our focus on Indigenous voices, this book aims to prompt states to move beyond narrow legalistic framings and explore new ways to develop and design institutions that empower Indigenous peoples on their own terms.

Reflecting its focus on contemporary constitutional reform in Australia, the book is concerned with structural reform of the state. In this sense, it lies within scholarship that is broadly understood as reflecting a paradigm of reconciliation as opposed to resurgence.[40] That said, it understands reconciliation as imposing real burdens. Assimilating or incorporating Aboriginal and Torres Strait Islander peoples into the prevailing legal and political framework will not suffice, for reconciliation requires a 'genuine accommodation'[41] that makes space for Indigenous peoples and communities.

[37] *United Nations Declaration on the Rights of Indigenous Peoples*, GA Res 61/295, 61st sess, 107th plen mtg, Supp No 49, UN Doc A/RES/61295 (13 September 2007).

[38] R Kuokkanen, *Restructuring Relations: Indigenous Self-Determination, Governance, and Gender* (Oxford, Oxford University Press, 2019) 3.

[39] Canada, Royal Commission on Aboriginal People, *Volume 2: Restructuring the Relationship* (1996) 18.

[40] These terms are both 'contested and contestable': J Borrows and J Tully, 'Introduction' in M Asch, J Borrows and J Tully (eds), *Resurgence and Reconciliation: Indigenous – Settler Relations and Earth Teachings* (Toronto, University of Toronto Press, 2018) 3, 4. I note also that reconciliation remains a problematic metaphor in this context.

[41] A Mills, 'Rooted Constitutionalism: Growing Political Community' in M Asch, J Borrows and J Tully (eds), *Resurgence and Reconciliation: Indigenous – Settler Relations and Earth Teachings*

Critical Indigenous scholars and activists' question whether such an approach can lead to transformational change.[42] These scholars recognise that practical realities inhibit the ability of Indigenous peoples and nations to entirely avoid or extricate themselves from relationships with the state(s) that claims jurisdiction over their lands, but fundamentally challenge state-sponsored efforts at accommodating their position within reformed politico-legal structures. These are powerful interventions that must be taken seriously, particularly by non-Indigenous people working in the field.[43] Nonetheless, as it is incumbent on non-Indigenous peoples to consider how existing constitutional frameworks can be reconceptualised to do justice to Indigenous claims, I contend that structural reform is defensible in at least three ways.

First, while sympathetic to the position of critical Indigenous scholars, it is not clear to me whether and how entrenched power imbalances can be displaced. In this light, scholars like Eualeyai and Kamillaroi professor Larissa Behrendt have urged Indigenous peoples to adopt a *modus viviendi* that allows them to respond to the world as it is.[44] After all, the issue facing Indigenous peoples is not a question between one choice and another, but 'about how to secure the best of both worlds'.[45] Indigenous participation within state institutions does not discount or prevent alternative oppositional strategies or the building of culturally resurgent institutions of self-government outside of the state. Rather, participation in culturally appropriate institutions 'can be viewed as simply one additional means of facilitating Aboriginal control over Aboriginal affairs' and of incorporating Indigenous voices in decisions that affect the state as a whole.[46] This is important not least because it is a brute fact that many significant issues facing Indigenous communities may most effectively be addressed by leveraging the power of the state, including its coercive powers of redistribution. Resurgence scholar, Yellowknives Dene political theorist Glen Coulthard,

(Toronto, University of Toronto Press, 2018) 133, 145; Independent Working Group on Constitutional Transformation, 'The Report of Matike Mai Aotearoa' (2016).

[42] See, eg: I Watson, *Aboriginal Peoples, Colonialism and International Law: Raw Law* (Abingdon, Routledge, 2014); A Moreton-Robinson, *The White Possessive: Property, Power, and Indigenous Sovereignty* (Minneapolis, University of Minnesota Press, 2015); G Coulthard, *Red Skin White Masks: Rejecting the Colonial Politics of Recognition* (Minneapolis, University of Minnesota Press, 2014); T Alfred, *Wasáse: Indigenous Pathways of Action and Freedom* (Toronto, University of Toronto Press, 2005); and A Simpson, *Mohawk Interruptus: Political Life Across the Border of Settler States* (Durham, Duke University Press, 2014).

[43] This scholarship is explored in greater detail in ch 3.

[44] L Behrendt, *Achieving Social Justice: Indigenous Rights and Australia's Future* (Annandale, Federation Press, 2003).

[45] G Slowey, 'A Fine Balance? Aboriginal Peoples in the Canadian North and the Dilemma of Development' in AM Timpson (ed), *First Nations, First Thoughts: The Impact of Indigenous Thought in Canada* (Vancouver, University of British Columbia Press, 2009) 229, 229.

[46] M Murphy, 'Relational Self-Determination and Federal Reform' in M Murphy (ed), *Canada: State of the Federation 2003 – Reconfiguring Aboriginal-State Relations* (Montreal, McGill-Queen's University Press 2003) 3, 16; M Murphy, 'Representing Indigenous Self-Determination' (2008) 58 *University of Toronto Law Journal* 185.

recognises this challenge, acknowledging that Indigenous struggles 'for land and freedom' require Indigenous peoples to 'continue to engage with the state's legal and political system', even if they should do so with 'caution'.[47] Affirming both this principle and its qualification, this book explores why Indigenous peoples might be rightly sceptical of engagement.

Second, participation does not simply reflect hard-headed pragmatism, but may also bring principled benefits. In exploring American Indian participation in the American political system, Yak Tityu Tityu Northern Chumash and Yokut political scientist Kouslaa Kessler-Mata has highlighted that 'the relationships and interests of tribes and states are not easily separated'.[48] As Kessler-Mata explains, increasing interdependence means that in practice, American Indian participation in non-Indian politics can 'improve the relationships between tribes and non-tribal governments' and influence Congress's exercise of plenary power over Native American affairs. Participation is thus responsive to some of the 'structural constraints placed on tribal authority, as well as out of the exercise of sovereignty itself'.[49] Engaging in and with state political systems can develop productive relationships and improve substantive outcomes.

Third, as chapter three will explore in detail, many – though not all – Aboriginal and Torres Strait Islander people agree that it is worthwhile to seek reform of the state. In the Uluru Statement, Indigenous Australians documented their desire for 'substantive constitutional change and structural reform' so that their 'ancient sovereignty can shine through as a fuller expression of Australia's nationhood', and that they may take '*a rightful place* in our own country'.[50] Although participants at each regional dialogue that preceded and led to the First Nations National Convention at Uluru were invited by the organisers rather than selected by their communities,[51] the dialogues were structured around free and informed discussion, and the resulting Statement from the Heart stands as a clear Aboriginal and Torres Strait Islander position. It must be taken seriously.

In engaging seriously with those aspirations, this book also contributes to a growing literature that examines state institutions aimed at empowering Indigenous peoples' participation in public governance. Many states have recognised the moral force of Indigenous peoples' claims and a diverse array of mechanisms that empower Indigenous peoples with the capacity to have their voices heard in the processes of government have been established, and others

[47] Coulthard, *Red Skin White Masks* (2014) 179.

[48] K Kessler-Mata, *American Indians and the Trouble with Sovereignty: A Turn Toward Structural Self-Determination* (Cambridge, Cambridge University Press, 2017) 103.

[49] ibid 104.

[50] Uluru Statement (n 17) (emphasis in original).

[51] For criticism of this approach see: Joint Select Committee on Constitutional Recognition Relating to Aboriginal and Torres Strait Islander Peoples, Parliament of Australia, 'Final Report' (2018) 68 [2.268].

proposed, in recent years.[52] In status and scope, these mechanisms range from appointed or elected administrative agencies to representative bodies exercising limited policy-making functions, to relatively self-governing autonomous units within federations. Depending on their mandate, powers and authority, these institutional arrangements provide a measure of input into and control over public decision-making, ensuring that government remains responsive to the interests of Indigenous peoples.

The emergence of these institutions and mechanisms suggests a growing recognition and acknowledgement of Indigenous rights. Considered as an element of a burgeoning or emergent notion of shared rule, these bodies signal, even if they do not necessarily demonstrate in practice, the public and political equality of Indigenous peoples within the state.[53] At the same time, however, the development of these bodies gives rise to a range of concerns over their capacity to meet Indigenous aspirations for structural reform. This book explores these concerns by close examination of the institutional mechanism called for in the Uluru Statement; an Indigenous representative body.

Indigenous representative bodies are not uncommon across the globe, but they are largely unexamined in the scholarly literature. Several have existed from time to time in Australia,[54] while they also operate in different forms across Scandinavia,[55] South Africa[56] and New Caledonia.[57] Generally speaking, these bodies are separate from the ordinary parliament, but are constitutionally or statutorily incorporated into the parliamentary process and empowered to advise that assembly or government in certain contexts. These institutions differ in important respects from related bodies. In contrast to non-government representative organisations, their formal connection to the state is intended to guarantee an opportunity to be consulted and to have their voices heard on relevant issues. While consultation might not always occur, the organisation's structural link to government ensures that it retains a preeminent position within the architecture of public governance. They also differ from government appointed advisory bodies. Although their status as 'representative' institutions does not necessarily mean their members are elected, it does denote that they are primarily (though not solely) accountable to their community rather than the state. As this book finds, whether and how this delicate balance can be managed in practice is key to the effectiveness and success of such institutions.

[52] Human Rights Council, 'Final Report of the Study on Indigenous Peoples and the Right to Participate in Decision-Making: Report of the Expert Mechanism on the Rights of Indigenous Peoples', 18th sess, Agenda Item 5, UN Doc A/HRC/18/42 (17 August 2011) 5–11, [16]–[39].

[53] P Macklem, 'Distributing Sovereignty: Indian Nations and Equality of Peoples' (1993) 45 *Stanford Law Review* 1311.

[54] See ch 5.

[55] See ch 6.

[56] Traditional Leadership and Governance Framework Act 2003 (SA), ss 16(1)(a), 18(1).

[57] Nouméa Accord, signed 5 May 1998 (entered into force 8 November 1998) art 1.2.5.

III. THE STRUCTURE OF THIS BOOK

I approach this topic in eight chapters. In chapter two, I examine Australia's existing governance framework, assessing whether it empowers Aboriginal and Torres Strait Islander peoples with the capacity to have their voices heard and their interests considered in the processes of government at the Commonwealth level. As I demonstrate, Aboriginal and Torres Strait Islander peoples may participate in democratic politics as Australian citizens, but the absence of a treaty relationship or constitutional protection of Indigenous rights, the dominance of majoritarian parliamentary governance and pervasive ideological commitment to a notion of formal equality, inhibits Indigenous Australians' capacity to speak and be heard as *Indigenous* Australians.

Australia has vigorously debated the constitutional relationship of Aboriginal and Torres Strait Islander communities and non-Indigenous peoples for many years. Only recently however, has that discussion centred on the aspirations of Indigenous Australians.[58] This is alarming for many reasons, not least because, as Behrendt has remarked, 'The appropriate and best starting point for protection of Indigenous rights is assessing what it is that Indigenous people want'.[59] Chapter three continues and deepens this focus. It explores Aboriginal and Torres Strait Islander peoples' nuanced and complex political thought with the aim of developing an understanding of their aspirations for structural reform. By centring its analysis on Indigenous positions and perspectives, chapter three responds to persistent Indigenous feelings of 'being done to'.[60] Although it is impossible to distil the multiplicity of Indigenous aspirations into a set of clear proposals, key themes do emerge.

Exploration of Indigenous political thought in chapter three is not limited to Aboriginal and Torres Strait Islander sources but draws on the lived experience of Indigenous peoples across time and space. This is because Indigenous peoples are transnational actors, constructing and sharing ideas, values and norms at a global level that rebound and influence local communities in diverse ways. Australia is a 'space criss-crossed' and enriched by these relationships. While the specific challenge facing every Indigenous community is distinct, it is impossible to understand Aboriginal and Torres Strait Islander peoples' activism, ambitions, and aspirations without attention to those 'transnational dimensions'.[61]

[58] See generally H Hobbs, 'The Road to Uluru: Constitutional Recognition and the UN *Declaration on the Rights of Indigenous Peoples*' (2020) 66 *Australian Journal of Politics and History* (forthcoming).

[59] Behrendt, *Achieving Social Justice* (2003) 85.

[60] K Gilbert, *Because a White Man'll Never Do It* (Sydney, Angus and Robertson, 1973) 82, 158, 188, 198, 204.

[61] R de Costa, *A Higher Authority: Indigenous Transnationalism and Australia* (Sydney, UNSW Press, 2006) 3.

In chapter four, those themes are articulated into a set of criteria to assess institutions and mechanisms designed to empower Indigenous peoples to have their interests considered in the processes of government. The four criteria that emerge – *voices*, *power*, *ownership* and *integrity* – are informed and infused by the rich and nuanced thought of Indigenous peoples, but are expressed in a manner comprehensible to Australia's public law framework.[62] As a non-Indigenous person undertaking this task, I am conscious that my approach may concern some Indigenous peoples, wary that it could constrain or constrict their aspirations by misidentifying or mischaracterising their goals. While that is a risk, I see the articulation of these criteria as a challenge to the state, both urging it to take seriously Indigenous aspirations and surveying a path through a tangled thicket for that possibility. This is only feasible because, although cognisable to public law values, the criteria remain firmly grounded in Indigenous aspirations.

The criteria are framed in broad terms to allow considerable room for innovation and variety in institutional design. Indigenous peoples are differently situated – it is natural that political and legal solutions will respond to those distinctions. It is also consistent with the values that underlie self-determination. As contemporary proposals for structural reform in Australia have coalesced around the idea of a First Nations Voice to advise the Commonwealth Parliament, however, the remainder of the book focuses attention on Indigenous representative bodies. Chapter five examines the Aboriginal and Torres Strait Islander Commission (ATSIC), while chapter six explores the Swedish Sámi Parliament (the Sámediggi). In shifting from abstract principles to concrete assessment of institutions, these chapters reveal the tensions and trade-offs inherent within the criteria. Indigenous Australians will have to make hard choices to determine their priorities.

My choice of these two case studies has been guided by pragmatic functionalism.[63] Functionalism rests on three central premises: legal systems face similar problems; different legal systems adopt different measures to address those problems; and, despite those different measures, each legal system should reach similar results. In other words, because 'institutions are contingent while problems are universal', the function or social purpose of a law can serve as the object of comparison.[64] Each of these premises is contestable, but a pragmatic functionalism recognises and seeks to avoid functionalism's limitations. As I outline in chapters five and six, while ATSIC and

[62] This is not to suggest that Indigenous scholarship is inherently illegible to Australia's legal framework.

[63] O Brand, 'Conceptual Comparisons: Towards a Coherent Methodology of Comparative Legal Studies' (2007) 32 *Brooklyn Journal of International Law* 405.

[64] R Michaels, 'The Functional Method of Comparative Law' in M Reimann and R Zimmerman (eds), *The Oxford Handbook of Comparative Law* (Oxford, Oxford University Press, 2006) 339, 346.

the Sámediggi serve independent purposes, they also serve a common social function. Both institutions are provisional responses to the central and enduring challenge facing all settler states: how the specific interests of Indigenous peoples can be considered in public decision-making. For this reason, they are worthwhile comparators.

ATSIC was a national Indigenous representative body that commenced operation with great hope in 1990. Signalling a 'new era' in the administration of Aboriginal affairs,[65] the Commission was abolished with bipartisan support in 2005. Nonetheless, the Commission remains Australia's most significant institutional attempt to empower Indigenous peoples to have their interests considered in the processes of government. ATSIC imbued elected Indigenous representatives with considerable authority: they could identify local funding priorities, formulate and implement regional plans, make decisions over public expenditure, protect cultural material and information, and speak directly to government. Ultimately, as chapter five reveals, design problems, ideological opposition and serious concerns over the probity of some of its leaders led to the Commission's eventual closure. As efforts to establish a new national Indigenous representative body continue, however, it is worth reassessing the Commission. In this chapter I examine whether ATSIC empowered Indigenous Australians effectively.

What does this examination mean for contemporary institutional design? Direct observations are difficult to draw given the significant political and legal developments following the Commission's establishment and abolition. This includes the recognition and regulation of native title,[66] protection of Aboriginal and Torres Strait Islander heritage,[67] and most recently, the emergence of State and Territory-driven treaty processes.[68] It also includes less prominent but no less substantial developments, such as the ideology of mainstreaming in the public administration of Indigenous affairs,[69] and the prioritisation of ameliorating socio-economic disadvantage at the expense of the Indigenous rights agenda. A major challenge today is therefore not simply the lack of Indigenous representation in Parliament but the absence of clear and direct avenues for Aboriginal and Torres Strait Islander peoples to provide input in and make decisions over Aboriginal affairs. ATSIC cannot simply be re-established and strengthened because the channels for policy-making have shifted. Nonetheless, close examination of the Commission is vital to assess the strengths and weaknesses

[65] 'Federal Government Introduces ATSIC' *Torres News* (30 November 1989) 4.

[66] *Mabo v Queensland (No 2)* (1992) 175 CLR 1; Native Title Act 1993 (Cth).

[67] Commonwealth protection was legislated in 1984, but state protection did not immediately follow. See, eg: Aboriginal Cultural Heritage Act 2003 (Qld).

[68] Williams and Hobbs, *Treaty* (2020) ch 8.

[69] J Hunt, 'Between a Rock and a Hard Place: Self-Determination, Mainstreaming and Indigenous Community Governance' in J Hunt, D Smith, S Garling and W Sanders (eds), *Contested Governance: Culture, Power and Institutions in Indigenous Australia* (Canberra, ANU Press, 2008) 27.

of Indigenous representative bodies as institutional mechanisms to empower Indigenous peoples. If ATSIC did not succeed, what changes should be made to a contemporary body?

Similar questions are often asked about the Swedish Sámediggi. The Sámediggi was established three years after ATSIC, but it continues to operate today. As an institutional mechanism designed to empower the Indigenous people of Sweden with the capacity to have their interests considered in the processes of government, the Sámediggi serves a similar role to ATSIC. It also undertakes similar, albeit more limited, responsibilities. Through the Sámediggi elected Sámi representatives speak to government and administer certain functions, primarily relating to reindeer herding. Examination of the Sámediggi broadens and deepens the book's focus on Indigenous aspirations and structural reform. It demonstrates the wider utility of the four criteria by applying them to an international case study, while detailed analysis of a second Indigenous representative body strengthens my assessment of the potential advantages and disadvantages of this particular institutional mechanism.

Several Indigenous representative bodies exist across the world. I focus on the Swedish Sámediggi for four reasons. First, although Sweden and Australia are both developed Western liberal democracies, they differ considerably in important respects relating to colonial history, diversity and breadth of Indigenous nations, and political culture and legal traditions. These marked distinctions allow detailed examination of ATSIC and the Sámediggi to draw out the inherent strengths and weaknesses of Indigenous representative bodies. This is important because the focus of this chapter is not to directly inform debate in Australia but to develop our understanding of Indigenous representative bodies as an institutional mechanism to further the interests of Indigenous peoples.

Second, comparative English-language legal scholarship on Indigenous peoples' rights generally focuses on the 'natural' grouping of Canada, Australia, Aotearoa New Zealand and the United States.[70] While there are strong methodological reasons for this focus, it also risks offering only a 'limited and partial understanding of the nature of Indigenous self-determination and Indigenous-state relations'.[71] Exploration of the approach taken in Sweden both expands knowledge and provokes novel institutional developments. This is especially important as the Sámediggi is sometimes casually identified as inspiration for institutional design in Australia.[72] Third, unlike many other Indigenous representative bodies, including those in South Africa and New Caledonia, the Sámediggi is not simply an advisory body, but enjoys a real, though imperfect, domain of executive responsibility. This is critical, for as chapters three and four

[70] K Gover, 'Settler-State Political Theory, "CANZUS" and the UN Declaration on the Rights of Indigenous Peoples' (2015) 26 *European Journal of International Law* 345, 356.

[71] Kuokkanen, *Restructuring Relations* (2019) 7.

[72] See, eg: S Morris, 'False Equality' in S Morris (ed), *A Rightful Place: A Road Map to Recognition* (Melbourne, Black Inc, 2017) 209, 216, 231.

demonstrate, desire for some form of *power* is a key theme that recurs across Indigenous political thought. Finally, while Sámi representative bodies exist in Sweden, Norway and Finland, the Swedish institution is comparatively under-studied. Drawing on a large number of untranslated Swedish sources (both primary and secondary), the chapter provides the most detailed examination of the Parliament yet undertaken in English.

The case studies reveal that Indigenous representative bodies can provide an enhanced opportunity to participate in the processes of government, but that they are also beset by tensions. In chapter seven these complexities are unravelled to provide an accurate sense of the challenges and potential value of a First Nations Voice in Australia. I argue that careful institutional design is critical in developing an institution capable of influencing legislation and policy, but it is not sufficient. To give an Indigenous representative body the best prospect of success it should be integrated within a broader complementary framework that empowers Indigenous peoples and communities. A layered approach consisting of interlocking institutions and mechanisms targeted at realising different goals could reaffirm and strengthen each process, empowering Aboriginal and Torres Strait Islander peoples with the capacity to be heard. Emerging treaty processes offer one way that Australia's governance framework could be restructured in this manner. Whether it will succeed ultimately relies on state attitudes towards Indigenous peoples.

That the effectiveness of a First Nations Voice will ultimately rest on community support exposes the limits of structural reform. Although empowering Aboriginal and Torres Strait Islander peoples with the capacity to be heard requires amendment to the framework of the Australian state, such reform is unlikely to be sufficient. For lasting change to be effective, innovative institutional design must be combined with and grounded in attitudinal and relational shifts within government and the public at large, such that decision-makers *listen* to Indigenous voices.[73] The broader challenge of fomenting relations based on mutual respect and equal partnership goes beyond this work, but structural reform can play a crucial role in this wider project. As Behrendt reminds us, 'the institutional form given to the recognition of Indigenous rights and democratic ideals'[74] shapes societal and cultural attitudes. Imaginative institutional design may not directly engender respectful relationships or force government to listen, but it can enhance that prospect. It is to that task we now proceed.

[73] W Connolly, 'The Liberal Image of the Nation' in D Ivison, P Patton and W Sanders (eds), *Political Theory and the Rights of Indigenous Peoples* (Cambridge, Cambridge University Press, 2000) 183, 191; M Asch, *On Being Here to Stay: Treaties and Aboriginal Rights in Canada* (Toronto, University of Toronto Press, 2014) 140.

[74] Behrendt (n 44) 16.

2

Aboriginal and Torres Strait Islander Peoples and Australian Governance

I. INTRODUCTION

CONSIDERABLE CHANGE HAS occurred in the years since William Cooper circulated his petition. In stark contrast to those earlier times, institutional mechanisms to empower people to have their interests considered in the processes of government are today open on a non-discriminatory basis to all Australians. As citizens with rights,[1] Aboriginal and Torres Strait Islander people may vote, stand for Parliament and serve at the highest levels of the institutions of government. However, while formal legal equality represents a sizeable improvement on previous arrangements, Indigenous Australians argue that a formally equal opportunity to participate is insufficient. Indigenous scholars and activists assert that the structure and operation of Australian governance inhibits their ability to have their distinctive interests considered in the processes of government.[2]

This chapter assesses whether Australia's framework of governance empowers Aboriginal and Torres Strait Islander peoples to have their voices heard in the processes of government at the Commonwealth level. It does so by analysing in detail the structure and operation of Australian governance. It explores whether and how the judiciary is capable of protecting and promoting Indigenous peoples' rights as citizens and as collective political communities. It then examines the opportunities available for Indigenous peoples to participate in, and influence decisions of, Australia's representative democracy. The chapter focuses on formal mechanisms of political participation. I do not examine opportunities for Indigenous peoples to influence government via informal channels, such as public protest or through the media. In the latter case, it is sufficient to note that while dominant representations of Aboriginal and Torres Strait Islander people in the public domain both echo and contribute

[1] J Chesterman and B Galligan, *Citizens Without Rights: Aborigines and Australian Citizenship* (Cambridge, Cambridge University Press, 1997).

[2] See, eg: Uluru Statement from the Heart, Uluru, 26 May 2017; M Mansell, *Treaty and Statehood: Aboriginal Self-Determination* (Annandale, Federation Press, 2016).

to Indigenous disempowerment,[3] a growing Indigenous participatory media sphere offers potential to critique, challenge and reframe issues around Indigenous priorities.[4]

Australia's three arms of government are set out in Chapters I, II and III of the Australian Constitution. These institutions do not exist or operate on their own, however. While the Constitution sets out their key powers and responsibilities, its text was drafted against a set of theories and assumptions about the proper exercise and functions of public authority, and a range of unwritten, informal principles constituting the 'sinews and nerves of our body politic'[5] guide the behaviour of those exercising public power. Some of these take the form of constitutional or parliamentary conventions; binding but judicially unenforceable rules, which fill 'the important vacuums left between the words and phrases in the text' of the instrument.[6] Other norms and values that play a similar role arise from the history or structure of the instrument itself, imbuing those political institutions and their relationships with meaning.[7] Examination of the judiciary, the legislature and the executive therefore requires both doctrinal analysis, as well as attention to the underlying constitutional norms and values, those 'deep substantive commitments',[8] that give Australia's governance institutions meaning and channel political practice.

Analysis is carried out in three parts. I begin with the judiciary, outlining two foundational principles that construct, as well as constrict, Aboriginal and Torres Strait Islander participation. It is important to note at the outset that Australia has no history of treaty-making, and there is no larger record of treating Aboriginal and Torres Strait Islander communities as sovereign entities entitled to exercise an inherent right to govern themselves.[9] The Australian

[3] C Fforde, L Bamblett, R Lovett, S Gorringe and B Fogarty, 'Discourse, Deficit and Identity: Aboriginality, the Race Paradigm and the Language of Representation in Contemporary Australia' (2013) 149 *Media International Australia* 162; A Thomas, A Jakubowicz and H Norman, *Does the Media Fail Aboriginal Political Aspirations? 45 Years of News Media Reporting of Key Political Moments* (Canberra, Aboriginal Studies Press, 2020).

[4] K McCallum, L Waller and T Dreher, 'Mediatisation, Marginalisation and Disruption in Australian Indigenous Affairs' (2016) 4 *Media and Communication* 30; J Latimore, 'Changing the Channel: Social Media and the Information Wars' (2018) 60 *Griffith Review* 50.

[5] E Forsey, 'The Courts and the Conventions of the Constitution' (1984) 33 *University of New Brunswick Law Journal* 11, 12.

[6] I Killey, *Constitutional Conventions in Australia: An Introduction to the Unwritten Rules of Australia's Constitutions* (London, Anthem Press, 2014) 10.

[7] *Palmer v Ayers; Ferguson v Ayers* (2017) 259 CLR 478, 495 [42] (Gageler J); citing *Baxter v Commissioner of Taxation (NSW)* (1907) 4 CLR 1087, 1109.

[8] E Arcioni and A Stone, 'The Small Brown Bird: Values and Aspirations in the Australian Constitution' (2016) 14 *International Journal of Constitutional Law* 60, 60–61.

[9] *Love v Commonwealth; Thoms v Commonwealth* (2020) 94 ALJR 198, 235 [178] (Keane J): Aboriginal and Torres Strait Islander peoples do not 'enjoy a constitutionally privileged political relationship with the Australian body politic' (*Love; Thoms*). On the historical absence of a treaty-relationship see: H Hobbs and G Williams, 'The Noongar Settlement: Australia's First Treaty' (2018) 40 *Sydney Law Review* 1, 22–24.

Constitution simply ignored hundreds of existing Indigenous governing orders, blanketing multiple complex normative systems in a single legal framework that denied the reality and continuing vitality of those self-governing communities. Against this background, attempts to pluralise Australian law by recognising the continuing existence and significance of Aboriginal law and dispute resolution practices, let alone Indigenous communities' identity as collective political groups, face ongoing challenges. Those challenges are amplified by the fact that the Constitution imposed a 'strongly democratic and popular framework' of governance, 'predicated on the absence of … minorities within the polity'.[10] Although gradual removal of discriminatory legislation and practices has secured democratic goals, that underlying structure has not changed. The dominance of political constitutionalism and absence of comprehensive rights protection prioritises the electoral process as the chief means of influence and accountability, posing problems for a marginalised community comprising only three per cent of Australia's population.[11]

The structure of the Commonwealth Parliament does not respond to these challenges. As the 'heart of Australia's constitutional system',[12] it is vital that Indigenous voices are heard in Parliament. Low electoral participation and electoral system design, however, combine to inhibit the capacity of Aboriginal and Torres Strait Islander peoples to elect representatives of their choice, while strict party discipline constrains the capacity of those representatives to persistently advocate for Indigenous interests. The committee system offers an alternative avenue for voices to be heard by the legislature, but its capacity to empower Indigenous Australians is also imperfect. Like the legislature, the parliamentary committee system is not designed to ameliorate or rectify challenges specifically faced by Indigenous peoples.

Australian governance largely operates under a strict conception of formal equality. Indigenous peoples' interests as Australian citizens may be heard and protected, but their continuing existence as collective political units is marginalised. Recognition is ad hoc and limited. Greater effort is made in the executive branch, where specific mechanisms and processes to hear Indigenous voices do exist. Nonetheless, reflecting the formal equality that pervades Australia's governing institutions, such recognition is underdeveloped and premised on a thin account aimed at legitimating government action, rather than substantively enabling Indigenous peoples to express their views in the processes of government. Those views will be heard in the following chapter.

[10] P Emerton, 'Ideas' in C Saunders and A Stone (eds), *The Oxford Handbook of the Australian Constitution* (Oxford, Oxford University Press, 2018) 143, 156.

[11] K Gover, 'From the Heart: The Indigenous Challenge to Australian Public Law' in J Varuhas and S Wilson Stark (eds), *The Frontiers of Public Law* (Oxford, Hart Publishing, 2020) 205, 218.

[12] A Simpson, 'Parliaments' in C Saunders and A Stone (eds), *The Oxford Handbook of the Australian Constitution* (Oxford, Oxford University Press, 2018) 563, 563.

II. THE JUDICIARY

The judiciary is tasked with interpreting and applying the law. In Australia, that law is ultimately the Australian Constitution. This poses immediate challenges for Aboriginal and Torres Strait Islander peoples; the Constitution imposed a foreign system of law and government, displacing diverse normative orders across the continent with a single legal framework predicated on their exclusion.[13] Exclusion operated in two ways. It denied the existence and operation of Aboriginal law and dispute resolution practices and it cast Indigenous peoples out of the 'constitutional community'.[14] Legal reform has since welcomed Indigenous peoples into the Australian polity,[15] but recognition of Aboriginal law remains inchoate, subsumed within dominant conceptions of national unity and formal equality. These two underlying values continue to affect Aboriginal and Torres Strait Islander peoples' participation in the processes of government in other ways. Indigenous peoples may today form part of the Australian community, but their inclusion was not accompanied by amendment to the framework of governance. Consequently, although exceptions exist, the Australian legal system is not designed to empower Indigenous peoples to be heard as Indigenous peoples.

A. Aboriginal Law

Aboriginal societies have inhabited the Australian continent for at least 60,000 years.[16] As distinct communities, they developed a body of norms, values and traditions, a 'system of rules of conduct',[17] to settle disputes that might arise. The elaborate bodies of law that evolved across the land differ from Western conceptions. Aboriginal law is holistic and pervasive; intimately connected to the particular tracts of country that each community is connected to and is responsible for; it 'flows from the living heart[]' of country, and sustains that country.[18] As Kombumerri and Munaljahlai legal scholar Christine

[13] D Lino, 'Indigenous Recognition' in R Dixon (ed), *Australian Constitutional Values* (Oxford, Hart Publishing, 2018) 243, 243–47.

[14] E Arcioni, 'Excluding Indigenous Australians from "The People": A Reconsideration of s 25 and 127 of the Constitution' (2014) 40 *Federal Law Review* 1, 18.

[15] Although positive, this reform fails to do justice to Indigenous claims for differentiated citizenship status: H Hobbs, 'Constitutional Recognition and Reform: Developing an Inclusive Australian Citizenship through Treaty' (2018) 53 *Australian Journal of Political Science* 176.

[16] P Veth and S O'Connor, 'The Past 50,000 Years: An Archaeological View' in A Bashford and S Macintyre (eds), *The Cambridge History of Australia: Volume 1: Indigenous and Colonial Australia* (Cambridge, Cambridge University Press, 2013) 17, 19.

[17] *Milirrpum v Nabalco Pty Ltd* (1971) 17 FLR 141, 266 (Blackburn J).

[18] A Kwaymullina and B Kwaymullina, 'Learning to Read the Signs: Law in an Indigenous Reality' (2010) 34 *Journal of Australian Studies* 195, 202–03; J Gurrwanngu Gaykamangu, 'Ngarra Law: Aboriginal Customary Law from Arnhem Land' (2012) 2 *Northern Territory Law Journal* 236, 247.

Black has explained, 'the Land is the source of Law'.[19] Colonial dispossession and European settlement undermined traditional authority and dislocated members from their community, their country and their law. Despite considerable challenges, however, anthropological work and successive comprehensive inquiries have recognised the continuing dynamism and vitality of Aboriginal law. Adapting and responding to accommodate and utilise non-Indigenous law and practice, Aboriginal law 'exists as a real force, influencing or controlling the acts and lives' of Indigenous peoples across the country.[20]

The Constitution ignores these multiple intricate bodies of social ordering and there remains no systemic or general recognition of Aboriginal law within the Australian legal system. Rather, reflecting prevailing conceptions of national unity and formal equality, concerns are not infrequently raised that expressly acknowledging separate normative systems would be 'divisive' or discriminatory.[21] Nonetheless, because Aboriginal law still exists, recognition occurs in practice, albeit in a limited and 'haphazard' manner.[22]

Aboriginal law is sometimes incorporated by the judiciary. In *Mabo v Queensland (No 2)* the High Court held that the common law recognises native title,[23] a form of Indigenous land tenure that 'has its origin in the traditional laws acknowledged and the customs observed by the [relevant] indigenous people'.[24] Individual judges have also acknowledged the existence of Aboriginal law in reaching their decisions; in *R v Jungarai*, for instance, Forster CJ of the Northern Territory Supreme Court granted bail to an Aboriginal defendant accused of murder to enable him to undergo tribal punishment.[25] Although the fact that the defendant was sanctioned under Aboriginal law did not prevent Australian courts from sentencing him to a period of imprisonment, it appears to have been taken into account in determining that sentence.[26] These cases reveal the judiciary's capacity to consider Indigenous interests and hear Indigenous voices in certain fields, but Australian courts have proven unwilling to acknowledge

[19] C Black, *The Land is the Source of Law: A Dialogic Encounter with Indigenous Jurisprudence* (Abingdon, Routledge, 2010).

[20] Australian Law Reform Commission, 'Recognition of Aboriginal Customary Laws' (Report No 31, 1986) vol 1, 79 [103]; Northern Territory Law Reform Committee, 'Report on Aboriginal Customary Law' (2003); Law Reform Commission of Western Australia, 'Aboriginal Customary Laws: The Interaction of Western Australian Law with Aboriginal Law and Culture' (Final Report Project 94, 2006) 80.

[21] See, eg ALRC, 'Aboriginal Customary Laws' (1986) vol 1, ch 9.

[22] M Davis and H McGlade, 'International Human Rights Law and the Recognition of Aboriginal Customary Law' (Aboriginal Customary Laws Background Paper 10, Law Reform Commission of Western Australia, 2006) 381, 382.

[23] *Mabo v Queensland (No 2)* (1992) 175 CLR 1.

[24] *Fejo v Northern Territory* (1998) 195 CLR 96, 128 [46] (Gleeson CJ, Gaudron, McHugh, Gummow, Hayne and Callinan J).

[25] *R v Jungarai* (1981) 9 NTR 30, 31–32.

[26] *Jungarai v R* [1982] FCA (1 June 1982). See also *Jadurin v The Queen* (1982) 44 ALR 242 (1982). Judicial tolerance for tribal punishment has dissipated: T Anthony, *Indigenous People, Crime and Punishment* (Abingdon, Routledge, 2013) 128–35.

the continuing existence of Aboriginal law at a more general level. In *Walker v New South Wales*, the High Court rejected a submission that Aboriginal criminal law continues to function today, holding that 'Australian criminal law does not … accommodate an alternative body of law operating alongside it',[27] while in the *Yorta Yorta* case, three members of the High Court held that the assertion of sovereignty by the British Crown 'necessarily entailed … that there could thereafter be no parallel law-making system'.[28]

In some cases, the limits of the common law have been overcome by legislation. Statutory provisions across a wide field of law, including, land rights, family law, the criminal justice system, cultural heritage and intellectual property, direct courts to consider Aboriginal law as part of their decision-making process. For example, s 69 of the Aboriginal Land Rights (Northern Territory) Act 1975 (Cth) criminalises the entry on land that is a sacred site, except where entry is conducted by an Aboriginal person 'in accordance with Aboriginal tradition'. Similarly, the Family Law Act 1975 (Cth) requires judges to consider the cultural rights of Indigenous children and Indigenous kinship obligations and child-rearing practices in making parenting orders.[29] These provisions are significant, having imposed 'a far greater imperative' on courts to consider cultural issues,[30] but legislation in other areas has reduced scope for Indigenous voices to be heard in the Australian legal system. In *Western Australia v Ward*, for instance, the High Court held that the Native Title Act 1993 (Cth) (NTA) does not protect cultural knowledge.[31] More directly, amendments to the Crimes Act 1914 (Cth) as part of the Northern Territory Intervention explicitly preclude Northern Territory courts from considering customary law or cultural practices as a reason for certain behaviour in bail applications and sentencing.[32]

Overall, these examples paint a mixed picture. While they demonstrate that there is no legal or political obstacle to recognising Aboriginal law, they also reveal that existing recognition is irregular and unstructured. This is largely because, Greg McIntyre explains, recognition is conducted via a process that 'reinforces a[n unequal] power relationship', whereby the 'dominant system chooses when and how to incorporate compatible portions' of Aboriginal laws,[33] failing to accord Aboriginal law the respect or status it deserves *as law*.

[27] *Walker v New South Wales* (1994) 182 CLR 45, 50 (Mason CJ).

[28] *Members of the Yorta Yorta Aboriginal Community v Victoria* (2002) 214 CLR 422, 444 [44] (Gleeson CJ, Gummow and Hayne JJ). For a recent affirmation see: *Love; Thoms* (n 9) 209 [25] (Kiefel CJ), 223 [102] (Gageler J), 237 [199] (Keane J), 250 [264] (Nettle J), 268 [356] (Gordon J).

[29] Family Law Act 1975 (Cth), ss 60B(3), 60CC(3)(h), 60CC(6), 61F.

[30] *Davis v Davis* (2007) 38 Fam LR 671, 691 [79].

[31] *Western Australia v Ward* (2002) 213 CLR 1, 209 [468].

[32] Crimes Act 1914 (Cth) ss 15AB(1)(b), 16AA (subject to certain exceptions).

[33] G McIntyre, 'Aboriginal Customary Law: Can it be Recognised?' (Aboriginal Customary Laws Background Paper 9, Law Reform Commission of Western Australia, 2006) 341, 345.

The legal fiction of *terra nullius* may have been erased, but the larger governance system built on that fiction has not been restructured.[34]

This problem is also present in relation to dispute resolution systems. Research reveals that Indigenous peoples feel disempowered and alienated by mainstream court processes,[35] which differ markedly from their own forms of dispute resolution. Attempts to establish dispute resolution practices that embody Indigenous peoples' cultural values, however, are complicated by Australia's governance system. The Constitution imposes strict constraints on the capacity of the Commonwealth to establish bodies exercising adjudicatory power; the judicial power of the Commonwealth may only be exercised by courts established in accordance with Ch III of the Constitution,[36] and those courts may only exercise judicial power.[37] This precludes a putative federal Indigenous Court from exercising a combination of conciliatory or mediatory and judicial functions, and would impose strict security of tenure requirements on judicial officers, contrary to traditional Indigenous practices.

The situation is more complex at the state level. The restrictions noted above are impliedly drawn from the separation of legislative, executive and judicial powers in Chs I, II and III of the Constitution. This structural separation is not present at the state level, suggesting constitutional space for innovative Indigenous dispute resolution systems exercising a mix of adjudicatory and non-adjudicatory functions. Such space exists, but is limited. The High Court has drawn on Ch III to place constitutional limits on the capacity of state parliaments to alter their courts in a manner that would impair their institutional integrity as repositories of federal jurisdiction.[38] Consequently, an Indigenous state court exercising a combination of judicial and non-judicial functions could not be empowered with federal jurisdiction.

Constitutional complications have so far been avoided by making only a limited effort to formally incorporate Indigenous peoples and values into the Australian court system. Indigenous Sentencing and Circle Courts exist in all states and territories except Tasmania. These 'Aboriginal Courts' are informal, allowing Elders and community members to take part and influence the process by providing information to the judicial officer on the offender and the impact the offence has had on the community, with the aim of reducing cultural alienation and ensuring community support for sentencing outcomes.[39]

[34] L Behrendt, *Achieving Social Justice: Indigenous Rights and Australia's Future* (Annandale, Federation Press, 2003) 120.

[35] ALRC, 'Incarceration Rates of Aboriginal and Torres Strait Islander Peoples' (Discussion Paper No 84, 2017) 191–94 [11.18]–[11.34].

[36] *New South Wales v Commonwealth (The Wheat Case)* (1915) 20 CLR 54; *Waterside Workers' Federation of Australia v J W Alexander Ltd* (1918) 25 CLR 434.

[37] *R v Kirby; Ex parte Boilermakers' Society of Australia* (1956) 94 CLR 254.

[38] *Kable v DPP (NSW)* (1996) 189 CLR 1; see J Stellios, *Zines's The High Court and the Constitution*, 6th edn (Annandale, Federation Press, 2015) 275–99.

[39] E Marchetti and K Daly, 'Indigenous Sentencing Courts: Towards a Theoretical and Jurisprudential Model' (2007) 29 *Sydney Law Review* 415.

Empirical evidence suggests that Indigenous communities are generally supportive of these processes,[40] but it is clear that they are inadequate mechanisms. In addition to only being available for sentencing offences at the Magistrates level, these courts are not based on 'Aboriginal authority structures'[41] but modified western processes. Like state recognition of Aboriginal law, Aboriginal Courts 'can only represent the Indigenous systems of laws to the extent permitted by the non-Indigenous courts'.[42]

B. Judicially Enforceable Rights Protection

Non-recognition of Aboriginal law and dispute resolution practices is 'interwoven with colonial history and Australia's claim to sovereignty',[43] but it also reflects a formal conception of equality predicated on the notion that all persons within the Australian community constitute a unified national polity. These two underlying values similarly manifest themselves in the continuing absence of comprehensive judicially enforceable rights protections, although the initial absence also stems from a desire to exclude. As contemporary prevailing conceptions of Australian identity largely perceive Aboriginal and Torres Strait Islander peoples as undifferentiated members of the community,[44] institutional structures to specifically empower them are lacking. Consequently, although judicial review offers the potential to ensure that Indigenous peoples are heard in the processes of government by providing 'the basic institutional check on majority rule',[45] the Constitution contains few express rights protections, leaving the courts with limited scope to protect and promote Indigenous interests.

Faith in Parliament and electoral accountability as a protector of rights is often identified as a key reason for the absence of a comprehensive bill of rights. Chief Justice Mason, for instance, has explained that this sentiment was 'one of the unexpressed assumptions on which the Constitution was drafted'.[46] However, while British constitutional theorists and traditions heavily influenced the drafters – leading them to disclaim the need for incorporated rights guarantees in favour of relying on 'the common law and political processes'[47] – the absence of rights guarantees also reflects the racist attitudes

[40] G Wallace, 'Nowra Circle Sentencing – Seven Years Down the Track' (2010) 7(16) *Indigenous Law Bulletin* 13.

[41] ALRC (n 20) vol 2, 30, [721].

[42] M Harris, 'From Australian Courts to Aboriginal Courts in Australia – Bridging the Gap?' (2004) 16 *Current Issues in Criminal Justice* 26, 35.

[43] H Blagg, *Crime, Aboriginality and the Decolonisation of Justice*, 2nd edn (Annandale, Federation Press, 2016) 131.

[44] Hobbs, 'Constitutional Recognition and Reform' (2018).

[45] B Galligan, 'Judicial Review in the Australian Federal System: Its Origins and Function' (1979) 10 *Federal Law Review* 367, 367.

[46] *Australian Capital Television v Commonwealth* (1992) 177 CLR 106, 136 (Mason CJ) (*ACTV*).

[47] G Williams and D Hume, *Human Rights under the Australian Constitution*, 2nd edn (Oxford, Oxford University Press, 2013) 67.

of the day. As George Williams and David Hume have argued, the 'prevailing sentiment' Chief Justice Mason identified, 'was not [solely] due to a belief that rights across the whole community were generally well protected', but rather, was 'driven by a desire to maintain race-based distinctions'.[48] The drafters specifically empowered the Parliament with plenary legislative authority to make laws that discriminate on the basis of 'race',[49] and were careful to ensure any legal constraints on this power were avoided.

In this light, statements by the drafters that it would be 'utterly impossible to conceive that … Parliament will proceed to infringe any of the liberties of the citizens',[50] exposes the ethno-cultural identity of the citizenry.[51] These attitudes were also reflected in early decisions of the High Court. In the *Engineers* case, for example, the majority suggested that discriminatory legislation was highly improbable, but if it were enacted, would swiftly be resolved through the normal processes of electoral accountability:

> [I]f it be conceivable that the representatives of the people of Australia as a whole would ever proceed to use their national powers to injure the people of Australia considered sectionally, it is certainly within the power of the people themselves to resent and reverse what may be done. No protection of this Court in such a case is necessary or proper.[52]

Though an accurate account of the constitutional values that underpin Australian governance, this statement ignores the position of Indigenous peoples. Aboriginal and Torres Strait Islander peoples *were* entirely unable to protect themselves through the normal processes of electoral accountability because they were denied the vote in federal elections in several states until as late as 1962.[53] Further, as I demonstrate below, simply extending the franchise has not been sufficient. Electoral system design, party discipline and a commitment to formal equality means Aboriginal and Torres Strait Islander people are generally unable to exert meaningful influence on the political process; they may 'resent', but they cannot 'reverse' what may be done.

48 ibid 52.

49 Constitution, s 51(xxvi). The scope of this head of power is expansive. The Court has never ruled definitively on this point, but the orthodox position is that it permits Parliament to enact legislation imposing a disadvantage on Aboriginal and Torres Strait Islander people: *Kartinyeri v Commonwealth* (1998) 195 CLR 337, 378–79 (Gummow and Hayne JJ).

50 *Official Records of the Convention Debates*, Melbourne, 2 March 1898, 1761 (W Trenwith).

51 E Arcioni, 'Tracing the Ethno-Cultural or Racial Identity of the Australian Constitutional People' (2015) 15 *Oxford University Commonwealth Law Journal* 173, 175.

52 *Amalgamated Society of Engineers v Adelaide Steamship Co Ltd* (1920) 28 CLR 129, 151–52 (Knox CJ, Isaacs, Rich and Starke JJ).

53 Commonwealth Franchise Act 1902 (Cth), s 4; Commonwealth Electoral Act 1962 (Cth), s 2. Aboriginal and Torres Strait Islander peoples entitled to vote in state elections were enfranchised at the federal level in 1949: Commonwealth Electoral Act 1949 (Cth), s 3. As Indigenous peoples in Queensland, Western Australia, and the Northern Territory were precluded from voting in state elections, they remained unable to vote in Commonwealth elections until 1962: M Goot, 'The Aboriginal Franchise and its Consequences' (2006) 52 *Australian Journal of Politics and History* 517, 525.

Constitutional values can change, even if the text does not.[54] Notwithstanding limited express rights protections, the High Court has uncovered several rights implied by the text and structure of the Constitution, some of which have proven effective in protecting Aboriginal and Torres Strait Islander peoples' interests. In particular, drawing on provisions that mandate that the legislative and executive branches of government are 'ultimately answerable to the Australian people',[55] the Court has held that the Constitution implicitly protects freedom of political communication as 'indispensable to that accountability'.[56] While the act of casting a ballot is the principal moment at which an elector 'holds her representative accountable',[57] the Court has employed a broader notion of democratic accountability, declaring that the implied right operates across the electoral process and on all political matters.[58] In several cases, this approach has provided some protection for Indigenous Australians. For example, although the principle of representative government did not mandate universal adult suffrage in 1901, High Court justices have suggested that today it would prevent Parliament from legislating to disenfranchise Indigenous citizens.[59] The Court has also relied on this implied right to strike down legislation that purported to prevent prisoners from voting. As Indigenous peoples are 'markedly over-represented in the prison population',[60] the decision indirectly protected Indigenous Australians.

Protection is significant, but it is also limited.[61] The implied right protects Aboriginal and Torres Strait Islander people only in their status as Australian *electors* because its underlying justification is to ensure the 'efficacy of electoral accountability',[62] and not to empower Indigenous peoples' participation in the processes of government. This limitation can produce perverse outcomes. In *Kruger v Commonwealth*, for instance, five Aboriginal plaintiffs forcibly removed from their homes and communities as children unsuccessfully sought a declaration that the 1918 Ordinance authorising their removal was invalid.[63]

[54] R Dixon, 'Amending Constitutional Identity' (2012) 33 *Cardozo Law Review* 1847, 1852.

[55] *Nationwide News v Wills* (1992) 177 CLR 1, 47 [17] (Brennan J); *ACTV* (n 46) 137 [36] (Mason CJ).

[56] *ACTV* (n 46) 138 [38] (Mason CJ).

[57] H Pitkin, *The Concept of Representation* (Berkeley, University of California Press, 1967) 43.

[58] *Brown v Tasmania* (2017) 261 CLR 328 (*Brown*).

[59] *Roach v Electoral Commissioner* (2007) 233 CLR 162, 197 [78] (Gummow, Kirby and Crennan JJ) (*Roach*).

[60] ibid 223 [173] (Hayne J). See further *Murphy v Electoral Commissioner* (2016) 90 ALJR 1027, 1050–51 [106]–[107] (Gageler J).

[61] It does not appear that a similar indirect benefit has occurred following *Coleman v Power* (2004) 220 CLR 1. In *Coleman*, the Court held that public order or public nuisance offences should be interpreted in light of the implied freedom. As Aboriginal and Torres Strait Islander people are disproportionately charged with these offences the decision could have reduced the numbers of Indigenous peoples caught up in the criminal law. Empirical studies suggest that this has not happened: T Walsh, 'The Impact of *Coleman v Power* on the Policing, Defence and Sentencing of Public Nuisance Cases in Queensland' (2006) 30 *Melbourne University Law Review* 191.

[62] *Brown* (n 58) 377–78 [162] (Gageler J).

[63] *Kruger v Commonwealth* (1997) 190 CLR 1.

The plaintiffs challenged the Ordinance on several grounds, including that removal breached an implied right to freedom of movement and association, drawn from the implied freedom of political communication. Justice McHugh accepted that this implied right may exist, but held that it must be connected to the process of voting. As no Aboriginal person in the Northern Territory had the right to vote during the life of the Ordinance, they enjoyed no 'freedom or immunity from laws affecting their common law rights of association or travel'.[64] In other words, the plaintiffs were unable to succeed *because* they were discriminately denied the franchise.

Some statutory rights protections do exist. The Racial Discrimination Act 1975 (Cth) (RDA) prohibits acts or legislation that discriminate on the basis of race, except where such discrimination is a 'special measure' designed to secure the advancement of members of a particular race.[65] The RDA has been effective in protecting Indigenous peoples by rendering discriminatory legislation in Queensland[66] and Western Australia[67] inoperative. Once again, however, its protections are narrow. As ordinary Commonwealth legislation, the RDA is not entrenched against the Commonwealth, and the federal Parliament has passed at least three laws that override or exclude its protections over the last two decades.[68] In each case, that legislation has expressly discriminated against Aboriginal and Torres Strait Islander peoples. This practice suggests that any argument that the RDA has acquired quasi-constitutional status, such that it forms part of the background norms and values of the Australian constitutional framework, ignores the position of Indigenous people.

The RDA's limitations extend further. In contrast to the situation at international law,[69] there is no requirement that beneficial legislation designed to secure the advancement of Indigenous peoples either has their support or has been drafted in accordance with their wishes. In *Maloney v The Queen*, the High Court held that, while, 'as a matter of common sense, prior consultation … is likely to be essential to the practical implementation' of any measure,[70] the existence or adequacy of consultation is not relevant to the determination of

[64] ibid 144 (McHugh J).

[65] Racial Discrimination Act 1975 (Cth), ss 8, 9; *Gerhardy v Brown* (1985) 159 CLR 70.

[66] *Mabo v Queensland (No 1)* (1988) 166 CLR 186.

[67] *Western Australia v Commonwealth* (1995) 183 CLR 373.

[68] Native Title Act 1993 (Cth), Pt 2, Div 2; Native Title Amendment Act 1998 (Cth), Sch 1, s 3; Northern Territory National Emergency Response Act 2007 (Cth), Pt IV.

[69] United Nations Declaration on the Rights of Indigenous Peoples, GA Res 61/295, UN GAOR, 61st sess, 107th plen mtg, Supp No 49, UN Doc A/RES/61/295 (13 September 2007) arts 10–11, 19, 28–29, 32; Committee on the Elimination of Racial Discrimination, 'General Comment No. 32: The Meaning and Scope of Special Measures in the International Covenant on the Elimination of Racial Discrimination', 75th sess, UN Doc CERD/C/GC/32 (24 September 2009) [18]; Committee on the Elimination of Racial Discrimination, 'General Recommendation No. 23: Indigenous Peoples', 51st sess, UN Doc. A/52/18, annex V (18 August 1997) [4(d)].

[70] *Maloney v The Queen* (2013) 252 CLR 168, 186 [25] (French CJ) (*Maloney*).

whether legislation can be categorised as a special measure, and therefore validly enacted.[71]

Maloney turned on the question of the appropriate role of international law in interpreting legislative provisions, but the decision reflects the primacy of electoral accountability as the chief protector of rights in Australia and formal equality as an underlying structural value. This is most prominent in Crennan J's judgment. Her Honour notes that 'ordinarily neither consultation with constituents nor their consent to a law is a precondition to the legality of a statute'.[72] This is because robust 'democratic mechanisms' such as a 'free, informed public debate, a free press and regular elections', through 'which representative governments resolve contested policy'[73] permit the electorate to issue their judgment at the end of a parliamentary term. This is an accurate description of Australia's system of government, but like the *Engineers* decision, it ignores the distinctive position of Aboriginal and Torres Strait Islander peoples. As a marginalised, extreme numerical minority, territorially dispersed across the country, the absence of a requirement of consultation, even when implementing coercive measures supposedly targeted at improving their lives, inhibits Indigenous Australians' capacity to contest and challenge government action. Consistent with the fact that 'electoral choice ... constitutes the principal constraint' on the exercise of legislative and executive power in Australia,[74] the Court is limited to merely 'determin[ing] whether the assessment made by the political branch could reasonably be made'.[75] This is the case even if Indigenous peoples were not heard by the political branch.

Judicial review is an important mechanism to ensure the legality of legislation and executive action, but whether it can protect specific interests depends on the existence of a constitutional or statutory hook. Plenary legislative power in Indigenous affairs, the primacy of electoral accountability, and the corresponding absence of a comprehensive rights framework, means that hook is often absent, limiting the capacity of the judiciary to 'prevent unfair and racist policy-making'.[76] An evolutionary approach to constitutional interpretation has uncovered several implied rights that have proven effective at protecting the ability of Aboriginal and Torres Strait Islander peoples to participate in the processes of government in individual cases, but such protection is indirect and coincidental. The Australian legal system is not designed to empower Aboriginal and Torres Strait Islander peoples to be heard in the processes of government, and generally does not do so.

[71] ibid 185–86 [24] (French CJ); 208 [91] (Hayne J); 222 [136] (Crennan J); 238 [186] (Kiefel J); 257 [240] (Bell J).

[72] ibid 222 [135] (Crennan J).

[73] ibid.

[74] *McCloy v New South Wales* (2015) 257 CLR 178, 226 [111] (Gageler J) (*McCloy*).

[75] *Maloney* (n 70) 183–85 [19]–[21], 193 [45] (French CJ); 222–23 [137] (Crennan J); 260 [248] (Bell J); 298–99 [351] (Gageler J).

[76] Behrendt, *Achieving Social Justice* (2003) 11.

III. THE LEGISLATURE

The electoral process lies 'at the very heart of the system of government for which the Constitution provides'.[77] As the High Court has explained, the legitimacy of that system is premised on its accessibility; 'equality of opportunity to participate in the exercise of political sovereignty is … guaranteed by our Constitution'.[78] The design of the Australian Parliament reflects this position. Consistent with a commitment to formal legal equality, meaningful institutional opportunities to participate are enjoyed on a non-discriminatory basis. Aboriginal and Torres Strait Islander people may not enjoy dedicated mechanisms to ensure their interests are considered in the legislature, but as Australian citizens, they are guaranteed a formally equal opportunity to have their voices heard via general mechanisms and processes. This is insufficient. As I demonstrate here, the three major institutional opportunities for citizens to have their interests heard in the processes of the Australian legislature – voting, standing for Parliament, and the committee system – do not take account of the distinctive position and circumstances of Aboriginal and Torres Strait Islander peoples, inhibiting in practice their ability to be heard.

A. Electoral Participation

Indigenous Australians enjoy a formally equal opportunity to participate in the electoral process but political and structural factors, including electoral design, inhibit their capacity to ensure their interests are present and debated in Parliament. Exercising the right to vote is distinct from its formal entitlement. Despite an ability to participate in Australia's electoral system, many Aboriginal and Torres Strait Islander people fail to enrol or fail to vote. It is difficult to quantify the precise figure because the electoral roll does not require people to identify as Indigenous; in 2019, however, the Australian Electoral Commission (AEC) reported that across Australia, Indigenous enrolment sat at around 76 per cent.[79] This number is disputed. Writing in 2016, *Guardian Australia* journalist Paul Daley suggests that the AEC figure 'is a generous assessment'; reporting that 'the real enrolment figure is said to be closer to 50 per cent' and that 'private assessment by some Indigenous leaders, non-government and government agencies' put turnout at around 25 to 30 per cent of the entire population.[80] Unsurprisingly, discrepancies exist across the country: in Western

[77] *Roach* (n 59) 198 [81] (Gummow, Kirby and Crennan JJ).

[78] *McCloy* (n 74) 207 [45] (French CJ, Kiefel, Bell and Keane JJ).

[79] Australian Electoral Commission, Submission No 120 to Joint Standing Committee on Electoral Matters, 'Inquiry into and Report on All Aspects of the Conduct of the 2019 Federal Election and Matters Related Thereto' (20 September 2019) 10.

[80] P Daley, 'Only 58% of Indigenous Australians are Registered to Vote. We Should be Asking Why' *Guardian Australia* (30 June 2016), available at www.theguardian.com/commentisfree/2016/jun/30/only-58-of-indigenous-australians-are-registered-to-vote-we-should-be-asking-why.

Australia the AEC estimates that only about 63 per cent of Indigenous people are currently on the roll.[81] In contrast, the AEC estimates that 97 per cent of all eligible Australians are registered.[82]

Many reasons have been proffered as to why electoral registration and participation rates among Aboriginal and Torres Strait Islander people lag considerably those of non-Indigenous citizens. For some Indigenous peoples, actively choosing not to register or vote is a form of conscientious objection or protest. Former secretary of the Aboriginal Provisional Government (APG), Michael Mansell (Palawa), has argued that compulsory voting is 'aimed at containing Aboriginal political development', and forcibly incorporating Indigenous people within Australia's political system.[83] In the United States, Jeff Corntassel (Cherokee Nation) and Richard Witmar II have made a similar point, arguing that there is a 'fine line' between participation and co-option.[84] Reflecting these philosophical and political objections, prosecution for Indigenous non-participation is rare in Australia. Although Mansell was convicted and fined $25 in 1992,[85] the Electoral Commissioner of Queensland waived a $174 fine issued to the Chairperson of the APG, Callum Clayton-Dixon, in 2015. In a statutory declaration, Clayton-Dixon had argued that he has a 'religious obligation, as a member of the Anaiwan Aboriginal tribe not to participate in Australian elections'.[86]

Political objections undoubtedly account for a proportion of non-participation, but research suggests that structural factors are also significant. In its report on the conduct of the 2013 federal election, the Joint Select Committee on Electoral Matters recognised that Indigenous electors face significant barriers to electoral participation, including language difficulties and access to polling booths.[87] Other studies paint a similar picture. In October 2007, Lisa Hill and Kate Alport conducted a series of interviews with A<u>n</u>angu women of the Iwantja Community at Indulkana in the A<u>n</u>angu Pitjantjatjara Yankunytjiatjara Lands. Their results suggest that, at least among this community, voting abstention is often a result of practical obstacles such as insufficient electoral education and

[81] W Sanders, 'Electoral Administration and Aboriginal Voting Power in the Northern Territory: Reality and Potential Viewed from the 2019 Federal Election' (Centre for Aboriginal Economic Policy Research, Working Paper No 132, 2019) 12.

[82] Australian Electoral Commission (n 79) 9.

[83] M Mansell, 'Aborigines and the Constitution' (1993) 2 *Human Rights Defender* 5, 6.

[84] J Corntassel and RC Witmar II, *Forced Federalism: Contemporary Challenges to Indigenous Nationhood* (Norman, University of Oklahoma Press, 2008) 137.

[85] Mansell, 'Aborigines' (1993) 6.

[86] S Armbruster, 'Qld Election Non-Voter's Fine Dropped Over Aboriginal Religious Beliefs' *SBS News* (10 November 2015), available at www.sbs.com.au/news/qld-election-non-voter-s-fine-dropped-over-aboriginal-religious-belief.

[87] Parliamentary Joint Standing Committee on Electoral Matters, 'The 2013 Federal Election: Report on the Conduct of the 2013 Election and Matters Related Thereto' (April 2015) 110–111 [5.34]–[5.46], 114 [5.53], 117 [5.67]. See further Parliamentary Joint Standing Committee on Electoral Matters, 'Report on the Conduct of the 2016 Federal Election and Matters Related Thereto' (November 2018) 64–69 [3.143]–[3.164].

language literacy, as well as cultural obligations that prevent potential voters from attending polling day.[88] Hill and Alport also note, however, that many of the community members interviewed felt alienated and disempowered by the electoral process. There was a strong desire for candidates to visit and explain their policies in a language they understood.[89]

Low levels of trust in government run through Hill and Alport's study, with many interviewees noting that they 'don't believe government listens to them'.[90] Although it is difficult to extrapolate from one series of interviews in a single community, the 2017 Referendum Council regional dialogues revealed that these attitudes are replicated throughout Indigenous communities across the nation,[91] potentially accounting more generally for lower rates of participation. Failure by candidates and parties to meaningfully engage, as highlighted by the women of the Iwantja Community, likely plays a role in fomenting these practices. However, non-participation may also reflect a 'rational calculation that the Aboriginal vote is not generally decisive at election time'.[92] This is not an inevitable consequence of the numerically small, geographically dispersed nature of the Indigenous population in Australia, but a powerful yet subtle effect of the electoral system.

Electoral systems are not neutral but recognise and affirm 'different categories of difference'.[93] Single-member electorates of roughly equal size emphasise individual voting equality, while the dominance of political parties accentuates ideology as the foundational cleavage in political contests. Australia's electoral system is geared towards these two categories of difference. As a numerically small community, territorially dispersed across the continent, Aboriginal and Torres Strait Islander people do not constitute a majority in any Commonwealth electorate, and in any case, have considerably lower levels of electoral participation. Electoral system design and demographics combine to encourage politicians and parties to develop policy to attract non-Indigenous voters, inhibiting the ability of Indigenous peoples to elect representatives who will act in their interests. This challenge has flow on effects for electoral participation. While evidence is mixed, many empirical studies suggest that electoral participation is linked to the extent to which people believe they can influence policy and perceive government to be responsive to their interests.[94] In New Zealand,

[88] L Hill and K Alport, 'Voting Attitudes and Behaviour Among Aboriginal Peoples: Reports from Anangu Women' (2010) 56 *Australian Journal of Politics and History* 242, 251.

[89] ibid 248, 251.

[90] ibid.

[91] Referendum Council, 'Final Report of the Referendum Council' (Commonwealth, 2017) 163.

[92] Hill and Alport, 'Voting Attitudes' (2010) 246. But see Sanders, 'Electoral Administration' (2019).

[93] A Reilly, 'Dedicated Seats in the Federal Parliament for Indigenous Australians: The Theoretical Case and its Practical Possibility' (2001) 2 *Balayi: Culture Law and Colonialism* 73, 90.

[94] K Smets and C van Ham, 'The Embarrassment of Riches? A Meta-Analysis of Individual-Level Research on Voter Turnout' (2013) 32 *Electoral Studies* 344, 355.

research has found that Māori people are 'more likely to vote', and 'more likely to believe that they have a say in government', when represented by a Māori politician.[95] It should not be surprising then that some Indigenous Australians disengage from the electoral process entirely.

It is difficult to know for certain the extent of, or reasons for, Aboriginal and Torres Strait Islander electoral non-participation. What is clear is that registration and turnout estimates reveal a considerable number of Indigenous peoples are either unable or choose not to exercise their right to vote. In doing so, they are registering a judgment on Australia's governance framework: either it actively excludes them, or it does not try hard enough to include them on their own terms. In both cases, it inhibits Indigenous Australians' interests from being heard in the processes of government.

B. Parliamentary Representation

Members of Parliament have substantial authority and capacity to directly and indirectly influence legislation and policy as well as catalyse and lead public debate. Election of Aboriginal and Torres Strait Islander people to Parliament has therefore long been identified as a key mechanism to improve the capacity of Indigenous Australians to have their distinctive interests considered in the processes of government. Indeed, as we saw in the Introduction, William Cooper believed that dedicated representation could influence the design and content of laws to benefit Indigenous peoples and protect them from discriminatory or detrimental provisions. Parliamentary committees and scholars have suggested that representation could also have broader advantages, including enhancing community knowledge and awareness of Indigenous culture and concerns.[96]

Consistent with the underlying conception of equality that pervades Australia's governing institutions, no mechanism or process guarantees Indigenous voices in the Parliament. Rather, Indigenous Australians may stand for any seat on the same basis as all other citizens. For many years this model failed to lead to the election of Indigenous people, but this has changed more recently. Although only nine politicians who identify as Indigenous have served across the life of the federal Parliament, seven of those were elected in or following the 2010 election, and five are serving in the current forty-sixth Parliament.[97] Three are members of the Australian Labor Party (ALP),

[95] S Banducci, T Donovan and J Karp, 'Minority Representation, Empowerment and Participation' (2004) 66 *The Journal of Politics* 534, 552.

[96] See, eg: New South Wales Legislative Council Standing Committee on Social Issues, 'Enhancing Aboriginal Political Representation: Inquiry into Dedicated Seats in the New South Wales Parliament' (1998) 43–49.

[97] They are: Noongar, Wangai and Yamatji Member for Hasluck, Ken Wyatt; Yawuru Senator, Patrick Dodson; Yanyuwa Senator, Malarndirri McCarthy; Gunnai-Gunditjmara Senator, Lidia Thorpe; and Wiradjuri Member for Barton, Linda Burney.

one of the country's two main political parties, which since 2015 has committed to preselect Indigenous peoples for public office.[98] These are positive developments that carry the possibility of greater engagement and consideration of issues that affect Indigenous peoples. Nonetheless, it does not alter the fact that electoral system design and strict party discipline fosters a model of representation that inhibits the ability of Indigenous Members of Parliament to represent Indigenous peoples, let alone encourage parliamentary debate on their distinctive concerns.[99]

It is often assumed that Indigenous Members of Parliament will act as representatives for their Indigenous nation or Indigenous peoples across Australia more generally. In announcing his government's decision to reject the Referendum Council's recommendation to establish a constitutionally enshrined Indigenous representative body, for instance, Prime Minister Malcolm Turnbull acknowledged that 'people who ask for a voice feel voiceless', but contended that alienation could be rectified with 'more Aboriginal and Torres Strait Islander Australians serving in the House and the Senate'.[100] While greater numbers of Indigenous parliamentarians will undoubtedly enhance awareness and consideration of Indigenous peoples' priorities, statements such as this fundamentally misconstrue the nature of parliamentary representation in Australia. As the previous section noted, Australia's electoral system ensures that an Indigenous politician cannot be elected without the support of non-Indigenous voters. Their political platform must consequently cater to non-Indigenous persons, 'temper[ing]' the ability of parliamentary representation 'to actually deliver meaningful change for Aboriginal people'.[101]

This structural factor combines with a political practice that sees representatives almost always vote along party lines. Australia has one of the world's highest levels of party discipline,[102] meaning that Indigenous Members of Parliament serving in a party must ordinarily support the party platform. Discipline is particularly strong in the ALP, which binds members of the parliamentary party to vote in accordance with the decision of caucus.[103] Members who 'cross the floor' are expelled. This is a real threat; in 3,020 divisions between 1974 and 1998, only 'a single vote' was cast by an ALP member against the party in the

[98] Australian Labor Party, 'National Platform: A Smart, Modern, Fair Australia' (2015) 238. This commitment remains in the most recent national platform: Australian Labor Party, 'National Platform: A Fair Go for Australia' (2018) 308.

[99] In relation to Canada see: M Morden, 'Parliament and the Representation of Indigenous Issues: The Canadian Case' (2018) 71 *Parliamentary Affairs* 124, 139–41.

[100] Prime Minister, Attorney-General, Minister for Indigenous Affairs, 'Response to Referendum Council's report on Constitutional Recognition' (media release, 26 October 2017).

[101] S Maddison, 'White Parliament, Black Politics: The Dilemmas of Indigenous Parliamentary Representation' (2010) 45 *Australian Journal of Political Science* 663, 668; Mansell, *Treaty and Statehood* (2016) 21.

[102] C Kam, *Party Discipline and Parliamentary Politics* (Cambridge, Cambridge University Press, 2009) 8.

[103] ALP National Constitution (adopted 18 December 2018), ss 14 (d)(ii), 25.

House of Representatives.[104] Although the Liberal and National parties have historically been more forgiving, crossing the floor remains rare. Analysis by the Parliamentary Library reveals that in 14,243 divisions between 1950 and 2004, only 439 saw a member vote against their party.[105] For Indigenous representatives to persistently advocate for Indigenous interests they must first convince their party to change its policy.

In a series of interviews with current and former parliamentarians, Sarah Maddison has explored the challenges faced by Aboriginal and Torres Strait Islander representatives, who at times emphasise their heritage by speaking for an Indigenous constituency, and at other times feel compelled to prioritise the interests of their party or wider electorate. These tensions are particularly pronounced in inaugural speeches, as by convention, it is here where parliamentarians detail their background and outline their philosophy. Maddison traces several of these speeches, identifying the fine line that their speakers tread. For instance, Eric Deeral (Guugu Yimithirr), the first Indigenous representative in the Queensland Legislative Assembly, acknowledged that he had 'a feeling and an understanding for the people of my birth', but 'reassured the House'[106] that he possessed a 'similar understanding of the problems and feelings of all members of my electorate' and would not 'press for the advantage of any particular group', but would implement the policies of the Government.[107] Similarly, Ernie Bridge, the first Indigenous parliamentarian in Western Australia, informed the House that he entered 'wearing two hats'; Bridge would speak up for both the Aboriginal and Caucasian people of the Kimberly.[108]

More recent first speeches by Indigenous representatives have followed a similar pattern. Members may have more directly paid tribute to their indigeneity, but they have also remained careful to subsume its potential influence within their larger institutional role. For example, Senator Malarndirri McCarthy (Yanyuwa) began her inaugural speech speaking in Yanyuwa, her first language, and giving thanks to the Ngunawal and Ngambri, the traditional owners of the land where Parliament sits. At the same time, however, Senator McCarthy explained that she is 'standing here in this place … to represent not just my own people – the Yanyuwa, the Garrwa, the Mara and the Kudanji peoples – but to stand for all people of the Northern Territory'.[109] Linda Burney (Wiradjuri), the first Indigenous woman in the House of Representatives, walked a similar line. Burney expressed pride in her Aboriginal heritage, noting her intention to 'bring the fighting Wiradjuri spirit into this place', and declaring that 'these

[104] Kam, *Party Discipline* (2009) 47.

[105] D McKeown and R Lundie, 'Crossing the Floor in the Federal Parliament 1950 – August 2004' (Parliamentary Library Research Note, 10 October 2005) 1.

[106] Maddison, 'White Parliament, Black Politics' (2016) 672.

[107] Queensland, *Parliamentary Debates*, Legislative Assembly, 18 March 1975, 371.

[108] Western Australia, *Parliamentary Debates*, Legislative Assembly, 7 August 1980, 178–79.

[109] Commonwealth, *Parliamentary Debates*, Senate, 14 September 2016, 944.

lands are, always were and always will be Aboriginal land – sovereignty never ceded'. Burney also explained, however, that while 'The Aboriginal part of my story is important. It is the core of who I am … I will not be stereotyped and I will not be pigeonholed', forcefully asserting that, ultimately, 'I enter this place as a representative of the people of Barton', and am 'proud to carry [Labor] values into this place'.[110]

These tensions create real challenges. As Senator Aden Ridgeway (Gumbaynggirr) notes, the political career of Senator Neville Bonner (Jagera), the first Indigenous member of the federal Parliament, exemplifies some of the 'unique difficulties facing Indigenous people' forced to 'choose between their political parties and the priorities of their people'.[111] Representing Queensland as a member of the Liberal Party between 1971 and 1983, Bonner rejected criticism that he was a 'tame cat',[112] pointing to the fact that he 'voted against … [his] … government against … [his] … party … on 23 occasions'.[113] He acknowledged, however, that dissension was only possible once he had 'consolidate[d his] bona fides' by ordering his priorities along God, nation, state, and party.[114] Nonetheless, these tensions ultimately overwhelmed him. In 1983 Bonner was demoted to the unwinnable third spot on the Liberal ticket because, as Queensland Premier Joh Bjelke-Petersen explained, 'his position on Aboriginal issues had got right out of hand'.[115] In a 1995 interview, Bonner reflected on his experiences and urged Indigenous candidates not to join the major political parties, because you lose the 'freedom to express yourself against the party'.[116]

Australia's electoral system complicates the ability of Indigenous parliamentarians to effectively advocate for Indigenous interests where they differ from their party's priorities, but a further complication is equally challenging. Aboriginal and Torres Strait Islander peoples are diverse, with considerable cultural and linguistic heterogeneity, reflecting the existence of hundreds of distinct, 'intensely local', political communities.[117] As noted above, localism stems from the fact that spiritual and political authority is connected to country. While this does not conflict with Australia's geography-based conception of representation, it does create additional layers of extra-Parliamentary responsibility, problematising

[110] Commonwealth, *Parliamentary Debates*, House of Representatives, 31 August 2016, 163–70.

[111] A Ridgeway, 'We Must All Act to Build on the Legacy of Senator Neville Bonner' *Online Opinion* (7 October 2003), available at www.onlineopinion.com.au/view.asp?article=769.

[112] R Hughes, Interview with Neville Bonner (Australian Biography Project, 13 January 1992) Tape 8.

[113] ibid, Tape 3.

[114] ibid.

[115] T Rowse, '"Out of Hand" – The Battles of Neville Bonner' (1997) 21 *Journal of Australian Studies* 96, 106.

[116] C Griffith, 'Interview with Neville Bonner', *Land Rights Queensland* (April 1995).

[117] L Behrendt, *Aboriginal Dispute Resolution: A Step Towards Self-Determination and Community Autonomy* (Annandale, Federation Press, 1995) 27.

Parliament's position as the centre of political decision-making. John Ah Kit (Jawoyn) articulated the tension he felt as a member of the Northern Territory Legislative Assembly:

> I try to represent and advance the interest of my constituents, most of whom are Aboriginal … I cannot 'speak for country'. I cannot usurp this role for the traditional owners and elders of the country. I would not choose to do so, nor would it be tolerated if I tried.[118]

Indigenous leadership roles are dispersed, but it is not constitutionally permissible to include representatives for each issue from each Indigenous community. These complications will therefore persist.

The existence of Aboriginal and Torres Strait Islander parliamentarians undoubtedly enhances the presence of Indigenous voices and interests in legislative processes and public debate. Their capacity to promote Indigenous interests is, however, constrained by electoral system design and strict party discipline. Indigenous Members of Parliament rely on the support of non-Indigenous voters to secure election and retain their position. They must balance advocacy for Indigenous interests against the priorities of the broader non-Indigenous community and their political party. As Neville Bonner's experience reveals, this can be politically fatal.

C. Committee System

Low rates of electoral participation, conceptual difficulties surrounding the desirability or capacity of Aboriginal and Torres Strait Islander Members of Parliament to represent diverse Indigenous communities, and strict party discipline, suggest that the views and interests of Indigenous peoples can struggle to be considered in the legislature. The Parliamentary committee system offers an alternative means for the voices of Indigenous peoples to be heard in a manner that does not rely on either of these avenues.[119] Parliamentary committees may assist in two ways. First, committees travel extensively throughout the country, enabling direct engagement between representatives and underserviced or alienated communities where otherwise-unheard concerns may be aired. Second, in undertaking their integrity functions, Parliamentary committees, particularly Senate committees, provide critical oversight of legislation, government agencies, and policies, including those dealing with Indigenous affairs.

[118] J Ah Kit, 'Reconciliation and Constitutional Issues: Participation in Government – Sovereignty or Subjugation?' (Speech delivered to the Australian Reconciliation Convention, Melbourne, 26 May 1997).

[119] Constitution, s 49; T Matulick, A Palmer and A Westgate, 'Engaging Indigenous People with the Australian Parliament through the Senate Committee System' (Australia and New Zealand Association of Clerks at the Table Conference, Wellington, 19 January 2016).

A Parliamentary committee is a group of Members or Senators (or both in the case of joint committees) appointed by one or both Houses of Parliament. Committees have considerable powers to undertake work on behalf of the Parliament and monitor government activities. They may compel people and documents to come before them, gather evidence from experts, discover facts and produce a report. They may also call members of the government or public service to account or answer for their actions.[120] The committee system thus enables parliamentarians to question and challenge the executive, as well as to ensure focus is retained on matters that might otherwise not be considered by the legislature. Members take this responsibility seriously, using the committee system to test and develop alternative policy proposals. Output is extensive; between its inception in 1970 and 31 July 2020, the Senate committee office has produced 5284 reports, 104 on matters solely and specifically relating to Indigenous Affairs.[121]

Parliamentary committees are an important mechanism of citizen participation in law-making and policy review. Any person may make a submission and committees regularly meet outside Canberra, taking oral evidence from witnesses and 'gaining firsthand knowledge of and exposure to issues of concern to the public'.[122] In this way, the committee system allows 'a direct line of communication with … legislators'.[123] These features are useful in promoting engagement with Indigenous Australians, who, as we have seen, participate at lower rates through other formal mechanisms. Committees can also leverage their capacity to travel and procedural flexibility to smooth hierarchical relations, promote conversations, lower distrust of government, and improve the scrutiny of legislation and policy that affects Indigenous peoples. For instance, the Joint Select Committee on Constitutional Recognition Relating to Aboriginal and Torres Strait Islander Peoples held a public hearing at the Northern Territory Combined Land Councils meeting at the remote Barunga community, prior to the culturally significant Barunga Festival in June 2018. At the hearing, the Co-Chair, Senator Patrick Dodson (Yawuru), spoke in a conversational tone and gently encouraged all attendees to have their say. Recognising that social or cultural mores may inhibit some people from speaking, Senator Dodson also invited Indigenous women to speak candidly in private with female committee members after the conclusion of the hearing.[124] Although these conversations

[120] House of Representatives, *Standing Orders* (13 September 2016) ch 16; Senate, *Standing Orders* (August 2018) ch 5.

[121] Parliament of Australia, *Register of Senate Committee Reports* (31 July 2020).

[122] R Laing (ed), *Odgers' Australian Senate Practice: As revised by Harry Evans*, 14th edn (Department of the Senate, 2016) 462; BC Wright and PE Fowler (eds), *House of Representatives Practice*, 6th edn (Department of the House of Representatives, 2012) 639.

[123] Matulick, Palmer and Westgate, 'Engaging Indigenous People with the Australian Parliament' (2016) 12.

[124] Personal observation.

would not be recorded in *Hansard*, they provided an enhanced and respectful opportunity for Indigenous voices to be heard.

Senate committees also undertake an important scrutiny function. Several committees assess bills and delegated legislation for their compatibility with certain rights, while others examine the proposed annual expenditure of government departments and agencies. Committees undertaking these functions rarely hold public hearings or accept submissions from the public,[125] preventing non-parliamentarians from influencing their deliberations, but Indigenous interests are considered where relevant. For example, the Parliamentary Joint Committee on Human Rights assesses all bills and legislative instruments against a set of seven international covenants signed by Australia.[126] Although the United Nations Declaration on the Rights of Indigenous Peoples is not included,[127] the Committee has relied on complementary protections to assess legislation that affects Aboriginal and Torres Strait Islander people.[128] Similarly, estimates hearings, held three times a year, provide an opportunity for Senators to assess the performance of government. Since 2008, a cross-portfolio Indigenous matters estimates hearing has been held, enabling clearer lines of accountability to be identified in an otherwise complex and multifarious portfolio.[129] Nonetheless, while allowing closer examination of the performance of government in Indigenous affairs, scrutiny is ultimately conducted by parliamentarians whom are overwhelmingly non-Indigenous, and accountability relies on government responding to those queries – something that does not always occur.

The committee system presents an opportunity to empower Aboriginal and Torres Strait Islander peoples. The Joint Select Committee noted above travelled extensively across the country providing Indigenous Australians with a real chance to have their voices heard by parliamentarians. Participants are grateful, often thanking committees for the opportunity to speak,[130] as members commit to transmit those voices to colleagues in Canberra. This is important and should be acknowledged. All the same, however, parliamentary committees remain an imperfect mechanism. A committee report may faithfully and sensitively record Indigenous views, but if it fails to lead to meaningful change, participants may regard the endeavour as worthless. More problematically,

[125] This has been criticised: L Grenfell and S Moulds, 'The Role of Committees in Rights Protection in Federal and State Parliaments in Australia' (2018) 41 *UNSW Law Journal* 40, 74.

[126] Human Rights (Parliamentary Scrutiny) Act 2011 (Cth), s 3.

[127] But see: Joint Select Committee on Constitutional Recognition of Aboriginal and Torres Strait Islander Peoples, 'Final Report' (June 2015) 68 [6.18] Recommendation 6.

[128] See, eg: Parliamentary Joint Committee on Human Rights, '2016 Review of Stronger Futures Measures' (Commonwealth of Australia, 16 March 2016).

[129] Commonwealth, *Journals of the Senate* (No 22–26 August 2008) 671, 683 (Item 21).

[130] See, eg: Evidence to Joint Select Committee on Constitutional Recognition Relating to Aboriginal and Torres Strait Islander Peoples, Parliament of Australia, Kununurra, 11 June 2018, 23 (Selina Newry); Evidence to Joint Select Committee on Constitutional Recognition Relating to Aboriginal and Torres Strait Islander Peoples, Parliament of Australia, Dubbo, 2 July 2018, 9 (Alastair Ferguson).

if the committee process raises expectations that go unrealised, participants may choose not to engage in future processes.[131] Unfortunately, Cobble Cobble professor of law Megan Davis argues that the 'universal' perception within Indigenous communities is that parliamentary committees are ineffective at resulting in legislative change.[132] Although disappointing, this is unsurprising. Low electoral participation rates and an electoral system ordered by geography and dominated by parties means that Aboriginal and Torres Strait Islander peoples' interests are rarely considered in the processes of the Parliament. Committees are a subset of this body; any recommendation must secure the support of the legislature.

This reality reveals the difficulty in relying on the committee system to ensure Indigenous Australians' interests are considered in the processes of government. The system is not structured to specifically channel Indigenous voices – though that may occur at times – but to ensure all citizens have an opportunity to be heard on an equal basis. For this reason, recent scholarly work arguing that committees need to 'deepen and broaden' their public engagement, become more deliberative, and/or augment their powers,[133] may offer some improvement for Aboriginal and Torres Strait Islander people, but it will not rectify the fundamental problem of the committee system: their matters are directed by terms of references adopted by parliamentarians and voices are chosen by committee members. They are useful but limited. It is for this reason that Indigenous Australians consistently advocate for 'a new review requirement for laws with respect to Aboriginal and Torres Strait Islander people';[134] an 'institutional tension or brake' on government power,[135] to truly rectify feelings of being dictated to. Such an institution would challenge the formal equality that pervades the legislature.

IV. THE EXECUTIVE

Law and public policy in Australia are determined and driven by popularly elected governments. If the interests of Aboriginal and Torres Strait Islander peoples are to be considered in the processes of government, those interests must be heard by

131 Evidence to Joint Select Committee on Constitutional Recognition Relating to Aboriginal and Torres Strait Islander Peoples, Parliament of Australia, Melbourne, 17 April 2018, 26 (Megan Davis).

132 M Davis, 'Self-Determination and the Right to be Heard' in S Morris (ed), *A Rightful Place: A Road Map to Recognition* (Melbourne, Black Books, 2017) 119, 130.

133 C Hendriks and A Kay, 'From "Opening Up" to Democratic Renewal: Deepening Public Engagement in Legislative Committees' (2019) 54 *Government and Opposition* 25; I Marsh and R Miller, *Democratic Decline and Democratic Renewal: Political Change in Britain, Australia and New Zealand* (Cambridge, Cambridge University Press, 2012) 310–14.

134 Commonwealth, 'Recognising Aboriginal and Torres Strait Islander Peoples in the Constitution: Report of the Expert Panel' (January 2012) 185.

135 M Davis, 'A Rightful Place: Correspondence' (2014) 56 *Quarterly Essay* 73, 79.

the executive. Under Australia's constitutional system, members of the executive are drawn directly from the legislature.[136] Lower rates of electoral participation as well as a structural design that favours territorially concentrated broad-based parties, places Indigenous peoples at a disadvantage in securing representatives of their choice. However, while ministers may enjoy greater capacity than ordinary members of the legislature to design and implement policy, they face similar limitations arising from their obligations to their electorate, their party and the country, complicating the capacity of Indigenous members of government to drive law and public policy that accords with Indigenous priorities.

In contrast to the strict formal equality that exists in the legislative branch, there is some recognition of the distinctive position of Indigenous people at the executive level. Here, several specific formal mechanisms or processes for channelling Indigenous interests and ensuring Indigenous voices are heard exist. These range from government-sponsored efforts to increase the number of Indigenous public servants, the establishment of formal extra-parliamentary bodies to advise government or departments on specific issues, to organisations with Indigenous-specific scrutiny functions.[137] As I demonstrate, however, each of these processes is inadequate at empowering Aboriginal and Torres Strait Islander peoples with the capacity to have their interests considered in the processes of government. Rather, they reflect limited efforts at incorporating Indigenous voices on non-Indigenous terms.

A. Ministers and Cabinet

Executive government is carried out by ministers and the Cabinet. A minister is a member of Parliament allocated a department of state, such as Defence, Health or Education. As head of a department, ministers have 'the most profound, ultimate responsibilities for the design, implementation and administration of policies on behalf of the community'.[138] Working closely with and seeking advice from their department, ministers develop and implement legislation and policy and are responsible for ensuring agencies within their portfolio are accountable and effective. By convention, the Ministry is divided into the Outer Ministry, which is comprised of more junior ministers, and Cabinet, which consists of both senior ministers and key portfolios. The Cabinet is the 'core'[139] of Australia's constitutional system and the 'focal point'[140] of government decision-making processes, as it is here that the government's legislative

[136] Constitution, s 64.

[137] Of course, a wide range of informal mechanisms aimed at influencing the executive exist, including political lobbying and campaign contributions.

[138] K Coghill, 'Ministers in Office: Preparation and Performance' (lecture delivered at the Department of the Senate Occasional Lecture Series, Parliament House, 29 September 2000) 3.

[139] I Jennings, *Cabinet Government*, 3rd edn (Cambridge, Cambridge University Press, 1959) 1.

[140] Wright and Fowler, *House of Representatives* (2012) 73.

program is controlled and directed.[141] While detailed empirical analysis suggests that legislatures in parliamentary systems are not necessarily 'dominated' by the executive,[142] considerable power certainly lies with the executive.[143] For this reason, Aboriginal and Torres Strait Islander peoples seeking to have their interests considered in the processes of government must ensure that their voices are heard in the ministry and Cabinet.

Only one Indigenous person has ever served in the federal ministry. Ken Wyatt (Noongar, Wangai and Yamatji), the member for Hasluck in Western Australia, was appointed Minister for Aged Care and Indigenous Health on 24 January 2017, a position in the outer ministry.[144] Demonstrating both the considerable authority that comes with ministerial appointment and the significance of Indigenous peoples serving in this role, Wyatt declared that he intended to focus on issues of concern to Indigenous communities.[145] Among other achievements, Wyatt drove the establishment of an $8 million taskforce aimed at responding to the blood-borne virus HTLV-1, found in Aboriginal communities at 1,000 times the rate of anywhere else in the world.[146] Following the 2019 federal election, Wyatt was appointed Minister for Indigenous Australians, a Cabinet position.[147]

The general or historical absence of Indigenous Australians in the executive does not mean that Indigenous interests are not considered. Ministers developing law and policy study how proposed reforms will affect all Australian residents, including Indigenous peoples.[148] More directly, as Indigenous affairs spending constitutes a considerable component of the federal budget, governments have often appointed a minister with specific responsibility for this domain. At times that position has been a dedicated role, while at others, it has been conceived or subsumed within a broader portfolio.[149] Wyatt is the first Aboriginal and

[141] C Foster, 'Cabinet Government in the Twentieth Century' (2004) 67 *Modern Law Review* 753, 753–54; T Daintith and Y-F Ng, 'Executives' in C Saunders and A Stone (eds), *The Oxford Handbook of the Australian Constitution* (Oxford, Oxford University Press, 2018) 587, 607.

[142] M Russell, D Glover and K Wollter, 'Does the Executive Dominate the Westminster Legislative Process? Six Reasons for Doubt' (2016) 69 *Parliamentary Affairs* 286.

[143] Though note recent decisions restraining the executive in relation to appropriations: *Pape v Commissioner of Taxation* (2009) 238 CLR 1; *Williams v Commonwealth (No 1)* (2012) 248 CLR 156; *Williams v Commonwealth (No 2)* (2012) 252 CLR 416.

[144] Commonwealth Government, 'Turnbull Ministry', 24 January 2017.

[145] P Karp, 'Ken Wyatt: New Minister to Tackle how Indigenous Health Funding Used' *Guardian Australia* (19 January 2017), available at www.theguardian.com/australia-news/2017/jan/19/key-wyatt-new-minister-to-tackle-how-indigenous-health-funding-used.

[146] B Brennan, 'Ancient HTLV-1 Virus Affecting Millions to Receive "Rapid Action", Health Minister Greg Hunt Signals' *ABC News* (25 May 2018), available at abc.net.au/news/2018-05-25/government-signals-rapid-action-on-deadly-virus-htlv-1/9797790?pfmredir=sm.

[147] Commonwealth Government, 'Second Morrison Ministry', 29 May 2019.

[148] The value of this consideration can be questioned; without a committed or effective advocate, Indigenous peoples' unique interests may not be articulated in an appropriate way, nor receive the attention they deserve.

[149] Aboriginal affairs are currently dealt with by the Department of Prime Minister and Cabinet: Administrative Arrangements Order, 1 February 2020, Sch, Pt 11.

Torres Strait Islander person to have held this portfolio. The position does not guarantee Cabinet status,[150] but the presence of a minister – whether they are Indigenous or not – responsible for government agencies serving Aboriginal and Torres Strait Islander peoples offers a heightened opportunity for Indigenous interests to be heard in the processes of government. The relevant minister will receive advice from his or her Department and will also meet Indigenous peoples and organisations across the country, acting as an adviser to government by carrying their concerns and priorities.

There are limits to the extent that that individual ministers – whether in Cabinet or the outer ministry – can affect or influence government legislation or policy. As Wyatt noted in his inaugural speech, although he can 'advocate for Indigenous Australians' he must assume the 'mantle of responsibility to represent the people of Hasluck'.[151] Similarly, though a dedicated Indigenous Affairs Minister may promote and advocate for Indigenous views in government, the executive serves to implement its platform and ultimately represents all Australians, making decisions on that basis. To that end, Cabinet ministers are bound by the principle of collective Cabinet responsibility, which requires all members publicly support Cabinet decisions.[152] Wyatt himself has acknowledged the tensions that arise from his position in managing competing expectations from Indigenous peoples, his party and the nation.[153] Fewer Indigenous ministers make this task harder.

The absence of Indigenous ministers is consequential in other ways. Power to enact laws ordinarily resides in the legislature. In practice, however, legislation is generated by ministers, and the necessity of dealing quickly and appropriately with changing circumstances requires empowering the executive, specified ministers, or agency heads, to enact subordinate legislation that operates with the force of law. Over the later decades of the twentieth century the volume of delegated legislation increased significantly and now averages between 1,500 and 2,000 instruments a year.[154] In increasingly prevalent cases, primary legislation is expressed in a framework form with broad powers delegated to the executive.[155] In addition to weakening visibility and public accountability, such practices further emphasise the necessity of ensuring Indigenous voices are present within the executive.

[150] Though by convention the minister will be present in cabinet in all discussions that concern the portfolio: Commonwealth, *Cabinet Handbook*, 10th edn (Department of Prime Minister and Cabinet, 2017) s 3(45).

[151] Commonwealth, *Parliamentary Debates*, House of Representatives, 29 September 2010, 211.

[152] Commonwealth, *Cabinet Handbook* (n 150) s 2(19)–(21).

[153] L Allam, 'Man in the Middle: Ken Wyatt on Being Caught Between the Uluru Statement and his Party' *Guardian Australia* (2 February 2020), available at www.theguardian.com/australia-news/2020/feb/02/man-in-the-middle-ken-wyatt-on-being-caught-between-the-uluru-statement-and-his-party.

[154] Laing, *Odgers' Australian Senate Practice* (2016) 432.

[155] Senate Standing Committee for the Scrutiny of Bills, Parliament of Australia, 'Final Report – Inquiry into the Future Role and Direction of the Senate Scrutiny of Bills Committee' (May 2012) 35 [5.13].

Delegated legislation is subject to scrutiny, but not in a manner that responds to the absence of Indigenous parliamentarians. Rule-makers are required to consult with interested stakeholders prior to making instruments,[156] offering the potential for extra-parliamentary actors to influence its content, but failure to consult does not affect its validity.[157] Every instrument is assessed by the Standing Committee on Regulations and Ordinances,[158] but an instrument will only be disallowed on a vote by a House of Parliament within a specified timeframe.[159] The reactive and parliamentary nature of these scrutiny measures emphasises that the presence of Indigenous peoples in the ministry is critical for ensuring issues that affect them are considered.

B. The Public Service

Ministerial and Cabinet decisions are carried out by the Australian Public Service. Even if the interests of Aboriginal and Torres Strait Islander people are not directly conveyed by ministers or considered within Cabinet, Indigenous public servants may be able to affect or influence the design of legislation and policy as well as how that policy is implemented in practice.[160] This can occur in two ways. First, in designing legislation and policy, Ministers rely on the technical, complex, and specialised knowledge of their departments. That 'frank, honest [and] timely advice'[161] concerning law and policy formation may lead to drafting amendment to the principal act, or subsequent regulatory change via delegated legislation.[162] Second, depending on their position, mandate and stakeholder expectations, senior members of the bureaucracy may enjoy a limited but real domain of formal or de facto policy autonomy, permitting room for flexibility in policy implementation and delivery.[163]

Traditional accounts of public administration sought to identify and preserve a clear conceptual distinction between ministers and bureaucrats. Consistent with principles of ministerial responsibility, scholars argued that, 'ministers make policy; public servants administer it'.[164] Whether this position

[156] Legislation Act 2003 (Cth), s 17 ('Legislation Act').

[157] ibid s 19.

[158] Senate, *Standing Orders* (n 120) O 23(3).

[159] Legislation Act (n 156), s 42(1). Some instruments are not subject to disallowance.

[160] See generally E Page, *Policy without Politicians: Bureaucratic Influence in Comparative Perspective* (Oxford, Oxford University Press, 2012).

[161] Public Service Act 1999 (Cth), s 10(5).

[162] K Kernaghan, 'Politics, Policy and Public Servants: Political Neutrality Revisited' (1976) 16 *Canadian Public Administration* 432, 436.

[163] A Roman, 'The Determinants of Public Administrators' Participation in Policy Formulation' (2017) 47 *American Review of Public Administration* 102, 115.

[164] J Svara, 'The Politics-Administration Dichotomy Model as Aberration' (1998) 58 *Public Administration Review* 51, 52; R Mulgan, 'Assessing Ministerial Responsibility in Australia' in K Dowling and C Lewis (eds), *Ministerial Careers and Accountability in the Australian Commonwealth Government* (Canberra, ANU Press, 2012) 177, 179.

was ever accurate is difficult to ascertain, but it certainly became untenable as the complexity of governance increased, and it has long been regarded as a fallacy.[165] As Sir John Crawford noted in 1960, 'civil servants are not merely doers; they are part of the complete *process* of government including the task of making policy decisions';[166] they 'participate in policy making' and sometimes even 'initiate and carry through policy decisions … without formal clearance by Ministers'.[167] More recent scholarly work suggests that public servants operate under significant formal and informal constraints inhibiting the scope of their discretion,[168] but opportunities remain for powerful senior public servants or specific agencies to develop and 'channel policy imperatives … that transcend the formal program of parties in office'.[169] Can Indigenous public servants play this role?

Aboriginal and Torres Strait Islander people have historically been underrepresented in the Commonwealth public service. Cognisant of this underrepresentation and of the policy development role that public servants perform, governments have promoted employment of Indigenous Australians in the bureaucracy as a mechanism to 'enable effective contribution to policy and decision making affecting Indigenous people',[170] and thereby 'capably respond to the needs of the community'.[171] Such strategies appear to be working. As of 30 June 2018, Indigenous Australians comprised 2.9 per cent of the Commonwealth public service.[172] However, while this avenue offers potential, it is beset by tensions and complications that echo those faced by Indigenous parliamentarians. In a series of interviews with senior Indigenous public servants in the Northern Territory, Elizabeth Ganter reveals that the absence of a 'theory of action' inhibits the effectiveness of these employment strategies. Without substantive change to the structure, operation and 'norms' of the public service, the simple incorporation of Indigenous employees fails to result in meaningful accommodation of Indigenous views and perspectives.[173]

Authenticity was a recurrent issue in Ganter's interviews, with many perceiving themselves as 'betwixt and between' government and community.[174]

[165] Y-F Ng, *Ministerial Advisers in Australia: The Modern Legal Context* (Annandale, Federation Press, 2016) 53.

[166] J Crawford, 'Relations between Civil Servants and Ministers in Policy-Making' (1960) 19 *Australian Journal of Public Administration* 99, 100 (emphasis in original).

[167] ibid 101.

[168] Ng, *Ministerial Advisers in Australia* (2016) 53–55; Page, *Policy without Politicians* (2012) 175.

[169] E Jones, 'The Purse Strings and the Policy Process: Bureaucratic Shaping of Industry Policy Capacity after 1945' (2001) 60 *Australian Journal of Public Administration* 21, 21.

[170] Office of the Commissioner for Public Employment, 'Northern Territory Public Sector Indigenous Employment and Career Development Strategy 2010–2012' (Northern Territory, 2010) 12.

[171] Commonwealth, 'Commonwealth Aboriginal and Torres Strait Islander Employment Strategy' (Australian Public Service Commission, 2015) 1 [3].

[172] National Indigenous Affairs Agency, 'Indigenous Representation in the Commonwealth Public Sector', available at www.niaa.gov.au/indigenous-affairs/employment/indigenous-representation-commonwealth-public-sector.

[173] E Ganter, *Reluctant Representatives* (Canberra, ANU Press, 2017) 182–83.

[174] ibid 81.

Interviewees explained that they are often 'invited, or feel compelled ... to speak for their people',[175] 'even if the pressure of circumstances demanded that they sometimes had to construct their communities imaginatively'.[176] Aware that their position provided a perspective that might otherwise be absent, interviewees were concerned that they did not have authority to speak for other people or communities and 'felt their lack of accountability to the absent keenly'.[177] Indeed, almost half of Ganter's 50 interviewees did not consider that they represented Indigenous Australians,[178] and objected to being seen by colleagues as 'objects of consultation', or 'repositories of a uniform, incontestable Aboriginal expertise'.[179] Interviewees considered that external consultation with communities rather than informal internal discussions with Indigenous staff would be more appropriate and effective at incorporating Indigenous interests.

The development and implementation of the Indigenous Advancement Strategy (IAS) in 2013 highlights the consequences of limited substantive consultation and engagement with Indigenous communities. The strategy rationalised 150 programmes and activities previously run by eight different departments into five broad-based themes implemented by the Department of the Prime Minister and Cabinet. Designed to 'streamline arrangements, reduce red tape and prioritise expenditure to achieve practical outcomes on the ground',[180] the IAS was the Tony Abbott Liberal–National Government's key strategy to work with Indigenous peoples and communities. All organisations working with Indigenous communities, even those who had already secured funding, were required to reapply through one of these streams. Adding further complications was the fact that these significant changes were accompanied by an $534.4 million budget cut over five years.[181]

In 2017, the Australian National Audit Office (ANAO) released a scathing report, finding that the IAS was planned and designed in just seven weeks, seriously impeding the Department's ability to consult and prioritise the needs of Indigenous communities.[182] Manifestly inadequate planning had important consequences. In a submission to a Senate Committee inquiry, the Government admitted that the majority of funding secured through the IAS went to non-Indigenous organisations,[183] some with little or questionable experience in delivering services to Aboriginal and Torres Strait Islander people.[184] In fact,

[175] ibid 181.
[176] ibid 156.
[177] ibid 174.
[178] ibid 71.
[179] ibid 98.
[180] M Gooda, 'Social Justice and Native Title Report' (Australian Human Rights Commission, 2014) 18.
[181] Australian Government, 'Budget 2014–15: Budget Measures, Budget Paper No 2' (2014) 185.
[182] Australian National Audit Office, 'Indigenous Advancement Strategy' (Report No 35, 2017) 26 [2.21], 33–35 [3.18]–[3.28].
[183] Senate Finance and Public Administration References Committee, Parliament of Australia, 'Commonwealth Indigenous Advancement Strategy Tendering Process' (March 2016) 24 [2.50].
[184] ibid [2.49].

some funding was directed to groups opposed to Aboriginal interests. In 2018, Senate estimates revealed that the Northern Territory Amateur Fishermen's Association, the Northern Territory Cattlemen's Association and the Northern Territory Seafood Council received almost $500,000 in IAS grants to obtain legal advice about how they would be adversely impacted by Aboriginal land claims.[185] Unfortunately, as the Department 'did not maintain sufficient records', the ANAO explained that 'it is not possible' to determine how funding recommendations were made.[186]

In many respects the IAS continues and extends the broader shift that emerged with the Howard Government's election in 1996. As Will Sanders argues, this period has seen the re-emergence of a 'guardianship principle' within Indigenous affairs, which sees Indigenous Australians as 'vulnerable or exploited, as not knowing their own best interests, and hence as in need of guidance and direction'.[187] Characterised by Abbott as 'the new paternalism',[188] this policy agenda has reduced Indigenous Australians' agency and scope within public administration. It includes the widespread mainstreaming of Indigenous affairs, under which Indigenous-specific programmes were moved to mainstream departments, even though they had 'demonstrated little capacity to meet Indigenous needs'.[189] It also encompasses an eschewal of rights-based approaches to Indigenous affairs in favour of socio-economic indicators of development.

A further challenge is the shift in the nature of public administration more broadly. Over the last three decades, outsourcing of government services has increased significantly across the globe.[190] Australia is not immune to these changes. A 2017 ANAO report found that the Australian Government spent almost $40 billion on 'management and business professionals and administrative services' between 2012/13 and 2016/17.[191] While outsourcing can produce economic efficiencies, scholars have noted that the extensive use of consultants and contractors in the design and delivery of public policy and services may weaken traditional accountability mechanisms.[192] For instance,

[185] Senate Finance and Public Administration Legislation Committee, Parliament of Australia, 'Estimates' (26 October 2018) 68–71.

[186] ANAO, 'Indigenous Advancement Strategy' (2017) 10 [24].

[187] W Sanders, 'Changing Agendas in Australian Indigenous Policy: Federalism, Competing Principles and Generational Dynamics' (2013) 72 *Australian Journal of Public Administration* 156, 166.

[188] ABC Radio National, 'Abbott Suggests "New Paternalism" Solution to Indigenous Disadvantage', *AM* (21 June 2006).

[189] J Hunt, 'Between a Rock and a Hard Place: Self-Determination, Mainstreaming and Indigenous Community Governance' in J Hunt, D Smith, S Garling and W Sanders (eds), *Contested Governance: Culture, Power and Institutions in Indigenous Australia* (Canberra, ANU Press, 2008) 27, 30.

[190] OECD, 'Contracting Out Government Services: Best Practice Guidelines and Case Studies' (Public Management Occasional Papers No 20, 1997).

[191] ANAO, 'Australian Government Procurement Contract Reporting' (Report No 19, 2017) 12.

[192] R Mulgan, 'Transparency and the Performance of Outsourced Government Services' (Australia and New Zealand School of Government, Occasional Paper No 5, 2015) 11.

commercial-in-confidence contracts inhibit parliamentary and democratic scrutiny,[193] while private contractors are not required to act in accordance with administrative law principles, leaving citizens with reduced scope to challenge decisions.[194] As a marginalised community, Indigenous peoples are even less likely to be able to challenge these arrangements. To some extent this is ameliorated by a considerable 'Indigenous sector'[195] of Indigenous-controlled organisations that provide public services to Indigenous communities. As the IAS demonstrates, however, their capacity to operate is tied to Cabinet decisions; decisions often made with little Indigenous input.

C. Formal Advisory Bodies

Opportunities for Indigenous Australians to directly voice their interests within government as ministers or via the public service may be complicated, but a broad and diffuse range of indirect formal channels exist. Although by convention, ministers rely on advice from their departments, the increasing complexity of public policy issues, as well as the need to demonstrate community support for legislation and policy initiatives, has led the executive to rely on a wide network of external sources of advice. Today, government no longer sits at the top of a vertically integrated policy advice system but is situated 'at the centre of a complex "horizontal" web of policy advisors',[196] which extends beyond the public service. Included within this web are government-run or sponsored institutions, such as policy units within, or advisory bodies attached to, departments, political advisers and consultants, as well as more independent and (potentially) critical voices arising from intergovernmental bodies, such as the National Cabinet (the successor body to the Council for Australian Governments), parliamentary committees, public inquiries, and organisations providing a scrutiny function. A wide range of external organisations lacking formal access to government but exploiting opportunities for contact provided by lobbying or parliamentary committees also exist.

At the policy implementation or management level, government departments and statutory agencies have increasingly provided a formal role for Indigenous peoples to advise the executive. One example is the Indigenous Advisory Committee established under the Environment Protection and Biodiversity

[193] A Barton, 'Public Sector Accountability and Commercial-in-Confidence Outsourcing Contracts' (2006) 19 *Accounting, Auditing & Accountability Journal* 256.

[194] J McMillan, 'Ten Challenges for Administrative Justice' (2010) 61 *Australian Institute of Administrative Law Forum* 23, 28. Note that the Ombudsman has jurisdiction to inquire into complaints concerning outsourced service delivery: Ombudsman Act 1976 (Cth), s 3BA.

[195] T Rowse, 'The Indigenous Sector' in D Austin-Broos and G Macdonald (eds), *Culture, Economy and Governance in Aboriginal Australia* (Sydney, Sydney University Press, 2005) 213.

[196] J Craft and M Howlett, 'Policy Formation, Governance Shifts and Policy Influence: Location and Content in Policy Advisory Systems' (2012) 32 *Journal of Public Policy* 79, 85.

Conservation Act 1999 (Cth). Comprised solely of Aboriginal and Torres Strait Islander people, the Committee advises the Minister and Department on the operation of the Act, 'taking into account the significance of Indigenous peoples' knowledge of the management of land and the conservation and sustainable use of biodiversity'.[197] These forums provide an enhanced capacity for Indigenous interests to be conveyed to decision-makers. At its 33rd meeting, for instance, the Committee met with senior departmental staff and the Minister's Senior Adviser for the Environment and resolved to prioritise increasing the size and scope of the managed Indigenous estate in Australia.[198] The capacity of these bodies to affect decisions is limited, however. Members are appointed by the Minister and provide advice 'as and when requested by the Minister'; they are 'not a decision-making body' and they do not 'advocate on behalf of Indigenous communities'.[199] In short, they are effective to the extent that their priorities align with the strategic and policy direction of the Minister.

More general policy advisory bodies have existed at the national level. Chapter five examines three of these institutions, revealing that they too are often beset by inherent challenges. Consider the existing national body. At present, the Prime Minister and Minister for Indigenous Australians are advised by the Prime Minister's Indigenous Advisory Council. The Council comprises of up to 12 'highly regarded, pre-eminent thinkers and practitioners', appointed 'for the depth of their experience in their respective field' and is intended to 'advise Government on practical changes which can be made to improve the lives of Indigenous peoples'.[200] There is no question that the Council's members are distinguished individuals with the considerable knowledge and expertise necessary to provide advice to government. The problem is, staffed by 'hand-picked' appointees with limited ability to independently consult with Indigenous peoples, the body enjoys little credibility within the community.[201] As members owe their position to the Prime Minister and not the broader Indigenous constituency, the Government is able to deal with Indigenous peoples 'on its own terms',[202] and the Council is incentivised to 'spend its time telling the government what it wants to hear, not what it needs to know'.[203]

[197] Environment Protection and Biodiversity Conservation Act 1999 (Cth), s 505B(1).

[198] Indigenous Advisory Committee, 'Indigenous Advisory Committee Bulletin No 9 Meeting 33' (Canberra, 27–28 July 2017) 1.

[199] Department of Energy and Environment, 'Indigenous Advisory Committee', available at www.environment.gov.au/epbc/advisory-committees/iac.

[200] National Indigenous Advancement Agency, 'Prime Minister's Indigenous Advisory Council', available at www.niaa.gov.au/indigenous-affairs/prime-ministers-indigenous-advisory-council.

[201] Aboriginal and Torres Strait Islander Social Justice Commissioner, 'Building a Sustainable National Indigenous Representative Body' (2008) 43.

[202] W Jonas and D Dick, 'Ensuring Meaningful Participation of Indigenous Peoples in Government Processes: The Implications of the Decline of ATSIC' (2004) 23 *Dialogue: Academy of the Social Sciences* 4, 14.

[203] S Bellear, 'The Case for Indigenous Self-Determination' *ABC News* (21 October 2013), available at www.abc.net.au/news/2013-10-21/bellear-indigenous-sovereignty/5032294.

All government-established or supported stakeholder organisations tread this tension between authenticity and influence, but challenges are particularly pronounced for Indigenous advisory bodies as their interests often diverge widely from the state. In Australia, these tensions have sometimes exploded into public forums, as Indigenous representatives have sought stronger forms of autonomy or advocated for priorities not supported by government, catalysing state efforts to abolish the body. Yet, as these bodies explicitly recognise that Aboriginal and Torres Strait Islander peoples' interests are distinct and should play an enhanced role in the policy process, their existence counters the formal equality that pervades Australia's governance framework. Nonetheless, in practice, the experience in Australia reveals the dominance of formal equality. Rather than a conduit of Indigenous Australians' political voice, government generally conceives Indigenous advisory bodies as representing a sectional interest to be informed on policy development and implementation and seeks to use their imprimatur to legitimise government action. If a First Nations Voice is to be effective at empowering Aboriginal and Torres Strait Islander peoples and ensuring their diverse interests are considered in the processes of government, close attention should be paid to its design.

D. Scrutiny Institutions

The three mechanisms examined so far all clearly operate within the executive. Individuals and communities seeking to ensure their interests are considered in the processes of government are not restricted to these processes; a range of institutions that examine and scrutinise the operation of the executive exist. These organisations may have multiple functions but are primarily focused on assessing existing legislation and policy and, based on their knowledge or expertise, recommending reform. Operating independent of government to some degree, scrutiny institutions do not have the authority to mandate changes, but may nonetheless be successful in leading to legislative or policy reform. Problematically, and suggesting that executive scrutiny institutions may have limited salience for Indigenous Australians, government engagement appears to be inversely related to independence.

Scrutiny institutions are formally independent of and separate from government but may be empowered to speak directly to the executive, enhancing the potential for reform. The Australian Human Rights Commission (AHRC), for instance, is an independent statutory body empowered with individual complaints conciliation functions, a broader research and educative role, and the responsibility to advise parliament and the executive on international human rights law.[204] Although the Commission advocates for the protection

[204] Australian Human Rights Commission Act 1986 (Cth), s 11. See, generally, E Santow, 'The Australian Human Rights Commission' in M Groves, J Boughey and D Meagher (eds), *The Legal Protection of Rights in Australia* (Oxford, Hart Publishing, 2019) 123.

and enjoyment of human rights generally, a discrete Aboriginal and Torres Strait Islander Social Justice Commissioner has also been established. This Commissioner is empowered to assess whether bills and legislation 'recognise and protect' the human rights of Indigenous peoples and to report their findings to the Minister,[205] as well as to report to the federal Parliament on the operation of the NTA.[206] The Australian Law Reform Commission (ALRC), a statutory agency operating within the Attorney-General's Department, also enjoys a formal relationship with government. The ALRC's primary role is to advise the Attorney-General on options for the systemic development and reform of Commonwealth law.[207] The Commission has produced 135 reports since 1975, including several specifically concerning legal issues relating to Aboriginal and Torres Strait Islander people.[208] Neither the AHRC nor the ALRC are entirely structurally independent of government. Commissioners are appointed by the Minister, staff are employed under the Public Service Act 1999 (Cth), and the ALRC is limited to assessing matters referred to it by the Attorney-General.[209] Although this relationship does not necessarily inhibit the capacity of scrutiny institutions to meaningfully critique law and policy, it does impose some important constraints. And yet, at the same time, it does establish a formal channel between each organisation and government, ensuring a level of access that may not otherwise be available.

The experience of the National Congress of Australia's First Peoples ('Congress') highlights the compromises and challenges inherent to scrutiny institutions. A private company, owned and controlled by its 8,500 individual members and over 180 community organisations nationwide, Congress was legally and structurally independent of government. Independence allowed Congress to develop innovative and distinctive policy, advocate for Indigenous interests, and serve as a conduit between government and other stakeholders to ensure decision-makers act in the best interests of Indigenous Australians. As Sam Jeffries (Moorawarri and Wiradjuri) noted at its establishment, Congress could provide Indigenous Australians with 'a national platform and voice to advance issues important to our peoples'.[210] Independence came at a cost, however. While Congress was effective at times, its leaders acknowledged that it generally was 'not treated by government with the respect and genuine engagement that a national Indigenous representative institution deserves'.[211] Lack of

[205] Australian Human Rights Commission Act 1986 (Cth), s 46C.

[206] Native Title Act 1993 (Cth), s 209.

[207] Australian Law Reform Commission Act 1996 (Cth), ss 21(1)(a), 21(2) (ALRC).

[208] See, eg: ALRC (n 20); ALRC, 'Connection to Country: Review of the Native Title Act 1993' (Cth) (Report 126, 2015); ALRC, 'Pathways to Justice – Inquiry into the Incarceration Rate of Aboriginal and Torres Strait Islander People' (Report 133, 2018).

[209] ALRC Act (n 207), s 20.

[210] Australian Human Rights Commission, 'New Congress to Represent Aboriginal and Torres Strait Islanders' (press release, 2 May 2010).

[211] J Huggins and R Little, 'A Rightful Place at the Table' in S Morris (ed), *A Rightful Place: A Road Map to Recognition* (Melbourne, Black Books, 2017) 147, 168–69.

respect translated into operational difficulties; in 2014, the Federal Government withdrew earmarked funding, leaving the organisation on the brink of collapse.[212] In 2019, Congress was placed in voluntary administration.[213] Congress' experience suggests that in Australia an institution with a formal connection to government may be more effective at ensuring Indigenous voices are heard in relevant forums, even if this carries its own challenges.

V. CONCLUSION

Law is an expression of political, cultural and social values. Australia's system of governance provides all citizens with a formally equal opportunity to make their voices heard. As Indigenous activists and scholars have highlighted and this chapter has demonstrated, however, the structure of Australian governance fails to empower Aboriginal and Torres Strait Islander peoples and communities with the capacity to have their distinct voices heard and their unique interests considered in the processes of government. Australia's system of governance is 'built upon confidence in a system of parliamentary' representation,[214] but demographics, electoral system design and strict party discipline challenge Aboriginal and Torres Strait Islander peoples' capacity to elect representatives of their choice, let alone for those representatives to persistently advocate for Indigenous priorities. When combined with the absence of comprehensive rights protections, or a requirement that government 'listen to Indigenous peoples before passing laws that affect [them]',[215] the result is a government largely 'not accountable to Indigenous peoples',[216] who are left vulnerable to the 'wavering sympathies of the Australian community'.[217]

Of course, sometimes the political system does work for Indigenous peoples, and they can realise their aspirations by emphasising ties that bind the interests of the dominant non-Indigenous community to their own. The central problem remains, however, as intermittent, partial successes are often met with significant political backlash. In the case of the NTA, for instance, this manifested in the form of 'bucketloads of extinguishment',[218] and the continuing absence of

[212] National Congress of Australia's First Peoples, 'National Congress of Australia's First Peoples Strive to Survive' (media release, 2 November 2016).

[213] A Walker, 'Combined Notice of Appointment and First Meeting of Creditors of Company under Administration', 6 June 2019.

[214] *McKinlay v Commonwealth* (1975) 135 CLR 1, 24 (Barwick CJ).

[215] H Ludwick, 'Through Black Eyes' in M Davis and M Langton (eds), *It's Our Country: Indigenous Arguments for Meaningful Constitutional Recognition and Reform* (Melbourne, Melbourne University Press, 2016) 42, 45.

[216] D Cronin, 'Trapped by History: Democracy, Human Rights and Justice for Indigenous People in Australia' (2017) 23 *Australian Journal of Human Rights* 220, 235.

[217] Behrendt (n 34) 8.

[218] J Highfield, Interview with Tim Fisher, Deputy Prime Minister of Australia (radio interview, 4 September 1997); Native Title Amendment Act 1998 (Cth).

a promised social justice package. As chapter five will illustrate, a similar fate befell the Aboriginal and Torres Strait Islander Commission.

This is not to denigrate the many committed Indigenous peoples who agitate to have their voices heard in the processes of Australian government. It is merely to acknowledge what Indigenous Australians already know: the system is structured against them. As a numerically small community with distinct interests, the 'majoritarian arithmetic of electoral politics … le[aves] them with little leverage over government decision-making',[219] and real concerns over the fairness of existing decision-making processes. What should be done? How can Australia's governance system be restructured? Indigenous peoples have developed a complex and nuanced response to this question. The following chapter listens to their voices.

[219] S Brennan and M Davis, 'First Peoples' in C Saunders and A Stone (eds), *The Oxford Handbook of the Australian Constitution* (Oxford, Oxford University Press, 2018) 27, 30.

3

Exploring Indigenous Aspirations

I. INTRODUCTION

AUSTRALIA'S SYSTEM OF governance does not empower Aboriginal and Torres Strait Islander peoples with the capacity to have their distinct voices heard and their unique interests considered in the processes of government. How can constitutional or institutional design rectify this problem? This chapter explores the nuanced and complex political thought of Aboriginal and Torres Strait Islander peoples, as well as Indigenous peoples across the globe, with the aim of developing an understanding of Indigenous aspirations for structural reform. This issue is critical for many reasons, not least because institutions and processes aimed at empowering Indigenous peoples will not be effective unless they accord with the wishes of Indigenous peoples. As a 'fundamental discord' exists between what Indigenous peoples experience and discuss, and 'what well-intentioned non-Indigenous scholars think is important to Indigenous peoples',[1] questions of institutional design must begin, empirically, with a faithful exploration of Indigenous voices.

The plural is important. Indigenous peoples and communities are diverse and heterogeneous; there is no single 'Indigenous' perspective. Nonetheless, as Métis scholar Joyce Green has noted, diversity of opinion and disagreement 'does not mean that there is no agreement'.[2] Indigenous peoples are connected by a 'shared history of violent oppression and exclusion',[3] and consequently share experiences of 'collective trauma, disorientation, loss, and grief'.[4] While it is impossible to distil the multiplicity of Indigenous perspectives and positions into a set of clear proposals, within these shared experiences common themes can be discerned. The challenge facing all 'Original people', Kanien'kehá:ka

[1] A Ardill, 'Australian Sovereignty, Indigenous Standpoint Theory and Feminist Standpoint Theory: First Peoples' Sovereignties Matter' (2013) 22 *Griffith Law Review* 315, 318.

[2] J Green, 'Indigenous Feminism: From Symposium to Book' in J Green (ed), *Making Space for Indigenous Feminism* (Winnipeg, Fernwood, 2007) 14, 18.

[3] P Dodson, 'Foreword' in S Maddison, *Black Politics: Inside the Complexity of Aboriginal Political Culture* (Crows Nest, Allen & Unwin, 2009) vii, ix.

[4] L Kirmayer and G Valaskakis, 'Preface' in L Kirmayer and G Valaskakis (eds), *Healing Traditions: The Mental Health of Aboriginal People in Canada* (Vancouver, University of British Columbia Press, 2009) xiii, xv.

professor Taiaiake Alfred explains, 'is the same'; it is the challenge of 'regaining freedom and becoming self-sufficient'.[5]

Those common themes are articulated in two parts. I begin with sovereignty. Indigenous peoples often speak in the language of sovereignty, but what do they mean by this word? Is sovereignty a legal concept or is it something else, and what does it mean for the exercise of political authority and governmental decision-making? Exploring Indigenous peoples' use of this powerful yet malleable term highlights three major elements that are employed to articulate a relationship with the state that distinguishes Indigenous peoples from other citizens. Although sovereignty means different things to different people, assertions of sovereignty generally conceive of it in peoplehood, political and cultural dimensions. Institutional design must be sensitive to these diverse practices.

Sovereignty is a critical theme that pervades Indigenous political activism, but Indigenous peoples also place important value on relationships. As distinct political communities whose inherent sovereignty has been denied, Indigenous peoples desire a new relationship with the state built on principles of trust and mutual respect. This new relationship requires breaking down existing governance structures built on colonial foundations, constructing a more equitable framework of interactions reflective of Indigenous peoples' status, and embedding attitudinal changes among and within non-Indigenous communities.

In privileging Indigenous voices, in allowing Indigenous aspirations to drive the argument, this chapter aims to push constitutional and democratic theorists to understand the limits of their presumptions. In this, it is guided by the work of Torres Strait Islander scholar Martin Nakata, who has explained that a critique of Western epistemologies is 'not sufficient for the defence of Indigenous systems of thought or the re-building of Indigenous lives and communities'.[6] A central task of academics is therefore to 're-assert[] and draw[] in concepts and meanings from Indigenous knowledge and systems of thought and experience of the colonial'.[7] While, as a non-Indigenous person, I am unable to reassert or draw on Indigenous knowledge, I can attempt to faithfully and with sensitivity draw in Indigenous thinking and aspirations and carry these to other non-Indigenous persons. The aim here is not to problematise Indigeneity, a practice Māori professor Linda Tuhiwai Smith condemns as a 'Western obsession',[8] but to challenge constitutional design. That challenge is carried on in the following chapter, where the themes explored here are formulated into four public law principles to assess and guide the development of mechanisms and processes aimed at empowering Indigenous peoples with the capacity to have their voices heard in the processes of government.

[5] T Alfred, *Wasáse: Indigenous Pathways of Action and Freedom* (Toronto, University of Toronto Press, 2005) 20.

[6] M Nakata, V Nakata, S Keech and R Bolt, 'Decolonial Goals and Pedagogies for Indigenous Students' (2012) 1 *Decolonisation: Indigeneity, Education & Society* 120, 124.

[7] ibid.

[8] LT Smith, *Decolonizing Methodologies: Research and Indigenous Peoples* (Dunedin, University of Otago Press, 1999) 91–92.

II. DIVERSE ASPIRATIONS

The United Nations estimates that there are approximately 370 million Indigenous people in the world, belonging to 5,000 different communities, in 90 countries.[9] Unsurprisingly then, despite 'persistent tendencies to imagine Indigenous peoples as a monolithic bloc',[10] to distil them into some essential form, there is no single 'Indigenous' identity, characteristic, idea or aspiration.[11] Rather, Indigenous peoples are diverse and pluralistic, 'criss-crossing geographies, languages, culture areas, faiths, legally divided identities, politics' as well as 'personal socio-economic circumstances and perspectives'.[12] Indeed, while the label 'Indigenous' has proven flexible for diverse communities to articulate their local claims as part of a broader transnational social movement, it elides significant and substantial variance. Almost all Indigenous peoples have and continue to experience colonial intrusion, but such intrusion manifests itself in different forms; even in Australia, there is no single Indigenous account of colonialism.

Doing justice to this diversity of thought is challenging. To begin with, it requires reckoning with the reality that although Indigenous peoples aim to transcend this context, the catalyst for their activism is the political and legal structure of the settler state (or states) which claims their lands. Indigenous peoples' desires are therefore intimately connected to specific localised colonial processes and contemporary politico-legal frameworks; their aspirations are 'often shaped by the very hegemonic structures they seek to resist'.[13] This fact points to another challenge. Aspirations are not static. While Indigenous peoples' demands are culturally grounded, they are also historically contingent, context-specific, and responsive to changing political, social and legal conditions. Where many Aboriginal and Torres Strait Islander peoples in Australia once fought for civic inclusion and 'welcomed the acculturation presaged by enfranchisement',[14] for instance, disappointment at a lack of substantive change and shifting international and national dynamics, have subsequently led many to favouring expressing their claims via a call for distinct citizenship rights. These complications need to be borne in mind when drawing from a range of

[9] United Nations, *State of the World's Indigenous Peoples* (Department of Economic and Social Affairs, 2009) 8.

[10] E Coburn, 'Alternatives: Theorising Colonialism and Indigenous Liberation: Contemporary Indigenous Scholarship from Lands Claimed by Canada' (2016) 97 *Studies in Political Economy* 285, 288.

[11] J Borrows, *Freedom and Indigenous Constitutionalism* (Toronto, University of Toronto Press, 2016) 3.

[12] E LaRoque, *When the Other is Me: Native Resistance Discourse, 1850–1990* (Winnipeg, University of Manitoba Press, 2010) 32; P Monture-Angus, *Journeying Forward: Dreaming Aboriginal People's Independence* (Halifax, Fernwood, 1999) 21.

[13] T LeFevre, 'Settler Colonialism' in J Jackson (ed), *Oxford Bibliographies in Anthropology* (Oxford University Press, 2015), available at www.oxfordbibliographies.com/view/document/obo-9780199766567/obo-9780199766567-0125.xml.

[14] D Lino, 'The Indigenous Franchise and Assimilation' (2017) 48 *Australian Historical Studies* 363, 363.

Indigenous political thought across time and space. That said, as Wiradjuri activist and poet Kevin Gilbert explained in 1973, although 'fine detail' may change rapidly, 'the gut things, the underlying principles' persist.[15]

Complicating matters further, even if all Indigenous peoples were similarly situated, their aspirations would vary, as truth is not universal but is experienced and understood in differing ways. Reflecting on her peoples' traditions, for example, Leanne Simpson highlights that for Anishinaabe, what constitutes truth is personal. Simpson explains that the Nishnaabeg word *dae'b'ingaewin* does not easily translate to Western understandings of 'truth', but something akin to 'the sound of the heart', or, in individual cases, 'the sound of my heart'.[16] *Dae'b'ingaewin* reveals that one person's truth will be different to another's, reflecting both that truth is multifarious and that unlike traditional Western philosophy, there is no objective view from nowhere. Simpson cites Neyaashiinigmiing writer, Basil Johnston's explanation:

> [T]he person whom is said to be *dae'b'wae* is acknowledged to be telling what he or she knows only insofar as he or she has perceived what he or she is reporting, and only according to his or her command of the language. In other words, the speaker is exercising the highest degree of accuracy possible given what he or she knows.[17]

Drawing on Johnston's work, John Borrows (Anishinaabe/Ojibway) has explained that we should understand difference and diversity not as division and untruth, but as a part of the larger story.[18] This chapter does not shy away from disagreement; disagreement is to be expected from 'dynamic and culturally diverse' communities.[19] Instead, it embraces it, exploring a significant cross-section of Indigenous peoples' views with the aim not of elucidating all Indigenous aspirations, but key themes that reappear. As my focus is on structural reform in Australia, my attention is primarily on Aboriginal and Torres Strait Islander peoples, but this focus cannot encapsulate the variety or intensity of Indigenous thought,[20] and so, where relevant, I draw on the work of Indigenous peoples across the globe.

This task has been greatly informed by two recent localised substantive consultations with Indigenous Australians. In 2016 and 2017, the Victorian Aboriginal Treaty Working Group undertook community consultations on the design of an Indigenous representative body. These discussions took place at

[15] K Gilbert, *Because a White Man'll Never Do It* (Sydney, Angus and Robertson, 1973) 165.

[16] L Simpson, *Dancing On Our Turtle's Back: Stories of Nishnaabeg Re-Creation, Resurgence and a New Emergence* (Winnipeg, ARP Books, 2011) 59.

[17] ibid; B Johnston, *Anishinaubae Thesaurus* (East Lansing, Michigan State University Press, 2007) 73.

[18] Borrows, *Freedom* (2016) 11. See also R Austin, *Navajo Court and Navajo Common Law: A Tradition of Tribal Governance* (Minneapolis, University of Minnesota Press, 2009) 58–59.

[19] G Yunupingu, 'Introduction' in G Yunupingu (ed), *Our Land Is Our Life: Land Rights – Past, Present and Future* (Brisbane, University of Queensland Press, 1997) xv, xv.

[20] R de Costa, *A Higher Authority: Indigenous Transnationalism and Australia* (Sydney, UNSW Press, 2005).

16 locations across the state and were designed to enable Aboriginal people to discuss what principles should ground a body to represent them in Treaty negotiations with the state. Despite its narrow focus, the Victorian consultations are useful because they revealed broader feelings of disempowerment and alienation from political and governmental processes. Participants conceived the putative representative body as 'more than just an entity that negotiate[s] Treaty', but as capable of playing a longer-term role as 'a true representative voice for the Aboriginal Community that advocates and negotiates for and on behalf of, unites and represents the' community.[21]

Similar consultations have occurred recently at the national level. In the first half of 2017, a series of Indigenous-designed and led deliberative forums on reform of Australia's Constitution were held across 'all points of the southern sky'. Conducted under the auspices of the Referendum Council, a body established with bipartisan support to 'advise … on progress and next steps towards a referendum' on constitutional recognition of Aboriginal and Torres Strait Islander peoples,[22] these regional dialogues for the first time centred discussion and debate about democratic design and structural reform on Indigenous aspirations.

Each regional dialogue was organised in the same manner.[23] Attendance was by invitation and meetings were capped at 100 participants to promote discussion. Around 60 per cent of places were reserved for traditional owner groups; 20 per cent for community organisations; and 20 per cent for key individuals. A balance was sought between gender and across age groups, with members of the Stolen Generations also represented. The Referendum Council worked in partnership with a host organisation at each location to ensure the local community was appropriately represented in the process. The dialogues were conducted as a deliberative forum. Each took place over three days and included opportunities for large and small group discussions. The Council assisted delegates by providing information on the Constitution and the history of constitutional reform. This allowed delegates to discuss and assess reform options in an informed manner, and to explain what constitutional recognition would mean for their communities. At the end of the three days, delegates confirmed a statement of their discussion and selected ten representatives for a final convention at Uluru.

At Uluru, delegates issued a powerful Statement from the Heart. Grounded in their inherent right to sovereignty, the statement calls for constitutional reform to empower Indigenous peoples by establishing a national representative body

[21] Aboriginal Treaty Working Group, 'Aboriginal Community Consultations on the Design of a Representative Body' (December 2016) 6. See also Aboriginal Treaty Working Group, 'Aboriginal Community Consultations on the Design of a Representative Body – Phase 2' (June 2017). On the treaty process in Victoria see: G Williams and H Hobbs, *Treaty*, 2nd edn (Annandale, Federation Press, 2020) ch 8.

[22] M Turnbull and B Shorten, 'Referendum Council' (media release, 7 December 2015).

[23] M Davis, 'The Long Road to Uluru: Walking Together: Truth Before Justice' (2018) 60 *Griffith Review* 13, 27.

with the power to advise Parliament on laws that affect Indigenous people and a Makarrata Commission to supervise a process of agreement-making between governments and First Nations, and truth-telling.[24] Makarrata is a Yolŋu word of the people from north-east Arnhem Land that has been used since the late 1970s to refer to a negotiated settlement between Indigenous and non-Indigenous peoples. It means 'a coming together after a struggle', which the delegates explained, 'captures our aspirations for a fair and truthful relationship with the people of Australia'.[25] The Uluru Statement is not a unanimous position. Seven delegates walked out in protest the day before it was agreed to, concerned that any reform would lead to a loss of sovereignty, and not all returned.[26] Nonetheless, the statement reflects formidable consensus reached through a process of deliberation unmatched in Australian history, and has therefore been helpful in exploring Indigenous aspirations.

Before delving into this issue, however, it is important to note a final challenge. As Goenpul scholar Aileen Moreton-Robinson explains, Indigenous acts of resistance 'can be visible and invisible, conscious and unconscious, explicit and covert, partial and incomplete and intentional and unintentional'.[27] They often contain 'a logic that is incomprehensible to most white folk (of the right and left political persuasions), who want us to perform our politics according to their ideas about what constitutes correct and proper political action'.[28]

Moreton-Robinson's intervention points to a methodological challenge. In considering Indigenous peoples' conception and articulations of their goals, non-Indigenous theorists must avoid simply relating 'easily translatable' aspirations and obscuring or discarding the incomprehensible.[29] Although potentially innocuous, this is not always an innocent mistake. Megan Davis (Cobble Cobble) and Marcia Langton (Yiman and Bidjara) have noted that the state often 'cherry-picks Aboriginal aspirations to suit their own agenda'.[30] As much as possible then, I emphasise Indigenous aspirations in their own terms, accounting for their actual demands. Nevertheless, while aiming at authentically recording Indigenous peoples' political thought, there is a risk that I will overlook or misinterpret acts of resistance and their significance. What follows is therefore necessarily incomplete.

[24] Uluru Statement from the Heart, Uluru, 26 May 2017 ('Uluru Statement').

[25] ibid.

[26] C Wahlquist, 'Uluru Talks: Indigenous Australians Reject "Symbolic" Recognition in Favour of Treaty', *Guardian Australia* (26 May 2017), available at www.theguardian.com/australia-news/2017/may/26/uluru-talks-opt-for-sovereign-treaty-not-symbolic-constitutional-recognition.

[27] A Moreton-Robinson, *Talkin' Up to the White Woman: Aboriginal Women and Feminism* (Brisbane, University of Queensland Press, 2000) xxiii.

[28] A Moreton-Robinson, 'Introduction: Resistance, Recovery and Revitalisation' in M Grossman (ed), *Blacklines: Contemporary Critical Writing by Indigenous Australians* (Melbourne, Melbourne University Press, 2003) 127, 127.

[29] C Anderson and B Hokowhitu, 'Whiteness: Naivety, Void and Control' (2007) 8 *Junctures* 39, 45.

[30] M Davis and M Langton, 'Constitutional Reform in Australia' in P Macklem and D Sanderson (eds), *From Recognition to Reconciliation* (Toronto, University of Toronto Press 2016) 449, 463.

III. SOVEREIGNTY

In her 2003 book, *Achieving Social Justice: Indigenous Rights and Australia's Future*, Eualeyai and Kamillaroi scholar Larissa Behrendt reviews and reflects on a long history of Aboriginal and Torres Strait Islander political activism. Acknowledging the difficulty in synthesising a diverse body of material, Behrendt argues that 'sovereignty' and 'self-determination' 'have been the two political aspirations that have been most centrally featured in the lexicon of Indigenous claims'.[31] Almost two decades later, notions of sovereignty and self-determination continue to reverberate throughout Indigenous communities, activism, and scholarly work. In Western Australia, the Noongar Settlement – the largest and most comprehensive agreement to settle native title rights and interests in Australia's history – has been characterised by politicians as a process whereby the Noongar people and the Western Australian Government 'recognis[e] each other's sovereignty'.[32] In the Northern Territory, in June 2018, the four Aboriginal Land Councils and Territory Government signed the Barunga Agreement committing the parties to a process of treaty consultations. As part of this process, the Government agreed that the First Nations peoples of the Territory 'never ceded sovereignty of their lands, seas and waters'.[33] Sovereignty talk is also present in Victoria, where the preamble to the country's first treaty Act acknowledges that 'Victorian traditional owners maintain that their sovereignty has never been ceded'.[34] At Uluru too, sovereignty was central; the Statement from the Heart begins by noting that Aboriginal and Torres Strait Islander peoples were 'the first Sovereign Nations of the Australian continent and its adjacent islands'.[35]

Sovereignty and self-determination have broader salience. These concepts have been identified as the 'the heart and soul' of the United Nations Declaration of the Rights of Indigenous Peoples (UNDRIP),[36] constituting the 'river in which all other rights swim'.[37] This is significant, for Indigenous peoples were directly and actively involved in drafting the UNDRIP.[38] While the Declaration is, of course, a compromise, reflecting tensions within Indigenous polities and

[31] L Behrendt, *Achieving Social Justice: Indigenous Rights and Australia's Future* (Annandale, Federation Press, 2003) 87.

[32] Western Australia, *Parliamentary Debates*, Legislative Assembly, 19 November 2015, 8688 (Roger Cook, Deputy Opposition Leader); H Hobbs and G Williams, 'The Noongar Settlement: Australia's First Treaty' (2018) 40 *Sydney Law Review* 1.

[33] The Barunga Agreement (8 June 2018), principle 6(c).

[34] Advancing the Treaty Process with Aboriginal Victorians Act 2018 (Vic), preamble.

[35] Uluru Statement (n 24).

[36] United Nations Declaration on the Rights of Indigenous Peoples, GA Res 61/295, UN GAOR, 61st sess, 107th plen mtg, Supp No 49, UN Doc A/RES/61/295 (13 September 2007) (UNDRIP).

[37] C Scott, 'Indigenous Self-Determination and Decolonisation of the International Imagination: A Plea' (1996) 18 *Human Rights Quarterly* 814, 814 citing M Dodson.

[38] M Davis, 'Indigenous Struggles in Standard-Setting: The United Nations Declaration on the Rights of Indigenous Peoples (2008) 9 *Melbourne Journal of International Law* 439.

between Indigenous political communities and states, James Anaya (Apache and Purépecha), the Special Rapporteur on the Rights of Indigenous Peoples, has remarked that its norms 'substantially reflect Indigenous peoples' own aspirations'.[39] As such, while negotiations challenged some claims and tempered several provisions, the UNDRIP stands as a critical instrument in ascertaining how Indigenous peoples conceive of their position and articulate their aspirations for structural reform within democratic states. One element of this tension is the absence of 'sovereignty'. The term does not appear in either the text or preamble, save for its invocation in the final Article 46. Rather than affirm Indigenous sovereignty, however, this provision is intended to qualify or condition the rights of Indigenous peoples, precluding any interpretation that would 'dismember or impair, totally or in part, the territorial integrity or political unity of sovereign and independent States'. The juxtaposition of Indigenous rights to 'autonomy' under Article 4, with the rights of 'sovereign' states, suggests a more limited application in the Declaration. Nonetheless, outside the Declaration sovereignty remains the key concept identified by Indigenous peoples throughout Australia and the world.

Sovereignty and self-determination 'are distinct and yet related'.[40] Sovereignty is a broader concept that encompasses self-determination, but also conveys additional and exclusive meanings that help elucidate criteria for institutional design. If self-determination 'is the right to make decisions',[41] assertions of sovereignty appear to temper or condition the exercise of that right by insisting that decisions be made in a particular way, a way that connects with land and is 'fortified by … law and culture'.[42]

Indigenous peoples consider sovereignty to be inherent to Indigenous political communities. It is 'a spiritual notion',[43] said to derive 'from within a people or culture',[44] with Indigenous laws emanating from 'the songs of creation'.[45] As Palawa activist and lawyer Michael Mansell explains, sovereignty is 'the bedrock on which Aboriginal rights and entitlements are based'; sovereignty 'goes at

[39] J Anaya, 'Situation of Human Rights and Fundamental Freedoms of Indigenous People', UN Doc A/65/264 (9 August 2010) 17 [59]–[61].

[40] H McGlade, 'Native Title, "Tides of History" and Our Continuing Claims for Justice – Sovereignty, Self Determination and Treaty' in H McGlade (ed), *Treaty: Let's Get It Right!* (Canberra, Aboriginal Studies Press, 2003) 118, 128.

[41] Human Rights and Equal Opportunity Commission, 'Aboriginal and Torres Strait Islander Social Justice Commission: First Report' (Commonwealth, 1993) 41.

[42] M Dodson, 'Mabo Lecture: Asserting our Sovereignty' in L Strelein (ed), *Dialogue about Land Justice: Papers from the National Native Title Conference* (Canberra, Aboriginal Studies Press, 2010) 13, 15–16. See also the Independent Working Group on Constitutional Transformation, 'The Report of Matike Mai Aotearoa' (2016) ch 1.

[43] Uluru Statement (n 24).

[44] K Kickingbird, L Kickingbird, C Chibitty and C Berkey, *Indian Sovereignty* (Washington DC, Indian Legal Curriculum and Training Program of the Institute for the Development of Indian Law, 1977) 1.

[45] I Watson, 'There is No Possibility of Rights without Law: So Until Then, Don't Thumb Print or Sign Anything!' (2000) 5 *Indigenous Law Bulletin* 4, 4.

the heart of the Aboriginal struggle. It sustains land rights, customary law and self-determination'.[46] For many Indigenous people, sovereignty is intimately intertwined with country; it entails 'being in relationship with, belonging and being responsible to the lands of our ancestors'.[47] Pekeri Ruska (Goenpul) and Callum Clayton-Dixon (Anaiwan), articulate this view, arguing that sovereignty stems from:

> [T]he ancient reciprocal relationship we have with our lands. This relationship finds its roots in our connection to kind and country, manifesting in our song, dance and story, our language, ceremony and law. It is vested in the individual, the tribe and the nation. Our sovereignty has endured since the first sunrise – it cannot be handed to us or taken from us. Aboriginal sovereignty can only be expressed or suppressed.[48]

As this brief exploration suggests, sovereignty is a complex and ambiguous term. Despite, or perhaps because of its normative power as an 'important component of Indigenous political culture',[49] a wide range of interpretations and attitudes towards and about sovereignty exist. Distilling the major elements of these diverse views reveals that sovereignty has peoplehood, political and cultural dimensions. By this, I mean that sovereignty is used to differentiate Indigenous peoples from other members of the settler state polity, to assert a right to self-governance either via a separate state or through enhanced autonomy and powers of decision-making within the state, and to declare that such authority should be conducted in an Indigenous way – what Osage scholar Robert Allen Warrior calls 'intellectual sovereignty'.[50] These categories are somewhat arbitrary; assertions of Indigenous sovereignty cannot always be neatly conceptualised within such a framework. Nonetheless, this division is useful in articulating the diverse meanings conveyed when Indigenous peoples speak in the language of sovereignty. If nothing else, these three dimensions of sovereignty are consistent, though described differently, with Mohawk lawyer Patricia Monture-Angus' view:

> [W]hat seems to be common to all Aboriginal Peoples, despite our vast differences, is a desire to continue to exercise our authority in political, social and legal ways, at least among our own people, following our own understandings of our (political authority).[51]

[46] M Mansell, *Treaty and Statehood: Aboriginal Self-Determination* (Annandale, Federation Press, 2016) 74.

[47] I Watson, 'The 2007 Declaration on the Rights of Indigenous Peoples: Indigenous Survival – Where to from Here?' (2011) 20 *Griffith Law Review* 507, 509.

[48] P Ruska and C Clayton-Dixon, 'Words of the Struggle' (2015) 1 *Black Nations Rising* 10, 10.

[49] Maddison, *Black Politics* (2009) 49.

[50] RA Warrior, 'Intellectual Sovereignty and the Struggle for an American Indian Future' (1992) 8 *Wicazo Sa Review* 1, 6.

[51] Monture-Angus, *Journeying Forward* (1999) 30. See also P Coe, 'The Struggle for Aboriginal Sovereignty' (1994) 13 *Social Alternatives* 1, 10: Sovereignty 'means having the power to govern your own affairs in regard to political, social and cultural aspects'.

Monture-Angus's emphasis on following Indigenous understandings of political authority is germane. Despite the various ways it is used by Indigenous peoples, as a Western notion, sovereignty may be unable to fully capture Indigenous epistemologies and perspectives on law, governance and culture.[52] But, 'sovereignty' is a semantic concept, an expression of Indigenous aspirations rather than the core of the idea itself. As such, it is through developing a meaning of sovereignty 'that respects the understanding of power in Indigenous cultures' – through understanding its peoplehood, political, and cultural dimensions – that sovereignty can 'be part of the language of liberation'.[53]

A. Peoplehood

Indigeneity is 'conceptually fraught'[54] because Indigenous peoples share many commonalities with ethnic or cultural minority groups.[55] In most settler states, Indigenous peoples belong to non-dominant communities, differentiate themselves by and are differentiated from the larger polity by culture, language and identity, and constitute a numerical minority within the state. Like other marginalised communities, Indigenous peoples may struggle to have their interests heard in the processes of settler state government. This is often the case even where the minority community outnumbers other inhabitants in a particular region as, critically, they remain separated from the corridors of power. Notwithstanding analytical ambiguity, however, the concepts are not analogous, and a recurrent theme within Indigenous political advocacy aims at securing recognition of this distinct status; recognition that Indigenous peoples are not minority groups but polities with concomitant rights. For many Indigenous peoples and scholars then, 'sovereignty' is connected to assertions of identity and difference.

Sovereignty as peoplehood takes on a critical role in the face of state efforts to deny Indigenous difference. Lenape professor Joanne Barker explains that

[52] T Alfred, 'Sovereignty' in J Barker (ed), *Sovereignty Matters: Locations of Contestations and Possibility in Indigenous Struggles for Self-Determination* (Lincoln, University of Nebraska Press, 2005) 33; L Emerson, 'Diné Sovereign Action: Rejecting Colonial Sovereignty and Invoking Diné Peacemaking' in L Lee (ed), *Navajo Sovereignty: Understandings and Visions of the Diné People* (Tucson, University of Arizona Press, 2017) 160; N Tomas, 'Māori Concepts and Practices of *Rangatirantanga*: "Sovereignty"?' in J Evans, A Genovese, A Reilly and P Wolfe (eds), *Sovereignty: Frontiers of Possibility* (Honolulu, University of Hawai'i Press, 2013) 220.

[53] T Alfred, *Peace, Power Righteousness: An Indigenous Manifesto*, 2nd edn (Oxford, Oxford University Press, 2009) 78. See also KKNP Ontai, 'A Spiritual Definition of Sovereignty from a Kanaka Maoli Perspective' in J Barker (ed), *Sovereignty Matters: Locations of Contestations and Possibility in Indigenous Struggles for Self-Determination* (Lincoln, University of Nebraska Press, 2005) 153, 154.

[54] K Gover, *Tribal Constitutionalism: States. Tribes, and the Governance of Membership* (Oxford, Oxford University Press, 2010) 3.

[55] J Anaya 'International Human Rights and Indigenous Peoples: The Move Towards the Multicultural State' (2004) 21 *Arizona Journal of International and Comparative Law* 13, 21.

the 'making ethnic' or 'ethnicisation' of Indigenous peoples is a political strategy that relegates Indigenous peoples' aspirations and demands to that of just another minority interest, erasing their sovereignty and robbing their calls of political force.[56] Native Hawaiian scholar Haunani-Kay Trask has made a similar point, arguing that this process transforms Indigenous peoples engaging in decolonising practices to ethnic minorities in the midst of a 'cultural revival', as these latter features and terms have no political or legal context.[57] It is this dynamic that leads Indigenous scholars like James (Sákéj) Youngblood Henderson (Chickasaw), Dale Turner (Anishinaabe), Taiaiake Alfred, and Aileen Moreton-Robinson, to reject undifferentiated citizenship rights bestowed by the settler state, which 'offer[] only the silence and anguish of minority interest group status',[58] and signal the 'defeat of the idea of an independent … existence'.[59] Instead, these scholars position Indigenous political rights as 'sui generis',[60] as 'not predicated on the same basis as everyone else',[61] but rather flowing from their status as Indigenous nations that predate the formation of settler states.[62]

Assertion of sovereignty is a way to resist the assimilative tendencies of the settler state that positions Indigenous peoples as a numerical minority within a larger polity. Implicit in the call of and for Indigenous sovereignty is the declaration that Indigenous peoples are not merely a subsection of the larger society, 'but a people with a distinct political status'.[63] Sovereignty is 'a plea for recognition',[64] grounding Indigenous claims for a distinctive relationship with the state. Sovereignty talk is an act of resistance and refusal; a challenge to the settler state's view of Indigenous political communities 'not as a people with a governmental system, a philosophical order, but as a remnant, a "culture", a minority within an ethnocultural mosaic of differences'.[65]

Sovereignty is a valuable concept for this task. As non-Indigenous Canadian scholar Patrick Macklem has explained, sovereignty establishes legal space for a

[56] J Barker, 'For Whom Sovereignty Matters' in J Barker (ed), *Sovereignty Matters: Locations of Contestations and Possibility in Indigenous Struggles for Self-Determination* (Lincoln, University of Nebraska Press, 2005) 1, 16.

[57] H-K Trask, *From A Native Daughter: Colonialism and Sovereignty in Hawai'i* (Honolulu, University of Hawai'i Press, 1999) 90. See further I Watson, *Aboriginal Peoples, Colonialism and International Law: Raw Law* (Abingdon, Routledge, 2015) 2–3.

[58] J Henderson, 'Sui Generis and Treaty Citizenship' (2002) 6 *Citizenship Studies* 415, 433.

[59] Alfred, *Wasáse* (2005) 23.

[60] Henderson, 'Sui Generis' (2002) 433; D Turner, *This is Not a Peace Pipe: Towards a Critical Indigenous Philosophy* (Toronto, University of Toronto Press, 2006) 7.

[61] A Moreton-Robinson, 'Writing off Indigenous Sovereignty: The Discourse of Security and Patriarchal White Sovereignty' in A Moreton-Robinson (ed), *Sovereign Subjects* (Crows Nest, Allen & Unwin, 2007) 86, 99.

[62] Turner, *This is Not a Peace Pipe* (2006) 37.

[63] Mansell, *Treaty and Statehood* (2016) 140.

[64] ME Turpel, 'Aboriginal Peoples and the Canadian Charter of Rights and Freedoms: Contradictions and Challenges' (1989) 10 *Canadian Women's Studies* 149, 150.

[65] A Simpson, *Mohawk Interruptus: Political Life Across the Borders of Settler States* (Durham, Duke University Press, 2014) 10.

community 'to construct, project, and transform its collective identity'.[66] That some Indigenous people refuse state forms of identity when travelling across borders in preference for an Indigenous passport, thereby wilfully choosing to be detained 'in a faraway place in order to assert this other form of emplacement',[67] represents both a rejection of settler state governing logics and an affirmation of a 'politically empowered self-identity within, besides, and against colonisation'.[68] Such an act is not merely protest or dissent (which recognises political authority as lawful), but a challenge to the legitimacy of the state.

In its peoplehood dimension, sovereignty asks a challenging question: What does it mean to be Indigenous? While Australian law no longer defines Aboriginality according to statutory definitions of blood quantum, its legacy persists in attitudes that contest whether a person is or is not a 'real' Aboriginal. Reflecting on this pathology, Bardi woman Pat Dudgeon argues that Australian society still assigns Aboriginal identity to those who are practicing 'traditional culture', dismissing those who have 'lost their culture' as 'unauthentic' or 'not real'.[69] In *Living Black*, Kevin Gilbert documented similar debates within the Aboriginal community;[70] debates that echo still today,[71] and remain inflected by state law.[72] Indigenous peoples and nations take differing approaches to this question: some adopt strict descent rules, while others embrace civic nationalism permitting non-Indigenous persons to naturalise and become citizens within their community.[73] In all cases, however, sovereignty means the right to decide rests with the people themselves.

This understanding of sovereignty is reflected in the UNDRIP. The Declaration affirms a multinational ordering of the state,[74] guaranteeing that Indigenous peoples have the right 'to a nationality',[75] as well as the right to 'belong to an Indigenous community or nation' determined in accordance with the 'traditions and customs of the community or nation concerned'.[76] Recognition of the plurinational basis of states that house Indigenous peoples is inherent to Article 33, which expressly guarantees that membership in an Indigenous nation

[66] P Macklem, *Indigenous Difference and the Constitution of Canada* (Toronto, University of Toronto Press, 2001) 111.

[67] Simpson, *Mohawk Interruptus* (2014) 182.

[68] Barker, 'Sovereignty' (2005) 20.

[69] P Dudgeon, 'Indigenous Identity' in P Dudgeon, D Garvey and H Pickett (eds), *Working with Indigenous Australians: A Handbook for Psychologists* (Perth, Gunada Press, 2000) 43, 45. See ch 6 for discussion of this problem within the Sámi community in Sweden.

[70] K Gilbert, *Living Black: Blacks Talk to Kevin Gilbert* (Melbourne, Penguin, 1977) chs 1, 14, 16.

[71] S Grant, *The Australian Dream: Blood, History and Becoming* (2016) 64 *Quarterly Essay* 1.

[72] A Whittaker, 'White Law, Blak Arbiters, Grey Legal Subjects: Deep Colonisation's Role and Impact in Defining Aboriginality at Law' (2017) 20 *Australian Indigenous Law Review* 4.

[73] Gover, *Tribal Constitutionalism* (2010) ch 3.

[74] W Kymlicka, 'Beyond the Indigenous/Minority Dichotomy?' in S Allen and A Xanthaki, *Reflections on the UN Declaration on the Rights of Indigenous Peoples* (Oxford, Hart Publishing, 2011) 183, 188.

[75] UNDRIP (n 36) art 6.

[76] ibid art 9.

'does not impair the right of Indigenous individuals to obtain citizenship of the States in which they live'. Likewise, Article 36(1) affirms that Indigenous peoples may maintain and develop contacts and relationships as well as cooperate with members of their Indigenous nation, irrespective of international borders. The Declaration also imposes restrictions on states and provides for rectification of injustice, declaring that Indigenous peoples must not be subjected to forced assimilation or cultural destruction, and that they have the right to receive redress for any acts that deprive them of their identity and integrity as distinct peoples.[77]

B. Political

The political dimension of sovereignty is most frequently heard by non-Indigenous peoples. Sovereignty in this sense most directly challenges the legitimacy of settler state governance, contending that alternative, prior, normative orders retain the right to exercise political authority over defined territory. Perhaps precisely because the political dimension of sovereignty is so recurrent in the language of Indigenous peoples' aspirations, however, it is subject to multifarious interpretation. For some, Indigenous sovereignty prevails over the entirety of lands claimed by settler states such that it necessitates secession and external self-determination, while for others, it requires a renegotiated constitutional order that guarantees a degree of autonomy from the state and a commitment to shared-rule in other domains.

Māori professor Roger Maaka and non-Indigenous Canadian academic Augie Fleras have noted that 'Indigenous claims to sovereignty rarely entail separation or secession but instead a reconstitutionalising of the first principles upon which Indigenous peoples-state relations are governed'.[78] While this is generally true, it elides the fact that for many Indigenous peoples, a first principles approach *necessarily* involves separation and secession. These scholars and activists challenge the belief that Indigenous-state relations can ever be adequately 'accommodated' within a settler politico-legal framework. As Glen Coulthard (Yellowknives Dene) explains, such an approach fails to comprehend that assertions of sovereignty and nationhood fundamentally question 'the legitimacy of the settler state's claim to sovereignty over Indigenous people and their territories'.[79] In other words, Indigenous sovereignty cannot coexist with settler state sovereignty.

[77] ibid art 8(1)–(2).

[78] R Maaka and A Fleras, 'Engaging with Indigneity: Tino Rangatiratanga in Aotearoa' in D Ivison, P Patton and W Sanders (eds), *Political Theory and the Rights of Indigenous Peoples* (Cambridge, Cambridge University Press, 2000) 89, 89.

[79] G Coulthard, *Red Skins, White Masks: Rejecting the Colonial Politics of Recognition* (Minneapolis, University of Minnesota Press, 2014) 36.

Taiaiake Alfred has cogently developed this position over two decades. Alfred conceives sovereignty as a struggle for 'recognition and respect' of a nation's 'right to exist as [a] people[], unencumbered by the demands, controls, and false identities imposed on them by others'.[80] While this form of sovereignty may no longer be possible in a globalised and interdependent world where regional and transnational governance bodies, human rights instruments, and multinational corporations constrain state action to various degrees, Alfred is clear that he envisages Indigenous sovereignty existing on the same plane, though not necessarily in the same form, as settler state nations, for self-governance or self-rule 'within the legal and structural confines of the state' is 'an assimilative goal',[81] and ends with the 'defeat of the idea of an independent Onkwehonwe [original person] existence'.[82] Irene Watson (Tanganekald, Meintangk and Boandik) agrees with Alfred, dismissing recognition of Indigenous self-determination by or within Australian law as 'inevitably reinstat[ing] colonial law',[83] leaving Indigenous peoples 'subservient to the rules of the state'.[84] In a persuasive critique of state-sponsored efforts at 'recognition' and 'reconciliation', Coulthard adopts a similar position. Coulthard argues that conceiving recognition as something that is 'granted' or 'accorded' by the state to subaltern groups, 'prefigures its failure to significantly modify, let alone transcend, the breadth of power at play in colonial relations'.[85] Instead, it is a form of 'domestication'[86] of Indigenous sovereignty, that 'subtly reproduce[s] nonmutual and unfree relations rather than free and mutual ones'.[87] Here Coulthard echoes Mohawk scholar Audra Simpson who contends that policies of state recognition are merely a 'gentler form' of continuing the perennial problem of 'managing Indians'.[88]

These scholars posit refusal as a political alternative to recognition, calling on Indigenous peoples to turn away from the oppressor and resist the act of recognition.[89] For Watson, enhanced decision-making or autonomy within the settler state and other internal forms of self-determination, cannot provide a place 'with the freedom for the song law to be sung without the power and interference of the muldarbi',[90] the demon spirit who takes the form of the coloniser. As Indigenous sovereignty has never been surrendered or extinguished, what is required is self-rule emanating not from delegated authority, but inhering in Indigenous nations themselves.[91]

[80] Alfred, *Peace, Power, Righteousness* (2009) 8; See also: Monture-Angus (n 12) 29.
[81] Alfred (n 53) 122.
[82] Alfred (n 5) 23.
[83] Watson, *Raw Law* (2015) 2.
[84] ibid 91.
[85] Coulthard, *Red Skins, White Masks* (2014) 30–31.
[86] ibid 40.
[87] ibid 17.
[88] Simpson (n 65) 20.
[89] G Coulthard, 'Subjects of Empire: Indigenous Peoples and the "Politics of Recognition" in Canada' (2007) 6 *Contemporary Political Theory* 437, 454–56. See also: Simpson (n 65) 11.
[90] Watson (n 57) 152.
[91] ibid 161; Moreton-Robinson, 'Writing off Indigenous Sovereignty' (2007) 99.

Calls for sovereignty in this sense are often made by Indigenous leaders and activists across the world. In July 2014, for instance, the hereditary chiefs of two tribal villages of the Gitx̲san nation, Gitwanga and Gitsegukla, issued an eviction notice, ordering Canadian National Rail and all non-native sports fisheries and forestry activities to cease and persons vacate Gitx̲san territory (approximately 33,000km^2 in north-west British Columbia).[92] Although the notice was not supported by all Gitx̲san peoples and was eventually stayed,[93] that its proponents issued it pursuant to their understanding of *ayokim Gitxsan* (Gitx̲san law) reveals the orientation of their claims. Similar logics permeate the Standing Rock Sioux challenge to the Dakota Access Pipeline. Despite being compelled to litigate and protest within the United States legal system, the Sioux continue to predicate their claims on their own legal norms and obligations.[94]

The apparent incompatibility between these competing contestations to political authority was highlighted in a recent challenge in British Columbia. Hereditary chiefs of the Wet'suwet'en First Nation unsuccessfully sought to overturn an injunction preventing them from blockading the construction of an oil pipeline. The intended route of the pipeline would travel through unceded Wet'suwet'en territory, but because no treaty has been signed between the Wet'suwet'en and Canadian officials, that territory is not recognised in Canadian law as Wet'suwet'en land. In dismissing the application, the British Columbia Supreme Court noted that

> the defendants may genuinely believe in their rights under indigenous law to prevent the plaintiff from entering Dark House territory, but [Canadian] law does not recognize any right to blockade and obstruct the plaintiff from pursuing lawfully authorized activities.[95]

Assertions of Indigenous sovereignty have also been made in Australia. On 26 January 1972, four young Aboriginal men drove from Redfern to Canberra and established a tent embassy on the lawns in front of Parliament House. While they, and the 2,000 supporters who swelled the site, may have looked like protestors exercising their right to civil disobedience,[96] their motivations were distinct; they challenged the state's authority to unilaterally settle Indigenous peoples' claims, insisting that agreement must be reached between two polities.[97]

[92] Gwaans, 'Gitxsan Eviction Notice to Sportsfishers, Forestry and CN Rail' (press release, 10 July 2014).

[93] A Woo and W Stueck, 'As Evictions Loom, Even a Landmark Court Ruling Can't Bring Certainty on Gitxsan Land' *The Globe and Mail* (1 August 2014), available at www.theglobeandmail.com/news/british-columbia/on-gitxsan-land-even-a-landmark-court-ruling-cant-bring-certainty/article19897595.

[94] S Young, 'The Sioux's Suits: Global Law and the Dakota Access Pipeline' (2017) 6 *American Indian Law Journal* 173.

[95] *Coastal GasLink Pipeline Ltd v Huson* (2019) BCSC 2264 (31 December 2019) [225] (Church J).

[96] Members of the Government conceived them as such: See P Howson, *The Howson Diaries: The Life of Politics* (Melbourne, Viking, 1984) 892.

[97] J Newfong, 'The Aboriginal Embassy: Its Purpose and Aims' (July 1972) *Identity* 4.

By styling the ramshackle collection of tents an 'embassy', the activists positioned Aboriginal and Torres Strait Islander peoples as 'aliens in [their] own land',[98] serving as a potent 'symbol of unextinguished Indigenous sovereignty'.[99] The next year, Kevin Gilbert drew on his experiences with the embassy, arguing in *Because a White Man'll Never Do It*, that 'what blacks really want' is a combination of 'land, compensation, discreet non-dictatorial help and *to be left alone* by white Australia'.[100] In 1992, the Aboriginal Provisional Government (APG) proposed such a model, calling for an 'Aboriginal Nation':

> [A] nation exercising total jurisdiction over its communities to the exclusion of all others. A nation whose land base is at least all crown lands, so called. A nation able to raise its own economy and provide for its peoples.[101]

Consistent with this vision, the APG began issuing Aboriginal passports in the 1980s, on the basis that the Aboriginal nation 'is separate to the Australian nation' and that Aboriginal people should take 'our place among the nations and peoples of the world, not beneath them'.[102] Persons travelling on such passports have been accepted into Libya (1987 and 1988), Norway and Switzerland (1990), the Mohawk Nation (2014), and the Solomon Islands and New Zealand (2015).[103] While the Australian Government officially refuses to recognise it, individuals have successfully re-entered the state using an Aboriginal passport.[104] Such passports have been issued by Indigenous nations across the world: the Haudenosaunee first issued them as early as 1923, and members continue to travel on them, affirming their claims to statehood.[105]

Care must be taken in assessing Indigenous assertions of sovereignty in its political dimension, for not all extend this far or are directed in this manner. In contrast to the APG's vision of pan-aboriginality,[106] several Indigenous communities in Australia have recently sought to separate from the Australian state. However, while groups like the Euahlayi Nation assert their 'pre-existing and

[98] Gary Foley (Gumbainggir), cited in E Howell, 'Black Power – By Any Means Necessary' in G Foley, A Schaap and E Howell (eds), *The Aboriginal Tent Embassy: Sovereignty, Black Power, Land Rights and the State* (Abingdon, Routledge, 2016) 67, 75.

[99] Williams and Hobbs, *Treaty* (2020) 35.

[100] Gilbert, *White Man* (1973) 177 (emphasis in original).

[101] Cited in S Brennan, B Gunn and G Williams, '"Sovereignty" and its Relevance to Treaty-Making Between Indigenous Peoples and Australian Governments' (2004) 26 *Sydney Law Review* 307, 315.

[102] Aboriginal Provisional Government, 'About the Aboriginal Provisional Government', available at www.apg.org.au/about.php.

[103] ibid.

[104] Callum Clayton-Dixon, Chairperson of the APG, argues that this amounts to de facto recognition of Aboriginal sovereignty; this assertion is rejected by customs and border protection: J Robertson, 'Tolerance of Travellers with Aboriginal Passports Amounts to Recognition, Says Activist' *Guardian Australia* (20 April 2015), available at www.theguardian.com/australia-news/2015/apr/20/tolerance-of-travellers-with-aboriginal-passports-amounts-to-recognition-says-activist.

[105] Simpson (n 65) 182–84.

[106] On pan-Aboriginality in Australia see: J Martinez, 'Problematising Aboriginal Nationalism' (1997) 21 *Aboriginal History* 133.

continuing statehood',[107] it is not always clear that secession is desired. For instance, in 2014, members of the Yidindji nation, led by Murrumu Walubara Yidindji (formerly Jeremy Geia), renounced their legal ties to Australia and announced the formation of the Sovereign Yidindji Government; a nation that 'already existed' but that Australia 'failed to notice'.[108] The Yidindji nation operates under Yidindji Tribal Law, and through the Nyangi Wanya (executive government), which is composed of 10 ministers headed by Chief Minister Gudju-Gudju Gimuybara. It has exercised its sovereignty in several ways, including by issuing its own identity documents,[109] and has sought to establish 'formal diplomatic relations with Australia and other nations'.[110] The Yidindji cannot speak for all purportedly independent Aboriginal nations, but despite the formal appearance of separatism and secessionism, their aspirations are more moderate. The Yidindji Government website notes that the nation 'has no plans to become a member of the United Nations',[111] and Murrumu has been reported as saying that 'The Yidindji wished to ultimately participate in the Australian state once a treaty had been agreed … but not until then'.[112]

For many, though not all, Indigenous peoples, sovereignty means just this: a desire to participate *within* the existing state, but on renegotiated terms. Larissa Behrendt, for instance, has argued that 'the notion of sovereignty' strikes at the heart of restructuring the political relationship between Indigenous and non-Indigenous peoples.[113] For Behrendt, it is 'underlined by a strong demand for control of decision-making processes',[114] for autonomy and decision-making.[115] Sovereignty then is not the 'aim of political advocacy', but 'a starting point … a footing' from which to exercise rights within the state.[116] Non-Indigenous Australian scholar Lisa Strelein agrees, arguing that sovereignty asserts ideas of 'identity, autonomy and authority', as well as 'recognition and respect'.[117]

[107] GM Anderson, 'Euahlayi Nation Declares Independence and Asserts Pre-Existing and Continuing Statehood' (press release, 12 August 2013).

[108] YB Melhern, 'There's Another Government in Australia and Murrumu is Taking it to the World' *Guardian Australia* (29 January 2016), available at www.theguardian.com/commentisfree/2016/jan/29/theres-another-government-in-australia-and-murrumu-is-taking-it-to-the-world.

[109] Currency Act 2014 (YSG); Yidindji Sovereign Government, 'Public Notice: Vehicle Driver Licence; Cars, Trucks, Motorcycles' (18 March 2015).

[110] P Daley, 'He Renounced Australia and Lives Solely by Tribal Law. Now Murrumu is Hitting the Road' *Guardian Australia* (9 January 2015), available at www.theguardian.com/commentisfree/2015/jan/09/he-renounced-australia-and-lives-solely-by-tribal-law-now-murrumu-is-hitting-the-road.

[111] Yidindji Sovereign Government, 'Frequently Asked Questions', available at www.yidindji.org.

[112] J Robertson, 'Murrumu Charged After Driving with Licence Issued by his Indigenous Nation' *Guardian Australia* (27 May 2015), available at www.theguardian.com/australia-news/2015/may/27/murrumu-charged-after-driving-with-licence-issued-by-his-indigenous-nation.

[113] Behrendt, *Achieving Social Justice* (2003) 96.

[114] ibid 89.

[115] ibid 106.

[116] ibid 99.

[117] L Strelein, 'Missed Meaning: The Language of Sovereignty in the Treaty Debate' (2002/03) 20 *Arena* 83, 85.

This understanding of sovereignty was frequently aired in community consultations undertaken by the 2012 Expert Panel on Constitutional Recognition. One participant in Newcastle in July 2011 explained:

> We want sovereignty along with recognition. It is not realistic for us to have our own government, but we can look at the positions within government and areas for us to have power over. If the consensus in the community is that we should have a say in how this country is run then we should have a piece of it.[118]

This approach is consistent with modern treaties signed between First Nations and the Canadian Crown. Since 1973, 26 comprehensive agreements have been reached in Canada, 18 of which include provisions related to self-government. While each is specific to the particular First Nation, as well as place, history and circumstance, they all recognise culturally appropriate forms of decision-making, amounting to a degree of self-government in internal and local affairs, and provide recurrent financing as a means to ensure their autonomous functioning.[119] Jurisdiction recognised under each treaty typically includes the administration of justice, family and social services, healthcare, and language and cultural education.[120] All agreements are, however, reached on the basis of overriding sovereignty of the state, and federal and provincial law applies where an inconsistency or conflict arises with Indigenous law-making.[121] Yet, First Nations participating in these negotiations do not see this condition as inhibiting their aspirations, but as a central element of their goals. On signing the Nisga'a Final Agreement, for example, Edward Allen, CEO of the Nisga'a Lisims Government declared that 'we have negotiated our way into Canada, to be full and equal participants of Canadian society'.[122] As the Final Agreement records, the treaty relationship is a symbol of equal partnership, based on 'mutual recognition and sharing'.[123] Preliminary treaty processes in several states and territories in Australia conceive sovereignty in an analogous manner. Any treaties that eventuate will be subject to Australian law, but as the Barunga Agreement notes, treaty still offers the potential to ground 'lasting

[118] Commonwealth of Australia, 'Recognising Aboriginal and Torres Strait Islander Peoples in the Constitution: Report of the Expert Panel' (January 2012) 97.

[119] In relation to the British Columbia Treaty Process see C Godlewska and J Webber, 'The *Calder* decision, Aboriginal title, and the Nisga'a' in H Foster, H Raven and J Webber (eds), *Let Right be Done: Aboriginal Title, the Calder Case, and the Future of Indigenous Rights* (Vancouver, University of British Columbia Press, 2007) 1, 17–18.

[120] See, eg: Yale First Nation Final Agreement, signed 12 March 2011 (entered into force 19 June 2013) ch 3; Tla'amin Final Agreement, signed 10 July 2012, (entered into force 5 April 2016) ch 15.

[121] See, eg: Yale First Nation Final Agreement, ch 3.11.3. For concerns relating to this issue see T Alfred, 'Deconstructing the British Columbia Treaty Process' (2001) 3 *Balayi: Culture, Law and Colonialism* 37, 39–43; J Tully, 'Reconsidering the B.C. Treaty Process' in *Speaking Truth to Power: A Treaty Forum* (British Columbia Treaty Commission, 2000) 3, 8.

[122] E Allen, 'Our Treaty, Our Inherent Right to Self-Government: An Overview of the Nisga'a Final Agreement' (2004) 11 *International Journal on Minority and Group Rights* 233, 234.

[123] Nisga'a Final Agreement, signed 4 May 1999 (entered into force 11 May 2000), preamble.

reconciliation between … First Nations … and other citizens with the object of achieving a united [Australia]'.[124]

This understanding of sovereignty is reflected in the UNDRIP. Article 3 provides that Indigenous people have the 'right to self-determination', meaning they may 'freely determine their political status and freely pursue their economic, social and cultural development', while Article 5 guarantees Indigenous peoples the right to maintain their distinct institutions. Although broadly framed and suggestive of a more expansive understanding of political sovereignty, this right is conditioned by Article 46(1) which protects the territorial integrity of existing states, and Article 4 which limits the right to self-determination to the 'right to autonomy or self-government' in relation to 'internal and local affairs'.

The fact that political sovereignty is elaborated as 'internal' has been challenged by critical Indigenous scholars.[125] Nonetheless, while the agreed-upon formulation may be 'an inherently pragmatic decision',[126] it reflects a strong, majority current of Indigenous thinking. Throughout negotiations Indigenous peoples involved in the drafting frequently asserted that they 'have no interest in secession' but desire greater autonomy and decision-making authority in order to 'finally become part of' the state.[127] For this reason, the UNDRIP's underlying principles of 'participation, engagement and consultation',[128] are based on the 'assumption of interdependence between states and Indigenous peoples'.[129] That same notion of interdependence is present in the Uluru Statement, which explicitly declares that Indigenous sovereignty 'co-exists with the sovereignty of the Crown'.[130]

At root in many, though not all, of these calls is not secession, but autonomy; a desire to 'get greater control over our lives and future',[131] by transferring 'decision making to Aboriginal people'.[132] As Guugu Yimidhirr lawyer Noel Pearson has explained, 'Indigenous people want to take charge of our own affairs and lead our own development agendas'.[133] Understood in this light, invocations of Indigenous sovereignty are not always intended as a precursor to secession,

[124] Barunga Agreement (n 33) Principle 1.

[125] See, eg: (2011) 20 *Griffith Law Review* 'Special Issue: The 2007 Declaration on the Rights of Indigenous Peoples: Indigenous Survival – Where to from Here?'

[126] M Davis, 'To Bind or not to Bind: The United Nations *Declaration on the Rights of Indigenous Peoples* Five Years On' (2012) 3 *Australian International Law Journal* 17, 47.

[127] Ted Moses (Cree), cited in R Niezen, *The Origins of Indigenism: Human Rights and the Politics of Identity* (Berkeley, University of California Press, 2003) 156.

[128] Davis, 'Indigenous Struggles in Standard-Setting' (2008) 470.

[129] R Pitty and S Smith, 'The Indigenous Challenge to Westphalian Sovereignty' (2011) 46 *Australian Journal of Political Science* 121, 128.

[130] Uluru Statement (n 24).

[131] L-A Baer, 'The Right of Self-Determination and the Case of the Sámi' in P Aiko and M Scheinin (eds), *Operationalising the Right of Indigenous Peoples to Self-Determination* (Turku, Institute for Human Rights, 2000) 223, 230.

[132] Mansell (n 46) 71.

[133] N Pearson, 'In Pursuit of Regional, Reciprocal Responsibility Settlement for Cape York' (speech delivered at the National Native Title Conference, Port Douglas, 18 June 2015).

but to highlight the illegitimacy of the state's exclusive assertion of authority. Sovereignty, then, has a moral aspect that cannot be remedied by 'meeting the physical needs of Indigenous peoples'.[134] With an emphasis on autonomy and respect, Indigenous peoples who conceive sovereignty in this manner see no contradiction in its existing 'internally' within a state 'provided that the fullest rights of self-determination are accorded'.[135] Though potentially shifting the semantic battle, it seems likely that the 'fullest rights' would include the ability to wield greater control over land and resources, as well as authority to ensure cultural preservation and integrity; all rights guaranteed in the UNDRIP, included in modern-day treaties in Canada,[136] and recognisable in generations of Aboriginal and Torres Strait Islander advocacy. As the Uluru Statement explains, it is through empowering Indigenous peoples that 'this ancient sovereignty can shine through as a fuller expression of Australia's nationhood'.[137] However, it must be remembered that while this understanding of political sovereignty commands widespread support, it is not accepted by all Indigenous peoples.

C. Cultural

When Indigenous peoples speak in the language of sovereignty, they do not only refer to its peoplehood or political components: sovereignty also has a cultural dimension. This connotation of sovereignty can be understood broadly as coming 'from the *na'au* (gut)',[138] as living 'a way of life',[139] or as living in an Indigenous way.[140] As Monture-Angus explains, in its cultural conception, sovereignty 'is a responsibility'; a responsibility to 'carry ourselves; collectively as nations, as clans, as families, as well as individually, as individual Mohawk citizens, in a good way'.[141] Standing Rock Sioux scholar and activist Vine Deloria Jr adopted a similar approach, holding that sovereignty 'consist[s] more of a continued cultural integrity than of political powers and to the degree that a nation loses its sense of cultural identity, to that degree it suffers a loss of sovereignty'.[142] Connecting cultural sovereignty to its political form, Deloria Jr

[134] M Dodson and L Strelein, 'Australia's Nation-Building: Renegotiating the Relationship between Indigenous Peoples and The State' (2001) 24 *UNSW Law Journal* 826, 838.

[135] N Pearson, 'Reconciliation: To Be or Not to Be – Nation, Self-Determination or Self-Government' (1993) 3 *Aboriginal Law Bulletin* 14, 15.

[136] UNDRIP (n 36) arts 8, 10–15, 25–26.

[137] Uluru Statement (n 24).

[138] Ontai, 'A Spiritual Definition of Sovereignty' (2005) 165.

[139] Warrior, 'Intellectual Sovereignty' (1992) 18.

[140] C Jones, *New Treaty, New Tradition: Reconciling New Zealand and Māori Law* (Vancouver, University of British Columbia Press, 2016) 23.

[141] Monture-Angus (n 12) 36.

[142] V Deloria, Jr, 'Self-Determination and the Concept of Sovereignty' in J Wunder (ed), *Native American Sovereignty* (New York, Routledge, 1999) 118, 123.

believed that political freedom 'will emerge' when individuals articulating group sovereignty become responsible to the group.[143]

In recent years, Taiaiake Alfred and Leanne Simpson have most clearly articulated the cultural dimension of sovereignty. While Alfred explicitly frames his work in sovereignty's political dimension, his project is borne within the cultural. Alfred argues that meaningful change in Indigenous–Settler relations is only possible after Indigenous communities 'regenerate ourselves and take back our dignity'.[144] Contending that 'continued cooperation with state power structures is morally unacceptable',[145] Alfred urges Indigenous communities to 'recreat[e] our existences, regenerat[e] our cultures',[146] and live as Onkwehonwe 'with integrity'.[147] This entails Indigenous peoples moving beyond Western-style institutions of self-government, and instead developing solutions 'within their own cultural frameworks, reuniting themselves as individuals with their collectivity'.[148] For Alfred, this begins with the right kind of leadership; 'native leaders must aspire to embody traditional values'.[149]

Leanne Simpson also stresses the primacy of Indigenous resistance and resurgence, but emphasises it as a bottom-up process. Simpson defines resistance broadly, understanding it to entail everyday acts of 'kitchen table resistance', including speaking in Indigenous languages, retelling creation stories, and looking after children's physical, mental and spiritual well-being. These everyday acts are culturally powerful; they ensured 'the stories were passed along',[150] enabling Indigenous peoples today to 'live as *Indigenous* peoples'.[151] Resistance is not racialised, nor does it lock Indigenous peoples to a past long passed. It does not require Indigenous peoples 'to "go back" to "hunting with bows and arrows"', but instead to 'practice ways of being and living in the world that are profoundly Nishnaabeg'.[152] It entails strengthening traditional forms of governance, political cultures, and intellectual traditions,[153] to 're-create the conditions for living as Nishnaabeg peoples following our own inherent processes and expressions of life'.[154] Like Alfred, Simpson frames Indigenous resistance and

[143] V Deloria Jr, *We Talk, You Listen: New Tribes, New Turf* (Lincoln, University of Nebraska Press, 2007) 124.

[144] Alfred (n 5) 38; T Alfred, 'Colonialism and State Dependency' (2009) 5 *Journal of Aboriginal Health* 42, 48.

[145] Alfred (n 5) 36.

[146] ibid 19.

[147] ibid 24.

[148] Alfred (n 53) 29.

[149] ibid 13.

[150] Simpson, *Dancing On Our Turtle's Back* (2011) 101.

[151] K Ladner and L Simpson, 'This is an Honour Song' in L Simpson and K Ladner (eds), *This is an Honour Song: Twenty Years Since the Blockades* (Winnipeg, ARP Books, 2010) 1, 8 (emphasis in original).

[152] Simpson (n 16) 52–53.

[153] ibid 53.

[154] ibid 144.

resurgence as a political project. It is only through strengthening Indigenous peoples and communities, through 'transforming ourselves, our communities and our nations', that Indigenous peoples will be able to 'transform[] our relationship with the state'.[155]

Cultural resurgence was also at the heart of Kevin Gilbert's work. Writing in 1970s Australia, Gilbert acknowledged the dire need for improved social, physical and economic conditions within Aboriginal communities, but considered that while material support will help it cannot heal, 'for the thing at issue is the ruin of a frame of reference, a culture, and the consequent devaluation of individuals'.[156] In talking with Aboriginals across New South Wales, Gilbert was convinced that restoring personal 'confidence' and 'pride' in self,[157] would rebuild Aboriginal society. This regenerated Aboriginal nation would be 'built on the backs of Aboriginal patriots' – those who know 'the inner feelings of Aboriginal people' – and consequently, 'would stand like a rock'.[158] The genesis of the nation would be its cultural moorings, for 'what do you profit if you gain better housing but lose your soul?'[159] Following Gilbert, many Aboriginal leaders identify cultural resurgence as a key element of sovereignty. Yawuru scholar Mick Dodson has argued that strong, community leadership 'based on cultural authority and moral standing' will 'push governments out of our lives', and compel them to 'pay us the respect that we deserve as sovereign people'.[160] Similarly, Wiradjuri activist Paul Coe considers that 'the re-learning, the re-instating of black culture', and the enthusing of 'a sense of Aboriginality' is the 'only way to counteract … this slow death'.[161] Of course, like Simpson and Alfred, Gilbert saw cultural resurgence as creating 'something meaningful in today's context', as 'building a modern Aboriginal culture'.[162]

Alfred, Simpson and Gilbert consider cultural sovereignty as entwined with its political form, but understandings of cultural sovereignty are not dependent on how one views its political manifestations. As Alfred explains, regardless of one's view:

> [I]t must be recognised that the cultural basis of our existence as Onkwehonwe has been nearly destroyed and that the cultural foundation of our nations must be restored or reimagined if there is going to be a successful assertion of political or economic rights.[163]

155 ibid 17, 66–67.
156 Gilbert, *Living Black* (1977) 184.
157 ibid 15 (Elizabeth Pearce).
158 Gilbert (n 15) 182. Middle quote comes from Frank Roberts, at 140.
159 Gilbert (n 70) 138.
160 Dodson, 'Mabo Lecture' (2010) 16.
161 Paul Coe in C Tatz (ed), *Black Viewpoints: The Aboriginal Experience* (Sydney, Australia and New Zealand Book Company, 1975) 103, 105, 110.
162 Gilbert (n 70) 3–4.
163 Alfred (n 5) 29.

The view that sovereignty in its cultural connotation is vitally important for Indigenous nations is accepted by both critical and moderate Indigenous thinkers. Irene Watson contends that an element of sovereignty involves withdrawing from the colonial state and 're-emerg[ing] as First Nations Peoples'.[164] Jeff Corntassel (Cherokee Nation) and Richard Witmer II argue that the strength of Indigenous nations comes from 'protecting indigenous homelands and regenerating our cultural and political forms of governance'.[165] Likewise, the 2015 Empowered Communities Report, a comprehensive proposal for an Indigenous empowerment agenda designed and led by eight Australian Indigenous communities, rejected the belief that development requires Indigenous peoples to discard their distinct cultures, languages and identities.[166] Writing for *IndigenousX*, Gunditjmara playwright Richard Frankland echoes these calls:

> We need our own voice, our own societal structure with our own doctrines, policies, processes and cultural shapes. In essence, we need a social order within a social order. We need the ability to establish and live by our own cultural protocols that are accepted across the board, by us.[167]

Indigenous peoples have long expressed the significance of sovereignty's cultural dimension. Kiowa lawyer Kirke Kickingbird, for instance, considered that sovereignty 'cannot be separated from people or their culture',[168] while Ned'u'ten scholar June McCue finds sovereignty as 'sourced or rooted in our creation stories, our spirituality and our organic and peaceful institutions'.[169] Similarly, reflecting on the work of Vine Deloria Jr and Osage author John Joseph Mathews, Robert Allen Warrior sees sovereignty not as 'a struggle to be free from the influence of anything outside of ourselves, but a process of asserting the power we possess as communities and individuals to make decisions that affect our lives'.[170]

Sovereignty's cultural dimension is replete throughout the UNDRIP. The Declaration provides that Indigenous peoples have the right to 'practice and revitalise their cultural traditions and customs', 'manifest, practice, develop and teach their spiritual and religious traditions', as well as transmit to future generations their 'histories, oral traditions, philosophies, writing systems and

[164] Watson (n 57) 164.

[165] J Corntassel and RC Witmer II, *Forced Federalism: Contemporary Challenges to Indigenous Nationhood* (Norman, University of Oklahoma Press, 2008) 148–49.

[166] Empowered Communities, 'Empowered Communities, Empowered Peoples: Design Report' (2015) 9.

[167] R Frankland, 'A Treaty Won't Solve Everything But It Could Change this Nation's Cultural Tapestry' *Guardian Australia* (6 March 2017), available at www.theguardian.com/commentisfree/2017/mar/06/a-treaty-wont-solve-everything-but-it-could-change-this-nations-cultural-tapestry.

[168] Kickingbird, Kickingbird, Chibitty and Berkey, *Indian Sovereignty* (1977) 2.

[169] J McCue, 'New Modalities of Sovereignty: An Indigenous Perspective' (2007) 2 *Intercultural Human Rights Law Review* 19, 25.

[170] Warrior (n 50) 19.

literature', through their own 'educational systems'.[171] Indigenous peoples have the right to 'promote', 'maintain and strengthen their distinct political, legal, economic, social and cultural institutions',[172] which includes the right to maintain and develop their 'cultural heritage, traditional knowledge … traditional cultural expressions' and 'traditional medicines', as well as their 'distinctive spiritual relationship with their traditionally owned … lands, territories, waters and coastal seas'.[173] Articulating this point further, Article 35 provides that Indigenous peoples 'have the right to determine the responsibilities of individuals to their communities', a sharp distinction from liberal approaches to rights. Together, these provisions protect the integrity of Indigenous communities, enabling individuals to 'live well in this world'.[174]

Conceiving culturally resurgent self-government structures that empower Indigenous communities to respond to contemporary challenges is difficult; we simply do not have a rich vocabulary of examples to draw on.[175] Although many historic governance models exist, self-government arrangements that work for Indigenous peoples and nations today will likely differ in key respects from previous arrangements. Nonetheless, Indigenous communities are creatively adapting those historic forms. Consider developments within the Ngarrindjeri. In the mid-1980s the Ngarrindjeri nation of the lower Murray River, western Fleurieu Peninsula and the Coorong of southern, central Australia, formally revived their endogenous representative structures. As non-Indigenous scholar Anna Dziedzic and Wiradjuri academic Mark McMillian explain, prior to European colonisation, the Ngarrindjeri nation:

> [C]onsisted of 18 lakklinyeris or tribes. Each lakkinyeri had a tendi, comprising elders and a rupelli (chief). Members of the tendi were qualified on the basis of community status, and were elected according to Ngarrindjeri law. The tendi made and interpreted Ngarrindjeri law, resolved disputes and administered justice according to customary law. Representatives of each tendi also met at meetings of the national tendi, where interclan and national matters were discussed and determined.[176]

Today, governance is conducted through the Ngarrindjeri Regional Authority (NRA). Operating as the peak body for all Ngarrindjeri organisations, the NRA is composed of representatives of Ngarrindjeri community organisations, corporations and associations, and elected community members; the rupelli of the tendi was the inaugural Chair. The Ngarrindjeri describe the NRA as

[171] UNDRIP (n 36) arts 11(1), 12(1), 13(1), 14(1).
[172] ibid art 5. See also arts 20(1), 34.
[173] ibid arts 31(1), 24(1), 25.
[174] Borrows (n 11) 6.
[175] I thank Douglas Sanderson (Amo Binashii) (Opaskwayak Cree Nation) for this point.
[176] A Dziedzic and M McMillan, 'Australian Indigenous Constitutions: Recognition and Renewal' (2016) 44 *Federal Law Review* 337, 345.

'a contemporary form of ongoing Ngarrindjeri government',[177] and through the NRA, they have developed strategies for 'protecting and sustaining'[178] their nation. It is in turning inward and revitalising their culture and traditions that the Ngarrindjeri effectively interact with the state.

Contemporary Ngarrindjeri self-governance draws on their historic forms, but also responds to the structure of Australia's governing systems. This may be problematic for some Indigenous communities, but it is not necessarily so. As Lester-Irabinna Rigney (Narungga/Kaurna/Ngarrindjeri) explains, living in an Indigenous way does not necessarily require jettisoning Western forms of governance for 'not all Indigenous communities that use dominant forms of Western governance fail'.[179] Instead, what is required is that a group wields authority to determine what constitutes its traditional culture and decides how it will 'honour and practice that culture',[180] in a manner appropriate to its contemporary situation.

D. Summary

Sovereignty is a complex term. In its peoplehood connotations, sovereignty asserts Indigenous difference. It contends that if Indigenous peoples are to be included within the state, it must be on terms distinct to other members of the polity. In its political sense, Indigenous declarations of sovereignty fundamentally challenge the legitimacy of the state, raising questions about how and whether Indigenous nations can exercise jurisdiction. Debate persists within Indigenous communities over whether sovereignty should be exercised along kinship lines or along a broader pan-Aboriginal basis, as well as over the extent of autonomy, but it clear that *some minimum level* of decision-making authority and jurisdiction is desired. Finally, in its cultural dimension, sovereignty asserts a right to live in an Indigenous way; to a culturally appropriate form of decision-making with Indigenous leaders accountable to Indigenous peoples. As explored further in chapter four, these aspirations should inform the design of institutions aimed at empowering Indigenous peoples with the capacity to be heard in the processes of government. While important, however, these elements do not entail the totality of Indigenous aspirations.

[177] Ngarrindjeri Regional Authority, 'Ngarrindjeri Kurangk Le:wunanangk Management Plan No 1' (2016) 5.

[178] Dziedzic and McMillan, 'Australian Indigenous Constitutions' (2016) 346.

[179] L-I Rigney, 'Epilogue: Can the Settler State Settle with Whom it Colonises? Reasons for Hope and Priorities for Action' in S Maddison and M Brigg (eds), *Unsettling the Settler State* (Annandale, Federation Press, 2011) 206, 209.

[180] R Miller, 'Tribal Cultural Self-Determination and the Makah Whaling Culture' in J Barker (ed), *Sovereignty Matters: Locations of Contestations and Possibility in Indigenous Struggles for Self-Determination* (Lincoln, University of Nebraska Press, 2005) 123, 123.

IV. EQUITABLE RELATIONSHIPS

Aboriginal and Torres Strait Islander peoples are not content with existing governance structures, but frequently assert their desire for a renegotiated relationship so that they may 'take *a rightful place* in our own country'.[181] This aspiration is grounded in the three dimensions of sovereignty explored above. As prior self-governing political communities whose sovereignty has never been lawfully extinguished, Indigenous peoples maintain that they are distinct from other members of the larger political community and therefore retain a right to exercise a degree of political authority in a culturally appropriate manner. A reconstituted relationship based on trust and mutual respect that empowers Indigenous peoples with the capacity to have their distinct voices heard in the processes of government, and 'participate fully … in the political, economic, social and cultural life of the state',[182] will enable them to 'walk in two worlds'.[183]

The importance of relationships based on reciprocity and mutual respect is often expressed through storytelling. The Yolŋu people describe the concept of *ganma*, a metaphor that illustrates the coming together of two distinct knowledge systems. *Ganma* is a coastal lagoon within the mangroves in which two streams of water flow and meet: one stream is tidal and salt from the sea; the other is fresh from rain on the land. As the streams enter the lagoon, there is ebb and flow as the water circulates silently underneath, catalysing a chaotic froth of foam on the surface. Eventually, the swelling and retreating of the tides establishes a recognisable pattern as the streams merge within the lagoon. But within this brackish water the separate identity of the streams is not entirely lost. Underneath the surface the streams continue to exist, complementing, interacting and relating to one another, 'but never los[ing] their distinctiveness as separate and opposed parts of one whole'.[184]

Ganma is a call for 'respect and understanding of each other's ways of knowing and doing'.[185] This is an enduring call as the meeting of the waters is not a single event in time, but a continuous process. It is also enduring in the sense that it is common to Indigenous storytelling and relationship-making across the globe. For example, the *Guswentah*, or Two Row Wampum Treaty, signed in 1613 by representatives of the Five Nations of the Haudenosaunee and

[181] Uluru Statement (n 24).
[182] UNDRIP (n 36) art 5.
[183] Uluru Statement (n 24).
[184] B Yunupingu and H Watson, 'The Ganma Project in Mathematics Curriculum: A Draft Proposal Outline' (discussion paper for the Laynhapuy Association, Yirrkala Community School and Homelands Centres Schools) cited in S Muller, '"Two-Ways": Bringing Indigenous and Non-Indigenous Knowledges Together' in J Weir (ed), *Country, Native Title and Ecology* (Canberra, ANU Press, 2012) 59, 61; Dr Marika, 'An Arnhem Land Story' in R Tonkinson (ed), *The Wentworth Lectures: Honouring Fifty Years of Australian Indigenous Studies* (Canberra, Aboriginal Studies Press, 2015) 180, 187–88.
[185] Muller, 'Two-Ways' (2012) 62.

representatives of the Dutch Government in what is now upstate New York is often upheld as an example of this more equitable relationship. The agreement recorded by the Haudenosaunee in a wampum belt, is 'vastly complex but … visually quite simple'.[186] It consists of two rows of purple shells embedded in a sea of white beads. Cayuga Chief Jacob Thomas explains:

> One of the two purple paths signifies the European sailing ship that came here. In that ship are all the European things – their laws, languages, institutions and forms of government. The other path is the Mohawk canoe and in it are all the Mohawk things – our laws, institutions and forms of government. For the entire length of that wampum, these two paths are separated by three white beads. Never do the two paths become one. They remain an equal distance apart. And those three white beads represent 'friendship, good minds, and everlasting peace'. It is by these three things that Aboriginal Peoples and the settler nations agreed to govern all of their future relationships.[187]

This interpretation is supported by Haudenosaunee tradition, which records their reply to the initial Dutch treaty proposal:

> You say that you are our Father and I am your Son. We Say, We will not be like Father and Son, but like Brothers … Neither of us will make compulsory laws or interfere in the internal affairs of the other. Neither of us will try to steer the other's vessel.[188]

Some Indigenous peoples draw on the separate rows of purple beads to emphasise principles of non-interference. Others argue that the three white beads highlight relational values like 'sharing, mutuality and interdependence'.[189] John Borrows explains:

> The ecology of contemporary politics teaches us that the rivers on which we sail our ships of state share the same waters. There is no river or boat that is not linked in a fundamental way to the others; that is, there is no land or government in the world that is not connected to and influenced by others.[190]

On both accounts the *Guswentah* speaks to a relationship predicated on equality and respect. In the words of Dale Turner, the wampum belt signifies that 'because we share the same space, we are inextricably entwined in a relationship of interdependence – but *we remain distinct political entities*'.[191]

The same themes of autonomy and interdependence are present in the Yolŋu concept of *ganma*, and the modern treaty processes in Canada and Australia.

[186] Monture-Angus (n 12) 37.
[187] Cited in ibid.
[188] Cited in R Williams Jr, *Linking Arms Together: American Indian Treaty Visions of Law and Peace, 1600–1800* (Oxford, Oxford University Press, 1997) 83.
[189] R Kuokkanen, *Restructuring Relations: Indigenous Self-Determination, Governance, and Gender* (Oxford, Oxford University Press, 2019) 31.
[190] J Borrows, *Recovering Canada: The Resurgence of Indigenous Law* (Toronto, University of Toronto Press, 2002) 149.
[191] Turner (n 60) 54 (emphasis in original).

These themes should inform the principles that ground a new relationship between Indigenous peoples and the state and the institutional structure that gives shape to that relationship. Of course, in practice, questions will persist over the scope of autonomy or self-governance that Indigenous peoples may be able to exercise, as well as how conflicts between Indigenous and non-Indigenous normative orders may be resolved. These questions arise because, as Turner notes, Indigenous peoples and the state are 'inextricably entwined'; as such, a shared-interface between polities is required. It is this shared interface that Indigenous peoples argue must be restructured.[192]

How should this relationship, or interface, be restructured? Among Indigenous scholars, there is almost unanimous agreement that colonialism 'is salient to, or fundamentally shaping, everyday life across lands claimed' by the settler state, 'even if this does not mean that colonialism defines the horizon of all Indigenous experience or Indigenous theorising'.[193] A new relationship must therefore begin by decolonising the 'architecture of colonial domination',[194] and recognising the constitutive flaw in the moral legitimacy of settler states: the absence of consent. This entails reimagining the state's politico-legal structure to ensure that it governs by principles that both Indigenous and non-Indigenous peoples can agree too, not simply the unilateral assertion of one party's political, cultural and legal system. Significantly, this requires not only change to the politico-legal structures of the state to ensure that Indigenous peoples have authority over matters of importance to them, but also attitudinal change; the relationship between Indigenous peoples and the state should be mediated by an ethic of respect.

A. Decolonisation

Almost all Indigenous peoples believe that 'colonialism has stained the legal and political relationship'[195] between Indigenous and non-Indigenous peoples. As chapter two explained, the politico-legal framework and conventions which govern settler states like Australia, have 'established structural inequalities that have blocked effective free association of the First Nations and participation and

[192] Note that even if an Indigenous nation achieved secession, separating entirely from several centuries of entwinement, there will still need to be some shared interface of decision-making to deal with relations between the two polities. Compared to more moderate conceptions of political sovereignty, it is merely the extent and scope of a shared framework, not its existence, that differs. For discussion of a range of approaches in Aotearoa New Zealand see Independent Working Group on Constitutional Transformation (n 42) ch 4.

[193] Coburn, 'Alternatives' (2016) 291.

[194] T Alfred, 'Sovereignty' in P Deloria and N Salisbury (eds), *A Companion to American Indian History* (Malden, MA, Blackwell, 2002) 460, 463.

[195] Turner (n 60) 30–31.

representation of Aboriginal peoples',[196] and 'physically, politically, and socially relegated' Indigenous peoples to the margins of society.[197] The experiences of Indigenous peoples, their situation, perspectives and aspirations are thus intertwined with colonialism. For Audra Simpson, even 'to speak of Indigeneity is to speak of colonialism', as it is through this lens that Indigenous peoples 'have been known and sometimes are still known'.[198]

Over the last several decades, settler states have adopted and adapted mechanisms of transitional justice in an attempt to come to terms with legacies of Indigenous dispossession, destruction and exclusion. As a starting point, these processes have involved measures such as truth-seeking, recognition and acknowledgment of past injustice, and institutional reforms, and have included public apologies, truth and reconciliation commissions, public inquiries, remedial legislation, and in some cases compensation and reparations.[199] Notwithstanding the multitude of these institutional forms, each measure is, at least implicitly, framed as marking a liminal moment; intended to delineate the temporal pre-reconciliation period from that of a post-colonial future. In some instances, this understanding is explicitly formulated. Australian Prime Minister Kevin Rudd's 2008 Apology to the Stolen Generations, twice called upon the nation to 'turn a new page' in 'Australia's history by righting the wrongs of the past and so moving forward with confidence to the future'.[200] Likewise, Canadian Prime Minister Stephen Harper's Apology to former students of Indian Residential Schools, referred to state-imposed forced separation of over 150,000 Aboriginal children from their families and communities, as 'a sad chapter in our history'.[201]

Despite attempts to conjure dispossession, destruction and exclusion as a 'past', however, the logic of settler colonialism persists, and its structures continue to check Indigenous aspirations and intrude upon Indigenous ways of knowing and being, pervading relations between non-Indigenous and Indigenous peoples. Like a 'spider web', colonisation is not linear but a 'horizontal and entangled relationship',[202] involving occupation of territory and the appropriation of 'political authority, cultural self-determination [and] economic capacity'.[203] As Albert Memmi has argued, a coloniser's identity 'is essentially that of a

[196] J Henderson, 'Empowering Treaty Federalism' (1994) 58 *Saskatchewan Law Review* 241, 311–12.

[197] Turner (n 60) 30–31.

[198] A Simpson, 'On Ethnographic Refusal: Indigeneity, "Voice" and Colonial Citizenship' (2007) 9 *Junctures* 67, 67.

[199] H Hobbs, 'Locating the Logic of Transitional Justice in Liberal Democracies: Native Title in Australia' (2016) 39 *UNSW Law Journal* 512, 513.

[200] Commonwealth, *Parliamentary Debates*, House of Representatives, 13 February 2008, 167.

[201] *House of Commons Debates*, 39th Parl, 2nd Sess, No 110 (11 June 2008) 1514.

[202] Monture-Angus (n 12) 11.

[203] J Green, 'Decolonisation and Recolonisation in Canada' in W Clement and L Vosko (eds), *Changing Canada: Political Economy as Transformation* (Montreal, McGill-Queen's University Press, 2003) 51, 52.

usurper' and 'colonisers are constantly concerned with trying to legitimate their usurpation'.[204] The result, as many Indigenous peoples have long identified, is an institutional governance structure that favours the coloniser at the expense of the colonised. This 'cultural logic' remains static beneath its 'changing operational modalities',[205] for settler colonialism is a 'structure not an event'.[206]

For this reason, many Indigenous peoples do not characterise contemporary setter states as 'postcolonial'. Anishinaabe theorist Gerald Vizenor, for instance, prefers the term 'paracolonial'.[207] Vizenor does not provide a clear definition, but reflecting on his work, Native American scholar Malea Powell conceives it as a 'colonialism beyond colonialism', where 'the occupying force has not, nor will it ever be, withdrawn'.[208] Elaborating further, Chidi Okonkwo describes paracolonialism as a situation in which a country exists as two separate societies, with an Indigenous minority 'existing as the Third World underbelly of the dominant European society'.[209] While non-Indigenous Australians may feel this language overstates the challenges facing Indigenous peoples, chapter two revealed that the Australian governance system persistently fails to empower Aboriginal and Torres Strait Islander peoples. Acknowledging these pervasive structures, Linda Tuhiwai Smith uses the term 'decolonial' and describes a process of 'decolonisation' to emphasise both the contemporary temporality of colonialism and that only active engagement by the colonised has the potential to level settler-colonialism.[210] This approach is also advocated for by Dale Turner, who argues that Indigenous peoples can only 'critically undermin[e] colonialism', by participating in settler state institutions and recalibrating them to reflect Indigenous approaches.[211] It is only through 'challeng[ing] the state at every level and in every way',[212] as Taiaiake Alfred urges, that settler colonialism can be destroyed.

Indigenous peoples agree that colonialism must be dismantled, but decolonisation is understood in many ways. Jeff Corntassel considers it an element of cultural sovereignty, requiring Indigenous peoples to 'actively engag[e] in everyday practices

[204] A Memmi, *The Colonizer and the Colonized* (New York, Howard Greenfeld trans, Orion Press, 1965) 52 [trans of: *Portrait du colonisé précédé du portrait du colonisateur* (first published 1957)], cited in R van Krieken, 'Rethinking Cultural Genocide: Aboriginal Child Removal and Settler-Colonial State Formation' (2004) 75 *Oceania* 125, 144.

[205] P Wolfe, 'Nation and MiscegeNation: Discursive Continuity in the Post-*Mabo* Era' (1994) 36 *Social Analysis* 93, 96.

[206] P Wolfe, 'Settler Colonialism and the Elimination of the Native' (2006) 8 *Journal of Genocide Research* 387, 388.

[207] G Vizenor, 'The Ruins of Representation: Shadow Survivance and the Literature of Dominance' (1993) 17 *American Indian Quarterly* 7, 7.

[208] M Powell, 'Rhetorics of Survivance: How American Indians Use Writing' (2002) 53 *College Composition and Communication* 396, 399.

[209] C Okonkwo, *Decolonization Agonistics in Postcolonial Fiction* (London, Palgrave Macmillan, 1999) x.

[210] Smith, *Decolonizing Methodologies* (1999).

[211] Turner (n 60) 30–31, ch 5.

[212] Alfred (n 53) 102.

of resurgence',[213] while Eve Tuck (Unangax) and Wayne Yang remind non-Indigenous peoples that decolonisation is 'unsettling'; 'it is not a metaphor' but is about the 'repatriation of Indigenous land and life'.[214] This is a significant challenge. As Sámi scholar Rauna Kuokkanen argues, decolonisation should involve the broader restructuring of all relations of domination, including 'heteropatriarchial neo-colonial agendas'.[215] As colonialism is intimately connected to state institutions and attitudes, decolonisation necessarily involves a challenge to both the state and its politico-legal structures. Notwithstanding diversity of opinion and intensity, then, decolonisation involves the restructuring of Indigenous–state relations along lines that accommodate coexisting sovereignties; peoplehood, political and cultural. As a form of 'belated state building',[216] Indigenous peoples must be involved in setting up the state's new governing structure.

B. Reflective of Status

A more equitable relationship between Indigenous peoples and the state would be reflective of Indigenous communities' status as polities with an inherent right to self-government. This status is an integral element of both historical and contemporary treaties signed between Indigenous peoples and colonial powers or the state, serving as an attempt to reconcile 'the pre-existence of aboriginal societies with the sovereignty of the Crown',[217] in a 'multicultural constitution'.[218] Consistent with this spirit, any shared-interface should formulate and institute politico-legal structures partially based on Indigenous ways of knowing and being, rather than existing unilateral non-Indigenous foundations that entrench a 'fundamental disrespect' for Indigenous peoples.[219] This is both an issue of decolonisation and democratisation. James (Sákéj) Youngblood Henderson connects these two strands of thought in explaining that:

> [W]ithout a balance between Aboriginal perspectives and the Eurocentric view, existing [governing systems] reflect[] political domination and oppression built on colonial misunderstandings. Without a proficiency in indigenous worldviews, languages, rights and treaties, the Canadian legal system cannot equitably talk about authentic democracy.[220]

[213] J Corntassel, 'Re-Envisioning Resurgence: Indigenous Pathways to Decolonisation and Sustainable Self-Determination' (2012) 1 *Decolonisation: Indigeneity, Education & Society* 86, 89.

[214] E Tuck and KW Yang, 'Decolonisation is Not a Metaphor' (2012) 1 *Decolonisation: Indigeneity, Education & Society* 1, 1.

[215] Kuokkanen, *Restructuring Relations* (2019) 220.

[216] EI Daes, 'An Overview of the History of Indigenous Peoples: Self-Determination and the United Nation' (2008) 21 *Cambridge Review of International Affairs* 7, 23.

[217] *Delgamuukw v British Columbia* [1997] 3 SCR 1010, 1124, [186] (Lamer CJ, Cory and Major JJ); *Beckman v Little Salmon/Carmacks First Nation* [2010] 3 SCR 103, 153 [103] (Le Bel and Deschamps JJ).

[218] Williams Jr, *Linking Arms Together* (1997) 99.

[219] Dodson and Strelein, 'Australia's Nation-Building' (2001) 826.

[220] Henderson, 'Empowering Treaty Federalism' (1994) 323.

This point has also been ably made by James Anaya, who distinguishes between two normative strains within substantive (as opposed to remedial) self-determination. For Anaya, constitutive self-determination requires that 'the governing institutional order be substantially the creation of processes guided by the will of the people[s]', while ongoing self-determination ignores the process of creation of the state, inquiring only whether it is one 'under which people may live and develop freely on a continuous basis'.[221] A restructured relationship would involve constitutive elements; broad consultative forums would be established to discover what Indigenous traditions and cultural principles should be incorporated into existing institutions and the politico-legal framework, as well as how this could be accomplished. It need not however, entail discarding that framework. A restructured relationship reflective of Indigenous status should therefore be judged by the standard of ongoing self-determination: is the state's democratic political order such that Indigenous peoples (as well as non-Indigenous peoples) are 'able to continue [their] distinct character and to have this character reflected in the institutions of government under which [they] live[]'?[222]

In broad strokes, Mick Dodson has explored how this relationship might look. Dodson has in mind a socio-political structure:

> [E]quivalent to some type of co-operative with enough cohesion to facilitate communication between different sections and to share certain institutions and resources where appropriate, but to nevertheless retain and ensure the recognition of the human rights of specific groups, and in particular Indigenous peoples.[223]

The next chapter will examine how the themes explored here can be conceptualised as principles of institutional design. It is worth noting, however, that a reconstituted framework built on Indigenous peoples' status as political communities is consistent with federal-type arrangements. While federalism has generally focused on territorial forms, in recent years scholarly work in Australia has proposed ways to reconceptualise understandings of federalism towards a 'multinational' approach.[224] Michael Mansell, for example, has advocated the establishment of an Aboriginal state within the Australian federation, comprising of existing Indigenous landholdings,[225] while non-Indigenous academic Dylan Lino has explored how this institutional mechanism may offer a 'valuable

[221] J Anaya, *Indigenous Peoples in International Law* (Oxford, Oxford University Press, 2004) 105.

[222] ibid 106 (citation deleted).

[223] M Dodson, 'Aboriginal and Torres Strait Islander People and Citizenship' (speech delivered to the Complex Notions of Civic Identity Conference, University of New South Wales, 20 August 1993). See also RL Barsh and J (Sákéj) Youngblood Henderson, *The Road: Indian Tribes and Political Liberty* (Berkeley, University of California Press, 1980) ix: 'To us, political liberty means an effective voice in national government, *and* the right of the people to establish local governments to exercise any and all of the powers they have reserved to themselves'.

[224] H Hobbs, Aboriginal and Torres Strait Islander Peoples and Multinational Federalism in Australia' (2018) 27 *Griffith Law Review* 307.

[225] Mansell (n 46).

conceptual language' for framing Indigenous peoplehood claims.[226] Although these approaches do not delve too deeply into institutional design, they share a commitment to a relationship based on a robust democratic constitutional system which divides powers equitably between distinct and interdependent polities. Such an approach could provide the building blocks for mechanisms designed to empower Indigenous Australians in a manner consistent with democratic ideals. Such an approach requires recognising Indigenous political communities as 'an equal partner in the state'.[227]

C. An Ethic of Respect

Amending governance structures is an important first step in establishing a more equitable relationship, but it is only a step, for relationships exist between people who staff institutions rather than institutions themselves. Put another way, state intervention into Indigenous affairs and communities is made possible by a politico-legal framework that denies Indigenous sovereignty, but it is a product of the attitudes of individuals. As Dodson and Strelein explain:

> Disrespect occurs not just in the relationship between the state and Indigenous peoples, but has engendered a more personal disrespect that is experienced by Indigenous people on a daily basis. It is the ongoing tolerance of disrespect that maintains racism as a core value of Australian society.[228]

Indigenous peoples have long identified a 'culture of disrespect'[229] that permeates Indigenous–state relations and constructs a 'wall of indifference'.[230] It exists in the discounting of Indigenous values and world views, as well as the formulation of legislative policy that remains 'largely a product of Settler-Colonial ideas, attitudes and institutions that have operated to deny Indigenous rights'.[231] These concerns were replete throughout the Referendum Council regional dialogues;[232] and as such, they lie behind the Uluru Statement's calls for a Makarrata Commission to supervise a process of 'truth-telling about our history'.

[226] D Lino, 'Towards Indigenous – Settler Federalism' (2017) 28 *Public Law Review* 118, 128.

[227] S Tierney, 'Federalism and the Plurinational Challenge' in A Lev (ed), *The Federal Idea: Public Law Between Governance and Political Life* (Oxford, Hart Publishing, 2017) 227, 236; U Mörkenstam 'Recognition *as if* Sovereigns? A Procedural Understanding of Indigenous Self-Determination' (2015) 19 *Citizenship Studies* 634, 641.

[228] Dodson and Strelein (n 134) 826.

[229] M Davis, 'A Culture of Disrespect: Indigenous Peoples and Australian Public Institutions' (2006) 9 *UTS Law Review* 135.

[230] Ken Colbung (Noongar) in Tatz, *Black Viewpoints* (1975) 22, 28.

[231] P Dodson and D Cronin, 'An Australian Dialogue: Decolonising the Country' in S Maddison and M Brigg (eds), *Unsettling the Settler State: Creativity and Resistance in Indigenous Settler-State Governance* (Annandale, Federation Press, 2011) 189, 189.

[232] See, eg: Referendum Council, 'Final Report of the Referendum Council' (Commonwealth, 2017) 17 (Brisbane).

Appreciating these dynamics is difficult for many non-Indigenous peoples. John Borrows has sought to foment such attitudinal change by playfully critiquing 'practical' approaches to Indigenous disadvantage that minimise or ignore rights-based approaches. Borrows calls on Indigenous peoples to 'recolonise' the Australian continent, defending his project by arguing that this process would merely provide Indigenous peoples with 'the same level of protection that non-Indigenous Australians enjoy'.[233] Borrows suggests several forms practical recolonisation could take, including extinguishment of non-Indigenous titles to land if incompatible with continued existence of Indigenous title, as well as the 'disestablishment of elected non-Indigenous political structures'.[234]

Borrows' intervention highlights that grounding the relationship between Indigenous peoples and the state on an ethic of respect requires more than non-discriminatory attitudes and policies; it requires recognising Indigenous peoples' distinctive status as polities. As non-Indigenous political theorist Bruce Buchan explains, it 'means that an acceptance needs to be made by the "sovereign" authorities that the collective *identities* of Indigenous people represent an essential part of this nation's constitutional foundation'.[235] This acknowledgement is at the heart of Indigenous peoples' aspirations. As the Swedish Sámediggi has explained, states must recognise that they are 'founded on the territory of two [or more] peoples' having 'to exercise their right to self-determination side by side', and that 'none of the [...] peoples' right to self-determination have priority over the other people's'.[236] It requires overturing the 'psychological terra nullius',[237] and understanding that Indigenous peoples

> are not simply demanding a general decentralisation of power, to promote administrative efficiency or local democracy. Rather, they are demanding recognition as distinct peoples and as founding partners in the ... state who have maintained the right to govern themselves and their land in certain areas.[238]

It requires recognising or establishing culturally appropriate governance structures and allowing them to succeed, as well as genuinely listening to Indigenous peoples' voices.

[233] J Borrows, 'Practical Recolonisation' (2005) 28 *UNSW Law Journal* 614, 639.

[234] ibid.

[235] B Buchan, *Empire of Political Thought: Indigenous Australians and the Language of Colonial Government* (London, Pickering & Chatto, 2008) 143 (emphasis in original).

[236] Cited in U Mörkenstam, 'The Constitution of the Swedish Sámi People: Swedish Sámi Policy and the Justification of the Inner Colonisation of Sweden' in J Tripathy and S Padmanabhan (eds), *Becoming Minority: How Discourses and Policies Produce Minorities in Europe and India* (New Delhi, Sage, 2014) 88, 102.

[237] Behrendt (n 31) 120; Watson (n 57) 42–43.

[238] W Kymlicka, *Finding Our Way: Rethinking Ethnocultural Relations in Canada* (Oxford, Oxford University Press, 1998) 6.

V. CONCLUSION

Indigenous peoples claim a distinctive relationship with the state based on their pre-colonial status as self-governing sovereign communities. But sovereignty means many different things to many different people. Perhaps the simplest definition is the best. Indigenous sovereignty, in the words of Robert Porter, Chief Justice of the Sac & Fox Nation of Missouri Supreme Court, means 'the freedom of a people to choose what their future will be'.[239] Although underdeveloped, this formulation encapsulates Indigenous sovereignty in its peoplehood, political, and cultural dimensions. It implies that Indigenous peoples are *different* from other members of the state and that this difference means they may exercise *political authority* in a *culturally appropriate* manner. This chapter has illustrated that despite a complex empirical picture, Indigenous political resistance is and always has been a struggle to reassert their sovereignty and build relationships with the state on this basis. Institutional structures to empower Aboriginal and Torres Strait Islander peoples with the capacity to have their voices heard and interests considered in the processes of government, must be built on those aspirations. The following chapter draws on these voices to identify four public law principles that should guide the design of structures and processes that accomplish this task.

[239] R Porter, 'The Meaning of Indigenous Nation Sovereignty' (2002) 34 *Arizona State Law Journal* 75, 75.

4

Principles of Institutional Design

I. INTRODUCTION

INDIGENOUS PEOPLES' ASPIRATIONS are nuanced, complex and contested, as is to be expected of a community of some 370 million people across the globe. Nonetheless, despite such diversity, common themes can be articulated. Aboriginal and Torres Strait Islander peoples, and Indigenous peoples more broadly, generally desire a renegotiated relationship with the state(s) in which they reside. This new relationship should be premised on a recognition of their status as distinct political communities who retain the right to exercise some minimum level of decision-making authority and jurisdiction in a culturally appropriate manner,[1] and who are entitled (if they choose) to participate fully in the life of the state.[2] Drawing on these goals, this chapter develops four criteria to assess whether an institution or mechanism empowers Indigenous peoples with the capacity to be heard in the processes of government.

Characterised as *voices*, *power*, *ownership* and *integrity*, these criteria are grounded in and animated by the rich and considered views of Indigenous scholars, theorists and political activists explored in chapter three. They are also informed by the two recent substantive community consultations with Aboriginal and Torres Strait Islander peoples discussed in that chapter: the Referendum Council's regional dialogues on constitutional reform;[3] and the Victorian Aboriginal Treaty Working Group's consultations on the design of an Indigenous representative body.[4] As community-centred discussions these consultative processes reveal broad congruence between the aspirations of Indigenous scholars and community members, and, as more practical documents, help to elucidate relevant design principles necessary to realise those aspirations.

[1] United Nations Declaration on the Rights of Indigenous Peoples, GA Res 61/295, UN GAOR, 61st sess, 107th plen mtg, Supp No 49, UN Doc A/RES/61/295 (13 September 2007) (UNDRIP) art 4.

[2] ibid art 5.

[3] Referendum Council, 'Final Report of the Referendum Council' (2017).

[4] Aboriginal Treaty Working Group, 'Aboriginal Community Consultations on the Design of a Representative Body' (December 2016) (ATWG 2016); Aboriginal Treaty Working Group, 'Aboriginal Community Consultations on the Design of a Representative Body – Phase 2' (June 2017) (ATWG 2017).

The criteria do not simply convey Indigenous claims to the state. Rather, drawing in and from Indigenous peoples' political thought,[5] they express those aspirations in a form comprehensible to the state, connecting to public law values and principles. Reflecting their foundation in the lived experiences and stated desires of Indigenous peoples, however, the criteria differ from traditional public law accounts, leading to new priorities and approaches to institutional design. Political and legal mechanisms aimed at empowering Indigenous peoples should be assessed against these criteria.

The criteria are framed in broad terms to allow considerable room for innovation and variety in institutional design. Indigenous peoples and communities are differently situated. It is both natural that political and legal solutions will respond to these distinctions, as well as being consistent with the values that underlie self-determination. Indigenous communities will consider their own distinctive aspirations as well as the particular political and legal framework within which they live before choosing to prioritise one or more of the criteria. Each can be realised in strong or weak forms, and it may be that a range of complementary and interrelated mechanisms offers the best prospect for grounding new relationships built on trust and respect. These challenges will be explored in more detail in chapters five and six, where I examine the Aboriginal and Torres Strait Islander Commission (ATSIC) and the Swedish Sámediggi.

II. VOICES

(1) Indigenous peoples must be heard when decisions that affect them are being made

Indigenous peoples assert their status as *peoples*, not minorities, via claims of sovereignty and in calls for a renewed relationship reflective of their status as distinct political communities. In part, these calls stem from the structural inequalities that Indigenous peoples face in expressing their interests to settler state governments. Formal legal inequities may no longer exist in many states. However, as chapter two demonstrated, the norms and values that construct and enliven the institutions that exercise and regulate public power in Australia, continue to operate to inhibit Indigenous peoples' ability to have their voices heard in the processes of government. As such, Indigenous peoples consistently exclaim their feelings of disempowerment and alienation from governmental processes.[6] These invocations are recorded in Article 18 of the UNDRIP, which provides that Indigenous peoples 'have the right to participate in decision-making

[5] M Nakata, V Nakata, S Keech and R Bolt, 'Decolonial Goals and Pedagogies for Indigenous Students' (2012) 1 *Decolonisation: Indigeneity, Education & Society* 120, 124.

[6] Uluru Statement from the Heart, Uluru, 26 May 2017 (Uluru Statement). See also M Davis and M Langton (eds), *It's Our Country: Indigenous Arguments for Meaningful Constitutional Recognition and Reform* (Melbourne, Melbourne University Press, 2016).

in matters which would affect their rights, through representatives chosen by themselves in accordance with their own procedures'. The public law concept of 'voices' encapsulates this right.

'Voices' is not uncontested. It inherently involves acceptance of some of the logic of the settler state. Nonetheless, as chapter three demonstrated, a strong majority current of Indigenous thinking on sovereignty acknowledges that its political elaboration should not inexorably manifest itself in secession, but autonomy. Such autonomy will necessarily entail some form of institutional or relational interface empowering Indigenous peoples to participate in state governmental processes. This view is reflected in the Uluru Statement, which expressly calls 'for the establishment of a First Nations Voice enshrined in the Constitution'.[7] A First Nations Voice was supported at each of the 12 regional dialogues that preceded the Uluru Convention. At Broome, delegates from across the Kimberley and Pilbara 'strongly supported' having an Indigenous voice to Parliament to 'empower the First Peoples of Australia' and give them a 'greater say in government decision-making on matters that affect them and their rights'.[8] Similarly, in Melbourne, delegates 'strongly backed' this option, understanding it as a pragmatic and substantive reform that 'helps with our day-to-day struggles'.[9] Voice was also seen as a priority by delegates at the Cairns Regional Dialogue, which brought together First Nations from the Cape, Gulf, the West and the Tropic of Capricorn. Delegates here argued that Indigenous affairs policies and programmes have been ineffective because Aboriginal and Torres Strait Islander peoples 'haven't been asked what is needed or been involved in the delivery of services'.[10]

Voice was also identified as a 'key role' of a putative Indigenous representative body in community consultations across Victoria. Participants from all parts of the state considered that a representative body should 'advocate on behalf of all Aboriginal people in all aspects of Aboriginal affairs, by representing Aboriginal visions and aspirations'.[11] At a community consultation in Bendigo, voice was understood to encompass providing policy and strategic advice 'to all levels of government', as well as advocating on behalf of all Aboriginal people 'in all aspects', 'locally, nationally and internationally'.[12] Similarly, in Melbourne, voice was considered essential if legislation and policies designed to benefit Aboriginal people was to be effective.[13]

[7] Uluru Statement (n 6).

[8] Referendum Council, 'Broome Regional Dialogue Discusses Constitutional Reform' (media release, 13 February 2017).

[9] Referendum Council, 'Constitutional Reform Must Lead to Real Change' (media release, 20 March 2017).

[10] Referendum Council, 'Delegates Determine Self-Determination is a Priority' (media release, 28 March 2017).

[11] ATWG 2016 (n 4) 18.

[12] ibid 25 (Bendigo).

[13] ibid 41 (Melbourne).

In both the Referendum Council regional dialogues and the Victorian community consultations, the public law principle of *voices* was identified as critical for two democratic reasons. First, it was recognised that an Indigenous representative body was necessary to 'convey our voice' to Parliament,[14] to combat feelings of 'powerlessness',[15] and to ensure that Indigenous peoples could be 'involved in driving policy making' on issues that affect them.[16] In this sense, voice was seen as necessary to enable Indigenous peoples to overcome their demographic disadvantage and exert meaningful influence on public policy such that the government reflects their interests and is responsive to changes in those interests – as delegates in the Torres Strait explained, a voice would be 'an "engine room" for change'.[17] Only through a dedicated political or legal institution could Indigenous peoples be involved in designing and developing culturally appropriate policies.[18]

The existence of such a body was also identified as serving as a mechanism to 'keep the government accountable'.[19] In a politico-legal framework dominated by political constitutionalism, a person's ability to keep the government accountable by influencing legislation and policy is largely determined by their capacity to have their interests represented in Parliament. This presents challenges for marginalised groups. An institution that provides Indigenous peoples with an enhanced capacity to be heard in decisions that affect them is therefore critical. That these two elements are interrelated was recognised by delegates in Perth and Sydney, who conceived voice as a concept that will 'enhance First People's participation in Australian democracy'[20] by ensuring that 'First Nations People have influence over policy and keep parliamentarians accountable'.[21]

Three practical considerations concerning *representativeness*, *access* and *hearing* are relevant. First, references to the importance of articulating the interests of 'all' Aboriginal people in the Victorian community consultations underscores that Indigenous peoples are characterised by significant heterogeneity. In Australia this diversity is both broad – encompassing several hundred nations across the continent with distinctive cultures, beliefs and languages, as well as historical and contemporary forms and intensities of colonial intrusion – and deep, as would be expected of a community of almost 800,000 people. Mechanisms to enhance First Nations' voices must therefore accurately reflect

[14] ibid.

[15] Referendum Council, 'Constitutional Reform: Speaking the Same Language' (media release, 7 April 2017).

[16] ATWG 2016 (n 4) 51 (Shepparton).

[17] Referendum Council, 'Final Report' (2017) 30.

[18] ATWG 2016 (n 4) 61 (Horsham).

[19] ibid 55 (Warrnambool).

[20] Referendum Council, 'First Nations Regional Dialogue in Perth' (media release, 3–5 March 2017).

[21] Referendum Council, 'First Nations Regional Dialogue in Sydney' (media release, 10–12 March 2017).

those voices in all their diversity.[22] This point was also emphasised by Aboriginal communities consulted by the South Australian Treaty Commissioner,[23] and delegates at Referendum Council regional dialogues across the country. At Ross River in Central Australia, delegates agreed that the body 'must represent communities across Australia and have legitimacy in remote, rural and urban areas', with some suggesting that it should also include 'representatives across generations'.[24] Similarly, in Adelaide, the First Nations Voice was conceived as being 'drawn from the First Nations and reflect[ing] the song lines of the country',[25] while in Perth, very strong support for the body was conditioned on it 'represent[ing] all lands and waters across Australia'.[26]

To ascertain and express the views of diverse communities, an institution or process designed to articulate voices in the processes of government requires an internal structure that channels distinctive local, regional and community views to the national body, as well as enabling members at the national level to report back to the community.[27] Simultaneously, reflecting the value of a politics of presence in expanding the range of ideas,[28] diverse groups within internally variegated polities could be empowered to have their interests heard. As Indigenous Australians have noted in consultations, a representative body should be inclusive and pluralistic, enabling the free and equal participation of distinct groups within Indigenous polities.[29] This could include women,[30] young people, traditional owners and, in Australia, members of the Stolen Generations and Torres Strait Islanders. Different Indigenous nations will have different cleavages that should be reflected.[31] In essence, the body must be genuinely representative of the Indigenous polity; all adult members should have the

[22] P Anderson, 'Our Hope for the Future: Voice. Treaty. Truth' (17th Vincent Lingiari Memorial Lecture, Darwin, 16 August 2017) 11.

[23] South Australian Treaty Commissioner, 'Talking Treaty: Summary of Engagements and Next Steps' (Office of the Treaty Commissioner, 2017) 14: 'One Aboriginal nation cannot speak for another, their interests and aspirations are different'.

[24] Referendum Council (n 3) 30.

[25] ibid.

[26] ibid.

[27] ATWG 2016 (n 4) 53 (Warrnambool), 59 (Horsham), 62 (Bairnsdale); Aboriginal and Torres Strait Islander Social Justice Commissioner (ATSISJC), 'Building a Sustainable Indigenous Representative Body' (2008) 39–40, 64, 82; Referendum Council (n 3) 30 (Hobart); (Darwin); (Brisbane).

[28] A Phillips, *The Politics of Presence* (Oxford, Oxford University Press, 1995) 176.

[29] See Cape York Institute, 'A First Nations Voice in the Constitution: Design Issues' (Report to the Referendum Council, June 2017) 39; South Australian Treaty Commissioner (n 23) 14. In Aotearoa New Zealand see, Independent Working Group on Constitutional Transformation, 'The Report of Matike Mai Aotearoa' (2016) 77.

[30] Simply adding women into existing structures is likely to be inadequate. As Rauna Kuokkanen explains, Indigenous women should be able to incorporate their own 'conception of self-determination into political institutions and practices', for otherwise women will be 'constructed as irrelevant or secondary in Indigenous governance and self-determination discourses': R Kuokkanen, *Restructuring Relations: Indigenous Self-Determination, Governance, and Gender* (Oxford, Oxford University Press, 2019) 139 and 157.

[31] For exploration of cleavages in the Sámi community see ch 6.

opportunity to participate in its affairs, and children and young people should be able to contribute through committees or similar processes.

An inherent tension exists within this principle. An institution or mechanism designed to transmit Indigenous interests to government will be pressured to speak in one voice in order to be effectively heard. In structuring a representative body to promote a diversity of views, however, there is a risk that that voice will be splintered, and unanimity will not be possible. In these circumstances, government may find it difficult – or choose to find it difficult – to work with the institution, and either ignore unfavourable perspectives, or find confirmatory support for its preferred course of action, 'effectively sidelin[ing] the body'.[32] This is a practical difficulty, but there is no principled reason why disagreement should not be permitted. The purpose of a representative institution is to provide *all* Indigenous peoples with the capacity to have their voices heard in legislation and policy that affects them. This aim would be defeated by prohibiting dissenting reports or imposing an unreasonable requirement of unanimity. Indeed, if it were otherwise, dissenting voices would be expressed in alternative forums, harming the credibility of the institution in other, no less damaging ways.

Resolving this tension is an ongoing challenge that will rely on the moral authority and political skills of the body's members, but creative institutional design can assist. Consider, for example, the Canadian territory of Nunavut. Nunavut governance largely follows Westminster traditions, but no political parties run or are present in the Legislative Assembly. Rather, the territory operates under a form of consensus government, where members are elected as independents and Cabinet is appointed by the legislature. Empirical studies suggest that this practice both contributes to and reflects Inuit values of respect, teamwork and sharing, while minimising adversarial and confrontational politics more common in partisan systems.[33] Even under consensus government, however, disagreement and dispute arise; non-unanimous votes are 'relatively uncommon',[34] but decisions in the legislature are ultimately reached by majority vote.[35] Nonetheless, the experience in Nunavut suggests while institutional design cannot entirely remove the possibility of dissent, it can channel disagreement in certain ways, potentially limiting the state's opportunity to marginalise Indigenous voices.

[32] G Appleby, Submission No 132 to Joint Select Committee on Constitutional Recognition of Aboriginal and Torres Strait Islander Peoples, 12 June 2015) 12.

[33] G White, 'Traditional Aboriginal Values in a Westminster Parliament: The Legislative Assembly of Nunavut' (2006) 12 *The Journal of Legislative Studies* 8, 29.

[34] A Henderson, *Nunavut: Rethinking Political Culture* (Vancouver, University of British Columbia Press, 2007) 134.

[35] Legislative Assembly and Executive Council Act, S.Nu. 2002, c.5, s 9(2). Vehement dissent has sometimes publicly erupted; in 2003, Jack Anawak was sacked from Cabinet for breaching cabinet solidarity: G White and J Hicks, *Made in Nunavut: An Experiment in Decentralised Government* (Vancouver, University of British Columbia, 2015) 238. A similar sacking occurred in October 2018: 'Nunavut Housing Minister Stripped of Portfolio After "Serious Breach", Says Premier' *CBC News* (24 October 2018), available at www.cbc.ca/news/canada/north/nunavut-minister-pat-angnakak-without-portfolio-1.4876494.

Second, Indigenous voices must be heard by all relevant actors in the policy development cycle. In a federation like Australia, where decisions that affect Aboriginal and Torres Strait Islander people are made at all levels of government and through policies given effect by both the legislature and executive, this can create some difficulties, but they are not insurmountable. For example, an elected Indigenous representative body providing advice directly to government has operated in the ACT since 2008 and another has recently been created in Victoria.[36] Similar localised bodies could be established in all states and territories.[37] A Commonwealth representative body could be drawn, or built up, from these state and territory-based institutions. Alternatively, a separate national representative body could reach agreement with state and territory governments providing it with access, power and responsibilities that mirror their authority at the Commonwealth level. While this may increase financial pressure on the national body, it could be accomplished in a relatively straightforward manner via specific state and territory or cross-cutting thematic policy committees under the national organisation. A third option is to decouple a national representative body from Australian governance institutions. Under this approach, such a body could function as an interface, facilitating engagement between individual First Nations and the relevant decision-maker.[38] Each of these examples carries complications, but they demonstrate that there are multiple approaches to resolving the challenge of developing durable channels of communication.

Access also requires opportunities for Indigenous views to be presented at a sufficiently early stage of public policy decision-making, where their position has the capacity to influence the decision adopted. If Indigenous interests are heard too late in the policy development cycle, decision-makers may be reticent to amend their action,[39] making consideration of Indigenous views largely a tokenistic, box-ticking exercise.[40] This consideration brings to mind the distinction between 'consultation' and 'negotiation'. Whereas consultation implies the views of Aboriginal and Torres Strait Islander people were sought, negotiation infers that those views were 'integral to the settlement of terms'.[41] This is impossible if Indigenous voices are not considered at an early stage in the process.

[36] Aboriginal and Torres Strait Islander Elected Body Act 2008 (ACT); Advancing the Treaty Process with Aboriginal Victorians Act 2018 (Vic) pt 2 (Victorian Treaty Act). There is no requirement that government consult with either of these bodies.

[37] W Mundine, 'Practical Recognition from the Mob's Perspective' (Uphold and Recognise, 2017); W Mundine, 'Recognising the First Nations' in S Morris (ed), *A Rightful Place: A Road Map to Recognition* (Melbourne, Black Inc., 2017) 195–208.

[38] Cape York Institute, 'A First Nations Voice in the Constitution' (2017) 40.

[39] C Saunders, 'Indigenous Constitutional Recognition: The Concept of Consultation' (2016) 8(19) *Indigenous Law Bulletin* 19, 20.

[40] Referendum Council (n 3) 30.

[41] House of Representatives Standing Committee on Aboriginal Affairs, Parliament of Australia, 'Our Future Our Selves: Aboriginal and Torres Strait Islander Community Control, Management and Resources' (1990) 48 [4.7], 59 [4.56].

Finally, and relatedly, as chapter three demonstrated, Indigenous peoples desire that decision-makers treat their views with a 'level of seriousness',[42] by acting with an ethic of respect for the equal status of Indigenous political communities as a constituent normative order within the state. Cheryl Saunders emphasises this point in arguing that consultation should be measured '*both* by the opportunity to make substantive (and timely) contributions; *and* in terms of the effect of the contributions on the final decisions made'.[43] Public law principles can provide institutional opportunities to be heard, and voices should be measured against Saunders' standard. Yet, in the absence of a veto power, public law principles cannot guarantee that those voices will be listened to. This reality is problematic. The history of settler state interaction with Indigenous polities reveals that politicians can gain political traction with the broader electorate by explicitly declaring that they will refuse to listen to Indigenous peoples.

It may not be possible to force a decision-maker to listen and therefore to resolve this legitimate apprehension. Nonetheless, institutional design can respond in novel and innovative ways to enhance the prospect that forums conducive to negotiation arise.[44] For instance, constitutional guarantees against racial discrimination may limit the field of political action by prohibiting law or policy that treats Indigenous peoples less favourably than non-Indigenous peoples. Alternative options, such as making the obligation to consult justiciable,[45] or by enhancing transparency surrounding the process of consultation, may also assist. These latter two options will be explored below; a veto power will be explored in the following part.

In Canada, the Supreme Court has held that the Crown has a duty to consult, and where appropriate, accommodate First Nations views, when contemplating conduct that might adversely impact potential or established Aboriginal or Treaty rights.[46] The standard of consultation differs in each circumstance, but in all cases consultation 'must be meaningful and performed in good faith, with the intention of substantially addressing the concerns of the affected Indigenous group'.[47] Meaningful consultation may require that the Crown 'make changes

[42] J Huggins and R Little, 'A Rightful Place at the Table' in S Morris (ed), *A Rightful Place: A Road Map to Recognition* (Melbourne, Black Inc, 2017) 147, 170.

[43] Saunders, 'Indigenous Constitutional Recognition' (2016) 21 (emphasis in original).

[44] J Sabin, 'A Federation within a Federation? Devolution and Indigenous Government in the Northwest Territories' (Institute for Research on Public Policy, No 66, November 2017) 17.

[45] M Davis and R Dixon, 'Constitutional Recognition through a (Justiciable) Duty to Consult? Towards Entrenched and Judicially Enforceable Norms of Indigenous Consultation' (2016) 27 *Public Law Review* 255.

[46] *R v Sparrow* (1990) 1 SCR 1075; *Haida Nation v British Columbia (Minister of Forests)* (2004) 3 SCR 511, 522–25 [16]–[25] (*Haida Nation*). See generally: D Newman, *Revisiting the Duty to Consult: New Relationships with Aboriginal Peoples* (Saskatoon, Purich, 2014).

[47] S Morales, 'Bridging the Incommensurable: Indigenous Legal Traditions and the Duty to Consult' in O Fitzgerald and R Schwartz (eds), *UNDRIP Implementation: Braiding International, Domestic and Indigenous Laws* (Waterloo, Centre for International Governance Innovation, 2017) 63, 66; *Taku River Tlingit First Nation v British Columbia (Project Assessment Director)* (2004) 3 SCR 550, 566 [29].

to its proposed action based on information obtained through consultations';[48] that is, to take interests and concerns voiced by the affected Indigenous group seriously, by 'substantially addressing'[49] them, and, 'wherever possible', ensuring they are 'demonstrably integrated into the proposed plan of action'.[50] The obligation to consult does not apply to legislative action,[51] and Canadian courts have not imposed a duty to agree,[52] thereby weakening First Nations' bargaining position. Nonetheless, a justiciable obligation to consult imposes a minimum standard and establishes the Court as a third-party arbiter on the genuineness of any process.

An alternative option involves enhancing transparency surrounding the process of voice. This could include tabling the report of the Indigenous body in Parliament and recording it in *Hansard*;[53] giving members of the body the right to address Parliament;[54] or setting out processes for regular communication between members of Parliament, the public service and Indigenous representatives.[55] Another approach involves creatively adapting requirements under the Human Rights (Parliamentary Scrutiny) Act 2011 (Cth). All Bills and legislative instruments introduced into the Commonwealth Parliament must be accompanied by a statement of compatibility that assesses how the Bill or instrument is compatible with the rights and freedoms recognised in seven core international human rights treaties to which Australia is a party.[56] Although the UNDRIP is not one of these seven international treaties,[57] a similar arrangement could be devised whereby the relevant department sets out whether and how the views articulated by the Indigenous representative body influenced the final version of the instrument. Concerns have been raised over the standard of statements of compatibility,[58] and while there is no evidence that they have led to more human rights compliant laws,[59] a burgeoning 'culture of justification' may

[48] *Haida Nation* (n 46) 534 [46].

[49] *Delgamuukw v British Columbia* (1997) 3 SCR 1010, 1113, [168]; *Mikisew Cree First Nation v Canada (Minister of Canadian Heritage)* (2005) 3 SCR 388, 419–20 [61]–[62].

[50] *Halfway River First Nation v BC* (1999) BCCA 470, [160].

[51] *Mikisew Cree First Nation v Canada (Governor-General in Council)* (2018) 2 SCR 765.

[52] *Haida Nation* (n 46) 532 [42].

[53] A Twomey, 'Putting Words to the Tune of Indigenous Constitutional Recognition' *The Conversation* (20 May 2015), available at theconversation.com/putting-words-to-the-tune-of-indigenous-constitutional-recognition-42038.

[54] Referendum Council (n 3) 30 (Broome).

[55] Cape York Institute, 'First Nations Voice' (2017) 40.

[56] Human Rights (Parliamentary Scrutiny) Act 2011 (Cth) s 8.

[57] A parliamentary committee has recommended the Human Rights (Parliamentary Scrutiny) Act 2011 (Cth) is amended to include the UNDRIP: see Parliamentary Joint Select Committee on Constitutional Recognition of Aboriginal and Torres Strait Islander Peoples, 'Final Report' (June 2015) 68 [6.18] Recommendation 6. See ch 2 for discussion on how the existing parliamentary committee process operates for Aboriginal and Torres Strait Islander peoples.

[58] S Rajanayagam, 'Does Parliament Do Enough? Evaluating Statements of Compatibility under the *Human Rights (Parliamentary Scrutiny) Act 2011*' (2015) 38 *UNSW Law Journal* 1046, 1077.

[59] L Grenfell and S Moulds, 'The Role of Committees in Rights Protection in Federal and State Parliaments in Australia' (2018) 41 *UNSW Law Journal* 40, 49.

be emerging.[60] A form of accountability consistent with political constitutionalism, this method would require the Government explain and justify its reasons for choosing not to listen to the views of Indigenous peoples. In contrast to a justiciable obligation, it would not ensure a minimum standard of consultation, but it could impose a political cost to ignoring Indigenous voices. Indeed, for many Indigenous people the hope is that by grounding an Indigenous institution in the political and legal framework of the state, the interests articulated by that body may carry significant moral and political force. Enhancing transparency around the consultation process may assist this.

As these examples illustrate, this condition is flexible. *Voices* requires institutional opportunities for Indigenous peoples to articulate and express their interests at appropriate times to relevant decision-makers in the processes of government. Those institutional opportunities may come in various forms. This malleability is intended to leave room for Indigenous peoples to exercise their right to self-determination by adopting their preferred mechanism. As such, it is process rather than outcome-oriented, and grounded in the belief that to have confidence in Parliament and in government policy-making, Indigenous peoples must have a sense of influence and ownership in the decisions that affect their lives. If this is realised, then regardless as to whether Indigenous interests are adopted on a specific policy issue, they will have been afforded due weight and will have been empowered by the process.

III. POWER

(2) Indigenous peoples must have the authority and financial capacity to exercise independent policy and decision-making power over matters relating to internal or local affairs

Indigenous peoples do not merely aspire to have their interests considered in the processes of government. Over certain matters, they desire real decision-making power. This condition is similar but distinct from voices. Whereas *voices* requires government listen in good faith to Indigenous peoples but does not mandate that their interests are afforded priority, *power* demands that over certain issues, Indigenous peoples' views *are* implemented. As the previous chapter illustrated, in its peoplehood conception, assertions of Indigenous sovereignty contend that Indigenous peoples' status as pre-existing nations differentiates them from other members of the state. By virtue of this differentiated status, Indigenous peoples argue that they should have the

[60] G Williams and D Reynolds, 'The Operation and Impact of Australia's Parliamentary Scrutiny Regime for Human Rights' (2016) 41 *Monash University Law Review* 469, 506. Although note that Adam Fletcher contends that the PJCHR has 'failed to engender good faith human rights debate in any significant measure': A Fletcher, *Australia's Human Rights Scrutiny Regime: Democratic Masterstroke or Mere Window Dressing?* (Melbourne, Melbourne University Press, 2018) 307.

authority to determine decisions over matters where their interests are more relevantly affected than non-Indigenous peoples. This claim is not violative of democracy, but is consistent with long-standing democratic principles such as subsidiarity and federalism.

Indigenous aspirations for decision-making authority are recorded in Article 4 of the UNDRIP. As that article provides, in exercising their right to self-determination, Indigenous peoples 'have the right to autonomy or self-governance in matters relating to their internal or local affairs'. This encompasses the ability to wield greater control over land and resources, authority to maintain, protect and develop religious, spiritual and cultural traditions, as well as the right to establish and control educational institutions.[61] Consistent with democratic theory, additional matters could be included where their resolution is considered to be more legitimately made by Indigenous peoples,[62] for it is through institutions that empower Indigenous peoples to make these decisions that the 'governing order' in which they live will more closely track their aspirations.[63]

Considering the diversity of Indigenous nations both across the globe and Australia, it is not possible to be prescriptive about the extent of self-government powers that could be recognised in any one case. Differently situated communities will have different aspirations and competencies. Partly for this reason debate persists within Indigenous nations over the extent of desired autonomy.[64] Although complex, this fact is not indicative of the impossibility of power as an essential condition of institutional design. As Patricia Monture-Angus (Mohawk) has noted, '*the* solution is *not* about constructing a single (national) model',[65] but in permitting Indigenous political communities the freedom to determine for themselves the extent of their authority, within a reworked overarching framework based on respect and partnership. That said, it is clear that *some minimum level* of decision-making authority and jurisdiction is desired. An Indigenous representative body, or alternative structure should therefore not merely provide Indigenous peoples with a voice in decision-making, enabling them to act as advisory or consultative committees, but, within a defined jurisdictional ambit, empower them as decision-making bodies.[66] Within this domain, Indigenous peoples must be free to steer their own vessel; articulating

[61] UNDRIP (n 1) arts 8, 10–15, 25–26.

[62] M Åhrén, *Indigenous Peoples' Status in the International Legal System* (Oxford, Oxford University Press, 2016) 139.

[63] J Anaya, 'The Right of Indigenous Peoples to Self-Determination in the Post-Declaration Era' in C Charters and R Stavenhagen (eds), *Making the Declaration Work: The United Nations Declaration on the Rights of Indigenous Peoples* (Copenhagen, International Work Group for Indigenous Affairs, 2009) 184, 189.

[64] Åhrén proposes a 'sliding scale' of jurisdiction based on the 'relative importance of the issue to the respective people': Åhrén Åhrén, *Indigenous Peoples' Status* (2016) 139.

[65] P Monture-Angus, *Journeying Forward: Dreaming First Nations' Independence* (Halifax, Fernwood, 1999) 12 (emphasis in original).

[66] K Gilbert, *Because a White Man'll Never Do It* (Sydney, Angus and Robertson, 1973) 186.

their own concerns, identifying their own priorities and developing solutions to address those challenges, independent of state action.

Participants in community consultations in Victoria, and delegates at regional dialogues across the country, repeatedly emphasised the importance of this condition. In Mildura, participants outlined that the representative body must be more than a consultative body; it must be able to 'write and make our own policies', and make decisions on behalf of the Aboriginal Community.[67] In Shepparton it was noted that over certain matters, the representative body 'should be able to make the final call'.[68] Similarly, in Hobart, delegates agreed that a First Nations Voice 'must be stronger than just an advisory body',[69] while in Dubbo in central New South Wales, delegates considered that a First Nations Voice 'must have real power', including 'a power of veto and the power to make a difference'.[70]

As these statements hint, power is 'not an absolute quality … [but] is something that is enjoyed in degrees'.[71] This is true even for state and federal governments in Australia, who 'are constrained in their capacity to govern themselves autonomously, both by one another and by the international sphere of power relations'.[72] It is helpful therefore to articulate gradations of power in order to understand the functions or capacities that an Indigenous-institution could exercise. Although these responsibilities range from weaker to stronger forms of autonomy they should not be considered hierarchal, but rather thought of as a 'bundle of dynamic legal [and political] relationships',[73] that provide diverse opportunities for differently situated Indigenous nations to 'develop answers to … questions based on the wishes of our people'.[74] In most cases, a layering of complementary and integrated processes is likely the optimum solution.

At one end sit forms of soft power. A capacity to effectuate outcomes does not necessarily require legal authority. Rather, relying on powers of persuasion and moral force,[75] an Indigenous institution could obtain its preferred outcomes even in the absence of legal compulsion. The concept of soft power emerged

[67] ATWG 2016 (n 4) 32 and 29 (Mildura). See also 36 (Swan Hill).

[68] ibid 51 (Shepparton).

[69] Referendum Council (n 3) 30 (Hobart).

[70] ibid (Dubbo).

[71] M Murphy, 'Relational Self-Determination and Federal Reform' in M Murphy (ed), *Canada: The State of the Federation 2003: Reconfiguring Aboriginal-State Relations* (Montreal, McGill-Queen's University Press, 2005) 3, 10.

[72] ibid.

[73] S Imai, 'Indigenous Self-Determination and the State' in BJ Richardson, S Imai and K McNeil (eds), *Indigenous Peoples and the Law: Comparative and Critical Perspectives* (Oxford, Hart Publishing, 2009) 285, 290.

[74] J Borrows, 'A Genealogy of Law: Inherent Sovereignty and First Nations Self-Government' (1992) 30 *Osgoode Hall Law Journal* 291, 352.

[75] Soft power is more than simply influence but conveys a sense of attraction or acculturation: J Nye Jr, 'Public Diplomacy and Soft Power' (2008) 616 *The ANNALS of the American Academy of Political and Social Science* 94.

within international relations theory during the 1980s, but it is relevant in considering the potential scope of authority available to Indigenous institutions in a politico-legal governance structure that provides Indigenous peoples with very little 'hard power' resources. Practical challenges exist, however. Soft power tends to 'work indirectly by shaping the environment for policy, and sometimes takes years to produce the desired outcomes'.[76] Whether an Indigenous body is effective in achieving its preferences via forms of soft power therefore relies on a combination of personal and institutional factors, including the qualities and actions of its members,[77] as well as the way that institutional structures or processes allow those members to control the political agenda.[78] While this latter element could be strengthened through procedural rights that empower members to be heard at sufficiently early stages of policy development, or by grounding a form of deliberative political reasoning, soft power ultimately relies on state actors accepting that the moral force of Indigenous claims outweigh non-Indigenous interests. Soft power is an important complementary dimension of Indigenous political strength, but its effectiveness is limited.

Shifting to 'harder' forms of power leads us to co- or joint management of lands and waters. This structure is extensively utilised in Australia, Canada and Aotearoa New Zealand. Typically, it involves the establishment of a board comprised of government-appointed Indigenous and non-Indigenous persons who oversee planning and management of certain areas. If conducted on a firm basis of formal recognition and active participation in decision-making processes, collaborative land and resource planning can empower local communities by ensuring that Indigenous values are considered and expressed in developing management strategies. One noteworthy example is the Te Urewera Act 2014 (NZ), which grants legal personality to Te Urewera, 'a fortress of nature, alive with history', and 'a place of spiritual value' in the north island of Aotearoa New Zealand.[79] The Act also establishes a board to manage the area. In undertaking its functions, the Te Urewera Board may give expression to Tūhoetanga and Tūhoe concepts of management, and must 'consider and provide appropriately for the relationship of iwi and hapū and their culture and traditions with Te Urewera when making decisions'.[80]

The Te Urewera Act has been recognised as an innovative politico-legal arrangement that re-envisages co-management regimes towards a 'bicultural'[81] model of preservation. Although the powers of Tūhoe representatives are

[76] J Nye Jr, *Soft Power: The Means to Success in World Politics* (New York, PublicAffairs, 2004) 99.

[77] G Gallarotti, 'Soft Power: What It Is, Why It's Important, and the Conditions for Its Effective Use' (2011) 4 *Journal of Political Power* 25, 28. See discussion under integrity below in pt V.

[78] Nye Jr, *Soft Power* (2004) 5–11.

[79] Te Urewera Act 2014 (NZ) s 3(1)–(2) (Te Urewera Act).

[80] ibid ss 18(2), 20(1).

[81] J Ruru, 'A Treaty in Another Context: Creating Reimagined Treaty Relationships in Aotearoa New Zealand' in J Borrows and M Coyle (eds), *The Right Relationship: Reimagining the Implementation of Historical Treaties* (Toronto, University of Toronto Press, 2017) 305, 320.

constrained in important respects, the Act 'recognises the way in which Māori … conceive of and relate to the particular places at issue'[82] and 'allows for the substantial incorporation of Māori law'.[83] As Andrew Geddis and Jacinta Ruru (Raukawa, Ngāti Ranginui and Ngāti Maniapoto) note, the 2017 Te Urewera Management Plan differs considerably from existing conservation management plans in Aotearoa New Zealand:

> It is centred on creating and applying rules to manage the people rather than the land. Its opening words include 'Deliberatively, we are resetting our human relationships and behaviour towards nature. Our disconnection from Te Urewera has changed our humanness. We wish for its return'.[84]

Considerable diversity exists within co- and joint management regimes. In some cases, a majority of members are Indigenous, and decisions can be made without the consent of non-Indigenous members,[85] providing significant scope for the maintenance and development of Indigenous land management priorities. Even where Indigenous members predominate, some boards must reach certain decisions by consensus or unanimity,[86] while in others still, membership is divided equally.[87] In these cases, the capacity for Indigenous values to guide decision-making relies on elements of soft power, including the political and cultural authority of Indigenous members as well as the attitudes of their non-Indigenous colleagues. In all cases however, co-management boards have limited jurisdictional authority; beyond the internal regulation of their procedures, decisions must legally be confirmed or acquiesced to by the responsible minister,[88] and the territorial scope of decision-making is strictly delimited.

Next, sit service delivery arrangements. Under this model, Indigenous organisations take control of the administration and delivery of programmes and services usually delivered by the state. This approach can provide real advantages. Compared to mainstream or universal service providers, Indigenous organisations are more likely to understand the felt needs of their target populations, enhancing the prospect that such programmes will be effective. Nonetheless, this model again provides a very limited scope of authority. While control over

[82] A Geddis and J Ruru, 'Places as Persons: Creating a New Framework for Maori–Crown Relations' in J Varuhas and SW Stark (eds), *The Frontiers of Public Law* (Oxford, Hart Publishing, 2020) 255, 256.

[83] ibid 270. See also C Jones, *New Treaty, New Tradition: Reconciling New Zealand and Māori Law* (Vancouver, University of British Columbia Press, 2016) 98.

[84] Geddis and Ruru, 'Places as Persons' (2020). Citing Te Kawa O Te Urewera (2017) 8.

[85] See, eg: Environment Protection and Biodiversity Conservation Act 1999 (Cth) ss 374–83; Conservation, Forests and Lands Act 1987 (Vic) s 82M(3)(a).

[86] See, eg: Te Urewera Act (n 79) ss 33–34.

[87] See, eg: Wagyl Kaip & Southern Noongar Indigenous Land Use Agreement, signed 8 June 2015 (registered 17 October 2018) annex N ss 3, 4.1.

[88] See, eg: the legal effect of decisions made by the Nunavut Wildlife Management Board: Agreement between the Inuit of the Nunavut Settlement Area and Her Majesty the Queen in Right of Canada (Minister of Indian Affairs and Northern Development and Tungavik, 1993) art 5.3.7–5.3.23.

service delivery may permit some degree of autonomy for Indigenous peoples to manoeuvre when implementing services, programmes are rarely designed by Indigenous peoples and communities themselves, but by public servants operating under the legislative and regulatory framework of the state. As we saw in chapter two, shifts in government policy can also radically alter the landscape of Indigenous service delivery arrangements.

The next two capacities provide more significant autonomy. In some cases, Indigenous communities are empowered to exercise regulatory powers. In Canada, for instance, First Nations operating under the Indian Act are authorised to enact delegated legislation on a range of internal matters, including, inter alia, to: prevent the spread of contagious disease; regulate traffic; observe law and order; remove and punish persons trespassing; and, regulate the sale of alcohol.[89] As delegated legislation, by-laws must not be inconsistent with any regulations made by the Governor in Council, or relevant minister.[90] In Australia, Land Councils established under the Aboriginal Land Rights (Northern Territory) Act 1976 (Cth) approach these powers. Under s 23(2) of this Act, 'with the approval of the Minister', a Land Council may:

> [P]erform any functions that may be conferred on it by a law of the Northern Territory, including, without limiting the foregoing, functions in relation to:
>
> (a) the protection of sacred sites;
> (b) access to Aboriginal land; and
> (c) schemes for the management of wildlife on Aboriginal land.

Although requiring ministerial approval, these powers are valuable. In 2018, for example, the Kenbi Open Area Declaration was gazetted, prohibiting public access to several islands on the Cox Peninsula because they contain important sacred sites.[91] Capacity to enact delegated legislation provides enhanced autonomy for Indigenous nations, but authority is legally and conceptually grounded in the sovereignty of the state. As the previous chapter demonstrated, this conflicts with Indigenous peoples' understanding of their own political authority, which does not flow from the state but is inherent in their status as prior, self-governing communities.

Australia has never acknowledged that Aboriginal and Torres Strait Islander nations possess an inherent authority to enact primary legislation over a defined territory, but in Canada and the United States, some Indigenous nations have secured recognition of rights approximating this scope of autonomy. In Canada, modern treaties negotiated between First Nations and the Crown recognise a

[89] RSC 1985, c I-5, s 81(1)–85(1).

[90] ibid s 81(1). See also the Metis Settlements Act, RSA 2000, c M-14 s 51, Sch 1, cl 2. Note also that significant sustained criticism of the Indian Act suggests that it would fail to satisfy the 'ownership' criteria discussed below in pt IV.

[91] Northern Territory, *Government Gazette*, No S20, 22 March 2018.

degree of self-government.[92] As noted in chapter three, jurisdiction recognised under these treaties typically includes the administration of justice, family and social services, healthcare, and language and cultural education. Under the Nisga'a Final Agreement, for example, the Nisga'a have principal authority over laws respecting Nisga'a Government, citizenship, culture, language, lands and assets;[93] but provincial or federal laws apply where an inconsistency arises in all other areas over which the Nisga'a have legislative authority.[94] In the United States, the Supreme Court recognised the inherent sovereignty of Native American tribes as early as 1823,[95] though that authority is limited. While it extends to the power to govern the nation's internal affairs, including by regulating the activities of non-Indians who enter 'consensual relationships' with the tribe or its members within tribal lands,[96] it is defeasible by Congressional action.[97]

Power may also include the authority to conclusively resolve disputes. Indigenous adjudicatory authority is rarely recognised by the state. Where it is recognised, its scope is often tightly constrained. In Canada, although the Nisga'a Final Agreement empowers the Nisga'a to constitute a court to adjudicate disputes, appeals will be heard in the British Columbia Supreme Court.[98] In the United States, Native American nations enjoy inherent authority to exercise civil and criminal jurisdiction over Indians (including non-member Indians) in Indian country,[99] but while they may exercise civil jurisdiction over non-Indians,[100] they have no criminal jurisdiction over non-Indian persons who commit crimes.[101] Nevertheless, such adjudicatory power remains valuable. Raymond Austin, a former Navajo Nation Supreme Court Justice, has documented the way Navajo Courts are reinscribing traditional laws and values in a 'Navajo adjudicatory system designed and equipped for American-style litigation'.[102] The Navajo experience illustrates how Native American 'tribes are

[92] C Godlewska and J Webber, 'The *Calder* decision, Aboriginal title, and the Nisga'a' in H Foster, H Raven and J Webber (eds), *Let Right be Done: Aboriginal Title, the Calder Case, and the Future of Indigenous Rights* (Vancouver, University of British Columbia Press, 2007) 1, 17–18.

[93] Nisga'a Final Agreement, signed 4 May 1999 (entered into force 11 May 2000) ch 2(22) (Nisga'a Treaty); Nisga'a Final Agreement Act, SC 2000, c 7, ch 11(33).

[94] Nisga'a Treaty (n 93) ch 11(30)–(129).

[95] *Johnson v M'Intosh*, 21 US (8 Wheat) 543 (1823). See also *Worcester v Georgia*, 31 US (6 Pet) 515 (1832).

[96] *Montana v United States*, 450 US 544, 565 (1981).

[97] *United States v Wheeler*, 435 US 313, 323 (Stewart J) (1978).

[98] Nisga'a Treaty (n 93) ch 12(45).

[99] 25 USC § 1301 (2018); *United States v Lara*, 541 US 193 (2004).

[100] *Navajo Nation v Daley* (10th Cir, No 16-2205, 24 July 2018). See also *Dollar General Corporation v Mississippi Band of Choctaw Indians*, 136 S Ct 2159 (2016); *Dolgencorp Inc v Mississippi Band of Choctaw Indians*, 746 F 3d 588 (5th Cir, 2014).

[101] *Oliphant v Suquamish*, 435 US 191 (1978).

[102] R Austin, *Navajo Court and Navajo Common Law: A Tradition of Tribal Governance* (Minneapolis, University of Minnesota Press, 2009) 62.

slowly subverting' these limitations and 'making courts vehicles for self-determination'.[103] This does not appear to be the case in Australia, where, as chapter two revealed, 'Aboriginal Courts' are precluded from applying non-Indigenous laws and limited to sentencing for offences at the magistrates' level.

Finally, as highlighted by some delegates to the Referendum Council regional dialogues, power may also involve the capacity to veto legislative or executive action. Article 19 of the UNDRIP provides that states must obtain the 'free, prior and informed consent' of Indigenous peoples before adopting and implementing legislative or administrative measures that may affect them. While this article suggests that Indigenous peoples retain a right of veto in some cases, states have been reticent to recognise such power,[104] and the UN Permanent Forum on Indigenous Issues has stressed that it should be understood in terms of meaningful participation and good faith consultation.[105] Veto powers are not alien to Australian governance. Judicial review essentially provides the courts with a veto power over legislation or executive actions that breaches constitutional or legal authority. Similarly, the vertical distribution of political power effectively empowers state and federal governments with veto powers over their exclusive legislative authority. Imaginative arrangements may well provide a carapace for Indigenous authority in certain domains.

Prospects for Indigenous federal arrangements in Australia may be weak,[106] but the preceding discussion illustrates that *power* encompasses several interrelated political and legal responsibilities or functions. These include: dimensions of moral persuasion and soft power; co- or joint management of lands and resources; service delivery arrangements; the authority to enact delegated, and/or primary legislation; dispute resolution; and the capacity to veto state or federal legislation or executive action. Articulating power in this manner reveals that this condition can be realised in several ways; it may be appropriate for different institutions to exercise different forms of authority.

Two further elements need to be examined within this condition. First, power requires some degree of *independence*. Colonial histories are replete with state efforts at marginalising Indigenous leadership and resistance, sparking legitimate contemporary anxiety that participation with or within the state is designed to co-opt Indigenous peoples in the ongoing project of settler governance.[107]

[103] J Borrows, *Freedom and Indigenous Constitutionalism* (Toronto, University of Toronto Press, 2016) 174.

[104] In Canada; see nn 48–52.

[105] Permanent Forum on Indigenous Issues, 'Report of the International Workshop on Methodologies Regarding Free, Prior and Informed Consent and Indigenous Peoples' (New York, 17–19 January 2005), UN Doc E/C.19/2005/3, 12 [47]. Though the PFII did elliptically note that 'this process may include the option of withholding consent'.

[106] Though note that emerging treaty processes in Australia may lead to a quasi-federal division of powers: H Hobbs, 'Aboriginal and Torres Strait Islander Peoples and Multinational Federalism in Australia' (2018) 27 *Griffith Law Review* 307. See further ch 7.

[107] J Corntassel and RC Witmer II, *Forced Federalism: Contemporary Challenges to Indigenous Nationhood* (Norman, University of Oklahoma Press, 2008).

Conscious of this history, participants in community consultations in Victoria and delegates at the Referendum Council's regional dialogues emphasised that any political or legal institution or process to empower Indigenous peoples, must be independent.[108]

Independence can be understood in several ways. It may mean that policy development and political advocacy should not be restricted to occurring within the confines of government policy, but represent actual Indigenous interests in all their diversity.[109] Alternatively, it may mean that the institution is legally or structurally separated from government. Indeed, being implicated in the state as an order of government can be problematic; Indigenous peoples working in such an institution may feel compromised and pressured from both their constituents and the state at large. As we saw with the experience of the National Congress of Australia's First Peoples in chapter two, however, strict legal and structural independence can be problematic. While it may enable an Indigenous institution to develop creative and culturally grounded policy, it may also conflict with other priorities, including the ability to effectively exercise its functions. As Mick Dodson (Yawuru) and Diane Smith have noted, 'Indigenous governance arrangements need to be informed by local cultural standards … [but they] also have to work'.[110]

Indigenous peoples must determine for themselves the appropriate institutional framework within which their aspirations can be realised, but formally embedding that institution in the constitutional or politico-legal structure of the state may produce advantages without necessarily weakening its ability to make decisions over internal and local affairs. Indeed, creative legislative arrangements have the potential to resolve this challenge. In Victoria, the Advancing the Treaty Process with Aboriginal Victorians Act 2018 requires the state recognise an Aboriginal Representative Body, on the recommendation of the Victorian Treaty Advancement Commissioner.[111] This statutory hook aims to ensure that the state will consult in 'partnership and good faith' with the body in the development of a treaty framework,[112] but leaves questions of structure and design to be determined by Aboriginal Victorians.[113] Independence permits the Aboriginal Representative Body to operate in a culturally appropriate manner, but that structural hook promotes institutional opportunities to discuss matters of shared concern. This body is intertwined to some degree with the state – government may revoke its recognition[114] – but it remains independent.

[108] ATWG 2016 (n 4) 30 (Mildura), 35 (Swan Hill), 39 (Melbourne), 44 (Ballarat), 50 (Shepparton), 59 (Warrnambool); Referendum Council (n 3) 31.

[109] ATSISJC (n 27) 64.

[110] M Dodson and D Smith, 'Governance for Sustainable Development: Strategic Issues and Principles for Indigenous Australian Communities' (Centre for Aboriginal Economic Policy Research, Discussion Paper No 250, 2003) 19.

[111] Victorian Treaty Act (n 36) ss 8, 10–11.

[112] ibid ss 20(2), 22.

[113] ibid s 11(2).

[114] In limited circumstances: ibid s 13.

Second, power also requires *financial capacity*. In order to exercise decision-making authority Indigenous peoples must have the financial capacity to do so.[115] This connection is underscored by Articles 4 and 39 of the UNDRIP, which provide that in exercising their right to self-determination, Indigenous peoples have the right to 'ways and means for financing' the autonomous functions of their institutions, and the right to 'have access to financial … assistance' in order to enjoy their rights. Participants at community consultations in Victoria and delegates at regional dialogues across Australia also highlighted this link. At Swan Hill participants considered that a representative body should have 'strong funding and resourcing',[116] while in Shepparton it was agreed that such a body should have 'ownership of the funding and how it is allocated'.[117] Similarly in Horsham, participants noted that an Indigenous body 'cannot be reliant on government funding'.[118] The Final Report of the Referendum Council echoed these calls. Citing discussions in Brisbane, Broome and Darwin, the report concluded that any Indigenous body 'must … be supported by a sufficient and guaranteed budget, with access to its own independent secretariat, experts and lawyers'.[119]

There are various ways that an institution's financial capacity can be made secure. For example, the New South Wales Land Council was established in 1983, funded by a 15-year 7.5 per cent levy of land taxes across the state. In each year, half of the collected amount was placed in an investment fund, and the remainder allocated to the Land Council's operation.[120] Alternatively, the Aboriginal and Torres Strait Islander Social Justice Commissioner has suggested that funding for an Indigenous body could be independently set by the Commonwealth Grants Commission, in the manner that Special Purpose Grants and General Purpose Payments were previously allocated to the states and territories.[121] Other approaches can be considered: Ole Henrik Magga, the first President of the Norwegian Sámi Parliament has suggested that Indigenous bodies could be funded through 'revenue derived from taxation or … exploitation of natural resources' in traditional Indigenous lands;[122] in Canada, Opaskwayak Cree Nation scholar Douglas Sanderson (Amo Binashii), has proposed including First Nations within horizontal fiscal equalisation formula.[123]

[115] Huggins and Little, 'A Rightful Place' (2017) 170; Gilbert, *White Man* (1972) 141–3.

[116] ATWG 2016 (n 4) 34 (Swan Hill).

[117] ibid 51 (Shepparton).

[118] ibid 59 (Horsham).

[119] Referendum Council (n 3) 30–31.

[120] Aboriginal Land Rights Act 1983 (NSW) s 28 (now repealed). At the Commonwealth level, an Indigenous capital fund was established under the Aboriginal Development Commission Act 1980 (Cth) ss 20–22, though sufficient resourcing was never allocated.

[121] ATSISJC (n 27) 104.

[122] OH Magga 'The Saami Parliament: Fulfilment of Self-Determination?' in J Erikkson and K Karppi (eds), *Conflict and Cooperation in the North* (Umeaå, Umeaå Universite, 2002) 299, 306.

[123] E Raymer, 'New Legal Framework for Indigenous Peoples Means "Sweeping" Legislative Changes', *Canadian Lawyer* (15 February 2018), available at www.canadianlawyermag.com/legalfeeds/author/elizabeth-raymer/new-legal-framework-for-indigenous-peoples-means-sweeping-legislative-changes-15334.

Apolitical and independent sources of funding are critical, because in practice an institution's financial capacity is likely to determine its independence and ability to effectively exercise its functions. In the absence of own-source, stable and secure financing, an Indigenous institution will be reliant to some degree on recurrent or conditional state funding. This is problematic, for it is impossible to be 'truly autonomous if each action and project requires state financial approval'.[124] As the Aboriginal and Torres Strait Islander Social Justice Commissioner has explained, government funding

> may be tied to certain functions not seen as a priority by the membership, they can put an organisation in the position of being a proxy for government, they often come with conditions attached such as limiting the organisation's ability for public comment on certain programs, and if withdrawn they can pull the rug out from under the organisation.[125]

Ultimately, in the absence of constitutional amendment empowering Indigenous communities with the power of taxation, security and stability of funding can only be guaranteed by public support. If an Indigenous institution is regarded as credible by both Indigenous and non-Indigenous peoples, it is likely to be financed appropriately. To protect its independence from government and properly exercise some minimum level of decision-making power, it should also have the authority to determine its own funding priorities and should not be denied the capacity to raise funds from alternative sources. As Jerald Sabin has noted, 'increasing … own-source revenues moves … [Indigenous institutions] … toward greater independence and replaces fiscal dependency with partnership'.[126] These conditions will enable an Indigenous-institution to pursue an Indigenous agenda.

IV. OWNERSHIP

(3) Institutions or processes that empower Indigenous peoples must be regarded by Indigenous peoples as legitimate

It is not enough that political or legal institutions that empower Indigenous peoples to be heard in the processes of government exist; such institutions must be recognised as legitimate in the eyes of their constituents. As the 'quality that leads people … to accept authority – independent of coercion, self-interest, or rational persuasion',[127] legitimacy has normative and sociological dimensions. An

[124] A Stepien, A Petrétei and T Koivurova, 'Sami Parliaments in Finland, Norway, and Sweden' in T Malloy, A Osipov and B Vizi (eds), *Managing Diversity through Non-Territorial Autonomy: Assessing Advantage, Deficiencies, and Risks* (Oxford, Oxford University Press, 2015) 117, 133.

[125] ATSISJC (n 27) 101–02.

[126] Sabin, 'A Federation within a Federation?' (2017) 18.

[127] D Bodansky, 'The Legitimacy of International Governance: A Coming Challenge for International Environmental Law?' (1999) 93 *American Journal of International Law* 596, 600.

Indigenous organisation may be normatively legitimate because it was established in accordance with legal requirements set out in an Act of Parliament, but if the relevant Indigenous nation or nations does not accept or perceive it as capable of representing their interests, accountable to them, or as reflecting their values,[128] it is unlikely to be sociologically legitimate. In this sense, sociological legitimacy is relational. It is concerned with the attitudes of individuals and focuses on whether a community considers a particular public institution as worthy of support or justifiable beyond its legal validity, mere habit or fear of sanction.[129]

Several articles of the UNDRIP speak to this distinction. The Declaration provides that Indigenous peoples have the right to 'freely determine their political status',[130] 'maintain and strengthen their distinct political, legal, economic, social and cultural institutions',[131] and 'maintain and develop their own indigenous decision-making institutions'.[132] These articles reflect what Bernard Williams characterised as the 'Basic Legitimation Demand'; the idea that in order for power to be exercised legitimately, one must live under an 'intelligible order of authority', where that structure 'makes sense' in language justifiable to each subject.[133] This language is important. As Mark Suchman notes, an institution must be more than simply understandable under the norms and values of a society but be cognitively justifiable; it will only 'have sense', when it and its actions are 'desirable, proper or appropriate' within those norms.[134] An Indigenous institution must therefore be both normatively legitimate, as well as recognisable to and justifiable within the norms of the relevant nation(s).[135]

The UNDRIP articles highlight a further key point. Indigenous values are not static, but are subject to interpretation and adaption. While the structure and operation of any institution must fit the cultural norms and values of the people it serves, there is no requirement that Indigenous institutions and processes be legitimate or traditional in a historical sense. As the Expert Mechanism on the Rights of Indigenous Peoples has explained, such processes and institutions may 'have evolved over time', including 'as a result of discussion and dialogue, or even agreement, with the State'.[136] What is critical is that irrespective as to the institutional form that *voices* or *power* takes, it is recognisable by Indigenous

[128] D Beetham, *The Legitimation of Power*, 2nd edn (London, Palgrave MacMillan, 2013) 15–19.

[129] R Fallon Jr, 'Legitimacy and the Constitution' (2005) 118 *Harvard Law Review* 1789, 1795.

[130] UNDRIP (n 1) art 3.

[131] ibid art 5.

[132] ibid art 18.

[133] B Williams, 'Realism and Moralism in Political Theory' in B Williams, *In the Beginning was the Deed: Realism and Moralism in Political Argument* (Princeton, Princeton University Press, 2007) 1, 10–11.

[134] M Suchman, 'Managing Legitimacy: Strategic and Institutional Approaches' (1995) 20 *Academy of Management Review* 571, 574–75; Beetham, *Legitimation of Power* (2013) 11.

[135] N Roughan, 'From Authority to Authorities: Bridging the Social/Normative Divide' in R Cotterrell and M Del Mar (eds), *Authority in Transnational Legal Theory: Theorising Across Disciplines* (Cheltenham, Edward Elgar, 2016) 280.

[136] Expert Mechanism on the Rights of Indigenous Peoples, 'Final Study on Indigenous Peoples and the Right to Participate in Decision-Making', UN Doc A/HRC/EMRIP/2011/2 (26 May 2011) 5 [16].

peoples as an *Indigenous* institution. Such a body may be 'an adaptation to the social and political circumstances of the state',[137] but it must nonetheless be culturally appropriate with Indigenous leaders accountable to Indigenous peoples, for 'self-government on its own', as Taiaiake Alfred (Kanien'kehá:ka) argues, 'is meaningless if it is not conducted in an Indigenous way'.[138] Indeed, if an Indigenous polity does not recognise the institution or process as reflecting its values, character and knowledge, members of that community may not regard it as legitimate and may not interact with it; in other words, it will not simply be meaningless, but will fail to be effective.[139]

The importance and dynamism of ownership is reflected in both the Victorian and Australia-wide consultative processes. Community consultations in Victoria saw frequent assertions of the desire that an Indigenous Representative Body be 'accountable to the Aboriginal Community', 'meaning the Representative Body must answer to the Aboriginal Community'.[140] At all locations, an institution that 'answers to the Aboriginal Community' was understood to be one built on cultural principles, processes and knowledge, but flexible enough to accommodate development of those principles and practices. For instance, in Mildura, participants considered that 'culture must underpin the foundation of the design of the Representative Body',[141] while in Melbourne participants explained that the body must 'respect[] and embed[] customs and values'.[142] The significance of grounding the design of any institution or process on cultural principles was also underscored in Shepparton and Ballarat. Here, the community agreed that culture is necessary 'if it is to hold any integrity in the community',[143] 'because if there is no culture base then it is not for black fellas'.[144] Similar views were expressed across the country as part of the Referendum Council's regional dialogues. Repeatedly emphasised was the desire that a First Nations Voice 'must not be a hand-picked, advisory government body, but have legitimacy in the eyes of the community',[145] and therefore be 'structured in a way that respects culture'.[146] As such, there was staunch support for a body 'elected from the grassroots'.[147]

[137] Jones, *New Treaty, New Tradition* (2016) 86; P Nadasdy, *Sovereignty's Entailments: First Nation State Formation in the Yukon* (Toronto, University of Toronto Press, 2017) 7.

[138] T Alfred, *Peace, Power, Righteousness: An Indigenous Manifesto*, 2nd edn (Oxford, Oxford University Press, 2009) 5.

[139] See generally, S Cornell and JP Kalt, 'Two Approaches to the Development of Native Nations: One Works, the Other Doesn't' in M Jorgensen (ed), *Rebuilding Native Nations: Strategies for Governance and Development* (Tucson, University of Arizona Press, 2007) 3.

[140] ATWG 2016 (n 4) 23 (Bendigo).

[141] ibid 29 (Mildura).

[142] ibid 39 (Melbourne).

[143] ibid 49 (Shepparton).

[144] ibid 44 (Ballarat), 53 (Warrnambool), 59 (Horsham), 62 (Bairnsdale).

[145] Referendum Council, 'First Nations Regional Dialogue in Dubbo' (media release, 17–19 February 2017). See also Referendum Council (n 8) (Broome).

[146] Referendum Council (n 3) 30.

[147] Referendum Council, 'First Nations Regional Dialogue in Darwin' (media release, 22–24 February 2017). See also Referendum Council (n 10) (Cairns); Referendum Council (n 15) (Ross River).

Ownership is connected to voices. To faithfully articulate the views and interests of disparate Indigenous political communities, distinctive local and regional arrangements to ascertain and channel that voice may need to be devised.[148] This was illustrated through the regional dialogue process. While delegates at all dialogues agreed that support from the grassroots was necessary to ground a First Nations Voice, some communities identified additional procedures to ensure cultural authority. Delegates in Darwin proposed a Tribal Elders Council be established as a supplementary body to the elected group.[149] At Ross River delegates explained that the voice 'would need to be a land-based representative body so that the representatives are drawn from the micro unit of land ownership across Australia which represents Aboriginal culture'.[150] These interventions highlight that a uniform approach to channelling diverse local interests and aspirations to the national level risks failing to accurately ascertain those interests. In some cases, for some communities, democratic election may not be suitable.

Ideally, in a reconstituted governance framework reflective of Indigenous peoples' status as a constituent normative order, Indigenous decision-making institutions could be accepted by the state in whatever manifestation they take. This is a simple condition of equality: Indigenous peoples have 'original teaching, original thoughts, original values, and original lifeways that contain original concepts of governance',[151] and they 'must be free, like other people, to choose the political structures suitable to their needs'.[152] As discussed above, the Advancing the Treaty Process with Aboriginal Victorians Act 2018 seeks to accomplish this by requiring the state recognise a representative body built by and on Aboriginal values. Even here, however, some degree of translation is necessary to ensure culturally appropriate forms of Indigenous governance are legible to the state. Jill Gallagher, the Victorian Treaty Advancement Commissioner, explains:

> Before colonisation, we had traditional ways of doing business. There was no need for a statewide Representative Body. Colonisation has changed this. We now need a way to talk Treaty with the state … Our unique situation needs a unique response. We have to make a body that fits our unique culture, history and traditions. But it must also represent us in the modern world.[153]

[148] ATSISJC (n 27) 39–40.

[149] Referendum Council (n 147) (Darwin).

[150] Referendum Council (n 15) (Ross River).

[151] L Emerson, 'Diné Sovereign Action: Rejecting Colonial Sovereignty and Invoking Diné Peacemaking' in L Lee (ed), *Navajo Sovereignty: Understandings and Visions of the Diné People* (Tucson, University of Arizona Press, 2017) 160, 165.

[152] M Mansell, *Treaty and Statehood: Aboriginal Self-Determination* (Annandale, Federation Press, 2016) 141.

[153] Victorian Treaty Advancement Commission, 'Treaty Statewide Gathering' (Melbourne Cricket Ground, 25 September 2018) 3. See further J Webber, 'Beyond Regret: Mabo's Implications for Australian Constitutionalism' in D Ivison, P Patton and W Sanders (eds), *Political Theory and the Rights of Indigenous Peoples* (Cambridge, Cambridge University Press, 2000) 60, 66.

Assessing the congruence of norms and values between an institution and its constituents can be approached in several ways. One method is to identify the extent to which Indigenous leaders, people and communities were involved in choices around the design of the body prior to its establishment.[154] Was consultation undertaken and, if so, what did it look like? Was it conducted in a respectful manner? Did Indigenous peoples and communities lead the debate, or were their voices limited to proposing minor amendments to an existing proposal? It may be difficult to precisely identify causality here, as it is not always clear why amendments to a proposal were adopted. It may be helpful, therefore, to adopt a different angle: is the institution materially distinct in its structure, powers or legal status from comparable public law bodies? The greater the distinction, the greater the likelihood the state has at least attempted to modify its own understandings of political authority to accommodate Indigenous peoples' values and traditions.

The consequences of failing to accommodate Indigenous values emphasises its importance. An Indigenous body built on the norms of the dominant community will not be accountable to Indigenous peoples and will therefore lack legitimacy. As Keith Smith, a member of the 1973 National Aboriginal Consultative Committee, an early Indigenous representative body in Australia, noted, such an organisation would merely replace 'white oppression with black oppression'.[155]

Institutions are not fixed. Just as values can change, support for, or belief in, an Indigenous institution may rise and fall depending on whether it becomes grounded within the community, irrespective as to the process of its design.[156] Studies in British Columbia suggest that while trust is positively correlated with instances where 'governing institutions reflect local institutions, norms, and values, fostering constituent "buy-in" or legitimacy',[157] trust 'co-evolves with the development of institutions'.[158] By acting in congruence with the political, cultural, and social values of their constituents, members of Indigenous bodies can shape their structure and operation. As this suggests, ownership is related to an institution's capacity to realise outcomes, but it also concerns internal procedures and approaches to decision-making. It understands that while jurisdictional authority is necessary to protect and promote Indigenous interests, the manner in which that authority is exercised is also important. Power and authority must be exercised in a culturally grounded and appropriate way.

[154] UNDRIP (n 1) art 19.

[155] Gilbert (n 66) 192. See further ch 5.

[156] J Anaya, *Indigenous Peoples in International Law* (Oxford, Oxford University Press, 2004) 105–06.

[157] W Nikolakis and H Nelson, 'Trust, Institutions, and Indigenous Self-Governance: An Exploratory Study' (2019) 32 *Governance* 331, 344.

[158] ibid.

The procedural component of ownership is identifiable in an example from Nunavut. Nunavut operates under a public rather than ethnic government. As Inuit people comprise around 85 per cent of the population, however, governance is largely conducted by Inuit people, allowing them to shape its structure, albeit within broader Canadian confines. Legislative and policy development in Nunavut is guided by the concept of Inuit Qaujimajatuqangit (IQ). Emerging from a conference on traditional knowledge held in 1998, aimed at identifying 'processes designed to ensure that Inuit culture, language and values are democratically reflected in the policies, programs, and day-to-day operations of the new Nunavut government',[159] IQ is understood as 'the very foundation' of Nunavut.[160] Translated literally as 'that which has long been known by Inuit',[161] the extent to which IQ has infused Nunavut governance and public administration has, for some, become 'the benchmark against which the success'[162] of Nunavut is judged.

In two cases in 2018, the Nunavut Court of Justice explored how IQ can be meaningfully developed and applied. The Court held that the judiciary must 'strive to incorporate the precepts of IQ into our judgments and practices',[163] and affirmed that 'Inuit norms *must* be considered by the judge when crafting a just and fit sentence'.[164] In *R v Itturiligaq*, Bychok J relied on IQ values of 'forgiveness, reconciliation, reintegration, restitution and understanding', to hold that a federal mandatory minimum penalty imposing a four-year sentence to be served in a federal gaol, thousands of miles from Nunavut, would be grossly disproportionate and thus in violation of the Charter of Rights and Freedoms.[165] As Bychok J explained, such a sentence 'would be considered intolerable by fair minded Nunavummiut'.[166] Challenges certainly exist. It is difficult to identify diffuse and diverse 'Inuit values', let alone articulate and apply them in a modern state bureaucracy. Nonetheless, the prioritisation of IQ reflects the right of the people of Nunavut to have a government they 'can recognise as embodying their values'.[167]

These examples are helpful in articulating how an Indigenous institution may act to ensure congruence with the norms and values of its constituents, but it is still necessary to formulate a way to assess success. For representative

[159] Nunavut Social Development Council, 'A Discussion Paper: Towards an Inuit Qaujimajatuqangit (IQ) Policy for Nunavut' (1998) 5.

[160] ibid 1.

[161] Pikialasorsuaq Commission, 'Inuit Knowledge' Inuit Circumpolar Council, available at www.pikialasorsuaq.org/en/Inuit-knowledge.

[162] Henderson, *Nunavut* (2007) 190.

[163] *R v Anugaa* [2018] NUCJ 2, [42].

[164] *R v Itturiligaq* [2018] NUCJ 31, [108] (emphasis in original).

[165] ibid [106], [113]–[114].

[166] ibid [124]. Nunavummiut is an Inuktitut word for 'the people inhabiting the territory of Nunavut'.

[167] G Dacks, 'Nunavut: Aboriginal Self-Determination through Public Government', Report prepared for the Royal Commission on Aboriginal Peoples (1993) 36.

bodies, success may be assessed through electoral turnout and nomination for office. Voter turnout is the 'most common and important act of political participation in any democracy'[168] and is often identified as a 'powerful symbol[] of … democratic legitimacy'.[169] As such, political scientists have sought to identify causal relationships between turnout, legitimacy and trust in political institutions. Despite difficulty in accounting for multiple variables, it is generally accepted that at the macro level, trust in democratic institutions and representatives increases the probability of voting.[170] Consequently, increased voter support and increased candidature nomination over time may indicate a growing acceptance of the institution. Conversely, low turnout and nomination may suggest that the body is not regarded as legitimate, either because its members fail to act in a culturally appropriate manner or, perhaps, in protest against its limited authority or effectiveness. If the latter, the solution will involve imbuing the body with real power and establishing new institutional mechanisms to exert that authority. This needs to be assessed with caution, however; these assessment tools are intended to be suggestive rather than definitive and different case studies will lend themselves to different approaches. In organisations or institutions not constituted through elections, alternative approaches to measuring the active support[171] among Indigenous peoples must be developed.

V. INTEGRITY

(4) Indigenous leaders must act according to the purposes and values for which they have been entrusted with authority, and must be accountable for their actions

The final criterion is concerned with notions of accountability, responsibility and organisational or corporate governance. This condition is not always expressly articulated in the aspirations of Indigenous peoples discussed in chapter three, but remains an underlying element embedded within those values.[172] Integrity is a familiar concept to Indigenous communities across the globe. Anishinaabe/Ojibway scholar John Borrows likens it to 'Aboriginal concepts of stewardship', the essence of which, he explains, 'is the assumption of responsibility for something given'.[173] As Borrows demonstrates, notions of trust and accountability

[168] J Aldrich, 'Rational Choice and Turnout' (1993) 37 *American Journal of Political Science* 246, 246.

[169] R Topf, 'Electoral Participation' in H-D Klingemann and D Fuchs (eds), *Citizens and the State: Beliefs in Government* (Oxford, Oxford University Press, 1995) 27, 27.

[170] K Gronlund and M Setala, 'Political Trust, Satisfaction and Voter Turnout' (2007) 5 *Comparative European Politics* 400, 416.

[171] Beetham (n 128) 18.

[172] See for example Independent Working Group on Constitutional Transformation (n 29) 92–93.

[173] J Borrows, 'Stewardship and the First Nations Governance Act' (2003) 29 *Queen's Law Journal* 103, 103–04.

are present in First Nations legal traditions across North America. The Carrier people of central British Columbia, for instance, appoint witnesses to endorse and confirm legal dealings.[174] By memorising transactions, clan members entrusted with this responsibility can be called upon to verify terms at ceremonial feasts, where formal business is conducted.[175]

Stewardship extends further. As chapter three noted, in many Indigenous nations, the assumption of leadership expressly encompasses responsibilities to act in and for the interests of the community. Failure to exercise these duties carries consequences.[176] For example, in 1989 the Navajo Nation Tribal Court considered whether the Tribal Council had the authority to place its chairperson on administrative leave after discovering that he had received 'secret bribes and kickbacks'[177] from contractors doing business with the nation. In finding for the Council, the Court drew on creation stories that embodied the 'Navajo traditional concept of fiduciary trust of a leader (*naat'aanii*)'. The Court explained that:

> A naat'aanii was chosen based on his ability to help the people survive and whatever authority he had was based upon that ability and the trust placed in him by the people. If naat'aanii lost the trust of his people, the people simply cease to follow him or even listen to his words … The Navajo Tribal Council can place a Chairman or Vice Chairman on administrative leave if they have reasonable grounds to believe that the official seriously breached his fiduciary trust to the Navajo people.[178]

Similar accounts exist among Indigenous communities in Australia. In Yolŋu society, instead of a 'head', a leader is described as a 'nose' (*ngurru*), implying 'a view of a leader as someone who carries others behind him'.[179] Likewise, among the Pintupi, a leader is someone who 'will look after (*kanyilku*) … people and country'.[180] As Wiradjuri politician Linda Burney explains, in Indigenous societies 'leadership is earned; it is given when you have proven you can deal with responsibility and you understand that responsibility'.[181]

[174] J Borrows, *Canada's Indigenous Constitution* (Toronto, University of Toronto Press, 2010) 96.

[175] A Mills, *Eagle Down is Our Law: Witsuwit'en Law, Feasts, and Land Claims* (Vancouver, University of British Columbia Press, 2014) 38.

[176] Borrows, 'Stewardship' (2003) 110.

[177] *Navajo Nation v Peter MacDonald Sr et al*, 885 P. 2d 1104, 180 Ariz 539, 542 (Ariz Ct App, 1994). See also Austin, *Navajo Court and Navajo Common Law* (2009) 95.

[178] *Re Certified Question II: Navajo Nation v MacDonald* (1989) *Indian Law Reporter* 6086 (Navajo Supreme Court), edited version A-CR-13-89, slip op at 24–25 (1989). Cited in J Borrows, *Recovering Canada: The Resurgence of Indigenous Law* (Toronto, University of Toronto Press, 2002) 13–14.

[179] F Morphy, 'Whose Governance, for Whose Good? The Laynhapuy Homelands Association and the Neo-Assimilationist Turn in Indigenous Policy' in J Hunt, D Smith, S Garling and W Sanders (eds), *Contested Governance* (Canberra, ANU Press, 2008) 113, 128.

[180] F Myers, *Pintupi Country, Pintupi Self: Sentiment, Place, and Politics Among Western Desert Aborigines* (Berkeley, University of California Press, 1991) 222–23.

[181] Linda Burney, in Office of the Director of Equal Opportunity in Public Employment, *Yarnin' Up: Aboriginal People's Careers in the NSW Public Sector* (Sydney, Office of the Director of Equal Opportunity in Public Employment, 2001) 5, 6.

Western accounts also centre on notions of stewardship and responsibility. In its 'simplest form', integrity 'refers to the absence of corruption, in the sense of using public powers for personal advantage or taking bribes',[182] but it conveys something more than this, including the notion of ensuring that public power is exercised in a 'healthy' manner.[183] In a comprehensive examination of 'the integrity function' in public law institutions, Lisa Burton and George Williams distil its key elements in an effort to concretise this 'amorphous, complex and value-laden concept'.[184] They argue that 'integrity' requires that public power be exercised lawfully, for the purposes for which it was conferred, and with fidelity to public values, such as fairness. Integrity further requires that all exercises of public power be justified to internal and external supervisory mechanisms when called to account, introducing an additional requirement of transparency, because 'public power cannot be scrutinised unless there is evidence about how and why it was used'.[185] Burton and Williams suggest further that a law reform component may be necessary to scrutinise legislation that confers public power,[186] to ensure that identified governance challenges are ironed out. Intriguingly, integrity as law reform suggests that western accounts do not differ substantially from Indigenous conceptions; integrity is a process rather than an event, it is conditional and must be assessed and reassessed.

Reflecting on Indigenous and western accounts of integrity helps to elucidate its key features. To satisfy this condition, an Indigenous institution must have in place a credible governance structure whereby corruption and mismanagement is constrained, decision-making processes are transparent, and representatives are accountable for their decisions internally to their community and externally to the public at large.[187] In other words, members of the body must act 'in an upright and reliable manner … true to the values, purposes and duties for which they have been entrusted with that power',[188] 'exercise wise judgments for the well-being of their lands, clans people, and future generations',[189] and

[182] L Burton and G Williams, 'The Integrity Function and ASIO's Extraordinary Questioning and Detention Powers' (2012) 38 *Monash University Law Review* 1, 24.

[183] J Spigelman, 'The Integrity Branch of Government' (2004) 78 *Australian Law Journal* 724, 724.

[184] AJ Brown, 'Putting Administrative Law Back into Integrity and Putting Integrity Back into Administrative Law' (2007) 53 *AIAL Forum* 32, 51.

[185] Burton and Williams, 'The Integrity Function' (2012) 24–26.

[186] ibid 28.

[187] N Sterritt 'Defining Indigenous Governance' (paper presented to the Building Effective Indigenous Governance Conference, Jabiru, 4–7 November 2003) cited in D Smith, 'Researching Australian Indigenous Governance: A Methodological and Conceptual Framework' (Centre for Aboriginal Economic Policy Research Working Paper No 29, 2005) 9.

[188] AJ Brown, 'What is a National Integrity System? From Temple Blueprint to Hip-Pocket Guide' in B Head, AJ Brown and C Connors (eds), *Promoting Integrity: Evaluating and Improving Public Institutions* (Farnham, Ashgate, 2008) 33, 33.

[189] J-A Fiske and B Patrick, *Cis Dideen Kat, When the Plumes Rise: The Way of the Lake Babine Nation* (Vancouver, University of British Columbia Press, 2000) 57.

be 'accountable and transparent to Community' as well as 'open and honest'.[190] Integrity is ultimately a question for the individual members charged with carrying out an institution's responsibilities, but internal structures and processes can provide an environment conducive to good governance practices.

Notions of stewardship and integrity may be common to both Indigenous and western normative systems, but the mechanisms through which these concepts are realised may differ. This can cause tensions because Indigenous governance structures are sometimes assumed to conflict with western accountability mechanisms. Aboriginal and Torres Strait Islander people are said to value reciprocity, mutual responsibility and internal mechanisms of accountability while, in contrast, non-Indigenous governments focus on 'upwards accountability, financial management and compliance reporting' to manage western-style institutions.[191] Operating within 'the ambiguous and fraught zone between the two political and cultural systems', Indigenous people may struggle to discharge their obligations to both polities,[192] with kinship obligations, for instance, potentially conflicting with financial compliance requirements.[193] The challenge here is determining whether an Indigenous institution should be subject to the full range of western-style accountability mechanisms. This may count against its independence from government and affect its level of ownership within the community,[194] but may be necessary to ensure the institution operates with integrity and is regarded as credible by government.

Fortunately, this framing presents a false binary and tensions can be resolved. Traditional Indigenous forms of accountability may differ from western approaches, but it is important not to overstate this distinction for there is significant room for 'different traditions and values to be accommodated in the definition of "good governance"'.[195] If good governance is about achieving 'desired results and achieving them in the right way', then the right way 'is largely shaped by the cultural norms and values of the organisation or society'.[196] Good governance is therefore predicated and 'based on each tribe's traditional and contemporary tribal culture'.[197] Indigenous principles of governance may emphasise culturally appropriate norms of internal accountability,

[190] Aboriginal Community Assembly, 'Final Statement and Recommendations to the Aboriginal Treaty Working Group' (December 2017) 11.

[191] D Smith, 'Organising Aboriginal Governance: Pathways to Self-Determination Success in the Northern Territory, Australia' (Final Report to the Aboriginal Governance and Management Program, Aboriginal Peak Organisations of the Northern Territory, March 2015) 14.

[192] D Martin and J Finlayson, 'Linking Accountability and Self-Determination in Aboriginal Organisations' (Centre for Aboriginal Economic Policy Research, Discussion Paper No 116, 1996) 10.

[193] W Sanders, 'Being a Good Senior Manager in Indigenous Community Governance: Working with Public Purpose and Private Benefit' (2008) 67 *Australian Journal of Public Administration* 173.

[194] Alfred, *Peace, Power, Righteousness* (2009) 11; Jones (n 83) 126.

[195] Smith, 'Researching Australian Indigenous Governance' (2005) 11.

[196] ibid. See also Martin and Finlayson 'Accountability and Self-Determination' (1996) 25.

[197] A Riley, 'Good (Native) Governance' (2007) 107 *Columbia Law Review* 1049, 1054–55.

while accepting and accommodating public law principles of external accountability. In fact, evidence suggests that Indigenous organisations with robust culturally appropriate mechanisms of accountability are more likely to satisfy western conceptions of accountability. For instance, case studies undertaken by David Martin and Julie Finlayson in a review of the Aboriginal Councils and Associations Act 1976 (Cth) found that:

> [T]hose organisations which had developed broadly representative structures, and had instituted procedures to maximise equity in service delivery, participation in decision-making, and accountability to their constituencies in achieving their objectives had also achieved at least reasonable fiscal accountability; conversely, those which had deficient or virtually non-existent mechanisms to ensure such principles were more likely to demonstrate poor financial accountability. That is, organisations which are accountable to their members or constituencies are more likely to be effective in what they undertake and more financially accountable.[198]

Reflecting on these findings, Martin and Finlayson argue that public law accountability mechanisms need not conflict with Indigenous self-determination: 'both can be promoted through developing more sophisticated and effective mechanisms to assist these organisations develop better internal accountability'.[199] This was recognised by participants at the Swan Hill community consultation in north-west Victoria, where it was argued that an Indigenous organisation should be 'able to live in two worlds'.[200]

Across Victoria communities were adamant that a credible governance structure was critical for an Indigenous representative body to succeed in carrying Indigenous interests to government. Significantly, participants understood integrity in terms of accountability to two polities. In Ballarat, for example, participants agreed that an Indigenous body should avoid conflicts of interest, enshrine trust and operate with transparency.[201] Transparency was also emphasised in Melbourne, Morwell, Shepparton and Warrnambool as an element imperative to the effectiveness of the body,[202] with effectiveness understood in terms of realising results for the community and retaining credibility with government. These community discussions echo statements articulated by the Aboriginal and Torres Strait Islander Social Justice Commissioner, who has argued that transparency in an Indigenous institution's policy-making process, as well as its financial decisions and mechanisms for determining representation, would ensure that it receives widespread support from both Indigenous constituents and government.[203] As participants in Swan Hill explained, this requires

198 Martin and Finlayson, 'Accountability and Self-Determination' (1996) 12–13.
199 ibid 23.
200 ATWG 2016 (n 4) 34 (Swan Hill).
201 ibid 44 (Ballarat).
202 ibid 39 (Melbourne), 47 (Morwell), 50 (Shepparton), 54 (Warrnambool).
203 ATSISJC (n 27) 64.

the 'best warriors at the table',[204] those with the requisite 'skills, connections and resources to discharge their responsibilities'.[205] It also requires oversight. For this reason, the Victorian Aboriginal Community Assembly proposed the establishment of an Ethics Council comprised of Elders and young people and entrusted with the responsibility to ensure the representative body 'operates to the highest standards, and adheres to the required standards of cultural accountability'.[206]

There is no single uniform approach to monitoring the exercise of public power.[207] Integrity mechanisms are routinely adapted to specific circumstances. The Australian Security Intelligence Organisation, for example, is subject to a novel supervisory regime consisting of several overlapping and complementary parts because it is recognised that national security issues necessitate a different approach.[208] While the operation of an Indigenous institution raises very different issues and it is entirely legitimate that public power wielded by Indigenous representatives is exercised lawfully and consistently with the purposes for which it was conferred, there is no reason why mechanisms to realise this cannot be adapted to meet the demands of Indigenous peoples.

VI. CONCLUSION

Indigenous peoples articulate their diverse aspirations in varied ways, not all of which are comprehensible to public law or appreciated by constitutional theorists. This can be problematic. If the state is to be restructured in a manner that does justice to Indigenous peoples' claims, it must genuinely hear their voices and understand their demands. Drawing on Indigenous peoples' aspirations explored in chapter three, this chapter has identified four criteria for institutional design in democratic states. The criteria are expressed in a manner legible to public law but remain grounded in and reflective of those aspirations. They are:

(1) Indigenous peoples must be heard when decisions that affect them are being made.
(2) Indigenous peoples must have the authority and financial capacity to exercise independent policy and decision-making power over matters relating to internal or local affairs.

[204] ATWG 2016 (n 4) 34 (Swan Hill).
[205] ibid 13. See also Cape York Institute (n 29) 44.
[206] Aboriginal Community Assembly, 'Final Statement and Recommendations' (2017) 9.
[207] JL Mashaw, 'Accountability and Institutional Design: Some Thoughts on the Grammar of Governance' in MW Dowdle (ed), *Public Accountability: Designs, Dilemmas and Experiences* (Cambridge, Cambridge University Press, 2006) 115, 120–22.
[208] Burton and Williams (n 182).

(3) Institutions or processes that empower Indigenous peoples must be regarded by Indigenous peoples as legitimate.
(4) Indigenous leaders must act according to the purposes and values for which they have been entrusted with authority, and must be accountable for their actions.

Characterised as *voices*, *power*, *ownership*, and *integrity*, the criteria rest on notions of legitimacy and credibility. An institution or process designed to empower Indigenous peoples with the capacity to be heard in the processes of government will not be effective if it is not regarded as legitimate or credible by Indigenous peoples, government and the public at large. An institution that does not articulate the diversity of, or provide institutional opportunities to express, Indigenous voices to government, that does not have any real authority or financial capacity, that is built on non-Indigenous ways of knowing and being, and is not operated with integrity, will fail.

Exploration of these criteria reveals that they are contested, variable and interlinked. At times they may strengthen and reaffirm each other, while at others, they may conflict; an institution might realise them in strong or weak forms. Indigenous peoples and communities will need to particularise their own unique aspirations and consider their own distinct position before determining the elements they should prioritise in their struggle. Bearing this in mind, the next two chapters will explore challenges in realising these principles in real world institutions. Recognising that the Uluru Statement from the Heart revealed widespread support for a First Nations Voice among Indigenous peoples across Australia, chapters five and six will assess two Indigenous representative bodies: ATSIC; and the Swedish Sámediggi. In doing so, these chapters will highlight the inherent tensions and challenges involved in seeking to design Indigenous institutions embedded within the state generally, and Indigenous representative bodies specifically.

5

The Aboriginal and Torres Strait Islander Commission

I. INTRODUCTION

THE ABORIGINAL AND Torres Strait Islander Commission Act 1989 (Cth) (ATSIC Act) received Royal Assent on 27 November 1989, and the Commission commenced operation the following March. The explicit rationale for its establishment was the policy of self-determination. Gerry Hand, the Minister for Aboriginal Affairs, announced that the Aboriginal and Torres Strait Islander Commission (ATSIC) was intended to give Indigenous Australians 'a real say in the management of their own affairs', and 'a real say in the decision-making process'.[1] ATSIC was 'an acknowledgement by all of us that it is no longer acceptable for governments to dictate what is best for the Aboriginal and Torres Strait Islander people; they should decide for themselves what needs to be done'.[2] Through the Commission, elected Indigenous representatives exercised substantial authority; they could identify local funding priorities, formulate and implement regional plans, make decisions over public expenditure, protect cultural material and information, and speak directly to government.

The Government viewed self-determination in a positive light, but this language was seized upon by opponents who saw the Commission as a threat to their own understanding of Australian identity. During debate on the ATSIC Bill in 1989, Opposition Leader John Howard condemned the concept as 'a monumental disservice to the Australian community' which 'strikes at the heart of the unity of the Australian people'.[3] Other members of the Opposition adopted similar attacks, criticising the proposed body as an 'unjustified, unnecessary'[4]

[1] Commonwealth, *Parliamentary Debates*, House of Representatives, 4 May 1989, 1994 (Gerry Hand).

[2] Commonwealth, *Parliamentary Debates*, House of Representatives, 24 August 1988, 251–52 (Gerry Hand).

[3] Commonwealth, *Parliamentary Debates*, House of Representatives, 11 April 1989, 1328 (John Howard).

[4] Senate Select Committee on the Administration of Aboriginal Affairs, Parliament of Australia, Administration of Aboriginal Affairs (1989) 'Dissenting Report by Senator Baume and Senator Boswell' 2.

'philosophically repugnant'[5] 'black parliament',[6] which 'smacks of separatism of the worst possible kind in a nation'.[7] These critiques periodically reappeared in debate over ATSIC throughout its life and ultimately served as a justification for its abolition in 2005. In announcing that decision, Prime Minister John Howard declared that 'the experiment in separate representation, elected representation, for Indigenous people has been a failure'.[8] ATSIC was replaced by the National Indigenous Council (NIC), a government-appointed advisory body, and funding returned to mainstream departments.

The abolition of ATSIC has had permanent consequences. Megan Davis (Cobble Cobble) argues that it has 'eviscerated' self-determination 'from the lexicon of Australian politicians, policymakers ... journalists and political commentators',[9] stymieing the contemporary development of an institution that empowers Aboriginal and Torres Strait Islander peoples with the capacity to have their voices heard in the processes of government. Noel Pearson (Guugu Yimithirr) laments that the spectre of ATSIC still haunts discussion of Indigenous issues; 'conjur[ing] up all that is bad and hopeless about Indigenous affairs and Indigenous people'.[10] In response to the Aboriginal and Torres Strait Islander Social Justice Commissioner's 2008 Issues Paper on a new national Indigenous representative body, for instance, Jenny Macklin, the Labor Minister for Indigenous Affairs, calmed nerves by explaining that the Government had no intention of creating 'another ATSIC'.[11] Eight years later, in the middle of a debate on constitutional reform, Nigel Scullion, the Country Liberal Indigenous Affairs Minister echoed these comments, declaring that ATSIC was gone for good.[12] These attitudes are unfortunate. Despite unwillingness among the political class for the creation of 'another ATSIC', there has been 'virtually no interrogation of whether ATSIC, in the minds of Indigenous Australians, was self-determination', or whether it 'actually failed'.[13]

This is problematic for two reasons. First, the Referendum Council's regional dialogues found that ATSIC retains currency within Indigenous communities

[5] Commonwealth, *Parliamentary Debates*, House of Representatives, 23 May 1989, 2719 (Warwick Smith, Shadow Minister for Aboriginal Affairs).

[6] Commonwealth, *Parliamentary Debates*, Senate, 18 August 1989, 395 (Jim Short); 30 August 1989, 641 (Florence Bjelke-Petersen); House of Representatives, 11 April 1989, 1341 (Chris Miles, Shadow Minister for Aboriginal Affairs) (a 'black power parliament'); 23 May 1989, 2727–28 (Michael Cobb).

[7] Commonwealth, *Parliamentary Debates*, Senate, 17 October 1989, 2014 (Jim Short).

[8] ABC Radio National, 'Fed Govt Plans to Abolish ATSIC' *PM*, 15 April 2004 (John Howard).

[9] M Davis, 'Aboriginal Women: The Right to Self-Determination' (2012) 16 *Australian Indigenous Law Review* 78, 78.

[10] N Pearson, 'Remote Control: Ten Years of Struggle and Success in Indigenous Australia' *The Monthly* (No 111, May 2015) 28, 30.

[11] FaHCSIA National Representative Body Unit, 'Report on the Outcomes of the First Phase of Consultation for a National Indigenous Representative Body (NIRB)' (December 2008) 2.

[12] R Lewis, 'ATSIC is Gone for Good, Nigel Scullion tells Noel Pearson' *The Australian* (29 January 2016).

[13] M Davis, 'Listening but not Hearing: When Process Trumps Substance' (2016) 51 *Griffith Review* 73, 75.

as an effective instrument of self-determination,[14] and the proposed constitutionally enshrined First Nations Voice mirrors the Commission in important respects. Second, there have been significant events since 2005, including Australia's endorsement of the United Nations Declaration on the Rights of Indigenous Peoples (UNDRIP). Although not legally binding, the UNDRIP signals momentous developments in Indigenous rights and global democratic standards. In affirming a pluralised account of the state where sovereignties are dispersed among multiple polities,[15] the Declaration extends and develops understandings of self-determination.

Contemporary debate on political and legal institutions to empower Aboriginal and Torres Strait Islander peoples with the capacity to have their voices heard in the processes of government should engage with best practices gleaned from former institutions and evolving understanding of self-determination, even if the legal and policy architecture within which those institutions operated has shifted. This chapter assists that debate by assessing whether ATSIC satisfied the criteria articulated in chapter four – *voices*, *power*, *ownership* and *integrity*.

The chapter is divided into three substantive parts. I first situate the analysis by setting out early institutional attempts at hearing 'the Aboriginal voice',[16] which informed ATSIC's design. I then measure the Commission against the four criteria. I ask whether ATSIC empowered Indigenous Australians with the: (1) capacity to be heard in decisions that affect them; and (2) authority and financial capacity to exercise independent policy and decision-making power over matters relating to internal or local affairs. I also examine whether: (3) Indigenous Australians recognised the Commission as legitimate; and (4) the Commission's leaders acted according to the purposes and values for which they had been entrusted with authority and were accountable for their actions. Drawing on this analysis, I reflect on the reasons for ATSIC's abolition. Recognising the significant political and legal changes that have occurred since 1989, I conclude by offering several observations for future institutional design. These observations are taken up and explored further in chapter seven.

II. THE COMMISSION IN CONTEXT

The Australian Constitution divides responsibilities between the several states and the Federal Government, with the powers of the Commonwealth Parliament

[14] See, eg: Referendum Council, 'Structural Reform Will Improve State and Commonwealth Decision Making' (media release, 10 April 2017).

[15] W Kymlicka, 'Beyond the Indigenous/Minority Dichotomy?' in S Allen and A Xanthaki (eds), *Reflections on the UN Declaration on the Rights of Indigenous Peoples* (Oxford, Hart Publishing, 2011) 183, 190.

[16] Commonwealth, *Parliamentary Debates*, House of Representatives, 24 November 1978, 3449 (Ian Viner, Minister for Aboriginal Affairs).

enumerated in ss 51 and 52. As initially drafted, s 51(xxvi), empowered the Parliament to make laws with respect to 'the people of any race, other than the aboriginal race, for whom it is deemed necessary to make special laws', leaving responsibility for Indigenous affairs entirely in the hands of the states. The clause excluding Indigenous peoples from the Commonwealth's domain was not cause for any debate during the Constitution's drafting.[17] Indigenous peoples were viewed as the concern of the colonies and attention was focused on whether, like the states, the Commonwealth should be permitted to discriminate on the basis of race. Consequently, the Federal Government's only involvement in Indigenous affairs was in the Northern Territory and the Australian Capital Territory. This changed in 1967, when the Australian public voted in a referendum to amend the Constitution. The amendments altered s 127 to include Aboriginal Australians in determinations of population, and s 51(xxvi) to empower the Federal Parliament to legislate specifically for Aboriginal and Torres Strait Islander peoples.[18]

Since 1967, successive Australian governments have created institutions, established forums, or designed processes to enable the state to consult with and seek advice from Aboriginal and Torres Strait Islander peoples. Such mechanisms have not always been well designed, and the advice proffered has not always been well received. As I argue, early national Indigenous advisory bodies largely failed because they were intended merely to incorporate Indigenous Australians into the processes of government without meaningfully restructuring the framework of governance. Rather than incipient mechanisms of Indigenous political control, the state conceived these institutions as means to legitimate decision-making in Indigenous affairs. Exploring this troubled history places the Commission in its socio-political and historical context, revealing why its creation was lauded as 'a radical and timely change in the administration of Aboriginal affairs in this country'.[19] Understanding ATSIC's legal architecture uncovers a more mixed evaluation.

A. Early National Indigenous Affairs Advisory Bodies

Prime Minister Harold Holt established the first body to advise the Federal Government on Indigenous affairs in September 1967. The Council of Aboriginal Affairs (CAA) consisted of three non-Indigenous men; Governor of the Reserve Bank of Australia, Dr HC 'Nugget' Coombs, anthropologist Bill Stanner, and

[17] H Hobbs and G Williams, 'Treaty-Making in the Australian Federation' (2019) 43 *Melbourne University Law Review* 178, 202.

[18] Constitution Alteration (Aboriginals) 1967.

[19] Commonwealth, *Parliamentary Debates*, House of Representatives, 24 August 1988, 251 (Gerry Hand).

head of the accompanying Office of Aboriginal Affairs (OAA), Barrie Dexter. The Council was tasked with advising government on 'national policies for the Aboriginal citizens of Australia' and recommending policy coordination between the states and Commonwealth.[20] It was served by the OAA, located within the Prime Minister's department and responsible for implementing policy, administering legislation and facilitating liaison. The OAA was small. While it employed four Aboriginal people, it consisted of only seven staff in total in 1968.[21] Consequently, the Department of Territories (renamed the Department of the Interior in 1969) retained a principal role in policy formulation and advice.[22] Indigenous involvement was minor, and buttressed against the department's anti-Indigenous views.[23] Nonetheless, the CAA consulted extensively with Indigenous communities, encouraged Aboriginal leadership and decision-making, and supported the protection of Indigenous cultural heritage.[24]

Prime Minister Holt's death in December 1967 proved consequential for the Council as his successors, John Gorton and Billy McMahon, were less receptive to Indigenous aspirations.[25] In 1968, Prime Minister Gorton appointed Bill Wentworth Minister in Charge of Aboriginal Affairs. This meant that CAA proposals had to be presented to Cabinet via Wentworth (rather than through the Prime Minister), diluting the Council's potential influence.[26] Compounding this challenge, the Council was never placed on a firm statutory footing and nor were its responsibilities ever set down in a formal charter or letter of instruction. Although an inchoate legal grounding permitted Council members to operate with wide latitude, it also left them operating in 'a sort of twilight existence',[27] with their role and authority uncertain. As a result, Coombs considered that the Council was largely unsuccessful in persuading successive governments to accept 'the right of Aborigines to choose the nature and extent of their involvement in Australian society',[28] or to provide the 'power and resources to make that choice

[20] Commonwealth, *Parliamentary Debates*, House of Representatives, 2 November 1967, 2625 (Harold Holt); LR Hiatt, 'Australian Committee of Inquiry into the Role of the National Aboriginal Consultative Committee' (Australian Government Publishing Service, 1976) 10; T Rowse, *Obliged to be Difficult: Nugget Coombs' Legacy in Indigenous Affairs* (Cambridge, Cambridge University Press, 2000) 30.

[21] National Aboriginal Conference, *Establishment, Role and Functions* (1983) 6; P Read, *Charles Perkins: A Biography* (Melbourne, Viking, 1990) 126.

[22] Commonwealth, *Parliamentary Debates*, House of Representatives, 7 September 1967, 974 (Harold Holt).

[23] B Dexter, *Pandora's Box: The Council for Aboriginal Affairs 1967–1976* (Brisbane, Keeaira Press, 2015) 175–76; C Perkins, *A Bastard Like Me* (Sydney, Ure Smith, 1975) 158.

[24] Read, *Charles Perkins* (1990) 143.

[25] I Hancock, *John Gorton: He Did it His Way* (Sydney, Hachette Australia, 2011) 181; Read (n 21) 126–27; Dexter, *Pandora's Box* (2015) 15–17, 28.

[26] Rowse, *Obliged to be Difficult* (2000) 53.

[27] Bill Stanner cited in B Dexter, 'Stanner: Reluctant Bureaucrat' in M Hinkson and J Beckett (eds), *An Appreciation of Difference: WEH Stanner and Aboriginal Australia* (Canberra, Aboriginal Studies Press, 2008) 76, 82.

[28] HC Coombs, *Aboriginal Autonomy: Issues and Strategies* (Cambridge, Cambridge University Press, 1994) 172.

a reality'.[29] In any case, notwithstanding the CAA's efforts, Indigenous peoples had no formal role in developing or delivering policy advice to the Liberal–Country Coalition Government from 1967 to 1972.

Government policy shifted considerably with the election of the Gough Whitlam Labor Government in 1972. The new Government established a Commonwealth Department of Aboriginal Affairs (DAA), headed by Dexter, which took over the functions of the OAA and Indigenous affairs within the Department of the Interior, advising government, as well as implementing and administering Indigenous policy.[30] Significantly, the DAA recruited and appointed Indigenous staff, giving Aboriginal and Torres Strait Islander people a nominal role in the administration of their own affairs.[31] This shift was positive, but recruitment was slow; Coombs' 1976 Royal Commission into Australian Government Administration found that 'a substantially higher proportion of Aboriginals' would need to be employed 'at all levels of work and responsibility' in order to satisfy 'legitimate Aboriginal aspirations'.[32]

The decision to increase recruitment of Indigenous staff within the public service reflected a marked shift in Indigenous policy-making from assimilation and integration to 'self-determination'. Whitlam and Jim Cavanagh, the Minister for Aboriginal Affairs, explained that self-determination would allow Indigenous people to 'take a real and effective responsibility for their own [economic, social and political] affairs',[33] satisfying their 'most important objective' of 'restor[ing] to Aboriginals the power to make their own decisions about their way of life'.[34] Although Whitlam lost office in 1975, this principle remained central to Indigenous policy-making until the election of the Howard Government in 1996.[35] As such, between 1972 and 1996, successive governments 'participated in the process of building the institutions and agencies of self-determination'.[36] This included enactment of statutory land rights regimes recognising varying levels of title to traditional owners across the country;[37] encouraging the widespread

[29] HC Coombs and CJ Robinson, 'Remembering the Roots: Lessons for ATSIC' in P Sullivan (ed), *Shooting the Banker: Essays on ATSIC and Self-Determination* (Darwin, North Australian Research Unit, 1996) 1, 6.

[30] Commonwealth, *Administrative Arrangements* No 131, 20 December 1972, 2.

[31] Coombs, *Aboriginal Autonomy* (1994) 138. The DAA also recruited staff from the Department of the Interior and the Northern Territory Welfare Branch: Read (n 21) 151.

[32] Commonwealth, Royal Commission on Australian Government Administration, 'Report' (1976) 342.

[33] J Cavanagh, 'Review of Aboriginal Progress' (5 December 1973) in *Selected Policy Statements on Aboriginal Affairs 1973–1974* (Canberra, Australian Government Publishing Service, 1974) 4.

[34] G Whitlam, 'Speech by the Prime Minister at the Opening of the National Seminar on Aboriginal Arts', 21 May 1973.

[35] The Fraser Government preferred the term 'self-management': N Peterson and W Sanders, 'Introduction' in N Peterson and W Sanders (eds), *Citizenship and Indigenous Australians: Changing Conceptions and Possibilities* (Cambridge, Cambridge University Press, 1998) 1, 20.

[36] V Watson, 'Axing ATSIC: Australian Liberalism and the "Government of Unfreedom"' (2005) 23 *Policy and Society* 57, 64–66.

[37] See, eg: Aboriginal Land Rights (Northern Territory) Act 1976 (Cth); Native Title Act 1993 (Cth).

incorporation of Indigenous community organisations funded to deliver their own services,[38] providing a 'carapace'[39] within which communities could develop culturally appropriate mechanisms of self-government; and the passage of the Racial Discrimination Act 1975 (Cth). Successive governments also experimented with nationally representative Indigenous bodies, designed to develop and channel policy advice to government.

In 1973, the Whitlam Government established the National Aboriginal Consultative Committee (NACC) by ministerial directive. Composed of 41 delegates directly elected from an Indigenous-specific electoral roll, paid an annual salary and allowance, the NACC was designed as 'a forum for the expression of Aboriginal opinion' as well as a mechanism 'to allow a healthy *two-way* communication between Aboriginals and the national government'.[40] Praised by non-Indigenous Australians as a 'bold, black experiment',[41] the 'most unusual'[42] nationally representative body gave Aboriginal and Torres Strait Islander peoples 'their own national voice – for the first time'.[43] Consisting of representatives chosen by Indigenous peoples themselves, the NACC was a step forward from the CAA, which it effectively replaced. Presciently, however, contemporaneous Indigenous activists were less fulsome in their praise. Reflecting on the structure of the NACC, Kevin Gilbert (Wiradjuri) lamented that 'everything will be done according to the white man's values, definitions, structures and (ultimately) interests',[44] while Aboriginal activists Ossie Cruse and Keith Smith identified 'a big vacuum in between [the national structure] and the grassroots people',[45] which would mean 'so-called' Aboriginal leaders would not consult with their people.[46]

The vacuum between Aboriginal communities and the national structure proved challenging for the NACC in articulating Indigenous views to government, but its real problem lay in its struggle to define its role. As Len Hiatt's 1976 Report identified, the crux of the difficulty was a disjuncture between Indigenous aspirations and government expectations. The NACC pushed for executive rather than advisory powers. It voted to rename itself the National Aboriginal Congress, sought policy-making power and control over the DAA

[38] Aboriginal Councils and Associations Act 1976 (Cth); J Altman, 'Practical Reconciliation and the New Mainstreaming: Will it Make a Difference to Indigenous Australians?' (2004) 23 *Dialogue* 35, 36; Coombs (n 28) 136–138, 172–75.

[39] C Rowley, *The Remote Aborigines: Aboriginal Policy and Practice – Volume III* (Canberra, ANU Press, 1971) 13, 189.

[40] G Whitlam, 'Elections of the National Aboriginal Consultative Committee (23 November 1973) 2 (emphasis in original).

[41] T Hill, 'A Bold, Black Experiment' *The Herald* (1 April 1974).

[42] H Prizell, 'Aborigines get a Foot in Canberra's Door' *Sydney Morning Herald* (24 November 1973).

[43] M Grattan, 'A Parliament for Blacks' *The Age* (Melbourne, 12 September 1973).

[44] K Gilbert, *Because a White Man'll Never Do It* (Sydney, Angus and Robertson, 1973) 209.

[45] K Gilbert, *Living Black: Blacks Talk to Kevin Gilbert* (Sydney, Penguin Press, 1977) 60.

[46] ibid 188–89.

budget, and consistently revealed a willingness to criticise government. Although the government equivocated, its actions demonstrated that it preferred a more compliant organisation,[47] refusing to tolerate what it perceived as 'radicals'. In its submission to the 1976 Hiatt Inquiry, the DAA condemned the 'hostile attitudes' adopted by members of the NACC, dismissively noting that it did not encourage the Minister or the Department 'to be forthcoming in responses to NACC requests, demands or advice'.[48] The breakdown of the relationship between the NACC and government ensured that it was not effective.[49] In 1977, the Malcolm Fraser-led Liberal-Country Coalition Government replaced it with a new body: The National Aboriginal Conference (NAC).

The NAC initially consisted of 35 (increased to 36 in 1980) members elected from an Indigenous-specific roll, meeting annually at a national level, and at least twice a year at their state or territory level. This two-tier arrangement reflected the challenges faced by its predecessor and was designed to more effectively 'analyse, interpret and articulate the felt needs and views of Aboriginal people' as well as 'interpret' and communicate government policy to their constituents.[50] In 1978, the Conference became the first Aboriginal body to be incorporated under the Aboriginal Councils and Associations Act 1976–78 (Cth),[51] providing it with a firmer structural basis than both the CAA and NACC. There was, however, no statutory provision establishing a communications channel with the Minister. Instead, a separate body, the Council for Aboriginal Development (CAD), would provide formal advice to government. The NAC would nominate five members to the CAD, with the Minister for Aboriginal Affairs nominating five others. All members would be Indigenous.[52] In 1980, the CAD was replaced by the Aboriginal Development Commission (ADC). The ADC retained the CAD's advisory functions but was also empowered to 'further the economic and social development of Aboriginals' by, inter alia, assisting with the acquisition of land, business enterprises, and finance for housing.[53]

The differentiation of roles between the NAC and the CAD/ADC was designed to make clear to Indigenous representatives that the new elected body was not an 'Aboriginal parliament'. Ian Viner, the Minister for Indigenous Affairs, explained that this mistaken belief contributed to the failure of the NACC to provide 'constructive advice' to government, and it was not the Government's intention to 'set up a quasi-parliamentary body outside the constitutional parliamentary system'. Rather, the NAC was to be 'a non-legislative forum in

[47] Hiatt, 'National Aboriginal Consultative Committee' (1976) 23–26, 34–36, 45.

[48] ibid 34.

[49] ibid 45. See also S Weaver, 'Australian Aboriginal Policy: Aboriginal Pressure Groups or Government Advisory Bodies? Part I' (1983) 54 *Oceania* 1, 7–8.

[50] National Aboriginal Conference (n 21) 12.

[51] ibid 5.

[52] Charter of the National Aboriginal Conference (1977) arts 2, 8–9.

[53] Aboriginal Development Commission Act 1980 (Cth) s 8. On the ADC see Read (n 21) 213–16.

which elected members will be free to debate and express, among other things, an Australia-wide Aboriginal view on long-term goals which the Government should pursue, programs which it should adopt and priorities for expenditure'.[54] The Minister for Aboriginal Affairs could ignore recommendations from the CAD, though Viner personally committed to providing written reasons for such a decision.[55]

The NAC was heavily involved in national debates during its existence. Its advocacy for a treaty between Indigenous Australians and the state, in particular, catalysed a 'new impetus for discussions of sovereignty',[56] propelling its members onto the national stage. Unfortunately, however, the NAC also ultimately proved unsuccessful as a mechanism of empowerment. Coombs' 1984 Review found that it failed to meaningfully bring about significant changes in government policy,[57] and identified 'almost unanimous agreement' among Aboriginal peoples that 'the NAC … is ineffective as an instrument of Aboriginal political influence or action';[58] it delivered no services, administered no programmes, and provided no funding.[59] Compounding frustration over the absence of executive responsibilities was the 'frequent' complaint that NAC members were not accountable to their local communities, failing to effectively present their needs and aspirations or provide information about its work to its constituents.[60] Although the Conference was often roiled by internal tensions, much of the blame for its ineffectiveness lies with government, which provided inadequate funding and did not meaningfully engage.[61] Shortfalls prevented representatives from satisfying their responsibilities, making it difficult to travel throughout their electorates and identify and articulate their communities' concerns, as well as to hire secretariat staff and lawyers to advocate for the interests of their constituents across all forums.[62] As Scott Bennett surmises, the NAC was designed 'to enhance the government's image' rather than give 'Aborigines a significant role in their own affairs'.[63] The Bob Hawke Labor Government wound it up in 1985.

[54] Commonwealth, *Parliamentary Debates*, House of Representatives, 30 May 1977, 2108 (Ian Viner).

[55] 'Statement on Council for Aboriginal Development' in *Charter of the National Aboriginal Conference* (1977) 7.

[56] J Fenley, 'The National Aboriginal Conference and the Makarrata: Sovereignty and Treaty Discussions, 1979–1981' (2011) 42 *Australian Historical Studies* 372, 372.

[57] HC Coombs, 'The Role of the National Aboriginal Conference' (Australian Government Publishing Service, 1984) 16.

[58] ibid 11.

[59] ibid 16.

[60] ibid 11. See also Coombs (n 28) 134.

[61] Q Beresford, *Rob Riley: An Aboriginal Leader's Quest for Justice* (Canberra, Aboriginal Studies Press, 2006) ch 7; S Weaver, 'Australian Aboriginal Policy: Aboriginal Pressure Groups or Government Advisory Bodies? Part II' (1983) 54 *Oceania* 85, 93, 105.

[62] Beresford, *Rob Riley* (2006) 176.

[63] S Bennett, *White Politics and Black Australians* (Crows Nest, Allen & Unwin, 1999) 94.

The NACC and NAC were a considerable step forward from the CAA. Despite their promise, however, these two government-sponsored Indigenous representative structures fell well short of empowering Aboriginal and Torres Strait Islander peoples with the capacity to have their voices heard in the processes of government. Structural failings, inadequate funding, and the challenges of mediating competing demands of constituents and government led to criticism that they failed to provide adequate representation or accountability to the communities they served. Heightening these difficulties, neither representative body was granted executive decision-making power or administrative responsibilities; instead, they were designed merely to channel information to government and advise on policy matters. Both were abolished when they sought greater authority.

B. ATSIC's Genesis and Structure

The NAC may have largely been ineffective, but its abolition left no national representative Indigenous advisory body. In 1986, the Hawke Government commissioned Lois O'Donoghue (Yunkunytjatjara) to consult with Indigenous organisations and communities and advise 'whether Aboriginal people wanted a replacement organisation'.[64] O'Donoghue undertook discussions at 65 locations across Australia, and found 'a very strong desire' for a new consultative body.[65] On 10 December 1987, Hand formally announced the Government's response. Unveiling the proposal for an 'Aboriginal Affairs Commission', Hand released a comprehensive policy statement, 'Foundations for the Future', which outlined the putative body's proposed structure and powers. Accepting that the effectiveness of the proposal 'rests on receiving a positive endorsement from the Aboriginal and Islander community of Australia',[66] Hand committed to an extensive consultation process.

Consultation was widespread, and the proposal received considerable engagement. In introducing the Bill into Parliament in May 1989, Hand declared that it had been subject to the 'most extensive' consultation undertaken on a single piece of legislation in recent history.[67] Over 21,000 copies of 'Foundations for the Future' had been distributed to 1,000 Indigenous communities and organisations, and the minister himself held 537 preliminary meetings involving 14,500 people to discuss the proposal. Hand continued:

> Between 23 January and 10 March of this year, I personally visited and spoke with some 6,000 Aboriginal and Torres Strait Islander representatives at 46 separate meetings. Subsequently, an options paper was prepared which identified a range of

[64] L O'Donoghue, *An Aboriginal and Islander Consultative Organisation* (Department of Aboriginal Affairs, 1986) 1.

[65] ibid.

[66] Commonwealth, *Parliamentary Debates*, House of Representatives, 10 December 1987, 3153.

[67] Commonwealth, *Parliamentary Debates*, House of Representatives, 4 May 1989, 1994.

> alternative proposals based on suggestions and recommendations received as a consequence of my consultations with the Aboriginal and Torres Strait Islander people. That paper was widely circulated and was discussed at another 88 meetings involving some 2,700 people.[68]

These consultations led to several changes in the Commission's design. The Bill developed further following successive amendments on the floor of Parliament.[69] The key rationale underlying the proposal, however, largely remained. Reflecting on his 1984 review, Coombs noted that 'only an organisation under Aboriginal control and capable of exercising real power could prove effective' at delivering meaningful change for Indigenous peoples.[70] Acknowledgement of this fact, as well as the struggles faced by previous representative bodies, pushed the Government to strike a different approach in developing ATSIC.

Established as an independent statutory commission rather than by ministerial directive or incorporation ensured ATSIC had clearly defined powers and responsibilities. Its objectives were set out in s 3 of the Act:

(a) to ensure maximum participation of Aboriginal and Torres Strait Islander people in government policy formulation and implementation;
(b) to promote indigenous self-management and self-sufficiency;
(c) to further indigenous economic, social and cultural development; and
(d) to ensure coordination of Commonwealth, state, territory and local government policy affecting indigenous people.

To achieve these objectives, ATSIC had three key roles. It advised governments at all levels on Indigenous issues; advocated for the recognition of Indigenous rights on behalf of Indigenous peoples regionally, nationally and internationally; and, following the abolition of the DAA, delivered and monitored most of the Commonwealth Government's Indigenous programs and services. Two key structural features distinguished the Commission from its predecessors.

i. Representative and Administrative Roles

The NACC and NAC enabled Indigenous peoples to articulate their aspirations to government. Both, however, had been criticised as offering elected Indigenous representatives' roles that were 'merely consultative',[71] and therefore 'fail[ing] to develop as a significant instrument of Aboriginal political influence and power'.[72] To alleviate this criticism, ATSIC combined representative and administrative responsibilities, 'ensur[ing] the place of the Indigenous peoples of this country

[68] Commonwealth, *Parliamentary Debates*, House of Representatives, 24 August 1988, 252.
[69] See below pt III.C–D.
[70] Cited in Rowse (n 20) 198–99.
[71] Hiatt (n 20) viii.
[72] Coombs, 'National Aboriginal Conference' (1984) 14.

in the decision-making processes of government'.[73] This was a significant decision, marking the first time that Indigenous Australians had been empowered with executive authority over Commonwealth programmes dedicated to their welfare. In practice, it meant that ATSIC initially comprised a representative arm of councillors and commissioners elected by Indigenous peoples, and an administrative arm that replaced the DAA and ADC.

The basis of ATSIC's representative structure was the 35 Regional Councils (originally 60),[74] directly elected every three years. The councils were grouped into 16 zones, each of which elected a full-time commissioner to the national board. Another commissioner was elected from the Torres Strait, which comprised its own zone.[75] Initially, two additional commissioners, as well as the chairperson, were appointed by the Federal Minister for Aboriginal Affairs.[76] This power was removed in 1993, though deferred until 1 July 1996, and the chairperson was subsequently elected by the commissioners themselves.[77] The zone from which the elected chairperson came elected a replacement zone commissioner, making a total of 18 commissioners.

Elections were run by the Australian Electoral Commission. Entitlement to vote and nominate for election was restricted to Aboriginal and Torres Strait Islander people over 18 years of age who were registered on the Commonwealth electoral roll. Unlike the NACC and NAC, no Indigenous-specific electoral roll was established. As the Commonwealth roll does not identify Indigenous peoples, voting and nomination was accompanied by a declaration of Indigeneity. Challenges to these declarations could be made at polling booths and in the courts.[78] As the site of a large number of challenges, an alternative arrangement was trialled in Tasmania in 2002, where an Indigenous subset of the Commonwealth electoral roll was drawn up. This attempt was not as successful as its proponents had hoped.[79] ATSIC's abolition prevented further development.

The administrative arm supported ATSIC's elected representatives and administered Commission programmes. As of 30 June 2003, it comprised 1,052 staff (of which 501 were Indigenous), employed under the Public Service Act and headed by a chief executive officer appointed by the minister.[80] Many of these public servants had worked within various incarnations of Aboriginal affairs

[73] Commonwealth, *Parliamentary Debates*, House of Representatives, 24 August 1988, 251 (Gerry Hand).

[74] Aboriginal and Torres Strait Islander Commission Amendment Act 1993 (Cth) cl 23, replacing Sch 1 of the Aboriginal and Torres Strait Islander Commission Act 1989 (Cth) (ATSIC Act).

[75] ATSIC Act (n 74) Sch 1.

[76] ibid s 27(2).

[77] Aboriginal and Torres Strait Islander Commission Act (No 3) 1993 (Cth) Pt 31 and Sch 4.

[78] *Gibbs v Capewell* (1995) 128 ALR 577; *Shaw v Wolf* (1998) 163 ALR 205.

[79] W Sanders, 'The Tasmanian Electoral Roll Trial in the 2002 ATSIC Elections' (Centre for Aboriginal Economic Policy Research, Discussion Paper No 245, 2003).

[80] Aboriginal and Torres Strait Islander Commission, 'Annual Report 2002–03' (2003) Appendix 5, 295.

departments over the years,[81] gathering necessary experience but also potentially carrying dated attitudes on Indigenous policy. Reflecting the diverse geographic need of Indigenous communities, it was divided into three tiers: a central office in Canberra; state offices in each capital city; and 27 regional offices located across Australia. Initially, the administrative arm reported to the minister through the CEO but took direction from ATSIC's elected officials.[82] This complex accountability framework was intended to harmonise the Government's commitment to Indigenous self-determination with the need to maintain proper stewardship of public funds but, as will be discussed below, also created an internal tension that was the focus for questions over the Commission's integrity.[83] It was revised in 2003, when the Government established a separate, independent, service delivery agency, Aboriginal and Torres Strait Islander Services (ATSIS),[84] and migrated most staff from the Commission. As at 25 September 2003, 49 people were employed directly by ATSIC, with ATSIS staff comprising 1,211 people, a majority of whom were distributed across mainstream agencies.[85]

ii. Regionalism

ATSIC's decentralised federal structure was lauded as a critical innovation, promising to transfer decision-making powers from 'remote governments in Canberra to the elected local representatives of Indigenous peoples'.[86] The genesis of this arrangement was the failings of the NACC and NAC. As noted above, successive inquiries had revealed concerns that these organisations were 'out of touch' with Indigenous communities, and that they consequently failed to effectively present 'the needs and aspirations of communities, groups and organisations to governments at State and Federal level'.[87] Drawing on consultations with Indigenous communities, these reviews recommended that an Indigenous representative body must 'be firmly based on, derive its Aboriginal authority from, and be accountable to local groups and communities and their organisations'.[88] Greater connectivity between a national executive and local and regional communities would increase the Commission's legitimacy among its constituents.

[81] M Ivanitz, 'Straddling Two Worlds: ATSIC and the Management of Indigenous Policy' (Centre for Australian Public Sector Management, Research Paper No 6, 1998) 4.

[82] ATSIC Act (n 74) ss 46, 55.

[83] See below pt III.D.

[84] Commonwealth, *Gazette* No S 183, 30 May 2003, 1.

[85] Senate Select Committee on the Administration of Aboriginal Affairs, Parliament of Australia, 'After ATSIC – Life in the Mainstream?' (2005) 12 [2.4]; J Hannaford, J Huggins and B Collins, 'In the Hands of the Regions – A New ATSIC' (Report of the Review of the Aboriginal and Torres Strait Islander Commission, 2003) 19.

[86] R Tickner, *Taking a Stand: Land Rights to Reconciliation* (Crows Nest, Allen & Unwin, 2001) 49.

[87] Coombs (n 57) 11; Hiatt (n 20) 32 and 48.

[88] Coombs (n 57) 33 [11(a)]; Hiatt (n 20) 48 and 129.

Each Regional Council was responsible for formulating and implementing a plan for improving the economic, social and cultural status of Indigenous peoples living in the region.[89] To ensure these plans reflected local concerns, they were developed through a process of community consultation.[90] Regional plans were submitted to the national board, which was required to determine financial priorities and develop an overall budget. The board then allocated funds to the regional councils in line with the priorities identified in their plans.[91] The emphasis on decentralisation, enabling Indigenous communities to devise and implement policy priorities, marked a clear change in government policy. Prior to the creation of ATSIC these functions were performed by the Minister for Aboriginal Affairs. Although somewhat tempered by consultation with the NACC and NAC (when they existed), the minister had been principally advised by a 'hierarchically organised department which was centrally focused and almost totally removed from the day to day realities of life for Indigenous people'.[92] Nonetheless, even under the ATSIC Act, the minister retained significant control.

III. ATSIC AND INDIGENOUS ASPIRATIONS

ATSIC was built on the NACC and NAC. Its dual roles and regional structure indicated a willingness to improve upon design flaws in those earlier experiments. Its executive powers were limited but considerable, reflecting a marked shift in government attitudes towards Indigenous Australians. And yet, as discussed below, its funding arrangements and public accountability regime suggested that these attitudes had not been entirely displaced. Nonetheless, ATSIC's structure granted a real opportunity for Aboriginal and Torres Strait Islander peoples to be heard in the processes of government. Whether it was successful in practice – and what this tells us about future institutional design in Australia – are separate questions. This part answers the first of those questions by assessing the Commission against the conditions drawn from chapter four. Those conditions are:

(1) Indigenous peoples must be heard when decisions that affect them are being made.
(2) Indigenous peoples must have the authority and financial capacity to exercise independent policy and decision-making power over matters relating to internal or local affairs.

[89] ATSIC Act (n 74) s 94.
[90] J Finlayson and A Dale, 'Negotiating Indigenous Self-Determination at the Regional Level' in P Sullivan (ed), *Shooting the Banker: Essays on ATSIC and Self-Determination* (Darwin, North Australian Research Unit, 1996) 70, 71.
[91] ATSIC Act (n 74) s 7(1).
[92] M Dillon, 'Institutional Structures in Indigenous Affairs' in P Sullivan (ed), *Shooting the Banker: Essays on ATSIC and Self-Determination* (Darwin, North Australian Research Unit, 1996) 89, 95.

(3) Institutions or processes that empower Indigenous peoples must be regarded by Indigenous peoples as legitimate.
(4) Indigenous leaders must act according to the purposes and values for which they have been entrusted with authority, and must be accountable for their actions.

A. Voices

Under s 7 of the Act, ATSIC was required to 'advise the Minister' on matters relating to Indigenous affairs, as well as develop policy and implement programmes for Indigenous peoples. Although the minister was not 'restricted to, nor bound by the advice received',[93] this statutory right provided significant advantages relative to the multiplicity of Indigenous organisations across the country,[94] guaranteeing Aboriginal and Torres Strait Islander representatives a place at the table. In fact, the Commission enjoyed an especially prominent position; unlike lobby groups, ATSIC could provide coordination comments on Cabinet submissions when requested, empowering the Commission to speak directly to the core of government decision-makers.[95] However, while the Commission's statutory powers left it well placed to convey Indigenous interests to government, two complications reveal challenges in satisfying this standard in practice. First, ATSIC struggled to articulate the voices of all Indigenous peoples, including remote communities and women. Second, as ATSIC discovered, institutional opportunities are necessary but insufficient to empower Indigenous peoples to have their voices heard in the processes of government. Equally vital is a government that commits to meaningfully engage.

The NACC and NAC had been accused of favouring urban Indigenous polities over more 'traditional' rural-based communities.[96] ATSIC's Regional Councils were intended to rectify this failing by connecting the localism of Indigenous politics to a national body. This connection was intended to be two-way. Regional Councils were tasked with developing plans that 'identify local needs, aspirations and priorities',[97] as well as serving as a forum for representatives 'to provide feedback to the community'.[98] In this way, the Commission would be able to express the voices of all Aboriginal and Torres Strait Islander

[93] Senate Select Committee on the Administration of Aboriginal Affairs, 'Administration of Aboriginal Affairs' (1989) 15 [2.15].
[94] Dillon, 'Institutional Structures' (1996) 100.
[95] J Hannaford, J Huggins and B Collins, 'Review of the Aboriginal and Torres Strait Islander Commission' (discussion paper, 2003) 36 [5.4].
[96] Aboriginal and Torres Strait Islander Social Justice Commissioner, 'Building a Sustainable National Indigenous Representative Body: An Issues Paper' (2008) 24.
[97] D Smith, 'The Fiscal Equalisation Model: Options for ATSIC: Future Funding Policy and Practice' (Centre for Aboriginal Economic Policy Research, Discussion Paper No 30, 1993) 8.
[98] O'Donoghue, *Aboriginal and Islander* (1986) 18.

peoples and be accountable to them. This structure was generally effective. Councils usually consulted widely to build capacity and develop strategies to 'empower Indigenous Australians to take control of their futures'.[99] However, this potential was not always realised; operational and structural challenges inhibited the capacity of the innovative federal structure to empower remote Indigenous polities. Among other complications, councils were not always resourced appropriately; relevant local government agencies did not provide input and were subsequently disinclined to consider the plans in their own decision-making processes; the plans themselves were often far too broad in scope; and, alarmingly, local communities were sometimes not involved in the planning process.[100] Additionally, very low voter turnout figures inhibited the Commission's ability to accurately ascertain and express all voices.

Operational problems made it difficult for the national board to express remote interests to government, but structural challenges also existed. In particular, difficulties were encountered in setting the borders of the regional councils and zones, which did not always correspond with or acknowledge traditional community boundaries.[101] The challenge here involved mediating two competing principles: ensuring that distinct Indigenous communities were empowered to represent themselves on their own terms, while maintaining administrative efficacy in a federation that divides responsibilities between state and federal governments.[102] As the 1995 Boundary Review Panel explained, aligning electoral and regional boundaries along tribal and group affiliations often conflicted with 'the pursuit and achievement of community and organisational objectives'.[103] Issues would need to be negotiated with multiple state and territory governments, and require several ATSIC offices to coordinate; a situation that caused 'extreme difficulties' and the Commission decried as 'unworkable'.[104] The Commission's decision to prioritise administrative ease is understandable, as electoral boundaries did not prevent or inhibit communities from continuing to observe those connections. It did, however, cause complications, alienating communities, and detaching councils, zones and the national board from the concerns of their constituents.[105] In some cases, communities refused to participate in ATSIC elections.[106] Although regular boundary reviews

[99] Aboriginal and Torres Strait Islander Social Justice Commissioner, 'Social Justice Report 2005' (Human Rights and Equal Opportunity Commission, 2005) Appendix 2, 271–72.

[100] Hannaford, Huggins and Collins, 'In the Hands of the Regions' (2003) 32–35. See further Aboriginal and Torres Strait Islander Commission, 'Strengthening ATSIC: The 1997 Review of the ATSIC Act' (1998) 25.

[101] P Coe, 'ATSIC: Self-determination or Otherwise' (1994) 4 *Race & Class* 35, 36.

[102] O'Donoghue (n 64) 29–30.

[103] Aboriginal and Torres Strait Islander Commission, 'Review of Boundaries' (Report of the Panel Convened by the Minister for Aboriginal and Torres Strait Islander Affairs to Review Matters Relating to the Boundaries of ATSIC's Zones, Regions and Wards, February 1995) 6.

[104] ibid.

[105] Hannaford, Huggins and Collins (n 85) 45.

[106] Bennett, *White Politics* (1999) 134; ATSIC (n 103) 9–10.

reveal continuing efforts to manage these competing priorities, they were unresolvable: choices had to be made.

Two other challenges relating to hearing internally variegated polities received distinct responses. The Commission failed to ensure that women were adequately represented on regional councils and the national board. While Hand's initial proposal provided for mandatory equal gender representation, 'this was not reflected' in the final Bill,[107] and ATSIC fought against its introduction.[108] The absence of a statutory requirement for gender balance had negative consequences for female representation; of the 35 regional councils elected in 1993, 1996, and 1999, four, seven, and one, had no women.[109] At the national level, only two women held positions on the 18-member board in 1989; both appointed by the minister. The situation did not improve: 'From 1991–1993, three women were elected; 1994-1996, there were two women elected and from 1996–1999 two women were elected. In 1999 there were four elected out of 18 Commissioners and in the final Board there was one woman elected'.[110]

Partially acknowledging this problem, the Commission established several sub-committees to provide advice to the national board on 'women's issues'. The influence of these bodies fluctuated, however, and the Commission was never truly able to integrate women's perspectives.[111] As if to emphasise this failing, in 1997 the Commission closed the Office of Indigenous Women. ATSIC's inability to meaningfully engage with women had practical consequences for the Commission's activities; a comprehensive review found that 'ATSIC programs and services have limited effectiveness in meeting the needs of Indigenous women'[112] because, interviewees argued, 'programs are planned by men for men'.[113]

In contrast, legislative amendment largely enabled the Commission to articulate the distinct interests of Torres Strait Islander peoples. Constituting around 10 per cent of the total number of Indigenous Australians and maintaining a distinct body of customs, traditions and beliefs described as *Ailan*

[107] Hannaford, Huggins and Collins, 'Review' (2003) 26 [4.19].

[108] Aboriginal and Torres Strait Islander Boundaries and Electoral System Review Panel, 'Review of Electoral Systems' (1997) 17, Recommendation 18.1.

[109] W Sanders, J Taylor and K Ross, 'Participation and Representation in ATSIC Elections: A 10 Year Perspective' (2000) 35 *Australian Journal of Political Science* 493, 510.

[110] M Davis, 'ATSIC and Indigenous Women: Lessons for the Future' (2008) 10 *Balayi: Culture, Law & Colonialism* 73, 77.

[111] ibid 84; H McGlade, *Our Greatest Challenge: Aboriginal Children and Human Rights* (Canberra, Aboriginal Studies Press, 2012) 78–79. On the challenge that 'masculinist political institutions' pose for Indigenous self-determination see: R Kuokkanen, *Restructuring Relations: Indigenous Self-Determination, Governance, and Gender* (Oxford, Oxford University Press, 2019).

[112] Aboriginal and Torres Strait Islander Commission Office of Evaluation and Audit, 'The Final Report of the Evaluation of the Effectiveness of ATSIC Programs in Meeting the Needs of Aboriginal Women and Torres Strait Islander Women' (1995) 104.

[113] ibid 40.

Kastom, separate arrangements were established to specifically empower this group.[114] The Torres Strait initially comprised a separate region and zone, but amendments in 1993 transformed the Torres Strait Regional Council into an independent statutory authority. The Torres Strait Regional Authority enjoyed similar powers and functions to ATSIC and survived the Commission's 2005 abolition, continuing today to advise the Minister on matters relating to Torres Strait Islanders as well as formulate, develop and monitor programmes for all Indigenous peoples living within the region.[115] ATSIC's board was also served by the Office of Torres Strait Islander Affairs, and a Torres Strait Islander Advisory Body, which respectively monitored the conduct and development of programmes and policies that affected, and represented, Torres Strait Islanders across Australia. Reviews suggested that Torres Strait Islander peoples generally considered these arrangements 'fair and reasonable',[116] reflecting and fuelling aspirations for greater autonomy.[117]

ATSIC sought to articulate the voices of diverse communities but struggled to effectively realise this responsibility. This problem may have contributed to the Commission's second major challenge: ensuring that government meaningfully engaged with their advice. Causality in policy formulation and legislative drafting is often difficult to ascertain. If the Commission commented on a legislative proposal and a draft Bill was subsequently amended or a proposal jettisoned, it is possible that government listened, but that shift may also have been coincidental. Nonetheless, several clear examples exist. For instance, Lois O'Donoghue, ATSIC's inaugural chair, was heavily involved in negotiations over the Native Title Act 1993 (Cth). The Commission's role 'within and without' government, operating inside intergovernmental channels while remaining responsive to its constituents proved challenging,[118] but by 'working co-operatively … in close alliance with Aboriginal organisations in Australia',[119] even critical Indigenous activists acknowledged that ATSIC 'extract[ed] the best deal from the government'.[120] The Commission had other successes. It progressed implementation of procedures to repatriate Indigenous remains from the United Kingdom and was successful in increasing the numbers of Indigenous leaders on national

[114] Australian Bureau of Statistics, 'Australia's Aboriginal and Torres Strait Islander Population' (Catalogue No 2740.0, 1991) 5.

[115] See now Aboriginal and Torres Strait Islander Act 2005 (Cth) pt 3A.

[116] ATSIC, 'Strengthening ATSIC' (1998) 35; Hannaford, Huggins and Collins (n 85) 43–44.

[117] W Sanders, 'Reshaping Governance in Torres Strait: The Torres Strait Regional Authority and Beyond' (Centre for Aboriginal Economic Policy Research, Discussion Paper No 74, 1994).

[118] Rowse (n 20) 204–09. But see: G Foley, 'The Road to Native Title: The Aboriginal Rights Movement and the Australian Labor Party 1973–1996', available at www.kooriweb.org/foley/resources/pdfs/227.pdf.

[119] ABC Radio National, 'Aborigines Welcome the New Native Title Bill' *PM*, 19 October 1993 (Lois O'Donoghue).

[120] Statement from the Aboriginal Provisional Government cited in F Brennan, 'One Land, One Nation: Mabo – Towards 2001' (Brisbane University of Queensland Press, 2001) 71. But see: Coe, 'ATSIC' (1994) 36.

policy bodies, as well as providing councillors and Commissioners a platform to develop a public profile and participate in public debate.[121]

These successes suggest that government engaged with ATSIC at least occasionally. In the absence of any formal requirement to be heard, or to document how the Commission's comments influenced government proposals, let alone clear procedures for engagement, however, it is impossible to state with any precision whether ATSIC was generally effective. The clearest evidence we have is not promising. The 2003 Hannaford Review found that although the Commission had once been a 'central player in policy development', there had been 'a significant decline over time in ATSIC's input and access to the Cabinet policy development process'.[122] Indeed, Patricia Turner (Arrernte/Gurdanji), ATSIC CEO from 1994 to 1998, has remarked that while she met regularly with the minister, 'in all of my four years we got one meeting with the Cabinet'.[123] Much like the NACC and NAC, it appears ATSIC representatives were not always present in the forum where public policies are debated, their voices were not always heard, and their interests were not always considered.

Further difficulties arose from Australia's federal structure. The Commonwealth Parliament enjoys only a concurrent power to legislate with respect to Aboriginal and Torres Strait Islander affairs, and responsibility for many issues of concern for Indigenous peoples lie with the states. Inexplicably, however, ATSIC initially had no structural interface with the states and territories, severely hampering its capacity to effectively articulate Indigenous interests within areas of state responsibility. The Commission was able to subsequently negotiate Memoranda of Understanding with each state and territory government, sector-specific bilateral agreements in key areas, such as housing and infrastructure,[124] and establish informal state advisory committees to coordinate relationships, but no general obligation on other bodies to cooperate with the Commission was ever established.[125] Various solutions were proposed,[126] though no amendment was forthcoming.

Did the Commission empower Indigenous Australians with the capacity to have their interests considered in decisions that affect them? At one level, the answer is clear: ATSIC had a statutory right to advise government on matters affecting Indigenous peoples. This right provided a guaranteed, direct

[121] W Sanders, 'ATSIC's Achievements and Strengths: Implications for Institutional Reform' (Centre for Aboriginal Economic Policy Research, 2004) 2; Senate Select Committee on the Administration of Aboriginal Affairs, 'After ATSIC' (2005) 38 [2.129].

[122] Hannaford, Huggins and Collins (n 95) 36 [5.6], [5.5].

[123] Evidence to Joint Select Committee on Constitutional Recognition Relating to Aboriginal and Torres Strait Islander People, Parliament of Australia, Canberra, 25 June 2018, 8.

[124] Senate Select Committee on the Administration of Aboriginal Affairs (n 85) 38 [2.131].

[125] Aboriginal and Torres Strait Islander Commission, Review of the Operation of the Aboriginal and Torres Strait Islander Commission Act 1989 (Cth) (1993) 9; ATSIC (n 100) 10.

[126] See, eg: Council for Aboriginal Reconciliation, 'Going Forward: Social Justice for the First Australians' (1996) Recommendation 18.

link, ensuring Indigenous peoples could be heard. In practice however, operational and structural challenges within the regional council framework, and ATSIC's inability to equitably accommodate Indigenous women, impoverished the Commission, weakening its ability to effectively express the diversity of Indigenous views, and leaving 'the cause of the advancement of Indigenous Australians' 'poorer'.[127]

The Commission also experienced considerable difficulties in exercising its key advantage: its connection to government. The absence of a statutory interface between the Commission and the states and territories inhibited its capacity to transmit Indigenous policy proposals to relevant decision-makers. More telling, however, is that despite individual successes, no genuine dialogue based on respectful deliberation ever developed. Although this owes much to the Howard Government's stated philosophical objection to the Commission, ATSIC's inability to articulate the views of important groups within the Indigenous community likely played a role. Indeed, while the Hannaford Review found ATSIC's influence dropped precipitously between the Keating and Howard eras, the Australian Labor Party also marginalised the Commission. After the 1993 election, Prime Minister Paul Keating established the Office of Indigenous Affairs within the Department of Prime Minister and Cabinet. As an alternative source of policy advice, the Office clearly undermined ATSIC.[128]

B. Power

ATSIC's chief advantage over previous national advisory bodies was its combination of representative and administrative roles. A central failing of both the NACC and the NAC was their inability to implement or administer policy decisions. Each was merely a sectional body consulted by government at its pleasure; their authority was limited to forms of soft power, relying on persuasion to achieve outcomes. In contrast, ATSIC enjoyed significant, though constrained, policy and decision-making authority. The Commission was not empowered with adjudicatory or legislative responsibilities, but it did imbue Indigenous Australians with considerable authority over matters that affected them, securing a vital domain for self-administration. Commissioners could identify funding priorities, formulate and implement policy and plans, make decisions over public expenditure, and protect cultural material and information. Yet, very real impediments to their exercise of authority existed, revealing that the Commission struggled to meet this standard.

Authority was primarily exercised through Regional Councils where elected Indigenous representatives developed community-based goals and strategies to

[127] Hannaford, Huggins and Collins (n 95) 27 [4.26].
[128] Tickner, *Taking a Stand* (2001) 109.

empower their constituents. Councils faced many practical challenges in developing their plans,[129] but genuine consultation both empowered communities as political actors and revealed distinct priorities and strategies for achieving those goals. For instance, the Mulga Mallee Regional Council identified early child development as a priority area, resolving to support the establishment of Indigenous childcare centres and improved access to Mother and Child Welfare Services to progress outcomes.[130] In contrast, the Townsville Regional Council found that improved transport and communications was a key goal for its community, and determined to negotiate with the state transport authority to develop a regional transport strategy that would lead to an affordable and reliable transport network that 'connects our people with one another and with essential services'.[131]

ATSIC may have had no structural interface with states and territories, but regional councils also exercised authority by engaging with subnational governments and organisations to reach creative agreements that secured valuable outcomes for communities. Neil Westbury and Will Sanders discuss a 1995 agreement between ATSIC and the Commonwealth and Northern Territory Governments that pooled dispersed funding for Indigenous housing programmes into a newly established cooperative organisation. The Indigenous Housing Authority of the Northern Territory (IHANT) comprised the seven elected Regional Council chairs and two elected ATSIC Commissioners for the Territory, as well as one Commonwealth government official and up to seven Northern Territory government nominees. As Westbury and Sanders note, IHANT's planning processes and deliberations 'introduced a new order and clarity to housing and infrastructure allocations for Aboriginal communities across the Northern Territory'.[132] They continue:

> Though there was still a bidding process and cause for argument, there was a much clearer, unified and coordinated framework within which this could occur. Indigenous representatives from the ATSIC elected arm were directly involved and could report back to their constituents. Housing and infrastructure provision in these communities was clearly better coordinated.[133]

[129] Finlayson and Dale, 'Negotiating' (1996); T Rowse, 'The Political Identity of Regional Councillors' in P Sullivan (ed), *Shooting the Banker: Essays on ATSIC and Self-Determination* (Darwin, North Australian Research Unit, 1996) 42.

[130] Mulga Mallee Regional Council, 'Strategic Plan 2004–2009'; cited in Aboriginal and Torres Strait Islander Social Justice Commissioner (n 99) Appendix 2, 323.

[131] Townsville Regional Council, 'Regional Plan 2001'; cited in ibid 302.

[132] N Westbury and W Sanders, 'Governance and Service Delivery for Remote Aboriginal Communities in the Northern Territory: Challenges and Opportunities' (Centre for Aboriginal Economic Policy Research, Working Paper No 6, 2000) 10.

[133] ibid. See further D Smith, 'Community Participation Agreements: A Model for Welfare Reform from Community-Based Research' (Centre for Aboriginal Economic Policy Research, Discussion Paper No 223, 2001).

The capacity to identify, prioritise and implement distinct projects led some scholars to characterise the Commission as exercising a form of regional autonomy,[134] while others argued that creative intergovernmental agreements were suggestive of an implicit recognition as an order of government.[135] Regional councils may well have developed in that vein, but as the examples above demonstrate, they remained primarily service-delivery organisations during ATSIC's existence. This is not to discount their achievements, but is to recognise that their capacity to exercise autonomy was statutorily limited.

It was also limited financially. Chapter four explained that financial capacity is critical for any organisation to exercise decision-making authority. As a statutory body, ATSIC enjoyed a guaranteed source of funding, and, as the central service delivery agency for Indigenous affairs, was well-financed to satisfy its responsibilities; in 2002–03, for instance, the Commission received around $1.3 billion from the Commonwealth Government. Some have pointed to the size of the Commission's budget to suggest both government support for the institution and its capacity to effectively exercise its powers. For example, Robert Tickner, Hand's successor as Minister for Aboriginal and Torres Strait Islander Affairs, favourably compared the protection of Indigenous rights in Australia to Canada and Aotearoa New Zealand, remarking that although treaties have secured important gains 'in the public administration of Indigenous affairs, no other government has been prepared to legislate to transfer executive control of an annual budget of over $1 billion to the elected representatives of Indigenous people'.[136] Tickner is correct, but focus on the headline figure is misleading. ATSIC did not have full control over its budget and was prohibited from developing independent sources of financing. As such, its capacity to exercise independent policy and decision-making power was seriously inhibited.

Contrary to the recommendations of the Coombs review,[137] substantial Commonwealth expenditure was spent on Indigenous affairs outside ATSIC. As Tim Rowse notes, although the Act outlined a scheme of regional government, it did so only 'in respect of those programs hitherto controlled by the DAA and ADC'.[138] ATSIC had no control over funding allocated via other Commonwealth departments, which were administered with 'none of the trappings of self-determination'.[139] This became particularly problematic in the

[134] W Arthur, 'Indigenous Autonomy in Australia: Some Concepts, Issues and Examples' (Centre for Aboriginal Economic Policy Research, Discussion Paper No 220, 2001) 7.

[135] W Sanders 'Towards an Indigenous Order of Government: Rethinking Self-Determination as Indigenous Affairs Policy' (Centre for Aboriginal Economic Policy Research, Discussion Paper No. 230, 2002).

[136] Tickner (n 86) 49.

[137] Coombs (n 57) 34, Recommendation 11(d).

[138] T Rowse, *Remote Possibilities: The Aboriginal Domain and the Administrative Imagination* (Darwin, North Australia Research Unit, 1992) 57.

[139] Commonwealth, Royal Commission into Aboriginal Deaths in Custody, 'National Report' (1991) vol 4, 8 [27.2.6].

early-1990s as Commonwealth expenditure on Indigenous-specific programmes was increasingly conducted through mainstream departments.[140] While in 1992–93, ATSIC's budget accounted for approximately two-thirds of the Federal Government's Indigenous programmes,[141] by 2000–01, the Commission administered just 48 per cent – including 'no education or health services and only some in housing and employment'.[142] This trend was continuing: in ATSIC's final year of operation, its budget accounted for only 46 per cent of the total identifiable Commonwealth expenditure on Indigenous affairs.[143] When state and territory expenditure is included, the overall proportion of funding controlled by ATSIC decreased further.

ATSIC did not administer a majority of Commonwealth expenditure on Indigenous Affairs, but it still retained responsibility over a significant quantum. However, budget cuts and paternalistic interference further challenged the Commission's capacity to exercise independent decision-making authority. In its first budget, the Howard Government cut ATSIC expenditure by 11 per cent,[144] and quarantined Commission expenditure on programmes that amounted to approximately 85 per cent of ATSIC's programme outlays. Many of these programmes, including the Community Development Employment Project and the Community Housing and Infrastructure Program realised important objectives.[145] Yet, quarantining meant that the proportion of ATSIC's budget that could be spent at its own discretion, on local programmes identified by regional councils to meet distinctive needs, was relatively small – amounting to only $195 million in 2003–2004 – severely inhibiting any semblance of self-determination.[146] This was displaced entirely in 2003, when the establishment of ATSIS stripped ATSIC of the power to allocate funding to individual projects. Instead, funding decisions were made by ATSIS staff under delegation from the government-appointed CEO, leaving elected representatives able only to make general directions on expenditure.[147]

Quarantined funding arrangements left ATSIC with authority over approximately 15 per cent of its budget and, therefore, only around seven per cent of

[140] Altman, 'Practical Reconciliation and the New Mainstreaming' (2004) 38.

[141] Hannaford, Huggins and Collins (n 85) 18: Amounting to over $800 million.

[142] Altman (n 38) 42: ATSIC administered $1,114 million of the total $2,329 million spent on Indigenous-specific programmes.

[143] J Gardiner-Garden and J Simon-Davies, 'Commonwealth Indigenous-Specific Expenditure, 1968–2010' (Parliamentary Library of Australia, 16 September 2010).

[144] M Ivanitz, 'The Politics of Accountability: ATSIC, the Coalition Government, and Public Sector Service Outcomes' (Centre for Australian Public Sector Management, Research Paper No 9, July 1999) 3.

[145] A Pratt, 'Make or Break? A Background to the ATSIC Changes and the ATSIC Review' (Parliamentary Library, Current Issues Brief No 29, 2003) 12.

[146] ATSIC (n 100) 2–3.

[147] Commonwealth, *Gazette* No S 183, 30 May 2003; Ministerial Directions to the CEO of ATSIS, 1 July 2003.

the total Commonwealth monies expended on Indigenous affairs.[148] Yet, control over even this minor proportion of funding was subject to broad ministerial supervision and stringent accountability requirements. Regional councils did not have autonomous control over expenditure as the Commission's budget required approval from the minister and Parliament. Parliamentary authorisation is, of course, necessary for the valid expenditure of public funds,[149] and good public administration requires public monies be properly accounted for, but extensive statutory accountability requirements led Mick Dodson (Yawuru) to view the arrangement as 'reminiscent of an earlier paternalistic time'.[150] The Act set out detailed provisions concerning how draft budgets were to be prepared and submitted to the minister;[151] money could not be spent without his or her approval;[152] and the minister could alter the Commission's budget provided they explained why in a statement to Parliament.[153] Concerns were heightened by the strictures placed on such expenditure. Funding was provided only on an annual basis with 'no guarantees of future funding (even when subject to satisfactory audit and performance review)'.[154] This funding model created considerable uncertainty, leading to 'difficulties in attracting and retaining skilled and qualified staff'.[155] Repeated recommendations to adopt a triennial funding model[156] were never adopted.

Compounding the Commission's financial challenges, ATSIC was prevented from developing independent sources of financing. The Commission was prevented from raising money except by borrowing, and strict limits were placed on its ability to do even this.[157] The failure to permit ATSIC a degree of financial security, either via raising money outside parliamentary control or via less restrictive constraints on state funding, further impeded its capacity to exercise its powers autonomously. The Commission was entirely reliant on government; a government that demonstrated its limited support for and lack of faith in the Commission through paternalistic control over expenditure.

ATSIC was a marked improvement on its predecessors. The Commission's regional structure established and empowered important and significant infrastructure at the local level. This architecture allowed Aboriginal and Torres

[148] J Cunningham and J Baeza, 'An "Experiment" in Indigenous Social Policy: The Rise and Fall of Australia's Aboriginal and Torres Strait Islander Commission (ATSIC)' (2005) 33 *Policy & Politics* 461, 466.

[149] Constitution, s 83; *Williams v Commonwealth (No 1)* (2012) 248 CLR 156; *Williams v Commonwealth (No 2)* (2014) 252 CLR 416.

[150] M Dodson, 'Assimilation versus Self-determination: No Contest' (North Australian Research Unit, Discussion Paper 1, 1996) 10.

[151] ATSIC Act (n 74) ss 63, 64.

[152] ibid s 61.

[153] ibid s 65.

[154] Council for Aboriginal Reconciliation (n 126) 65.

[155] ibid.

[156] ibid, Recommendation 41; Hannaford, Huggins and Collins (n 85) Recommendation 30.

[157] ATSIC Act (n 74) ss 69–70.

Strait Islander people to articulate their own concerns, identify their own priorities, and develop policy (though not law) to address those challenges. While their decisions, and their capacity to effectuate those decisions, were always subject to ministerial and parliamentary review, communities had some latitude in which they could steer their own vessel. That latitude was closely guarded. The Commission laboured under heavy public accountability obligations and had limited control over expenditure on Indigenous affairs, inhibiting its ability to make independent decisions. This subordinate role was intentional.[158] When introducing the ATSIC Bill to Parliament, Hand explained that the Commission was not to be an instrument of self-rule, but 'a solid foundation' for Indigenous Australians to 'use and build upon in their quest for self-determination'.[159] Tickner echoed these comments, framing ATSIC as 'the first step'[160] on this path. O'Donoghue understood this, and was at pains to point out that, although the Commission was 'a radical advance in the application of self-determination principles within Commonwealth government arrangements', it did not provide self-government.[161] Complete structural independence may not have been necessary for the Commission to exercise independent policy and decision-making authority, but that goal did require a respectful dialogue between government and the Commission. That dialogue never developed.

C. Ownership

Empowered with representative and administrative responsibilities, ATSIC promised Indigenous Australians the opportunity to participate within the processes of government and shape its actions to reflect their priorities. Its status as a government-created organisation caused difficulties, however, and ATSIC faced persistent criticism throughout its life: was it a culturally appropriate body, or was it simply an Indigenous-staffed institution built on western norms? For many Aboriginal and Torres Strait Islander peoples, the answer was simple: The Commission 'entrench[ed] white values and ways of being'[162] and was intended to 'impede', rather than promote self-determination.[163] Regional voter turnout figures complicate this picture. It is clear that notwithstanding its initial design the Commission sought – with some success – to ground itself

[158] ibid s 3(a).

[159] Commonwealth, *Parliamentary Debates*, House of Representatives, 24 August 1988, 252 (Gerry Hand).

[160] Tickner (n 86) 48.

[161] L O'Donoghue, 'Keynote Address: Australian Government and Self-Determination' in C Fletcher (ed), *Aboriginal Self-Determination in Australia* (Canberra, Aboriginal Studies Press, 1994) 3, 10.

[162] I Watson, 'Settled and Unsettled Spaces: Are we Free to Roam?' in A Moreton-Robinson (ed), *Sovereign Subjects: Indigenous Sovereignty Matters* (Crows Nest, Allen & Unwin, 2007) 15, 24.

[163] Coe (n 101) 39; Coombs (n 28) 183–84.

within Indigenous communities. Nonetheless, despite concerted effort, examination of the design and evolution of the Commission reveals that ATSIC was largely unable to satisfy this standard.

i. Design

Aboriginal and Torres Strait Islander people and communities were closely engaged in the development of the Commission. As noted above, the Government's extensive consultation process was encouraging; even ATSIC's detractors acknowledged that it 'was among the most exhaustive and protracted … ever undertaken'.[164] Nonetheless, the adequacy of the consultation process, and the extent to which Indigenous peoples had a determinative say over questions of institutional design, has been the subject of considerable controversy. Negotiation and compromise may be inherent to legislative enactment, but the Commission's development reveals challenges for future institutional design.

Indigenous involvement in the creation of ATSIC was more limited than appears. Most significantly, consultation with Indigenous Australians occurred only after the Government had already devised a substantial initial proposal. That proposal had been developed by 'an informal working party of consultants and staff from the office of the Minister of Aboriginal Affairs, in liaison with senior staff from portfolio agencies such as DAA'.[165] Although some Indigenous leaders had been involved in these discussions, including Rob Riley as Hand's Senior Adviser, the initial proposal as enumerated in 'Foundations for the Future', owed much to the model Coombs laid out in his 1984 report on the NAC.[166] Coombs' report had been informed by consultation with Indigenous peoples and communities, but engagement was severely limited – confined to 'a period of less than three months'.[167] There was thus little sustained scope for Indigenous Australians to design or propose key elements of the Commission.

Engaging with Aboriginal and Torres Strait Islander communities at this latter stage of the policy development process illustrates a failure to respect Indigenous Australians' status as polities with an inherent right to self-government. The views of Indigenous peoples were considered important – and considerable effort was taken to ascertain them – but not to the extent that they may derail the Government's proposal. Unlike the Indigenous-designed and led deliberative forums undertaken by the Referendum Council in 2017, Indigenous comment was sought on a consultative basis only, limited to discussing minor

[164] Tickner (n 86) 51. Referring to Charles Perkins.

[165] D Smith, 'From Cultural Diversity to Regionalism: The Political Culture of Difference in ATSIC', in P Sullivan (ed), *Shooting the Banker: Essays on ATSIC and Self-Determination* (North Australian Research Unit, 1996) 17, 23; Read (n 21) 274–75, 279.

[166] Beresford (n 61) 217–218.

[167] Coombs (n 57) 4.

details rather than proposing substantial amendments.[168] Unsurprisingly, this attitude may have infected the genuineness of the process. The Senate Select Committee inquiring into the ATSIC Bill characterised the process as a 'whistle-stop'[169] tour, while Gary Foley (Gumbainggir) derided the process as a 'lightning trip around the country', relating stories told by 'many Indigenous communities' of the Minister 'flitting in for 30 minutes and flitting out'.[170]

The Senate Select Committee was particularly damning, finding that the nature of the meetings 'precluded effective consultation'.[171] Meetings were only three hours long and were not conducted in a manner familiar to Indigenous Australians. The proposal was presented on a 'take it or leave it basis', communities were pressured to reach a quick decision that would bind all participants and senior departmental staff responsible for allocating funding to communities were present.[172] The Government was aware of these criticisms. Meeting reports drafted by DAA staff revealed considerable limitations. In April 1988, for instance, Brian Stacey, the DAA Darwin Regional Manager, noted that consultations with representatives from Maningrida, Oenpelli and Warruwi in West Arnhem Land were not effective: 'most Aboriginal people did not have any understanding of the concept … [because] the consultation process was too rushed'.[173] Changes to the process were not forthcoming. The Committee concluded that the 'failure to provide adequate time or resources for proper examination of the legislation constituted a 'glaring fault'.[174]

Problems existed with the Government's consultation process, but Indigenous peoples were able to influence some elements of ATSIC's design. Indigenous views were, for instance, integral in expanding the number of regional councils from 36 to 60,[175] more accurately reflecting their concerns with localism and regionalism (though subsequent amendments to the ATSIC Act revised the number of regional councils back down to 36).[176] Yet, successes were rare. Senior Indigenous executives of the DAA, including Charles Perkins (Arrernte and Kalkadoon), were not permitted to see a copy of the Bill until August 1988, and none of their proposed changes were accepted.[177] The limited ability of

[168] Senate Select Committee on the Administration of Aboriginal Affairs (n 4) ch 4.

[169] ibid 80 [4.36].

[170] G Foley, 'ATSIC: Flaws in the Machine' (15 November 1999), available at www.kooriweb.org/foley/essays/pdf_essays/atsic.pdf. Despite working hard to make them effective, Charles Perkins suggests that the consultations were not effective: Read (n 21) 283–84.

[171] Senate Select Committee on the Administration of Aboriginal Affairs (n 4) 71–72, [4.2]–[4.3].

[172] ibid 77–79, [4.25]–[4.30].

[173] ibid 83, [4.48].

[174] ibid 89, [4.76].

[175] Sanders, Taylor and Ross, 'Participation and Representation in ATSIC Elections' (2000) 497 n 6; Hannaford, Huggins and Collins (n 95) 13 [2.10].

[176] Aboriginal and Torres Strait Islander Commission Amendment Act 1993 (Cth) cl 23, replacing Sch 1 of the ATSIC Act (n 74). While this was at ATSIC's request, the result was 'an even more classically western structure': Hannaford, Huggins and Collins (n 95) 13 [2.12].

[177] Read (n 21) 289.

Indigenous peoples to effect change can be contrasted with the relative ease with which non-Indigenous peoples were able to make amendments once the Bill had been introduced into Parliament. As noted below, substantial amendments governing public accountability were made to the Bill before its eventual passage. The substance of these and other amendments led some Indigenous organisations to question whether it any longer 'resembled the original intention of ATSIC'.[178]

Several features of ATSIC's design raised concerns, most notably the electoral system. Many commentators have argued that ATSIC's electoral process was inappropriate and a 'primary cause[] of indigenous discontent'.[179] Coombs dismissed the system as merely 'mimicry of Australian electoral practice',[180] substantially different from the 'grass roots' approach he had proposed in the NAC review,[181] while Hal Wooten considered it a 'pre-emption of Aboriginal choice' premised on 'the assumptions of the Westminster system'.[182] Although the Hiatt review into the NACC had supported popular elections as consistent with 'the traditional egalitarian spirit of the Aboriginal people',[183] there is some evidence that Indigenous Australians supported a modified model. In her 1985–1986 consultations, O'Donoghue found that while 'a large majority' supported directly electing national representatives, a substantial majority supported a mixed-system at the regional level whereby two delegates would be elected from 'each Aboriginal community, Aboriginal service organisation and Aboriginal community organisation'.[184] This system was seen to strengthen members' accountability to their local communities.

Several Indigenous scholars also questioned the requirement that voters and candidates had to be registered on the Commonwealth electoral roll.[185] Registration may be compulsory, but chapter two revealed that Indigenous enrolment significantly lags that of non-Indigenous Australians. Reports suggest that the considerable gap is a combination of several factors, including education levels, health and social conditions, and the remoteness of some Indigenous communities.[186] However, it also reflects protest against the Australian state and constitutes an affirmation of Indigenous sovereignty. As Trudy Maluga, State

[178] John Ah Kit, Director Northern Land Council cited in F Brennan, 'ATSIC: Seeking a National Mouthpiece for Local Voices' (1990) 2(43) *Aboriginal Law Bulletin* 4, 5. See Part III.D.

[179] Foley, 'ATSIC' (1999) 6. See also: O'Donoghue Dissenting report in Hiatt (n 20) 117.

[180] Coombs (n 28) 183.

[181] Coombs (n 57).

[182] H Wooten, 'Self-Determination After ATSIC' (2004) 23 *Dialogue: Academy of the Social Sciences* 16, 17–18.

[183] Hiatt (n 20) 62. But see: O'Donoghue Dissenting report in Hiatt (n 20) 117.

[184] O'Donoghue (n 64) 16, 19. For more concerns see: House of Representatives Standing Committee on Aboriginal Affairs, Parliament of Australia, 'Our Future, Our Selves: Aboriginal and Torres Strait Islander Community Control, Management and Resources' (1990) 20 [2.18]–[2.19].

[185] See, eg: Foley (n 170) 6.

[186] Joint Standing Committee on Electoral Matters, Parliament of Australia, 'Civics and Electoral Education' (2007) 88 [5.8].

Secretary of the Tasmanian Aboriginal Centre explains, many Aboriginal and Torres Strait Islander peoples 'do not consider themselves part of the Australian nation and so have deliberately decided not to vote in white elections'.[187] Unlike earlier representative bodies, these individuals were prevented from interacting with the Commission on their own terms – meaning that the voices of a considerable number of people was not heard.[188]

ii. Evolution

Structural design choices had a direct impact as to whether Aboriginal and Torres Strait Islander people and communities initially viewed the Commission as a legitimate institution. For many, including Pat O'Shane (Yalangi), the first Indigenous magistrate, choices made at this stage meant that the Commission was a 'creation of non-Aboriginal Australia'.[189] Although effort was made to ensure Indigenous views were incorporated in its design, 'the values and priorities of the state'[190] predominated. The legitimacy of an institution is not static, however. It can rise and fall as its constituents come to accept it or nonetheless view it as securing important goals. Did Indigenous Australians come to perceive that ATSIC represented their interests, was accountable to them, and reflected their values?

Recognising the challenges inherent to its position as a government-established representative body, ATSIC strove to develop a sense of independence. It crafted important domestic policy on key areas,[191] and engaged in international advocacy; submitting communications, lodging comprehensive reports to international treaty bodies, and presenting views to UN forums. By directly articulating Indigenous aspirations, the Commission was able to distinguish and differentiate itself from government. Like its predecessors, however, ATSIC's increasingly independent action weakened its effectiveness as an operative within government and intensified attempts to marginalise and abolish it. Repeating Prime Minister Keating's strategy, in 2002 the Howard Government established

[187] ibid 88 [5.10].

[188] This requirement was initially adopted because reports found 'widespread resistance' to an Indigenous specific roll. By 1995 and 1997 ATSIC's Elections Review Panel found attitudes had 'altered significantly': Aboriginal and Torres Strait Islander Elections Review Panel, 'Review of Electoral Systems: A Report to the Minister for Aboriginal and Torres Strait Islander Affairs' (1995) 6, 7–9; Aboriginal and Torres Strait Islander Boundaries and Electoral System Review Panel (n 108) 10, Recommendation 2.1.

[189] P O'Shane, 'Aboriginal Political Movements: Some Observations' (13th Frank Archibald Memorial Lecture, University of New England, 14 October 1998) 6.

[190] J Robbins, 'Indigenous Political Representation in Liberal-Democratic Countries: A Comparative Analysis' in M Berg-Nordlie, J Saglie and A Sullivan (eds), *Indigenous Politics: Institutions, Representation, Mobilisation* (Colchester, ECPR Press, 2015) 61, 85.

[191] L Behrendt, 'Representative Structures – Lessons Learned from the ATSIC Era' (2009) 10 *Journal of Indigenous Policy* 35, 37.

an Office of Indigenous and Torres Strait Islander Affairs, 'to provide the Minister with a separate source of advice'.[192]

Consultations conducted by the Hannaford Review panel found considerable disquiet within Indigenous communities over attempts to marginalise ATSIC,[193] but it is not clear whether this ever translated into active support for the Commission. Indeed, while it is difficult to measure support, the political science literature discussed in chapter four suggests that voter turnout figures may indicate a causal relationship between trust in and support for the Commission. Examining voter turnout for the Regional Council elections reveals a complicated picture. At a national level, the Commission was largely unable to overcome its inauspicious start. Nationally, voting rates averaged around 20–25 per cent of estimated eligible voters across ATSIC's existence.[194] This figure compares favourably to similar non-compulsory local government elections held in South Australia and Western Australia in the early 1990s, suggesting that it is a 'respectable level of voter turnout … for voluntary elections',[195] but it hardly indicates widespread endorsement from the community. The figure also intensified concerns from the ideological right and left over the Commission's capacity to understand the interests of and speak for all Indigenous Australians.[196] This remained a recurrent problem. Even as the number of voters grew between 1990 and 2002, the voting rate improved only slightly,[197] revealing that the Commission struggled to obtain, or demonstrate, support across communities.

Focusing on the national figure elides distinctions across the country. The Commission's decentralised, regional structure meant each community played a significant role in the design and delivery of programmes and services tailored to their needs. In regional and remote areas, where ATSIC played a larger proportionate role in Indigenous communities, turnout was consistently higher.[198] In some places, this distinction was marked: in the 1993 elections, for instance, turnout in Cooktown in regional Queensland reached 79 per cent, evidencing significant support. In contrast, in Sydney turnout lagged at a dismal nine per cent.[199] It appears that this considerable regional distinction persisted throughout ATSIC's life: In 2002, the top 18 regions with turnout above 30 per cent were all in 'sparsely settled northern and central Australia'.[200]

[192] Senate Select Committee on the Administration of Aboriginal Affairs (n 85) 30 [2.90].
[193] Hannaford, Huggins and Collins (n 85) 51.
[194] Sanders, Taylor and Ross (n 109) 502.
[195] W Sanders, 'Participation and Representation in the 2002 ATSIC Elections' (Centre for Aboriginal Economic Policy Research, Discussion Paper No 252, 2003) 7.
[196] R Brunton, 'Low Turnout Undermines ATSIC' (1994) 46 *IPA Review* 8; Foley (n 170).
[197] Sanders, 'ATSIC's Achievements and Strengths' (2004) 1.
[198] Behrendt, 'Representative Structures' (2009) 58.
[199] W Sanders, 'Reconciling Public Accountability and Aboriginal Self-Determination/Self-Management: Is ATSIC Succeeding?' (1994) 53 *Australian Journal of Public Administration* 475, 486.
[200] Sanders, 'Participation and Representation' (2003) 7.

These figures should be treated carefully. In addition to the fact that many Aboriginal and Torres Strait Islander people did not support voting as the mechanism to choose representatives, no national register of people eligible to vote was ever created, complicating turnout figures. In the absence of an Indigenous-specific electoral roll, turnout was measured against estimates of the eligible Indigenous population as recorded in the census. This is problematic, as the Indigenous population enumerated in the five-yearly national censuses 'increased faster than can be explained by demographic factors alone', perhaps as the propensity of Indigenous people to identify as such increased, or enhanced enumeration methods were adopted.[201] It is not clear whether individuals who newly identified as being of Indigenous origin in the census considered themselves eligible to vote in ATSIC elections.[202] If this is the case, then the voting rate is lower than it should be. Indeed, in Tasmania in 2002, where a separate roll was drawn up, a more respectable 55 per cent of those enrolled, voted.[203]

Ownership assesses whether Indigenous people regard an institution designed to empower them with the capacity to be heard in the processes of government as legitimate. For many Aboriginal and Torres Strait Islander peoples, ATSIC could never satisfy this standard. In the words of Irene Watson (Tanganekald, Meintangk and Boandik), 'how could a structure, like ATSIC, based as it was upon hierarchy, patriarchy, and entrenched colonialism, serve the Aboriginal community?'[204] For individuals like Watson, this is likely to be true for any state-supported Indigenous institution, but a more generous view suggests two points.

First, although the extent to which Aboriginal and Torres Strait Islander communities and organisations were able to meaningfully influence the Commission's design was limited, consultation was more extensive than any previous reform effort. Those consultations allowed Indigenous Australians to engage with and challenge the proposal. In some cases, it led to minor amendments to the Bill. Second, despite its formal relationship with government, ATSIC increased its legitimacy in the eyes of Indigenous Australians. It worked hard to develop an independent streak, agitating for priorities meaningful to Indigenous peoples and challenging government policy. While turnout figures nationally and in urban areas remained poor, in regional and remote communities where ATSIC had the greatest footprint, it was rewarded by small yet steadily increased voter engagement at successive elections. These are positive and productive signs, suggesting that despite the Commission's broader challenges, some regional councils were regarded as effective and legitimate institutions. The Commission faced serious limitations, but future institutional design can learn from its experience.

[201] ibid.
[202] ibid.
[203] Sanders (n 121) 1–2.
[204] Watson, 'Settled and Unsettled Spaces' (2007) 24.

D. Integrity

Integrity connotes notions of responsibility, stewardship and accountability. It is concerned with whether ATSIC had a credible governance structure such that its leaders acted according to the purposes and values for which they were entrusted with authority. ATSIC was subject to an extensive stringent accountability regime. However, that regime was largely focused on controlling and checking Indigenous decision-making authority, rather than necessarily ensuring proper public administration. As such, while the majority of the Commission's members exercised their powers responsibly, the behaviour of two key individuals in the early 2000s revealed significant deficiencies. First, inadequate provisions managing conflicts of interests led to accusations that a Commissioner had misappropriated public funds.[205] Second, the Howard Government's longstanding opposition to ATSIC allowed leaders to frame criticism of their personal behaviour as part of a wider attack on the Commission and Indigenous Australians and refuse to stand down. Occurring simultaneously, these events revealed fatal weaknesses in the Commission's governance structure.

An affront to some conceptions of Australian identity, ATSIC served as a lightning rod for political criticism, leading public accountability to become one of the two 'key imperatives' of the Act.[206] Reflecting those familiar themes of formal equality and national unity, the legal accountability framework that was established largely aimed at inhibiting Indigenous decision-making authority rather than ensuring proper stewardship of public funds. Between 1988 and 1989, 'no less than 91 … amendments'[207] were made to the ATSIC Bill in response to five inquiries into the administration of Indigenous affairs. As Prime Minister Hawke explained in Parliament, these amendments were aimed at finding 'the right balance'[208] between the objectives of self-determination and accountability. Whether that balance was struck is open to question; Diane Smith contends that 'every stage in the devolution of powers' to ATSIC was 'met by increased requirements for public accountability measures'.[209] At its establishment the Commission operated under a more stringent accountability framework than any other department or statutory authority.[210]

Among other integrity provisions, the Commission was the only independent statutory authority with an internal Office of Evaluation and Audit (OEA).[211]

205 See eg, 'Robinson Seeks Source of Leak' *ABC News*, 26 June 2003, available at www.abc.net.au/news/2003-06-26/robinson-seeks-source-of-leak/1877108.

206 Sanders, 'Is ATSIC Succeeding?' (1994) 475 (the other being self-determination).

207 ibid 477.

208 Commonwealth, *Parliamentary Debates*, House of Representatives, 11 April 1989, 1325–26.

209 Smith, 'From Cultural Diversity to Regionalism' (1996) 27.

210 Commonwealth, *Parliamentary Debates*, House of Representatives, 23 May 1989, 2734 (Gerry Hand).

211 M Ivanitz, 'The Demise of ATSIC? Accountability and the Coalition Government' (2000) 59 *Australian Journal of Public Administration* 3, 6.

The OEA director was authorised to evaluate and audit the Commission's operations, and every programme conducted or funded by the Commission, at least once every three years.[212] Appointed directly by the minister, the director took instructions from the minister, not the ATSIC Board, though he or she was required to report in writing to both.[213] To comply with these statutory requirements, the Office 'undertook an average of nearly 60 audits, evaluations and reviews annually between 1993 and 2003'.[214] As the Commission noted, this extensive accountability framework was arguably inconsistent with 'the degree of autonomy that ATSIC should reasonably be expected to have'.[215]

Accountability requirements were enhanced by the Howard Government. In its first Cabinet meeting following the 1996 election, the Government initiated a comprehensive audit of ATSIC programmes on the basis that 'ATSIC [was] not accountable for the funds it receive[d]',[216] and appointed a special auditor to review all 1,122 ATSIC-funded organisations. The Federal Court subsequently determined that the appointment was ultra vires,[217] but the auditor had by then cleared 95 per cent of the organisations, with the remaining five per cent largely amounting to minor technical breaches.[218] Thereafter the Government unsuccessfully sought to amend the ATSIC Act to enable the minister to install an administrator if fraud or mismanagement was suspected, and to restore the minister's power to directly appoint the chairperson and two Commissioners, rather than allow Indigenous peoples themselves to select their leader.[219]

These examples detail the extent to which the Government employed accountability requirements to interfere and check Indigenous decision-making, but the Commission did face some inherent integrity challenges. Most significantly, the combination of representative and administrative roles empowered elected Indigenous leaders to make decisions over funding projects in communities. This constituted a marked change in Australian governance, but as the Shadow Minister for Aboriginal Affairs foreshadowed in 1989, this entitlement also placed Commissioners in 'an invidious position',[220] opening them up to situations of real and apparent conflicts of interests. ATSIC acknowledged the risk that councillors and Commissioners may participate in decisions over programmes in which they had a pecuniary or other interest but found widespread community support against legally separating these responsibilities. Noting that members will have specific knowledge of issues within their

[212] ATSIC Act (n 74) ss 76, 78.

[213] ibid s 76.

[214] Cunningham and Baeza, 'An "Experiment" in Indigenous Social Policy' (2005) 463–64.

[215] ATSIC (n 100) 46, Recommendation 33.

[216] I Anderson, 'The End of Aboriginal Self-Determination' (2007) 39 *Futures* 137, 144.

[217] *Aboriginal Services v Senator Herron* [1996] FCA 826.

[218] Ivanitz, 'The Politics of Accountability' (1999) 4.

[219] Aboriginal and Torres Strait Islander Commission Amendment Bill 1996 (Cth) Schedule 1, item 19.

[220] Commonwealth, *Parliamentary Debates*, House of Representatives, 23 May 1989, 2716–7 (Warwick Smith).

communities, the Commission recommended that the board and regional councils establish policies to govern the funding of individual projects,[221] suggesting that elected representatives with a pecuniary interest in a matter should be able to take part in discussion, but not in any decision, over funding.[222]

The inherent tension came to a head in late 2002 when it was revealed that 'Sugar' Ray Robinson, ATSIC's deputy chairperson, was subject to a series of investigations concerning his conduct as an administrator and board member of several Aboriginal organisations.[223] Responding to these allegations, the minister issued two general directions under the ATSIC Act to prevent Commissioners making grants or loans, or giving guarantees, to bodies on which full-time ATSIC officeholders or staff were directors or in a position to exercise control.[224] Protesting his innocence, Robinson resigned as deputy chair in June 2003 but remained a Commissioner, and was subsequently convicted of misappropriating $45,000 of taxpayer funds.[225] In the meantime, the Government legally separated ATSIC's dual responsibilities by establishing ATSIS.[226] This decision stripped ATSIC of its powers to make funding decisions, ensuring that no elected representative had an actual or apparent conflict of interest, but it also downgraded the Commission 'to the role of an advisory body'.[227]

The allegations against Robinson came only a few months after serious charges were levied against Geoff Clark, ATSIC's chairperson. In 2001, Clark was charged with historic sex offences. Although a magistrate found insufficient evidence to bring the case to trial it proved the catalyst for more women to come forward with rape allegations. Further criminal charges were dismissed but two civil cases were launched in 2002. The High Court allowed those cases to go ahead,[228] and ultimately in 2007, a six-member jury found Clark guilty of leading two gang rapes in 1971.[229] Around the same time, it was revealed that ATSIC had agreed to allocate $45,000 to fund Clark's legal defence relating to

[221] ATSIC (n 100) 18, Recommendation 11. O'Donoghue considered that the problem may be 'potentially insurmountable' as members are elected 'because they are prominent in Aboriginal organisations, but it is Aboriginal organisations that are the main recipients of ATSIC funding': L O'Donoghue, 'In Indigenous Affairs Nothing is New, Just Forgotten' (1997) 56 *Australian Journal of Public Administration* 5, 8.

[222] ATSIC (n 100) 2, 18–19.

[223] S Rintoul, 'This Time It's Do Or Die – The ATSIC Elections' *The Australian* (21 October 2002).

[224] Hon Philip Ruddock MP, 'Directions to ATSIC Concerning Conflicts of Interest' (media release, IPS 080/2002, 24 December 2002).

[225] T Koch and M McKenna, '"Sugar" Ray Robinson $45,000 No-Pay Order Reviewed' *The Australian* (15 April 2011).

[226] Commonwealth, *Gazette* No S 183, 30 May 2003; Hon Philip Ruddock MP, 'Good Governance and Conflicts of Interest in ATSIC' (media release, IPS 028/2003, 17 April 2003).

[227] Hannaford, Huggins and Collins (n 85) 73; Senate Select Committee on the Administration of Aboriginal Affairs (n 85) 21 [2.43].

[228] *Stingel v Clark* (2006) 228 ALR 229.

[229] S Rintoul, 'Leader of Rape Pack' *The Australian* (31 January 2007). Clark's appeal was dismissed: *Clark v Stingel* [2007] VSCA 292 (11 December 2007).

a stand-off with police in Warrnambool, Victoria in May 2002.[230] While the magistrate acknowledged that anti-Indigenous racism had sparked the incident, Clark was convicted of riotous behaviour and obstructing police as they sought to remove an intoxicated person.[231]

Throughout all this Clark remained in his position, damaging the Commission's credibility and revealing serious weaknesses in its mechanisms of legal and political accountability. The ATSIC Act did not require officers to stand down if charged with an offence, and Philip Ruddock, the Minister for Indigenous Affairs, was reticent to force Clark to do so before the legal process concluded. While Ruddock's successor, Amanda Vanstone, did suspend Clark for 'misbehaviour', the Federal Court ruled that the dismissal was racially discriminatory and unlawful,[232] forcing Vanstone to reinstate him. The Government's initial reluctance to interfere is understandable. Although it remained antagonistic towards the Commission, interference would strengthen Clark's position on the board. Indeed, Clark framed the allegations as part of a 'campaign against the Aboriginal leadership',[233] arguing that his 'only crime' was his 'audacity to question … the treatment of Aboriginal people'.[234] Characterising his travails as racially motivated allowed Clark to secure the backing of the national board,[235] and silence his internal critics.[236]

The Clark and Robinson scandals placed the Commission in an unenviable position. The absence of a clear legal requirement forcing Clark and Robinson to stand down, and/or the failure of their fellow Commissioners to compel that action, revealed serious weaknesses in the Commission's governance framework. As a political institution, the Commission's effectiveness relied on community support and its capacity to effectuate outcomes. That these two scandals occurred and that they could fester for so long clearly damaged ATSIC's credibility within government, the public and the broader Indigenous community. Poor governance had consequences for ATSIC's capacity to effectively undertake its roles. In these circumstances, why would government meaningfully and respectfully engage with the Commission?

IV. ABOLITION

At its establishment, ATSIC was lauded as marking 'the turning point' in Indigenous – non-Indigenous relations; a moment 'when Australia moved from a

[230] C Banham, 'Ruddock Steps in as ATSIC Debates Clark's Legal Fees' *Sydney Morning Herald* (26 February 2003).

[231] On appeal the riotous behaviour charge was dismissed: M Schwartz, *A Question of Power: The Geoff Clark Case* (Melbourne, Black Inc, 2008) 27.

[232] *Clark v Vanstone* (2004) 211 ALR 412; affirmed by the Full Federal Court in *Vanstone v Clark* (2005) 224 ALR 666.

[233] R Rennie-Gwaybilla, 'Clark Speaks Out' *The Koori Mail* (9 April 2003) 7.

[234] M Kingston, 'The Sound of Values Clashing' *Sydney Morning Herald* (20 June 2001).

[235] See, eg: T O'Shane et al, 'Chairs Support Leaders' *The Koori Mail* (9 April 2003) 18.

[236] McGlade, *Our Greatest Challenge* (2012) 82.

position of, firstly, contempt and ridicule of Aboriginal Australians; secondly, to a position of paternalism; and now to a period in which Aboriginal Australians are entitled to self-management, self-respect and self-determination'.[237] Just 15 years later, the Commission was abolished with bipartisan support. Why?

This chapter revealed that there are philosophical, structural and individual reasons for ATSIC's demise. Ultimately, while the Howard Government had long made clear its antipathy to the Commission, the antics of Clark and Robinson revealed an institution unable or unwilling to ensure that its leaders operated with integrity. Labor could no longer defend ATSIC. On 30 March 2004, the Labor caucus agreed that they would abolish the Commission if successful at the upcoming election. Opposition Leader Mark Latham explained:

> ATSIC is no longer capable of addressing endemic problems in Indigenous communities. It has lost the confidence of much of its own constituency and the wider community. Unhappily the current model has not delivered sufficient gains to Indigenous communities. It's been very much damaged by leadership turmoil, and I've publicly declared my lack of confidence in Geoff Clark in that capacity. It's also been damaged by the failure of the Howard Government to deliver reform effectively. ATSIC's been gutted by the Howard Government in recent times, and it is leaving very much a vacuum in terms of Indigenous policy.[238]

Bipartisan support may have existed for ATSIC's closure, but distinctions remained between the two major parties. While Labor agreed that the national board should be abolished, they rejected returning expenditure on Indigenous affairs to mainstream departments and argued that the Commission's regional structure should be retained and adapted to continue to empower Indigenous Australians with a voice in their own affairs.[239] They were unsuccessful. The Amendment Act that passed Parliament on 24 March 2005 abolished ATSIC in its entirety. All that remained was the separate Torres Strait Regional Authority, carved out in the mid-1990s.

In November 2004, the Government announced the formation of the NIC. A government-appointed 14-member body, the Council was intended to 'provide expert advice to the government on a range of matters that are of concern to Australia's Indigenous peoples'.[240] The Minister for Indigenous Affairs emphasised that the NIC 'is not intended to replace ATSIC',[241] though leaked Cabinet documents suggested otherwise.[242] In any case, the minister acknowledged that in the absence of the Commission, 'or any other national Indigenous body, the

[237] Commonwealth, *Parliamentary Debates*, House of Representatives, 2 November 1989, 2439 (Duncan Kerr).

[238] ABC Radio National, 'Labor would Abolish ATSIC *PM*, 30 March 2004 (Mark Latham).

[239] See AAP, 'Labor would abolish ATSIC: Latham' *Sydney Morning Herald* (30 March 2004).

[240] 'National Indigenous Council Terms of Reference' (2005) 9(3) *Australian Indigenous Law Reporter* 107.

[241] ibid.

[242] C Graham, 'NIC Claims False, Leaked Cabinet Document Reveals' *National Indigenous Times* (8 November 2004).

NIC may play an important role in Indigenous policy at the federal level'.[243] Aboriginal and Torres Strait Islander leaders across the political spectrum attacked the Council. Noel Pearson described it as a 'step backwards', while Patrick Dodson (Yawuru) considered that the Government had 'copped out' on giving Aboriginal people a 'real say' in their future.[244] Like all its predecessors, the NIC itself was wound up in 2008.

V. CONCLUSION

ATSIC had serious flaws. Operational and design challenges meant that the Commission struggled to include and express the diversity of Indigenous voices to government. Although some regional councils were effective at securing important local projects and programmes, nationally ATSIC never received more than lukewarm support, as evidenced by generally anaemic voter turnout and despite the Commission's best efforts advocating for Indigenous interests in local, national and international forums. While its enabling statute suggested a real capacity to exercise independent policy and decision-making power, in practice, successive governments burdened the Commission with extensive public accountability requirements targeted at impeding self-determination. Paternalistic control and the Howard Government's longstanding philosophical objection to the Commission, led some Commissioners to excuse the alleged criminal behaviour of its chair and deputy chair. Inability or indisposition to removing these individuals revealed serious weaknesses in ATSIC's integrity mechanisms, fatally damaging the Commission's credibility, and its consequent ability to effectively exercise its responsibilities. As Lenny Clarke, an Aboriginal Elder from Framlingham Aboriginal Community near Warrnambool, neatly summarised at the time: 'By the end, [ATSIC] wasn't effective and it wasn't delivering to the people who most needed help. It got caught up in a lot of issues that clouded its focus rather than the issues that really mattered'.[245] The Commission ended its days unloved by both major parties, the public and many Aboriginal and Torres Strait Islander people.

Today, however, a real sense of guarded nostalgia for the Commission exists among Indigenous Australians. That nostalgia permeated the Referendum Council regional dialogues and reappears in evidence to parliamentary inquiries.[246] The minister responsible for ATSIC's abolition also has regrets.[247] Perhaps this is unsurprising. The 15-year period without a national representative

[243] 'National Indigenous Council Terms of Reference' (n 240).

[244] Cited in G Ring, 'National Indigenous Council Knackered?' *Crikey* (5 December 2007), available at www.crikey.com.au/2007/12/05/national-indigenous-council-knackered.

[245] Cited in P Wilmoth, 'Under the Skin' *The Age* (20 March 2005).

[246] See, eg: Evidence to Joint Select Committee on Constitutional Recognition Relating to Aboriginal and Torres Strait Islander Peoples, Parliament of Australia, Dubbo, 2 July 2018, 11 (Alistair Ferguson).

[247] S Fitzpatrick, 'Dismantling ATSIC Probably a Mistake, Says Amanda Vanstone' *The Australian* (1 August 2018).

body for Indigenous Australians, without an institution designed to empower Indigenous peoples to have their voices heard in the processes of government, casts the Commission in a more favourable light. Despite its problems, the ATSIC Act was a 'direct recognition of the existence of Indigenous governance',[248] and an acknowledgement that the distinctive status of Aboriginal and Torres Strait Islander peoples necessitates a restructured relationship with the Australian state based on respect and mutual trust.

Chapter seven will draw on this material to outline how a contemporary national representative body could empower Aboriginal and Torres Strait Islander peoples to have their voices heard in the processes of government. That body may be better placed than the Commission as it will have the benefit of building on the significant developments that have occurred since 1989. Before that, however, it is worth emphasising four lessons for institutional design and structural reform.

First, and most importantly, the Commission's experiences reveal that integrity is critical. An institution that fails to ensure its leaders act according to the purposes and values for which they have been entrusted with authority will lose the support of its community and will not be effective in advocating for the interests of its constituents. Difficult questions surrounding the precise standard to adopt in monitoring the exercise of public power will remain, but whatever framework is employed must be effective at ensuring leaders exercise proper stewardship. ATSIC failed this test.

Second, while not all of the challenges ATSIC faced were problems of institutional design, many were. The decision to uniformly adopt electoral representation, for instance, caused some Indigenous peoples to question whether the Commission reflected their values. A design process centred on and driven by Aboriginal and Torres Strait Islander people and communities would likely have resulted in a mixed-member system, or at least a model that more directly drew on and affirmed diverse Indigenous communities' understandings of political authority. More than simply strengthening the initial legitimacy of the Commission, allowing Indigenous Australians to design ATSIC may have led to positive consequences into the future by enhancing the prospect that it expressed the diversity of Indigenous voices. A culturally appropriate body with broad support and evidence that it accurately reflects and articulates Indigenous peoples' interests would wield greater soft power and be more difficult to marginalise and ignore. In this sense, *ownership* is not just connected to *voices*, but also *power* and *integrity*.

[248] A Reilly, 'A Constitutional Framework for Indigenous Governance' (2006) 28 *Sydney Law Review* 403, 417. See also Sanders, 'Towards an Indigenous Order of Government' (2002) 11.

Third, ATSIC's experience underscores how important financial capacity is for an institution to effectively and independently exercise its decision-making powers. While mechanisms to ensure proper public administration are necessary, stringent public accountability and reporting requirements combined with extensive quarantined funding severely inhibited the Commission's ability to identify and fund distinctive local projects, reducing its role to an Indigenous-controlled 'government department'.[249] It also had several practical consequences. Fewer projects reduced opportunities for the Commission to ground itself within the Indigenous community by demonstrating its worth as budget cuts compelled the Board to rationalise programmes. That said, the decision to abolish the Office of Indigenous Women in 1997 and thereby further weaken its capacity to understand and address Indigenous women's distinctive concerns was clearly ill-advised.

Greater budgetary constraints may also have contributed to apparent conflicts of interest, as councillors and Commissioners could have felt more pressure to ensure that funding was delivered to their communities. Moreover, misinformation over the Commission's role and responsibilities enabled state and federal governments to 'fuel[] public perception' that ATSIC was responsible for all government-funded Indigenous programmes.[250] As the Hannaford Review found, 'time and again' the Commission was 'used as a scapegoat for poor Indigenous affairs outcomes (even when the program responsibility concerned clearly did not belong to ATSIC)'.[251] With greater control over their own finances, many of these problems may have been resolved. Perhaps a future body should 'accept responsibility only for discretionary funding that is allocated to them, and leave non-discretionary funding to be made through mainstream government departments'.[252]

A final lesson concerns the state. An Indigenous representative body with a formal relationship and statutory right to advise government on matters concerning Indigenous affairs must be allowed to advocate for interests different to and in contest with government policy. State anxiety over the approaches taken or issues adopted by such a body is self-defeating. These bodies are intended to empower Indigenous peoples to be heard in the processes of government. While it may not always be effective in persuading government, this role is impossible to carry out where interference weakens community trust and confidence in the institution to the extent that it is regarded as illegitimate.

[249] J Chesterman and B Galligan, *Citizens without Rights: Aborigines and Australian Citizenship* (Cambridge, Cambridge University Press, 1998) 213.

[250] Davis, 'ATSIC and Indigenous Women' (2008) 75.

[251] Hannaford, Huggins and Collins (n 95) 33 [4.59].

[252] Reilly, 'A Constitutional Framework' (2006) 433. This can be complicated in practice: see ch 6.

6

The Swedish Sámediggi

I. INTRODUCTION

On 26 August 1993, King Carl XVI Gustaf opened the first session of the Swedish Sámediggi[1] in a ceremony at the Town Hall in Kiruna, the northernmost city in Sweden. Intended to give Sámi living in Sweden a 'real ability to independently develop their culture on their own terms',[2] national newspapers reporting on the event remarked on the 'festive, crowded and colourful' atmosphere,[3] the performance of traditional joik,[4] and the contrasting receptions received by the Royal Family and the Minister responsible for the Parliament.[5]

The opening of the Sámediggi both reflected and contributed to a shift in the rights of Indigenous peoples across the Nordic states. Just four years earlier, on 9 October 1989, King Olav V of Norway presided over the first session of the Norwegian Sámediggi.[6] In neighbouring Finland, a Sámi representative body had existed since 1973,[7] but its authority was largely limited to issuing statements on Sámi affairs.[8] On 2 March 1996, less than three years after its Swedish counterpart was inaugurated, it was reconstituted and its role enhanced as the Finnish Sámediggi.[9] Ingwar Åhrén, the first President of the Swedish Sámediggi, warmly embraced these developments, hailing the creation of the representative bodies as marking a 'milestone in … Sámi endeavours to achieve self-determination'.[10] Non-Indigenous scholars observing this shift wondered

[1] 'Sámediggi' is the Northern Sámi word for the Sámi Parliament. There are three recognised Sámi languages in Sweden (though more exist), with Northern Sámi the most widely spoken.

[2] Sámi Rights Commission, *Samerätt och sameting* (SOU 1989:41) 147.

[3] A Reichwald, 'Festligt sameting under protest' *Dagens Nyheter* (27 August 1993) A14.

[4] 'Samer kräver unckels avgång' *Svenska Dagbladet* (27 August 1993) 16.

[5] C Hård, 'Kram, drottning silvia' *Expressen* (27 August 1993) A20–21.

[6] Sami Act 1987 (Norway).

[7] Cabinet Decree on a Sámi Assembly, No 824, 9 November 1973 (Finland).

[8] L Müller-Wille, 'The Sámi Parliament in Finland: A Model for Ethnic Minority Management?' (1979) 3 *Études/Inuit/Studies* 63, 68; L Sillanpää, *Political and Administrative Responses to Sámi Self-Determination: A Comparative Study of Public Administrations in Fennoscandia on the Issue of Sámi Land Title as an Aboriginal Right* (Helsinki, Finnish Society of Science and Letters, 1994) 114–15.

[9] Act on the Sámi Parliament (974/1995) (Finland).

[10] I Åhrén, 'Small Nations of the North in Constitutional and International Law' (1995) 64 *Nordic Journal of International Law* 457, 460.

whether these parliaments could lead to 'a meaningful consociational dialogue' between Sámi and the state.[11] Today, law and policy concerning the Sámi varies across the Nordic states, but these three institutions continue to serve as the principal vehicles for Sámi self-determination.

The Nordic Sámi Parliaments have attained prominence globally.[12] The United Nations Special Rapporteur on the Rights of Indigenous Peoples has described them as important models 'for Indigenous self-governance and participation in decision-making that could inspire the development of similar institutions elsewhere in the world'.[13] UN treaty bodies and the Expert Mechanism on the Rights of Indigenous Peoples agree, referring favourably to these institutional mechanisms of Indigenous participation and self-determination.[14] It is not surprising then that Indigenous peoples across the globe seeking structural change to the state(s) that claims their lands look to the Sámi Parliaments. In Australia, as debate over constitutional recognition and reform has intensified, the Nordic models have been identified as potentially valuable comparators.[15] For many Aboriginal and Torres Strait Islander people, the existence of a national representative body in Sweden, Norway, and Finland – an Indigenous Parliament no less – is a powerful reminder of their own voicelessness in the processes of Australian government. If the Nordic Sámediggi's are to be useful comparators for institutional design in Australia and elsewhere, however, it is imperative that they are well understood. This chapter aids this project by detailed examination of the Swedish Sámediggi.

The opening of the Sámediggi represented a new beginning for the relationship between Sweden and Sámi, but concerns were raised early over the substance of that relationship. On the very day the Parliament was inaugurated, three reindeer herders 'camped in a tepee-like shelter on a grassy slope outside the Town Hall', completed the fifth day of a hunger strike denouncing proposed legislation divesting Sámi of their right to be consulted in the issuing of hunting

[11] Sillanpää, *Political and Administrative Responses to Sámi Self-Determination* (1994) 84.

[12] A Stepien, A Petrétei and T Koivurova, 'Sámi Parliaments in Finland, Norway, and Sweden' in T Malloy, A Osipov and B Vizi (eds), *Managing Diversity through Non-Territorial Autonomy: Assessing Advantages, Deficiencies, and Risks* (Oxford, Oxford University Press, 2015) 117, 117. Owing to their significant distinctions, however, there is no 'unified Nordic model': E Josefsen, U Mörkenstam and R Nilsson, 'The Nordic Sámediggis and the Limits of Indigenous Self-Determination' (2016) 1 *Gáldu Čála – Journal of Indigenous Peoples Rights* 1, 39.

[13] J Anaya, 'The Situation of the Sámi People in the Sápmi Region of Norway, Sweden and Finland', UN Doc A/HRC/18/35/Add.2 (6 June 2011) 11 [37].

[14] Human Rights Committee, 'Consideration of Reports Submitted by States Parties under Article 40 of the Covenant: Norway', UN Doc CCPR/C/79/Add.27 (4 November 1993) 2 [6]; Expert Mechanism on the Rights of Indigenous Peoples, 'Final Study on Indigenous Peoples and the Right to Participate in Decision-Making', UN Doc A/HRC/EMRIP/2011/2 (26 May 2011) 6–7 [24]–[27].

[15] N Hunter, 'A Place at the Constitutional Table' in M Davis and M Langton (eds), *It's Our Country: Indigenous Arguments for Meaningful Constitutional Recognition and Reform* (Melbourne, Melbourne University Press, 2016) 114, 116; S Morris, 'False Equality' in S Morris (ed), *A Rightful Place: A Road Map to Recognition* (Melbourne, Black Inc, 2017) 209, 216, 231.

permits on their traditional lands. Josef Pittja, one of the hunger strikers, articulated their central concern as one of disempowerment, exclaiming: 'we have repeatedly asked to be given a say in the new rules but we have been ignored'.[16] The legislation was passed against the wishes of major Sámi organisations and before the new Sámi Parliament could consider it; 'a provocation' a national newspaper remarked, 'so rough that it is hard to believe that it was accidental'.[17]

Reflecting on this and similar experiences, many Sámi have long argued that their ability to participate and meaningfully influence decision-making on issues that affect their interests, let alone exercise genuine authority through the Sámediggi, is inadequate. Similarly, many scholars have remarked that its formal legal status and position within the Swedish constitutional and political system suggests that it may not be an appropriate vehicle to realise Sámi aspirations.[18] This chapter builds on this critical literature by assessing the Swedish Sámediggi against the broader set of criteria infused by Indigenous aspirations and consistent with public law principles drawn out in chapter four: *voices*; *power*; *ownership*; and *integrity*.

The chapter is divided into two substantive parts. I first situate the analysis by placing the Sámediggi in its social, political and legal context. I explain who the Sámi are, set out the Swedish constitutional and political system, and outline the legal basis and institutional design of the Parliament. This material provides vital background, enabling a clear assessment of the Sámediggi against the four criteria. I examine whether the Parliament empowers the Sámi with the: (1) capacity to be heard in decisions that affect them; and (2) authority and financial capacity to exercise independent policy and decision-making power over matters relating to internal or local affairs. I also ask whether: (3) the Sámi recognise the Parliament as legitimate; and (4) the Sámediggi's leaders act according to the purposes and values for which they have been entrusted with authority and are accountable for their actions. Close examination of the Sámediggi identifies several lessons for institutional design. These lessons are explored in more detail in chapter seven.

II. THE SÁMEDIGGI IN CONTEXT

A. The Sámi

The Sámi are an Indigenous people whose traditional lands, Sápmi, stretch approximately 600,000km^2 across northern Fenno-Scandinavia and the Kola Peninsula.

[16] G McIvor, 'Sweden: Hunting Row Clouds Opening of Sámi Parliament' *InterPress Third World News Agency* (29 August 1993).

[17] 'Sametinget kunde fått batter start' *Dagens Nyheter* (27 August 1993) A2.

[18] See, eg: R Lawrence and U Mörkenstam, 'Indigenous Self-Determination through a Government Agency? The Impossible Task of the Swedish Sámediggi' (2016) 23 *International Journal on Minority and Group Rights* 105; Anaya, 'The Situation of the Sámi People' (2011) 11 [37]; Stepien, Petrétei and Koivurova, 'Sámi Parliaments' (2015).

Although these lands are now claimed by four states – Norway, Sweden, Finland and Russia – the Sámi are 'one people residing across national borders',[19] 'enjoying a distinctive identity, language, history, culture and social structure, as well as unique traditions, livelihoods and aspirations'.[20] For thousands of years, Sámi have developed and maintained their society, uniquely adapted to the Arctic environment. Initially, Sámi practiced a nomadic lifestyle. Over time, those that settled permanently along the coast developed an extensive fishing industry, and supplemented this by farming, trapping and reindeer husbandry. Those in the interior of Sápmi generally pursued hunting and trapping.[21] Around the 1500s, these Sámi began to tame reindeer and form them into herding groups.[22] In following annual reindeer migrations across Sápmi, they came into conflict with Nordic communities colonising northern Scandinavia.

Sámi society was traditionally organised around the siida, a type of village assembly that played a key role in allocating resources and responding to societal issues within the community. The precise siida structure varied, reflecting differences in the main livelihoods across Sápmi,[23] but significant commonalities existed. Each siida was composed of several family groups, ranging from only a handful, to up to 20 or 30 and comprising several hundred people;[24] in reindeer herding areas, siidas were generally smaller, perhaps consisting of only a couple of households. Every siida had its own administrative council and territorial zone, delimited by natural boundaries, and by the early eleventh century it is believed that Sápmi was 'divided into an unbroken pattern of some 60–100 siidas'.[25] As large-scale reindeer herding commenced in the 1500s, the siida adapted to manage the shift to 'fully nomadic herding practices',[26] but no 'deep or permanent cooperation between independent siidas' developed, and this community remained the highest level of Sámi political society.[27]

The formal partition of Sápmi occurred gradually and unevenly, as competing states sought to extend northwards and consolidate their power. Initially,

[19] Seventh international Sámi Conference, Gällivare, Sweden, 1971. Reproduced in Sillanpää (n 8) 60.

[20] J Henriksen, 'The Continuous Process of Recognition and Implementation of the Sámi People's Right to Self-Determination' (2008) 21 *Cambridge Review of International Affairs* 27, 27.

[21] M Åhrén, 'Indigenous Peoples' Culture, Customs, and Traditions and Customary Law – The Saami People's Perspective' (2004) 21 *Arizona Journal of International and Comparative Law* 63, 65–68.

[22] D Muga, 'A Commentary on the Historical Transformation of the Sámi Communal Mode of Production' (1986) 14 *The Journal of Ethnic Studies* 111, 111.

[23] Åhrén, 'Indigenous Peoples' Culture, Customs, and Traditions and Customary Law' (2004) 67.

[24] T Ingold, 'The Transformation of the Siida' (1978) 43 *Ethnos* 146, 151.

[25] J Eriksson, *Partition and Redemption: A Machiavellian Analysis of Sámi and Basque Patriotism* (PhD thesis, Umea University, 1997) 82.

[26] MN Sara, 'Siida and Traditional Sámi Reindeer Herding Knowledge' (2009) 30 *The Northern Review* 153, 154.

[27] Eriksson, *Partition and Redemption* (1997) 82.

control was exercised via tax collection, but authority was inchoate and borders porous such that Sámi were often forced to pay tax to two or three states.[28] In 1751, the Strömstad Treaty demarcated the Norwegian–Swedish boundary, but the Lapp Codicil, an addendum to the Treaty, guaranteed Sámi access to their traditional lands on either side of the border in an effort to preserve 'the Lappish nation'.[29] Later treaties and state practice were not so generous; between 1809 and 1919 borders calcified. Notwithstanding some limited room for creative resistance, including changing their citizenship as they crossed borders,[30] this period saw traditional Sámi areas broken up and the disappearance of Sápmi. Across all four states, Sámi lands were legally considered unowned and appropriated by the respective Crown, despite centuries of taxpaying.

This remains the situation in Sweden today. Sámi reindeer herders have a constitutionally protected usufructuary right to their traditional lands based upon use and prescription from time immemorial,[31] but those lands are legally owned by the Crown or private parties. Although a National Boundary Commission identifying traditional Sámi territory released a report in 2006,[32] the Government has not implemented its findings,[33] and the state continues to assert that use rights cannot give rise to exclusive property rights. Sámi resist this contention in both political and judicial domains.

In 2016 they realised some success. That year, the Gällivare District Court dismissed the state's claim that traditional land occupied by the Girjas Sámi village was 'a borderless wilderness' and 'no-man's land' prior to the formation of the Swedish state, holding that Sámi have an exclusive right to hunt and fish on their traditional lands.[34] This decision was partially overruled by the Court of Appeal for Upper Norrland in 2018,[35] but in 2020 the Supreme Court affirmed the District Court judgment.[36] In a landmark decision, the Supreme Court recognised for the first time that Sámi reindeer herders possess an exclusive right

[28] K Nikul, *The Lappish Nation* (Bloomington, University of Indiana Press, 1977) 49.

[29] Eriksson (n 25) 84–86.

[30] P Lantto, 'Borders, Citizenship and Change: The Case of the Sámi People, 1751–2008' (2010) 14 *Citizenship Studies* 543, 549.

[31] *North Frostviken Sámi Village v State* (Högsta Domstolen, Case No 324/76, 29 January 1981) ('*Skattefjällsmålet*', or the '*Taxed Mountains Case*') reproduced in B Jahreskog (ed), *The Sámi National Minority in Sweden* (Stockholm, Almqvist and Wiksell International, 1982) 146.

[32] Betänkande av gränsdragningskommissionen för renskötselområdet, *Samernas sedvanemarker* (SOU 2006:14).

[33] Anaya (n 13) 14 [50].

[34] *Girjas sameby v Staten genom Justitiekanslern* (Gällivare Tingsrätt, Case No T 323-09, 3 February 2016). Discussed in R Lawrence and M Åhrén, 'Mining as Colonisation: The Need for Restorative Justice and Restitution of Traditional Sami Lands' in L Head, K Saltzman, G Setten and M Stenseke (eds), *Nature, Temporality and Environmental Management: Scandinavian and Australian Perspectives on Peoples and Landscapes* (New York, Routledge, 2016) 149.

[35] *Staten genom Justitiekanslern v Girjas sameby* (Hovrätten för Övre Norrlands, Case No T 214-16, 23 January 2018).

[36] *Staten genom Justitiekanslern v Girjas sameby* (Högsta Domstolen, Case No T 853-18, 23 January 2020).

to manage hunting and fishing within their territory. Although momentous, the Court did not consider whether Swedish law recognises Sámi rights to land. The Swedish Government's position also reveals ongoing tensions and contestation between Sámi and the state; the Government had sought an order dismissing Sami claims in their entirety, as well as costs.

Colonisation has left the Sámi a numerical minority within their traditional lands, but it is not possible to provide accurate figures of the Sámi population. Over many years, state policies encouraged their assimilation into the dominant Nordic communities, destroying languages and culture and forcing many to hide or reject their identity.[37] Today, no institution is responsible for systemic data collection, as the Nordic countries do not collect statistics on national minorities.[38] That said, various estimates exist, placing the total population of Sámi between 80,000 and 110,000, with around 50,000–65,000 in Norway, 20,000–40,000 in Sweden, 8,000–10,000 in Finland and around 2,000 in Russia.[39] The cloud over population figures makes it difficult to assess the distribution of Sámi people within each state, but it is clear that they are not only numerically small, but also territorially dispersed. Sámi constitute a numerical minority in most of Sápmi; only around the Tana River region in the Karasjok and Kautokeino municipalities within northern Finnmark County in Norway, and in the Utsjoki municipality in Finland, are Sámi a majority. In Sweden, most Sámi live in the northernmost Norrbotten and Västerbotten counties, but they do not constitute a majority in any municipality. Overall, Sámi constitute around just 0.5 per cent of the total Swedish population.

Compounding these demographic difficulties are cleavages that run through the Sámi community. A consequence of their historical division into independent siidas spread across a wide territory and differing experience of colonialism, Sámi are heterogeneous, with broad schisms along both livelihood and language. Despite the centrality of reindeer herding to Sámi identity, for instance, only around 10 per cent of Sámi who live in Sweden are members of a reindeer herding community.[40] Similarly, there are nine distinct Sámi language groups, some of which are mutually unintelligible, and many more local dialects. Those that speak a Sámi language at home are estimated to be between only one-quarter and one-half of the total population, and many languages are considered precarious, endangered or extinct.[41]

[37] H Minde, 'Assimilation of the Sámi – Implementation and Consequences' (2003) 20 *Acta Borealia* 121, 133.

[38] P Simon, 'Collecting Ethnic Statistics in Europe: A Review' (2012) 35 *Ethnic and Racial Studies* 1366, 1387.

[39] P Axelsson, '"In the National Registry, All People Are Equal": Sámi in Swedish Statistical Sources' in P Axelsson and P Sköld (eds), *Indigenous Peoples and Demography: The Complex Relation Between Identity and Demography* (New York, Berghan Books, 2011) 117, 117.

[40] A reindeer herding community is a state administrative unit created to manage the industry; it is not a modern version of the ancient siida.

[41] *Att Återta Mitt Språk: Åtgärder för att Stärka det Samiska Språket* (SOU 2006:19).

The occupational schism along reindeer herding has been created and exacerbated by the Swedish state. Its origins lie in government policies from the mid-1800s which constructed a homogenous Sámi identity around nomadic reindeer herding. Initially designed to maintain 'a peaceful cohabitation' between Sámi reindeer herders and Swedish farmers in Sápmi, this project introduced and reified an arbitrary distinction between 'real' and 'authentic' Sámi on the one hand, and Swedish citizens and non-reindeer herding Sámi on the other.[42] Early industry regulation characterised reindeer herding as '*the* Lappish occupation', or defined 'a Lapp' by their connection to reindeer herding,[43] imposing an exclusionary and artificial distinction. By 1928, this distinction gained coercive force, as state anxiety over 'overcrowd[ing]', led the Riksdag (Parliament) to enact legislation limiting the right to herd reindeer to people of 'Lappish origin', ie individuals descended patrilineally from nomadic reindeer herders.[44] The Act forcefully separated Sámi into two categories: reindeer herders and non-reindeer herders,[45] despite the fact that at this time, only about a third of Sámi people practiced this occupation.[46]

The rise of a minority rights discourse in the 1960s initially reinforced rather than challenged this dichotomy.[47] As the state considered that Sámi identity was inextricably bound to reindeer herding, legislation and policies were devised to protect and preserve 'authentic' and 'traditional' cultural practices. In the 1970s and 80s, Commissions of Inquiry recommended strengthening reindeer herding,[48] for it is 'the material prerequisite' of Sámi culture.[49] While language is today the key element of Sámi identity,[50] and the right to keep and herd reindeer is a 'collective right that belongs to all Sámi in Sweden',[51] imposed distinctions remain. To exercise this right an individual must be a member of a reindeer herding community.[52] In practice, this excludes a majority of Sámi living in Sweden from exercising their rights and 'creates a division between different Sámi rightholders' based on occupation.[53]

[42] U Mörkenstam, 'The Constitution of the Swedish Sámi People: Swedish Sámi Policy and the Justification of the Inner Colonisation of Sweden' in J Tripathy and S Padmanabhan (eds), *Becoming Minority: How Discourses and Policies Produce Minorities in Europe and India* (New Delhi, Sage, 2014) 88, 93; P Lantto and U Mörkenstam, 'Sámi Rights and Sámi Challenges: The Modernisation Process and the Swedish Sámi Movement, 1886–2006' (2008) 22 *Scandinavian Journal of History* 26, 30–31.

[43] Lantto and Mörkenstam, 'Sámi Rights and Sámi Challenges' (2008) 30–31 referring to 1886 and 1917 statutes.

[44] ibid 32. See further Axelsson, 'In the National Registry, All People Are Equal' (2011) 129.

[45] Mörkenstam, 'The Constitution of the Swedish Sámi People' (2014) 94.

[46] Lantto and Mörkenstam (n 42) 30.

[47] U Mörkenstam, 'Indigenous Peoples and the Right to Self-Determination: The Case of the Swedish Sámi People' (2005) 25 *The Canadian Journal of Native Studies* 433, 441.

[48] ibid 442. Citing *Samerna i Sverige: Stöd åt språk och kultur* (SOU 1975:99) 131.

[49] ibid 445. Citing *Rennäringens Ekonom* (SOU 1983:67) 135.

[50] Lantto and Mörkenstam (n 42) 40. Citing *Samerätt och samiskt språk slutbetänkande* (SOU 1990:91) 149.

[51] SOU 1989:41 (n 2) 264. See further: Instrument of Government (1974) ch 2, art 20 (Instrument of Government); Reindeer Husbandry Act (SFS 1971:437) s 1 (Reindeer Husbandry Act).

[52] Reindeer Husbandry Act (n 51), s 1.

[53] A Lof, 'Locking in and Locking out: A Critical Analysis of the Governance of Reindeer Husbandry in Sweden' (2016) 10 *Critical Policy Studies* 426, 427.

B. Framework of Swedish Governance

Sweden is a parliamentary constitutional monarchy, with three levels of government. At the national level, power is distributed between the Riksdag and the executive. The executive includes several ministries and around 400 government agencies and public authorities. Government agencies are state-controlled organisations empowered to carry out government policies, while ministries are relatively small and generally restricted to developing policy and monitoring agencies under their purview. The small size of the ministries reflects the Swedish administrative state's dualistic structure. Ministers are indirectly prohibited from governing their subordinate agencies, and explicitly prevented from interfering in individual cases,[54] enabling state agencies to operate with some degree of autonomy. That autonomy is limited. Annual Letters of Regulation set out specific guidelines for each agency, meaning autonomy is primarily exercised in a managerial rather than structural sense.[55] That said, distinctions exist across government; activities with 'high political saliency are usually more strongly monitored by the government'.[56]

Despite its formal status as a unitary state, Sweden has two levels of subnational government. At the local level, the state is divided into 290 municipalities. Each has an elected assembly that takes decisions on local matters through a municipal council and an executive committee.[57] Local government powers are provided under the Constitution and statute, though they are 'formulated in vague terms' and their scope is largely left to Parliament.[58] Nonetheless, local authorities may levy tax,[59] and comparative studies suggest that their authority is considerable.[60] At the regional level, Sweden is divided into 20 counties. Responsibilities are shared between county councils, which are directly elected and exercise a degree of municipal self-government (primarily in relation to healthcare), and county administrative boards, which are executive bodies appointed by the national government to progress party policies. In contrast to their municipal colleagues, the authority of county councils is severely restricted; they have no legislative powers and exercise no supervisory functions over municipalities.[61]

[54] Instrument of Government (n 51) ch 7, art 3 and ch 12, art 2.

[55] P Hall, 'The Swedish Administrative Model' in J Pierre (ed), *The Oxford Handbook of Swedish Politics* (Oxford, Oxford University Press, 2015) 299, 300.

[56] ibid 303.

[57] S Montin, 'Municipalities, Regions and County Councils: Actors and Institutions' in J Pierre (ed), *The Oxford Handbook of Swedish Politics* (Oxford, Oxford University Press, 2015) 367, 371.

[58] ibid 368.

[59] Instrument of Government (n 51) ch 14.

[60] J Sellers and A Lidström, 'Decentralisation, Local Government, and the Welfare State' (2007) 20 *Governance* 609.

[61] A Lidström, 'Swedish Local and Regional Government in a European Context' in J Pierre (ed), *The Oxford Handbook of Swedish Politics* (Oxford, Oxford University Press, 2015) 414, 419.

Institutions are vital to effectuate governance, but political culture infuses those institutions with a sense of purpose. Swedish political culture has historically been described as 'deliberative, rational, open and consensual'.[62] Among other things, this means that – in a governing system termed 'corporatism' or 'associative democracy' – organised interest groups and stakeholders play a prominent role within the legislative and administrative process,[63] as significant political and economic decisions are often 'reached via negotiation between or in consultation with peak-level representatives' of interest groups and the state.[64] Empirical evidence suggests that corporatism has declined in Sweden since the 1980s,[65] but policy development is still reliant on extra-parliamentary consultation and input. Most complicated policy proposals are first investigated by a Commission of Inquiry established by Cabinet, and state agencies and other interested parties (both public and private) comment on the report to the ministry. These reports are published as either Swedish Government Official Reports (*Statens Offentliga Utredningar* – SOU) or Ministerial Reports (*Departementsserien* – Ds). The most important arguments provided during this referral process are summarised in the government Bill prepared for Parliament, though the final Bill may differ in key respects.

Today, these Commissions are not as deliberative, rational, open and consensual, or influential, as they once were.[66] Nonetheless, the formal role of organised interests is safeguarded in the Constitution. The 1974 Instrument of Government, one of the four fundamental laws that form the Constitution of Sweden, provides that the state should listen to those affected when developing legislation and policy:

> In preparing Government business the necessary information and opinions shall be obtained from the public authorities concerned. Information and opinions shall be obtained from local authorities as necessary. Organisations and individuals shall also be given an opportunity to express an opinion as necessary.[67]

This constitutional requirement is critical in promoting broad input into policy development, but it distinguishes between three types of sources. While Cabinet is obligated to seek advice from 'public authorities concerned', other sources are afforded less weight. Cabinet may decide whether it is 'necessary' to seek information from municipal and regional governments, and private organisations

[62] T Anton, 'Policy-Making and Political Culture in Sweden' (1969) 4 *Scandinavian Political Studies* 88, 94.

[63] Hall, 'The Swedish Administrative Model' (2015) 309.

[64] L Kenworthy, 'Quantitative Indicators of Corporatism' (2003) 33 *International Journal of Sociology* 10, 11.

[65] J Lindvall and J Sebring, 'Policy Reform and the Decline of Corporatism in Sweden' (2005) 28 *West European Politics* 1057, 1070.

[66] B Jacobsson and G Sundström, 'Governing the State' in J Pierre (ed), *The Oxford Handbook of Swedish Politics* (Oxford, Oxford University Press, 2015) 347, 354.

[67] Instrument of Government (n 51) ch 7, art 2.

and individuals are only 'given an opportunity' to express views when 'necessary'. Constitutional silence over the specifics of the referral procedure means that, in practice, civil servants and the responsible minister maintain a large role in selecting which authorities and organisations are heard.[68]

Consistent with Sweden's political culture, the judiciary does not play a prominent role in political conflict. Constitutional or structural reform primarily arrives through administrative decisions rather than the courts. Indeed, until 1980 the judiciary was not empowered to review the constitutionality of legislation, and even today, this power 'has almost never been practiced'.[69] Instead, judicial oversight occurs in a different fashion. In a process termed 'judicial preview', all Bills are reviewed prior to their introduction to Parliament by the *Lagråd* (Law Council), a state agency composed of current and former justices of the Supreme Court and Supreme Administrative Court (the two highest courts in a parallel judicial hierarchy).[70] In considering proposed legislation, the council fulfills two distinct tasks: it operates as both a technical body assessing the statute's construction and effects, and as a constitutional review mechanism. The process is more akin to a Commission of Inquiry than a genuine strong-form review function, however. The council's determination is not binding though the expertise and moral authority of its members means that its decisions are usually adhered to.

Sámi aim to transcend the strictures of the Swedish state, but they have also leveraged its institutional framework and political culture to protect and promote their interests. Historically, the two largest Swedish Sámi organisations were *Same Ätnam* (SA) (the National Association of Samiland) and *Svenska Samernas Riksförbund* (SSR) (the National Union of Swedish Sámi). Established in 1945 and 1950 respectively, both organisations frequently comment on legislative proposals. Reflecting the occupational cleavage within the Sámi community, however, SA primarily seeks to further the interests of non-reindeer herding Sámi, while SSR pays special attention to the priorities of reindeer herders. SA has receded in significance in recent years, but alternative organisations and groups promoting the interests of 'all Sámi' have emerged, including *Landsförbundet Svenska Samer* (LSS) (the National Association of Swedish Sámi). The Sámediggi was intended both to formalise (and channel) the articulation of diverse Sámi interests under the referral process and decentralise state administration by transferring certain responsibilities relating to Sámi culture to the Sámi themselves. It was established in 1993, following a 1989 recommendation by the Sámi Rights Commission (SRC).

[68] O Petersson, 'Rational Politics: Commissions of Inquiry and the Referral System in Sweden' in J Pierre (ed), *The Oxford Handbook of Swedish Politics* (Oxford, Oxford University Press, 2015) 650, 652.

[69] M Wind, 'The Nordics, the EU and the Reluctance Towards Supranational Judicial Review' (2010) 48 *Journal of Common Market Studies* 1039, 1046.

[70] Instrument of Government (n 51) ch 8, arts 20, 21. The Government is not required to send all bills to the council, but it must provide a rationale if it chooses not to.

C. The Sámediggi's Structure

The Sámediggi is composed of three institutions, in a manner 'inspired by the organisation of Swedish municipalities': an elected plenary; a board; and a secretariat.[71] The plenary consists of 31 members.[72] Elections are held every four years on the third Sunday in May, with the entire country forming a single constituency.[73] Voting is conducted under a proportional representation system, with no minimum threshold required to secure a seat.[74] The elected members of the plenary choose a board of directors (with a maximum of seven members), which serves as the executive. The board prepares and presents motions, manages financial administration, and implements decisions of, and performs assignments referred to it by, the plenary.

The chair of the board, also known as the President of the Parliament, is elected by the plenary.[75] The current chair is Per-Olof Nutti, a member of *Sámiid Riikabellodat* (Sámi Party), an independent political party that initially emerged out of the SSR. The Swedish Government formally appoints a chair of the plenary, although by convention the Government acts on the nomination of that body.[76] This position is largely symbolic and functions in a similar role to that of a speaker of a national assembly.[77] Paul Kuoljok, also a member of *Sámiid Riikabellodat*, currently serves in this position. The plenary holds three sessions each year in locations across Sápmi.[78] Only the President serves full-time; since 2013, the Vice-President has been paid for three and a half days a week. There is no budget to employ parliamentary staff,[79] but representatives are compensated for loss of income during plenary sessions.

Voting for the Sámediggi is open to all people on the Sámi electoral roll.[80] As there is no official register of Sámi people in Sweden, a person must apply to be placed on the roll. A person will be enrolled if they are at least 18 years of age on election day and fulfil two criteria: they must subjectively identify as Sámi; and satisfy an objective language-based criterion – the voter, or one of his or her parents or grandparents, must have spoken a Sámi language at home, or

[71] Lawrence and Mörkenstam, 'Indigenous Self-Determination' (2016) 114; *Sametingets roll i det svenska folkstyret* (SOU 2002:77) 14.

[72] Sámi Parliament Act (SFS 1992:1433) ch 2, s 2 (Sámi Parliament Act).

[73] ibid ch 3, ss 1, 2.

[74] The Sámediggi has proposed setting a 4% minimum threshold: Sámediggi, *Ändringar i bestämmelser om val till Sametinget* (2018) 14 [32].

[75] Sámi Parliament Act (n 72) ch 2, s 4.

[76] ibid ch 2, s 2.

[77] Lawrence and Mörkenstam (n 18) 114.

[78] The author attended a plenary session in Kiruna, 3–5 October 2017.

[79] A-M Fjellström, U Mörkenstam, R Nilsson and M Knobloch, 'Sametingets formella ställning, valsystem och partier' in S Dahlberg, U Mörkenstam and R Nilsson (eds), *Sametingsval: Väljare, Partier och Media* (Stockholm, Santérus Förlag, 2016) 77, 80.

[80] *Sámi Parliament Act* (n 72) ch 3, s 3.

had a parent listed on the roll.[81] Voting is not restricted to Swedish citizens, but is open to non-Swedish Sámi who have been registered in the country for three consecutive years.[82] Applications for registration close on 20 October in the year preceding the election and a preliminary electoral roll is issued by 15 November. This roll is made available for scrutiny: any person who sought registration but is not listed can appeal their non-registration, and any person registered can challenge the registration of another person. Appeals are heard in public by the Norrbotten County Administrative Board, a government agency. No Sámi sit on the county board, leaving registration ultimately controlled by the state.[83]

Formally, the Sámediggi is an elected government agency.[84] Housed within the Swedish Ministry of Culture, its principal role is to 'monitor[] issues related to Sámi culture in Sweden'.[85] It works 'for a living Sámi culture' by: allocating state funds for Sámi organisations and cultural programmes; appointing the board of directors for the Sámi school system (a parallel public school system for Sámi children with six schools in Norrbotten and Västerbotten counties); guiding work to promote Sámi languages; participating in community development and ensuring that Sámi needs are considered in decision-making; and providing information about Sámi conditions to government.[86] Since 2007, it has served as the central agency for several tasks relating to the administration and management of reindeer herding, though the state maintains overall responsibility for the industry through both the Ministry of Enterprise and Innovation and regional county administrative boards north of the cultivation border.[87] Since 2009, the Sámediggi has also been tasked with evaluating and informing the Government on international developments on minority rights concerning the Sámi.[88]

The plenary is empowered to appoint various committees to investigate specific matters and undertake work on its behalf.[89] Currently five committees exist, relating to culture, nutrition, reindeer husbandry, language and elections. The Sámediggi also appoints a youth council composed of five members aged between 14 and 30 for a two-year term. The council aims to strengthen the influence of Sámi youth within the Parliament and encourage their engagement in politics, serving as an advisory body to the board and committees. The plenary and board are assisted by a secretariat. As of 31 December 2019, the

[81] ibid ch 1, s 2.
[82] ibid ch 3, s 3.
[83] See further pt III.C.
[84] Sámi Parliament Act (n 72) ch 1, s 1.
[85] ibid.
[86] ibid ch 2, s 1.
[87] The cultivation border is an administrative border established in 1867 dividing the mountainous regions in the west of Sweden from the eastern lowlands. The mountainous regions were reserved for Sámi reindeer herding and settlement was restricted.
[88] Law on National Minorities and Minority Languages (SFS 2009:724) s 3 (Languages Law).
[89] Sámi Parliament Act (n 72) ch 2, s 5.

secretariat consists of approximately 54 staff employed through the civil service and headed by a chief secretary.[90] Finally, as one people spread across four states, the Sámediggi cooperates and collaborates with its Norwegian and Finnish counterparts, as well as colleagues in Russia, to protect and promote Sámi rights across and beyond Sápmi. It is a member of the Sámi Parliamentary Council and enjoys observer status at several international forums.

The Sámediggi's institutional structure is a novel attempt at empowering Indigenous peoples with the capacity to have their voices heard in the processes of government. Its legal status however, suggests some complications. As an elected government agency, the Sámediggi serves two distinct functions. It is both a popularly elected Parliament representing the Sámi in Sweden and a state administrative authority required to 'observe objectivity'[91] and whose tasks are closely regulated. Does this conflicted legal position challenge Sámi aspirations or allow the state to undermine Sámi interests?

III. THE SÁMEDIGGI AND INDIGENOUS ASPIRATIONS

Sweden's constitutional framework and political culture suggests that the state may meaningfully accommodate Sámi interests in legislation and policy development. Corporatism grants organised interest groups without strong representation in the Riksdag superior opportunities to influence issues than they might otherwise enjoy, while the decentralised nature of Swedish administration means that state authorities and local governments may recognise and respond to distinctive Sámi views. The institutional structure and legal status of the Sámediggi appear to promote this; offering Sámi living in Sweden opportunities to affirm their identity, have their voices heard in decisions that affect them, and exercise a degree of control over certain matters. This part explores these issues by assessing the Parliament against the four criteria drawn from chapter four. Those conditions are:

(1) Indigenous peoples must be heard when decisions that affect them are being made.
(2) Indigenous peoples must have the authority and financial capacity to exercise independent policy and decision-making power over matters relating to internal or local affairs.
(3) Institutions or processes that empower Indigenous peoples must be regarded by Indigenous peoples as legitimate.
(4) Indigenous leaders must act according to the purposes and values for which they have been entrusted with authority, and must be accountable for their actions.

[90] Sámediggi, *Årsredovisning 2019* (2020) 73.

[91] SOU 1989:41 (n 2) 151–59, 305–11; *Sammanfattning av Samerättsutredningens: om samerna och samisk kultur m.m* (Prop 1992/93:32) 35.

It is necessary to note one qualification before commencing. Reflecting my focus on institutional reform in Australia, the criteria have been developed primarily to articulate Aboriginal and Torres Strait Islander peoples' aspirations in a form comprehensible to principles of Australian public law. They may not necessarily reflect Sámi priorities or be effective themes within Sweden's governance framework. Nonetheless, while the criteria are firmly grounded in the voices of Indigenous Australians, chapters three and four demonstrated that their reach is broader. Indigenous peoples are transnational actors and the political thought and activism that informs the criteria is not simply reflective of Aboriginal and Torres Strait Islander peoples. Drawn from the complex and nuanced views of Indigenous peoples across time and space, the criteria are valuable guides to assess institutions designed to empower Indigenous peoples to be heard in the processes of government across the globe. For this reason, they are employed to examine the Swedish Sámediggi.

A. Voices

The Sámediggi appears well-positioned to empower Sámi living in Sweden with the capacity to have their interests heard in decisions that affect them. The Sámi Parliament Act imbues the Parliament with responsibility for 'providing information on Sámi conditions' to relevant decision-makers, and 'ensuring that Sámi needs are considered'.[92] These obligations position the Sámediggi within the state's corporatist political culture; establishing it as a 'referral body',[93] and 'source of input into policy decisions'.[94] Nonetheless, notwithstanding this structural hook and ostensibly accommodative political culture, in practice the Sámediggi often struggles to ensure Sámi voices are heard. While the 'category cleavage'[95] within the Sámi community can complicate the Sámediggi's capacity to effectively articulate a clear position to government, the more significant challenge is the Swedish state's approach to the Parliament. The Sámediggi struggles to satisfy this condition because of an inadequate consultative framework, premised on the state's persistent refusal to engage with Sámi in a manner reflective of their position as an Indigenous people with a concomitant right to self-determination.

Like all substantial political communities, the Sámi are not homogenous in their outlook or political attitudes. The Sámediggi's proportional representation electoral system encourages heterogeneity, enabling a diverse cast of candidates and parties to secure seats. Diversity has long been a feature of the Parliament. In the first election held in 1993, the 31 seats were distributed among

[92] ch 2, s 1. See further Languages Law (n 88) s 5.
[93] SOU 1989:41 (n 2) 154.
[94] F Korsmo, 'Swedish Policy and Saami Rights' (1993) 11 *The Northern Review* 32, 49.
[95] I Ruong, *Samerna i historien och nutiden* (Stockholm, Bonnier Fakta, 1982) 187–88.

11 different parties, while in the most recent 2017 election, nine political parties secured a presence.[96] Pleasingly, despite a slight under-representation of women and indications that female representatives' influence is less than their male counterparts,[97] a comprehensive examination of the 2013 Sámediggi reveals that at a collective level, the Parliament is 'relatively representative of the electorate as a whole',[98] though the size of the potential electorate is uncertain.[99]

Multiplicity can make it difficult for the Sámediggi to speak authoritatively, weakening its ability to effectively be heard in decisions that affect Sámi interests. While this is a tension inherent to any representative institution it is more problematic for Indigenous representative bodies designed to channel distinctive, minority views to government. It is even more challenging for the Sámediggi, as many problems go beyond ordinary political disputes around the ordinal value of competing policy proposals. In particular, reproducing the category cleavage within the Swedish Sámi polity, distinctions between reindeer herders and non-reindeer herders has remained a lasting division within the parliament. In the 2017 election, for example, parties with strong support from reindeer herding communities secured 15 seats, while parties whose voters wish to reduce the influence of reindeer herding communities won 13 seats.[100] This division problematises the institution's ability to effectively articulate the views of all Sámi, and, at times, sparks challenges to its legitimacy.

Tensions emerge when issues directly concerning reindeer herders arise. For instance, predators are a major cause of losses of reindeer stock in Sweden, with suggestions that at least 60,000 reindeer (of an estimated population of 260,000) fall prey to predators each year. Swedish predator policy aims to facilitate viable populations of apex predators to maintain ecological systems, while providing monetary compensation for losses of livestock.[101] This can reach significant payouts; in 2009, €6.3 million was paid by the Sámediggi to reindeer herding communities.[102] Concern predator compensation was impacting on other budgetary priorities led the Sámediggi to reduce compensation that year; instead of receiving the full value of their lost stock, reindeer herding

[96] Norrbotten County Administrative Board, 'Elections to the Sámi Parliament 21 May 2017: Votes and Seats for Groups, Parties or Similar Associations' (2017) Annex I, 5.

[97] R Nilsson, M Jansson, U Mörkenstam and S Dahlberg, 'Kön och politik i sametingsvalet 2013' in S Dahlberg, U Mörkenstam and R Nilsson (eds), *Sametingsval: Väljare, Partier och Media* (Stockholm, Santérus Förlag, 2016) 201, 206. See further R Kuokkanen, *Restructuring Relations: Indigenous Self-Determination, Governance, and Gender* (Oxford, Oxford University Press, 2019) 167.

[98] A-M Fjellström, 'Partiernas rekrytering och nominering av kandidater inför valet 2013' in S Dahlberg, U Mörkenstam and R Nilsson (eds), *Sametingsval: Väljare, Partier och Media* (Stockholm, Santérus Förlag, 2016) 103, 126.

[99] See discussion in pt III.C.

[100] R Nilsson, U Mörkenstam and R Svensson, 'Politiska skiljelinjer vid val till Sametinget' in S Dahlberg, U Mörkenstam and R Nilsson (eds), *Sametingsval: Väljare, Partier och Media* (Stockholm, Santérus Förlag, 2016) 181, 195.

[101] *Rovdjuren och deras förvaltning* (SOU 2007:89).

[102] NT Hobbs, H Andrén, J Persson, M Aronsson and G Chapron, 'Native Predators Reduce Harvest of Reindeer by Sámi Pastoralists' (2012) 22 *Ecological Applications* 1640, 1641.

communities would receive 71 per cent of that figure. The affected communities successfully challenged this decision in the Norrbotten County Administrative Court, which ruled that they had the right to full compensation.[103] While the Sámediggi accepted this ruling (over the wishes of the Government),[104] reindeer herding communities remained disturbed with the Parliament's handling of the issue. In 2012, the SSR proposed that reindeer herding be removed from the Sámediggi's authority and managed under a new government agency.[105] As this dispute reveals, in issues that strike at the heart of the interests of reindeer herders, the SSR challenges the ability of the Sámediggi to accurately reflect their interests, and consequently its authority to speak on certain matters.

This foundational cleavage makes it difficult for any single representative body to effectively articulate Sámi interests and perspectives in all their diversity.[106] As such, alternative organisations, like the SSR, play a crucial role in expressing distinct and specific interests of Sámi groups by making submissions to government on particular issues. While individuals may organise themselves to promote their interests in any manner they choose, it challenges the political authority and legitimacy of the Sámediggi when it claims, as the pre-eminent national Sámi institution, to speak for all Sámi. Even so, despite this persistent challenge, scholars examining the Parliament have found that it has largely been successful at empowering 'previously neglected and marginalised Sámi groups' with the capacity to have their interests represented at a national level.[107] Of course, revealing the inherent tensions within this criterion, diversity may also have 'contributed to a divided and sometimes fragmented parliament', potentially impacting on the institution's effectiveness and credibility.[108]

The Sámediggi faces challenges, but in some instances, it has been effective in utilising its structural link to government to influence proposals. For example, in 2009 the Sámediggi heavily criticised a draft Bill purportedly aimed at bringing Swedish legislation into conformity with ILO Convention 169.[109] In response, the Government withdrew the Bill and announced its intention to substantially revise its proposal.[110] At other times, while the Sámediggi has been able

[103] *Gällivare Sameby v Sametinget* (Länsrätten i Norrbottens Län, Case No 1565–09, 9 September 2009).

[104] See further pt III.C.

[105] Svenska Samernas Riksförbund, *Förändring av Sametingets Funktion och Organisation* (2012) 6.

[106] This was recognised by the Sámi Rights Commission: SOU 1989:41 (n 2) 146.

[107] Lantto and Mörkenstam (n 42) 38–39. See also P Lantto and U Mörkenstam, 'Action, Organisation and Confrontation: Strategies of the Sámi Movement in Sweden during the Twentieth Century' in M Berg-Nordlie, J Saglie and A Sullivan (eds), *Indigenous Politics: Institutions, Representation, Mobilisation* (Colchester, ECPR Press, 2015) 131, 145.

[108] Lantto and Mörkenstam, 'Action, Organisation and Confrontation' (2015) 145. Many scholars suggest that the Parliament's limited authority may be the primary contributor to this instability: Fjellström, Mörkenstam, Nilsson and Knobloch, 'Sametingets formella ställning' (2016) 101–02.

[109] See *Vissa Samepolitiska Frågor* (Ds 2009:40).

[110] Anaya (n 13) 7 [22].

to exercise its institutional opportunity to be heard, its lobbying has not been as successful. In 2008, for instance, a proposal for a new Instrument of Government defined the Sámi as an Indigenous people, affording them a distinctive position within the state.[111] The Government rejected this, however, instead proposing to amend provisions of the Constitution protecting the rights of certain minorities so as to specifically include the Sámi people.[112] While the Sámediggi criticised this approach as misleading, arguing that minorities do not have the same rights as Indigenous peoples, the Government dismissed their push to adopt language that stipulates their special status.[113]

These examples suggest that although Sámi are not always successful, opportunities exist through the Sámediggi for their interests to be heard in decisions that affect them. Yet considerable gaps exist in this regime. For example, non-recognition of Sámi ownership rights to land leaves weak protection when it comes to resource extraction and development. Under the Minerals Act no consultation with the Sámediggi or relevant Sámi communities is required before an exploration permit is issued, even if the permit area covers traditional Sámi territory.[114] While affected Sámi communities are entitled to comment on proposed exploration work, the Chief Mining Inspector determines whether any project is approved under a test that strongly favours exploration.[115] Similarly, though consultation with affected communities must be undertaken for felling permits under the Forestry Act in year-round reindeer grazing areas, consultation is not required over winter grazing areas.[116] Even on year-round grazing areas, Sámi participants report that they are often presented with a completed plan and have 'very few opportunities to influence' proposals.[117]

Reflecting on these and other examples, many scholars and members of the Sámediggi have persistently decried the scope of the Parliament's voice, arguing that existing institutional opportunities are deficient. The UN Human Rights Committee, for example, has criticised the 'limited extent to which the Sámi Parliament may participate in the decision-making process on issues affecting land and traditional activities of the Sámi people'.[118] Similarly, the Special

[111] *En reformerad grundlag* (SOU 2008:125) 435.

[112] *En reformerad grundlag* (Prop 2009/10:80) 188.

[113] ibid 189; *Lag om ändring i regeringsformen* (SFS 2010:1408) ch 1, s 2. Note, however, that the amendment was nonetheless justified by their status as an Indigenous people.

[114] (SFS 1991:45) ch 2, s 2. See further Human Rights Committee, 'Concluding Observations on the Seventh Periodic Report of Sweden', UN Doc CCPR/C/SWE/CO/7 (28 April 2016) 8 [38].

[115] (SFS 1991:45) ch 3, ss 5, 5a. The Chief Mining Inspector assesses whether proposed measures are necessary and do not cause an affected party 'inconvenience of such magnitude as to outweigh the permit holder's interest in being allowed to carry out the work'.

[116] (SFS 1979:429) s 20.

[117] C Sandström and C Widmark, 'Stakeholders' Perceptions of Consultations as Tools for Co-Management: A Case Study of the Forestry and Reindeer Herding Sectors in Northern Sweden' (2007) 10 *Forest Policy and Economics* 25, 30.

[118] Human Rights Committee, 'Concluding Observations of the Human Rights Committee: Sweden', UN Doc CCPR/C/SWE/CO/6 (7 May 2009) 6 [20].

Rapporteur has reported that the Sámediggi has expressed concern over the degree to which it can 'genuinely participate in and influence decisions that affect the Sámi people', because it has no 'guaranteed genuine influence or decision-making power'.[119] Part of the problem may be an absence of structures to promote dialogue. A 2010 report by the Swedish Agency for Public Management found that informal contacts between the Government and the Sámediggi are 'limited', and that formal discussions have been infrequent, scheduled only annually and are not always well attended. It recommended 'quarterly meetings between the Cabinet Office and Sámi Parliament should take place'.[120] There are some indications that informal contacts and formal meetings with government officials have increased over the last few years. Problematically, however, the same law that provides government agencies with a measure of autonomous operation prevents Cabinet ministers from meeting Sámediggi representatives on an equal status.[121]

Whether a general responsibility to consult the Sámediggi should be imposed has been considered and rejected several times by the Swedish Government. It was first debated prior to the establishment of the Parliament but dismissed because the Government considered that consultation would occur naturally.[122] This was also the view of the SRC, which assumed that, over time, political practice would lead the Sámediggi to 'acquire the status of an obligatory advisory body'.[123] In 2002, the Government acknowledged that this had not occurred, but reiterated its position, explaining that Sámi views should be considered on issues only where 'really relevant'.[124] In 2006 and 2009, the Government again rejected proposals to impose a general consultative obligation, contending that such an obligation 'would take it too far',[125] and 'represent an excessive change'.[126]

There are some indications that this view may be shifting. In 2017, the Department of Culture released a ministerial report acknowledging that Sámi do not have adequate opportunities for effective participation in the processes of Swedish government.[127] In response, the Department proposed a draft consultation law that would oblige all levels of government and state administrative authorities to consult the Sámediggi and relevant Sámi communities in matters that are of particular relevance to them.[128] Consultation would be undertaken in good faith, with intent to reach an agreement, and discussions would be documented to reveal the genuineness of the process. While no freestanding

[119] Anaya (n 13) 11 [38].
[120] Statskontoret, *Myndighetsanalys av sametinget* (2010:15) 33–34.
[121] I thank Ulf Mörkenstam for this point.
[122] Prop 1992/93:32 (n 91) 43.
[123] SOU 1989:41 (n 2) 71.
[124] SOU 2002:77 (n 71) 18.
[125] *Ett ökat samiskt inflytande* (Prop 2005/06:86) 55.
[126] Ds 2009:40 (n 109) 101.
[127] *Konsultation i frågor som rör det samiska folket* (Ds 2017:43) 35.
[128] ibid 43, 46–47.

right to appeal the adequacy of the consultation would be introduced, such a right already exists in relation to certain decisions.[129] Significantly, the ministerial report recognised that the Sámediggi, and other Sámi organisations, would require increased funding to effectively manage an increased workload.[130] This proposal is promising, but consultation is distinct from consent. The report notes that while Sámi views would be accorded 'great importance',[131] their consent would not ultimately be required, as the aim of the law 'is to promote and enhance the Sámi people's influence over [their] own affairs in decision-making processes',[132] rather than to provide for self-rule.

The consultative arrangement fell off the agenda following the Swedish general election in 2018. Nonetheless, whether or not the proposal is adopted, it is unlikely that formalising rights to participate in the processes of government will entirely resolve concerns surrounding the extent (or genuineness) of the Sámediggi's voice. As we saw in chapter five, the state must also commit to engage in respectful dialogue. Even so, the existing absence of a general obligation to consult is consequential. The Sámediggi's opaque legal status as a referral body largely places the onus for initiating consultations on the Parliament itself,[133] with little guarantee that its position will be considered. A political agreement or legal requirement that decision-makers at the national, regional and municipal level consult on issues that affect Sámi interests at an early stage in the process, and publicly identify how those interests were considered and influenced the decision adopted, would enhance the capacity for Sámi voices to be heard. The Department of Culture's proposal is therefore promising.

Voices asks whether institutional opportunities exist to enable the Sámediggi to express Sámi interests to relevant decision-makers within the Swedish Government. As a representative institution elected on a proportional basis, the Sámediggi has been relatively successful in enabling internally variegated groups to articulate diverse views, notwithstanding the cleavage that cuts through its constituency. The key difficulty the Sámediggi faces is in its relationship with the state. Sweden acknowledged the Sámi as an Indigenous 'population' as early as 1977,[134] and has recognised their status an Indigenous 'people' in reports to UN treaty bodies,[135] but this acceptance has not been legally enshrined in the Constitution or relevant legislation,[136] and does not extend to specific rights of

[129] ibid 75–83.
[130] ibid 93. For discussion on the Sámediggi budget see below pt III.B.
[131] ibid 74–75.
[132] ibid 1.
[133] Statskontoret, *Myndighetsanalys av sametinget* (2010) 52.
[134] *Om insatser för samerna* (Prop 1976/77:80) 1.
[135] See, eg: Human Rights Committee, 'Consideration of Reports Submitted by State Parties under Article 40 of the Covenant: Sixth Periodic Report – Sweden', UN Doc. CCPR/C/SWE/6 (5 December 2007) 3–4 [6]–[7].
[136] Sámi are described as a 'national minority' in the Languages Law (n 88) s 2. In the Reindeer Husbandry Act (n 51) the term 'Sámi population' is used (s 1).

consultation. Rather, consistent with its corporatist political culture, they are treated in the same manner as all other major interest groups; they are – through the Sámediggi – entitled to comment on matters relevant to their interests, industry, or affiliation.

This entitlement is not supported by a political or legal obligation on the Government to listen. In treating the Sámi as a sectoral group rather than an Indigenous people, major historical and contemporary legal inequities continue to structure the Sámi–Swedish relationship. Even the Government recognises that consultation is not carried out in a 'consistent and comprehensive way' and is 'not sufficient to ensure Sámi influence'.[137] Close observers argue that it is likely that this limited influence contributes to division within the parliament; if the Sámi believed that their views would be accorded due weight, compromise on issues striking at the heart of internal divisions may be more likely to be struck.[138] Despite a promising framework, the Parliament struggles to satisfy this condition.

B. Power

Sweden's constitutional framework permits government agencies a degree of autonomy. The Sámediggi's legal status as an elected government agency suggests that it may wield a degree of independent policy and decision-making authority. Indeed, at its establishment, some advocates considered this a primary benefit of the proposed structure, contending that it would safeguard a stable financial base and ensure the Parliament would be invested with 'the proper powers to administer matters given over to its realm of responsibility'.[139] While this has proven partly true, the scope of the Sámediggi's autonomy has fallen far short of Sámi aspirations. As a state agency the Parliament is financed by yearly appropriations from the Swedish Government. Guaranteed resourcing from the state means that the Sámediggi does not need to solicit donations to fund its operations and the certainty that comes from regular financing should mean the Parliament is able to develop long-term priorities. In practice, however, the state's reluctance to meaningfully engage with Sámi political aspirations has influenced its approach to resourcing the Sámediggi and to recognising a degree of policy and decision-making authority. The state uses its legal and financial leverage to closely monitor and check Sámi autonomy. Despite some positives, the Sámediggi is largely unable to satisfy this condition.

[137] Ds 2017:43 (n 127) 35.

[138] Fjellström, Mörkenstam, Nilsson and Knobloch (n 79).

[139] H Beach, 'The New Swedish Sámi Policy – A Dismal Failure: Concerning the Swedish Government's Proposition 1992/93:32, *Samerna och Sámisk kultur m.m.* (Bill)' in E Gayim and K Myntti (eds), *Indigenous and Tribal Peoples' Rights – 1993 and After* (Rovaniemi, Northern Institute for Environmental and Minority Law, 1995) 109, 116 (describing, not arguing for this position).

Government agencies may operate with a degree of autonomy, but the extent of their authority is prescribed by the state. Unfortunately for the Sámediggi, the state has never countenanced granting it significant independent policy or decision-making powers. Indeed, the Sámi Rights Commission, whose report led to the Sámediggi's establishment, was precluded from considering certain significant matters. It was not empowered to examine veto rights over proposed land-use measures in Sápmi or whether the putative body should be invested with constitutionally protected powers of decision-making.[140] In the 1992 Bill establishing the body, the Government emphasised its subordinate status: 'despite the designation "ting" [meaning 'Parliament' in the word Sameting], there is no question of it being a body for self-determination that shall act instead [of] the Riksdag or the municipal council, or in competition with these bodies'.[141]

Instead, the Sámediggi was explicitly framed as a state agency that would protect Sámi culture and Sámi industries.[142] This purpose is reflected in the Sámi Parliament Act, which defines the 'primary task' of the Parliament as 'monitoring questions related to Sámi culture',[143] and assigns it responsibility to 'work for a living Sámi culture'.[144] Although the state has transferred several additional responsibilities to the Sámediggi in recent years, suggesting some enhancement of the Sámediggi's authority, all relate to cultural matters, indicating that the initial rationale for the Parliament has not substantially developed.

In fact, the state has actively resisted efforts to imbue the Parliament with any substantive powers of self-government. In a 2005 Bill, for example, the Government acknowledged that Sámi people should 'as far as possible' have the right to decide on issues relating to Sámi conditions, but narrowly prescribed this by situating it as a reference only to reindeer husbandry.[145] In that Bill the Government also rejected the Sámediggi's proposal that it investigate whether the Sámi could be granted greater self-government powers,[146] explaining that 'in our judgment' self-government can be enhanced via the gradual transfer of administrative tasks concerning Sámi affairs.[147]

The state's commitment to Sámi self-determination might be characterised as an inchoate pledge rather than a tangible promise. This leaves the Sámediggi in a tenuous position: while arguing for increased decision-making power and responsibility, it must simultaneously defend encroachments on its existing limited authority. For example, a 2010 report from the Swedish Agency for Public Management criticised the operation of the Parliament, arguing that it failed to measure targets, was beset by budgetary overruns, and struggled under

[140] SOU 1989:41 (n 2) 416. See further Korsmo, 'Swedish Policy' (1993) 40; Sillanpää (n 8) 108, 157, 189.
[141] Prop 1992/93:32 (n 91) 34.
[142] ibid 31. See also SOU 1989:41 (n 2) 147.
[143] Sámi Parliament Act (n 72) c 1, s 1.
[144] ibid ch 2, s 1.
[145] Prop 2005/06:86 (n 125) 34.
[146] ibid 35.
[147] ibid 38.

an unclear internal accountability framework. The report considered that a clearer accountability structure was necessary, recommending amendment to allow the Government to formally appoint the Parliament's board;[148] a proposal that would prove fatal to any notion of self-determination. Other challenges to the Sámediggi's autonomy are framed as enhancements. In 2007, for instance, responsibilities relating to reindeer husbandry were transferred to the Parliament – over the wishes of the Sámediggi, who had voted not to accept the duties.[149] Representatives correctly identified that the tasks transferred were limited and administrative in nature.[150] Burdened by additional administrative responsibilities, the Parliament now enjoys less scope for political and policy development.

State refusal to recognise significant policy and decision-making powers has not prevented the Sámediggi from exercising its limited authority to challenge government policy. Illustrating the Parliament's subordinate position, however, the state has often used its financial leverage to constrain acts of independence. For example, as noted above, the Sámediggi's decision to accept the Norrbotten County Administrative Court's ruling on predator compensation was made in the face of government opposition. While the Sámediggi's capacity to act contrary to state preference suggests that the Parliament enjoys a real, albeit marginal, domain of autonomy, its powers ultimately proved illusory. Unhappy with the Sámediggi's actions, the Government amended the Parliament's budget, merging two previous separate budget lines for predator compensation and the development of reindeer herding.[151] As Rebecca Lawrence and Ulf Mörkenstam note, conflating 'funds for general support and development of reindeer herding with financial compensation for the breach of a civil right, i.e. damage to property', reinforced the inferior status of the Parliament and 'effectively served to limit the role of the Sámediggi as a political representative of the Sámi people'.[152]

State control over the Sámediggi's budget further constrains the Parliament's ability to formulate and implement distinctive policies, priorities and long-term projects. Rather than adopt a hands-off approach, providing block grants and permitting the Parliament to identify and determine its own funding priorities (as is the case in Norway),[153] or legislate to enable the Parliament to raise funds from alternative sources, state oversight and control is employed to influence Sámi decision-making. The state has several levers through which it may undertake this task.[154] As it did to indicate its displeasure over the Parliament's handling of the predator compensation issue, the state can merge previously

[148] Statskontoret (n 120) 52.
[149] Lawrence and Mörkenstam (n 18) 117–18.
[150] Reindeer Husbandry Act (n 51) ss 86–88A.
[151] *Förslag till statsbudget för 2010, finansplan och skattefrågor m.m.*, (Prop 2009/10:1), Category 23, 1:28).
[152] Lawrence and Mörkenstam (n 18) 120–21.
[153] Josefsen, Mörkenstam and Nilsson, 'The Nordic Sámediggis' (2016) 16.
[154] These strategies are similar to those adopted by the Australian Government in checking the independent authority of the Aboriginal and Torres Strait Islander Commission: see ch 5.

separate budget lines to pressure the Sámediggi to change decisions. Alternatively, the state can entirely avoid limited Sámi autonomy by channelling Sámi-specific expenditure outside the Sámediggi – estimates suggest that up to 40 per cent of such funding is spent in this way.[155] Even funding that is directly allocated to the Sámediggi can be controlled. As former President Håkan Jonsson has argued, paternalistic strictures on funding mean that 'We cannot use the money that we receive as we would like to. When we get it, Sweden has already decided how we should use it'.[156] These restrictions are tightly formed. In 2011, the Special Rapporteur noted that state funding is principally directed to the Sámediggi's administrative tasks and responsibilities as a government agency, with only 'minimal funding' provided for its work as a representative self-determining institution.[157] Sámediggi annual reports reveal that this has not materially changed: in 2014, 2015 and 2016, approximately 94 per cent of state funding was directed to its administrative functions,[158] while in 2017, 2018 and 2019, that figure sat at around 90 per cent.[159] Of course, each of these approaches can be conducted somewhat surreptitiously; if it prefers, the state can simply reduce the Sámediggi's total budget.

Finally, it is important to note that state funding to the Sámediggi is minimal when assessed against resources extracted from traditional Sámi lands. Sweden does not recognise Sámi ownership rights to lands used for reindeer grazing. Consequently, mining projects are not required to pay royalties to affected Sámi communities or the Sámediggi for projects located on traditional Sámi territory. Thus, although in 2012 mines located on Sámi lands generated a total production value of approximately €4.3 billion, Sámi received nothing.[160] This compares unfavourably to Australia and Canada, where Indigenous peoples typically receive between two and three per cent of gross revenues from mining projects.[161] Based on these figures, Rebecca Lawrence and Sámi scholar Matthias Åhrén calculate that – in 2012 alone – Sámi were deprived of around €100 million,[162] almost five times the Sámediggi's 2016 budget of approximately €21.25 million.

State control over the Sámediggi's budget is a recurrent concern for Sámi politicians who have persistently argued that they should be granted greater authority to determine their own priorities. It seems that some within the Swedish

[155] J Henriksen (ed), 'Sámi Self-Determination – Scope and Implementation' (2008) 2 *Gáldu Čála – Journal of Indigenous Peoples Rights* 1, 15–16.

[156] Cited in L Fuchs, 'Understanding and Implementing Self-Determination for Indigenous Peoples: The Case of the Sami in Sweden' (MSc thesis, Linnaeus University, 2014) 40.

[157] Anaya (n 13) 12 [43].

[158] Sámediggi, *Årsredovisning 2016* (2017) 15.

[159] Sámediggi, *Årsredovisning 2019* (2020) 13.

[160] Lawrence and Åhrén, 'Mining as Colonisation' (2016) 184.

[161] C O'Faircheallaigh and G Gibson, 'Economic Risk and Mineral Taxation on Indigenous Lands' (2012) 37 *Resources Policy* 10, 11 fn 3.

[162] Lawrence and Åhrén (n 34) 184.

state agree. A 2002 Commission of Inquiry considered that the Sámediggi should be empowered to control its budget, arguing that such control would be consistent with their right to cultural autonomy, and likely to produce better allocative outcomes.[163] While the Commission explained that legal impediments prohibit granting the Sámediggi complete authority over public finances, it noted there is no reason why the Government could not provide funding as a single block grant to the Sámediggi to allocate itself.[164] The Government has not taken up this suggestion.[165]

The larger difficulty with the current arrangements is a simpler one. As identified by the UN Human Rights Committee and the Special Rapporteur, funding levels are both insufficient and inadequate for the Sámediggi to effectively exercise its self-governance functions.[166] The Sámediggi's budget is far less than that provided to ATSIC, but more significantly, only a very small proportion of that budget is allocated to its political role, inhibiting Sámi leaders' ability to conduct work outside plenary meetings. Without a budget to employ political advisers or secretarial staff for political offices, outreach, policy development, candidate recruitment and the establishment of effective party organisations all suffer.

The Sámediggi's legal status initially provided some promise that it could serve as an innovative institutional mechanism for the Sámi who live in Sweden to exercise independent policy and decision-making power over matters relating to internal or local affairs. In this light, the gradual expansion of the Sámediggi's competencies to include reindeer herding administration may suggest an 'incremental expansion of Sámi self-determination and autonomy'. Closer examination reveals that this is not the case.[167] The Sámediggi's limited authority stems from the state's failure to accept Sámi political aspirations. In practice, the state comprehends the Sámi people as a sectoral group with distinctive interests surrounding cultural activities, rather than as an Indigenous people entitled to an equitable relationship with the state. As such, it remains distrustful of recognising any authority over substantive issues.[168]

Sámi are not a sectoral group. Sámi do not merely aspire to express their views and interests through a representative body legally designated as a government agency, but desire and are entitled to 'the competency to make decisions of significance to Sámi situations'.[169] As Sámi scholar Nils Oskal has argued, the political inclusion of Sámi in Sweden requires 'far more than a granting of a

[163] SOU 2002:77 (n 71) 12.

[164] ibid 12–13.

[165] Prop 2005/06:86 (n 125) 36.

[166] Anaya (n 13) 20 [78]; Human Rights Committee (n 114) 8 [38].

[167] Stepien, Petrétei and Koivurova (n 12) 131.

[168] Lawrence and Mörkenstam (n 18) 118.

[169] EG Broderstad, 'Political Autonomy and Integration of Authority: The Understanding of Saami Self-Determination' (2001) 8 *International Journal on Minority and Group Rights* 151, 171. See further: R Nilsson, S Dahlberg and U Mörkenstam, 'Inledning' in S Dahlberg, U Mörkenstam and R Nilsson (eds), *Sametingsval: Väljare, Partier och Media* (Stockholm, Santérus Förlag, 2016) 27, 35.

right to be heard in the direction of institutionalisation of procedures for negotiations, and cooperation';[170] it requires an ability 'to act independently and to make autonomous decisions'.[171] Although the Sámediggi has sought to differentiate itself from the Government, at times creatively using its limited autonomy to make decisions contrary to government policy, its ability to act independently is inadequate. The state closely monitors the Sámediggi, controlling its operations through its financial dominance.

C. Ownership

The Sámediggi is perched in a difficult space. An institution or process aimed at empowering Indigenous peoples to be heard in the processes of government must be regarded as legitimate if it is to be effective. The Sámediggi satisfies this standard only to a weak degree. Although the state made some effort to meaningfully accommodate Sámi aspirations, the Parliament is largely a copy of existing Swedish public institutions, constraining representatives' ability to incorporate traditional governance structures or conventions.[172] More problematic, however, is that despite concerted effort to identify and develop long-term Sámi priorities and projects – attempts at grounding the Sámediggi within the community – the Parliament's limited authority and inherently compromised legal status inhibits its ability to meaningfully promote Sámi interests where they conflict with government concerns.

i. Design

Sámi activists drove the idea of a national representative institution.[173] In 1981, following a landmark Supreme Court decision holding that Sámi may enjoy ownership rights to their traditional lands,[174] the SSR called on the state to create a Commission of Inquiry to investigate the nature of Sámi rights to land and water and pass legislation to protect Sámi livelihoods, and SA requested the government establish a Sámi Parliament.[175] The state responded positively but the SRC tasked with developing a proposal struggled to satisfy competing priorities. Fae Korsmo argues that the Commission 'suffered from personal and philosophical disagreements, a lack of enthusiasm on the part of the central government, and a great degree of scepticism on the part of the Swedish Sámi'.[176]

[170] N Oskal, 'Political Inclusion of the Saami as Indigenous People in Norway' (2001) 8 *International Journal on Minority and Group Rights* 235, 256.
[171] Anaya (n 13) 12 [41].
[172] Kuokkanen, *Restructuring Relations* (2019) 91.
[173] SOU 1989:41 (n 2) 146. Sillanpää (n 8) 122.
[174] Taxed Mountains Case, in Jahreskog, *Sámi National Minority* (1982) 177–83.
[175] Korsmo (n 94) 40; Sillanpää (n 8) 108.
[176] Korsmo (n 94) 40.

Like most public inquiries, its final recommendations were the product of negotiation, contestation and compromise,[177] but its directives, which framed the outer limits of what the state would accept, precluded many Sámi aspirations from the outset. As noted above, there would be no veto right over proposed land-use measures in Sápmi, and no constitutionally based powers of decision-making. Although it had the benefit of studying the Norwegian Sámediggi, its proposals were consequently 'far less radical'.[178] '[N]one of the national Sámi associations in Sweden were very happy with the recommendations', remarking that they constituted the 'minimum acceptable'.[179]

The SRC also struggled to articulate how an institutional expression of Sámi political organisation could fit within the state's existing legal framework. In its 1989 report, the SRC explained that although the body shall be representative of the entire Sámi population in Sweden, 'it is not a question of creating Sámi self-government along the lines of local government'.[180] But neither, the Commission argued, could a putative Sámi representative body 'be compared to the Riksdag', or 'the convocation or church council'.[181] The SRC ultimately concluded that the responsibilities and mandate of the body meant that it should be legally situated as an executive agency with a representative role.[182] This hybrid structure indicates that there was some recognition that the organisation should be designed differently than traditional public bodies 'in order to get a real commitment from the Sámi people'.[183] To this degree, the SRC and government modified their own understandings of political authority to accommodate the distinctive character of Sámi political aspirations.

Their choice, however, challenges the assertion that the Sámediggi can empower Sámi representatives to develop long-term priorities and projects. As a body directly elected by Sámi people it should represent the will of its constituents, but, as a government agency, the Sámediggi is legally 'required to comply with regulations communicated by government',[184] even where they are contrary to the manifesto and promises of its elected members.[185] This institutional design has been criticised as setting up 'an inherent clash of interests'.[186] As Johan Eriksson explains, representatives are placed in 'an impossible situation': 'If a Parliament representing an ethnic minority is to enjoy any legitimacy and to show any kind of power, it is obvious that it cannot at the same time

[177] E Josefsen, U Mörkenstam and J Saglie, 'Different Institutions within Similar States: The Norwegian and Swedish Sámediggis' (2015) 14 *Ethnopolitics* 32, 33–34.

[178] R Kvist, 'Swedish Sámi Policy 1548–1992' in L Heininen (ed), *The Changing Circumpolar North: Opportunities for Academic Development* (Rovaniemi, Arctic Centre Publications No 6, 1994) 28, 39.

[179] Sillanpää (n 8) 91, 110–11.

[180] SOU 1989:41 (n 2) 159.

[181] ibid.

[182] ibid.

[183] Prop 1992/93 (n 91) 33.

[184] SOU 1989:41 (n 2) 160.

[185] Anaya (n 13) 12 [42].

[186] Mörkenstam (n 42) 102.

represent its major opponent, in this case the state'.[187] The Sámi Parliament itself acknowledges this tension, noting that the blending of responsibilities creates 'a built-in conflict between the Sámi's desire for increased independence and the government's restrictiveness and agency regulation'.[188] These strictures have, it explains, often left Sámi politicians feeling 'paralysed'.[189]

The SRC recognised the difficulties this would cause,[190] but did not recommend limitations on the potential for government interference. Rather, the Commission incorrectly considered that by virtue of its representative functions, one could assume the Government would generally refrain from issuing excessive directions to the Sámediggi.[191] A proposal by the SSR whereby the Sámediggi 'could be both a government authority in some capacities and fully independent in others',[192] was dismissed. Other suggestions that the body could be modelled on independent organisations granted a degree of authority to enable it to act independently of the state were also rejected.[193] The Sámediggi's institutional location carries further complications. As a government agency, the Parliament cannot sue the state, and nor has it been able to secure NGO status at the UN, inhibiting its ability to act independently in domestic and international forums.

This tension is also evident in the requirements governing registration and voting for the Sámediggi. As noted above, challenges to registration are heard by the Norrbotten County Administration Board, a state authority with no Sámi members. There is value in registration being settled by an impartial body, particularly in an environment where an occupation-based cleavage continues to split the Sámi community,[194] and there does not appear to be consistent support among the Sámi to change this arrangement. Nonetheless, it does conflict with the right of Sámi people to determine their own membership.

ii. Evolution

The inherent tension involved in establishing a Sámi representative body within the Swedish state challenges the capacity of the Sámediggi to accurately represent

[187] Eriksson (n 25) 162.

[188] Letter from the Sámediggi to James Anaya, 'Extract from the Written Compilation made for the Conference in Rovaniemi', 16 April 2010, 2.

[189] ibid.

[190] SOU 1989:41 (n 2) 160.

[191] ibid 160. Beach notes that Hans-Åke Wängberg, the Head of the Sámi Rights Commission considered that the 'Government should exercise great reserve in its right of directive to the Sameting': 'The New Swedish Sámi Policy' (1995) 117.

[192] ibid 117.

[193] Korsmo (n 94) 49.

[194] In the lead-up to the 2017 election, Per-Olof Nutti, the leader of the political branch of SSR, proposed an audit of the entire roll, arguing that many non-Sámi are currently registered: Sámediggi Motion 489 (16-05-31). Per Olof Nutti m fl. 'Upptagande av personer i röstlängden'. 1.1.8-2016-870. Cited in U Mörkenstam, 'Some Remarks on the Criteria to Register in the Sámi Electoral Roll in Sweden' in L Heinämäki, C Allard, S Kirchner, A Xanthaki, S Valkonen, U Mörkenstam, N Bankes, J Ruru, J Gilbert, P Selle, A Simpson and L Olsén (eds), *Actualizing Sámi Rights: International Comparative Research* (Finnish Prime Minister's Office, 4/2017) 361, 362.

Sámi interests and values in policy and decision-making. Notwithstanding these concerns, however, the Sámediggi has sought to prioritise its representative role by developing key policies on Sámi identity, seeking to strengthen and ground itself within Sámi society. Analysis of these policies uncovers concentrated effort to maintain and strengthen Sámi culture and traditions through the Sámediggi,[195] but also reveals tensions that inexorably arise. Sámi culture is dynamic and adaptable. These policy documents are both defensive measures to protect Sámi identity as well as attempts to reinterpret that identity and locate it in contemporary conditions, leading to internal conflicts as to what Sámi values are, and how they should be respected.

These tensions are identifiable within and across several policy statements. In *Eallinbiras*, the Sámediggi's environmental programme, the Parliament articulates the relationship between Sámi identity and the world. It explains that the Sámi are 'part of the landscape' and their identity is therefore premised on 'a living relationship to Sápmi'.[196] A resilient Sápmi is 'rooted in both healthy nature and a living Sámi culture'; 'what we take from nature should be in balance with what it can give', and 'all activities that contaminate air, land and water have to stop'.[197] This apparent categorical rejection of mineral resource extraction is tempered elsewhere, where the Sámediggi acknowledges the necessity of 'economic diversity' and 'a diversity of trades' to enable Sámi to protect and promote their identity in a changing environment, and envisages the development of new industrial activities.[198] This same tension is present in the Sámediggi's statement, 'Minerals and Mines in Sápmi', where the Parliament explains that resource extraction must not conflict with the overall goal of a 'viable and sustainable Sámi living environment'.[199] As the Swedish Minerals Act 'does not ensure or respect' Sámi rights, the Sámediggi calls for a 'moratorium on all exploitation in Sápmi'.[200] The Sámediggi's goal is not to prohibit all mining, but for the recognition of strict procedural and substantive rights over the issuing of permits and operations, to 'us[e], but not exhaust[]' natural resources;[201] mining should not occur without the consent of the Parliament and affected Sámi communities, and benefit-sharing and compensation agreements must be reached.[202]

At root here is a political position on land rights, self-determination, and governance. Expressed in more detail in a 2004 report, the Sámediggi premise

[195] See, eg: Sámediggi, *Árbediehtu: Policydokument för traditionell kunskap* (2010); Sámediggi, *Samisk språkhandbok för förvaltningsmyndigheter* (2010).

[196] Sámediggi, *The Sámi Parliament's Living Environment Program: Eallinbiras* (Adopted by the Parliament 19 February 2009) 4.

[197] ibid 11.

[198] ibid 5, 18.

[199] Sámediggi, *Minerals and Mines in Sápmi: The Viewpoint of the Swedish Sami Parliament* (Adopted by the Plenary Assembly in Åre, Sweden, 20 May 2014) 3.

[200] ibid 6–7.

[201] ibid 10.

[202] ibid 6–7.

their policies on the fact 'that Sweden is a state based on the territory of two people with equal rights'.[203] Implementation of this right must be adapted to specific contexts, but in essence the Sámediggi understands it as meaning that Sámi have the right to decide on issues of importance to their society, irrespective as to whether those issues relate to 'culture' or not.[204] Broad statements apparently rejecting mining wholesale, followed by moderating qualifications, serve this political strategy, providing an avenue for the state to accept Sámi rights while continuing to promote economic development.

The Sámediggi's political strategies raise tensions internally, but a further complication arises from the Parliament's subordinate legal status. Sámi identity is intimately connected to land and the Sámediggi therefore understands and articulates Sámi culture in a comprehensive fashion. Many of these policy statements, however, express views on matters that the Parliament does not have legal authority over, inhibiting elected representatives' ability to realise change and potentially damaging their credibility within the polity. In other cases, the state can constrict the ability of the Parliament to act in the best interests of their constituents. Consider the predator compensation example discussed earlier. Following the Norrbotten County Administrative Court's ruling that reindeer herding communities had a right to full compensation for stock losses occurring because of the Swedish Government's predator policy, the matter was debated in the Sámediggi Plenary. The board subsequently decided not to appeal the ruling, arguing that the decision was 'fundamentally in line with the Board's politics and in the Sámi people's interest'.[205] The Ministry of Agriculture disagreed, arguing that the board's decision politicised an administrative matter and that the Sámediggi had failed to act in accordance with its responsibilities as a government agency. In conversations with Rebecca Lawrence, members of the ministry 'maintained that the Parliament should have appealed the court's decision through the entire court system' noting that 'they had clearly communicated this view to the President of the Sámediggi and the chief secretary shortly after the ruling'.[206] A member of the Sámediggi explained the conflict facing the Parliament: 'We have to choose between following our hearts and seeing that reindeer herders are compensated for their loss, or following the government line and losing the Sámi people's confidence'.[207]

The predator compensation example highlights the interrelated nature of the four criteria. It reveals the difficulty in maintaining Sámi confidence in an institution built on a conflicted legal status and empowered with limited independent authority. In this sense, *ownership* is directly connected to *power*. Voter

[203] Svenska Sametingets Kommitté, *Förslag till strategi för en implementering av det samiska folkets rätt till självbestämmande påden svenska sidan av Sápmi* (May 2004) 10, 73.

[204] ibid 10.

[205] Lawrence and Mörkenstam (n 18) 119.

[206] ibid.

[207] ibid.

registration, turnout and electoral studies examining the motivation of voters and non-voters confirm this link and these challenges.

Table 6.1 sets out the number of persons registered on the Sámi electoral roll, and the number and percentage of those who cast a ballot in each election between 1993 and 2017. Several points are apparent. First, the number of voters registered has steadily increased since 1993. On average, around an additional 560 people enrolled at each subsequent election, bringing the total number of registered voters in 2017 to 8,766. This is positive, suggesting that over time, the Sámediggi has become recognisable as a legitimate institution of Sámi political authority. At the same time, however, while there are no accurate estimates of the population of Sámi living in Sweden, this figure is likely to still be less than 50 per cent of the total number of people entitled to register, tempering some of the positives associated with steadily increasing registration. In short, registration is growing, but perhaps not at a particularly impressive rate.

Table 6.1 Voter registration and turnout in Swedish Sámediggi elections

Year	1993	1997	2001	2005	2009	2013	2017
Registered voters	5,390	5,990	6,694	7,180	7,812	8,327	8,766
Change in registered voters	–	+600	+704	+486	+632	+515	+439
Number of voters	3,865	3,803	4,366	4,514	4,623	4,530	5,056
Turnout change	–	−62	+563	+148	+109	−93	+526
%	71.7	63.49	65.8	62.87	59.18	54.4	57.68
% change	–	−8.21	+2.31	−2.93	−3.69	−4.78	+3.28

Source: Swedish Electoral Authority, Norrbotten County Administrative Board.

Second, although registration has increased at each election, the number of people who cast a ballot has not. In 1997 and 2013, turnout in raw numbers decreased, notwithstanding a significant increase of people registered to vote. Similarly, while turnout in raw numbers increased in 2005 and 2009, as a percentage of those registered to vote, it decreased. This is particularly striking as registration on the Sámi electoral roll is not automatic; Sámi voters are a self-selecting group of the potential electorate. This suggests that registration may not necessarily indicate satisfaction or trust in the Sámediggi itself, but rather, an affirmation of Sámi identity.[208] A 2013 electoral survey confirms this hypothesis, finding that just over 52 per cent of respondents stated that the primary

[208] J Bergh, S Dahlberg, U Mörkenstam and J Saglie, 'Participation in Indigenous Democracy: Voter Turnout in Sámi Parliamentary Elections in Norway and Sweden' (2018) 41 *Scandinavian Political Studies* 263, 270.

reason for registering to vote was to express their Sámi identity, compared to 37 per cent who signed up to affect Sámi policy.[209]

Turnout figures for Sámediggi elections compare unfavourably with the rate for general Swedish elections, which, since 1944 has remained steady at around 85 per cent of the electorate.[210] Yet, as a 2002 Commission of Inquiry noted, it is 'not realistic' to assess voter turnout in Sámediggi elections against that for the Riksdag.[211] Indeed, several causal factors largely explain this disjuncture: national political parties – and their substantial campaign infrastructure – do not compete in Sámi elections; the elections themselves are not held concurrently with national elections; and, perhaps most determinative, the Sámediggi has little independent power.[212] In fact, compared to European elections (38.3 per cent) elections to parish councils (14.2 per cent),[213] and the average turnout rate for ATSIC elections (20–25 per cent), turnout for the Sámediggi is encouraging.

The real problem is not turnout, but credibility. Recent electoral survey results have revealed that trust and confidence in the Sámediggi is at staggeringly low levels. Only 16 per cent of respondents to a 2013 election survey reported that they were very, or fairly, confident in the Parliament; compared with 26 per cent for their city council, 32 per cent for the Government, and 36 per cent for the Riksdag.[214] This alarming figure reflects a precipitous fall from an already low 24 per cent who expressed a high or very high confidence in the Parliament in 2008.[215] These figures are concerning, but they raise an important question: why is registration steadily increasing and turnout remaining consistent around 55–65 per cent, if trust and confidence in the institution is so low? It is difficult to offer any firm conclusions, but close observers argue that it may simultaneously indicate support for a national representative body and protest against the existing institution's 'impotence'.[216] Findings from that 2013 election survey support this inference – a primary reason those registered gave for choosing not to vote was the Sámediggi's limited power.[217] Of course, as Sören Holmberg notes, even if the Parliament's limited authority explains these

[209] S Dahlberg and U Mörkenstam, 'Valdeltagande i valet till Sametinget 2013' in S Dahlberg, U Mörkenstam and R Nilsson (eds), *Sametingsval: Väljare, Partier och Media* (Stockholm, Santérus Förlag, 2016) 129, 144.

[210] S Dahlberg, 'Voter Turnout in Sweden' (Friedrich Ebert Stiftung, July 2016) 1.

[211] SOU 2002:77 (n 71) 18.

[212] Bergh, Dahlberg, Mörkenstam and Saglie, 'Participation in Indigenous Democracy' (2018).

[213] SOU 2002:77 (n 71) 18.

[214] S Holmberg, 'Politiskt förtroende' in S Dahlberg, U Mörkenstam and R Nilsson (eds), *Sametingsval: Väljare, Partier och Media* (Stockholm, antérus Förlag, 2016) 219, 219.

[215] U Mörkenstam, A Gottardis and H Roth, 'The Swedish Sámi Parliament: A Challenged Recognition?' (ACCEPT Pluralism, 2012) 10.

[216] Dahlberg and Morkenstam, 'Valdeltagande i valet till Sametinget 2013' (2016) 151; Bergh, Dahlberg, Mörkenstam and Saglie (n 208).

[217] Nilsson, Dahlberg and Mörkenstam, 'Inledning' (2016) 37.

survey results, they 'cannot be seen otherwise than as a very clear failing mark for the institution'.[218]

Ownership is concerned with cultural fit. It asks whether Sámi recognise the Sámediggi as a legitimate institution. The Sámediggi's conflicted legal status creates an inherent tension, but the critical difficulty facing the Parliament under this criterion is the state's willingness to intervene. Representatives are unable to act in a manner that reflects or promotes Sámi values if doing so conflicts with government policy or directives, seriously damaging trust and confidence in the Parliament. Playing on the Swedish word for the Sámediggi (Sameting), Lawrence and Mörkenstam note that it 'has been nicknamed "The Nothing" among the Sámi, since it is considered to be an extended arm of the Swedish state, rather than a representative body of the Sámi people'.[219] For this reason, despite concerted effort by Sámi representatives, this condition is satisfied only to a weak degree.

D. Integrity

The final criterion assesses whether the Sámediggi operates under a credible governance structure such that its members act according to the purposes and values for which they have been entrusted with authority and are accountable for their actions. The Sámediggi largely satisfies this standard but continues to experience intermittent criticism over its administration. Rather than simply exposing inadequacies in the Parliament's public accountability framework however, this criticism reveals a larger challenge. As this chapter has argued, a disjuncture exists between Sámi and state conceptions of the Sámediggi's purpose. In practice, elected representatives seek to prioritise their representative roles, understanding their primary duty as protecting and promoting Sámi interests. In contrast, consistent with its view of Sámi as a sectoral interest group, the state emphasises the Parliament's administrative responsibilities, underscoring its functions as a referral body on proposed legislation that affect Sámi and as a devolved agency specially tailored to undertake administrative functions on cultural matters. While managing conflicts of interest and fraud are relevant under both lenses, these distinct roles can sometimes conflict – especially when the state compels Sámi politicians to adopt policies in contention with their election promises and party manifestos. It is this contestation that sparks most criticism.

The state has long articulated the purposes and duties of the Sámediggi in terms of its administrative rather than representative responsibilities. Under this frame, two issues have arisen. First, the Sámediggi has often been described

[218] Holmberg, 'Politiskt förtroende' (2016) 230.
[219] Lawrence and Mörkenstam (n 18) 123–24.

as 'turbulent'.[220] Part of the problem is that the combination of proportional representation and the absence of a minimum threshold for election has meant no single party has ever enjoyed a majority in the plenary. The more serious difficulty, however, revolves around principles of responsible government. Prior to 2006, the executive did not require the ongoing confidence of the plenary: the 31-member plenary selected the board following an election but could not remove it from office if support shifted during the parliamentary term. This problem was pronounced in the 1997–2001 term, when the board lost the support of the plenary, sparking division and paralysing cooperation.[221] While it was rectified by amendment to the Sámi Parliament Act in 2006,[222] difficulties remain. For instance, during the 2009–2013 term, eight different political parties were represented in the plenary, causing 'an unstable balance between two main blocs' and leading to the Presidency changing four times in just over two years.[223] A revolving door presidency weakens the Parliament's ability to effectively agitate for Sámi interests, but for the state, the chief problem is the consequence for its capacity to manage its administrative responsibilities.

Second, the Sámediggi has been criticised for failing to exercise proper management of public funds. A 2010 report by the Swedish Agency for Public Management, for example, criticised the Sámediggi's internal accountability framework as inadequate. Among other issues, the report found that indicators for targets and objectives are often missing in the Parliament's annual reports,[224] limiting its ability to monitor programme effectiveness. It also noted that the plenary is responsible for determining the Parliament's budget, making it difficult for the board and secretariat to control and implement projects effectively.[225] These criticisms echoed a 2009 report by the National Audit Office, which noted that budgetary overruns revealed a need for significant improvements in internal financial management.[226]

Proper stewardship of public funds is a necessary component of public administration, and these reports are therefore concerning. It appears, however, that administrative problems identified by audit agencies are primarily the result of an inadequate legislative framework, rather than individual mismanagement. In 2017, the Swedish Financial Management Authority (ESV) released a damning report, finding that the Sámi Parliament Act divides responsibilities in complex and contradictory ways, contributing to difficulties in 'achieving satisfactory internal governance'.[227] The report recommended statutory amendment

[220] Josefsen, Mörkenstam and Saglie, 'Different Institutions within Similar States' (2015) 42.
[221] SOU 2002:77 (n 71) 16.
[222] (SFS 2006:803) amending Sámi Parliament Act (n 72) ch 2, s 5a.
[223] Josefsen, Mörkenstam and Saglie (n 177) 42.
[224] Statskontoret (n 120) 42.
[225] ibid 35–36, 42.
[226] Riksrevisionen, *Revisionsrapport Sametingets årsredovisning 2009* (2010).
[227] Ekonomistyrningsverket, *Analys av Sametinget: Finansiering och intern styrning och kontroll* (2017) 6.

to clarify management roles and resolve several uncertainties. It also criticised a 2015 Auditor-General report, which had censured the Parliament over its financial accounting.[228] In other areas, the legislative framework appears to be sound. Unlike ATSIC, Sámediggi representatives are precluded from participating in matters that concern them or their relatives or relate to a Sámi village of which they are a board member,[229] removing the risk of apparent or real conflicts of interest in public expenditure.

Reflecting on the ESV's report, it is difficult to avoid the conclusion that negative attitudes towards Sámi fuel or intensify criticism of the Parliament. In 2008, the Swedish Ombudsman against Ethnic Discrimination reported that Sámi experience 'harassment connected to their ethnic background' in 'all areas of society' as 'part of their day-to-day life'.[230] It is unsurprising then, that analysis of media coverage of the Sámediggi in eight national and local daily Swedish newspapers between 1993 and 2011 reveals a persistent concern among Swedes that the governance and integrity of the Sámediggi is inadequate. Ulf Mörkenstam, Andreas Gottardis, and Hans Roth identified that between 25 and 50 per cent of the articles surveyed 'portrayed the Sámi Parliament as problematic', highlighting political instability and poor administrative performance. Significantly, these articles conceived the problem as an 'internal' one, meaning that they considered that 'the Sámi officials are the ones to blame for the defects of the Parliament',[231] rather than the tensions inherent to its design, or state pressure on its capacity for independent decision-making. Mörkenstam, Gottardis and Roth argue that the media discourse has significant consequences, both reflecting and contributing to a belief that the Parliament is unstable as well as reproducing stereotypical images of Sámi as 'unable to handle their own affairs'. This discourse damages trust and credibility in the Parliament, but it also places further pressure on the state to closely monitor and control the Sámediggi's operations, reducing the likelihood that its autonomy will be enhanced.[232]

Dismissive attitudes are also prevalent in the framing of other supposed integrity challenges, which appear less problematic if the Sámediggi is understood primarily as a representative body. Take the charge of 'turbulence' as an example. Minority governments are common to most proportional systems and are a persistent feature of Swedish politics; only twice in Swedish history has a single party held an absolute majority of seats. Governance may be more challenging in these environments, but political conventions develop and evolve to

[228] ibid 43–44.

[229] Sámi Parliament Act (n 72) ch 2, s 6. Debate persists as to whether administrative tasks should be separated from the political body. See SOU 2002:77 (n 71) 14.

[230] H Pikkarainen and B Brodin, *Discrimination of the Sámi – The Rights of the Sámi from a Discrimination Perspective* (Discrimination Ombudsman, 2008) 24.

[231] Mörkenstam, Gottardis and Roth, 'The Swedish Sámi Parliament' (2012) 2–3, 14, 20.

[232] ibid 24.

accommodate those challenges. In the Riksdag, political scientists have observed a shift from 'positive parliamentarianism', in which the Government must win an investiture vote and actively maintain confidence to a 'negative parliamentarianism', whereby confidence is assumed so long as the Government does not suffer a loss on a key legislative item,[233] ensuring that an executive can exercise its powers as an agent of the Riksdag until and unless that delegation is actively rescinded. This important component of parliamentary governance was absent in the Sámediggi until 2006, damaging both the Sámediggi's administrative roles and representative functions, but this was a problem of design rather than inherent to the Sámi themselves. It was resolved by legislation.

The Sámediggi may sometimes fail to account for its activities in the standard required of Swedish government agencies and its administration may sometimes be affected by changes in political support. These are real challenges for an institution understood primarily as an administrative authority for a sectoral group, as they threaten the institution's effective ability to operate as a 'responsible or "objective" government agency', progress state priorities and clearly articulate views of organised interests.[234] For an institution understood as a representative body, however, these challenges – though they remain – are less problematic. Under this lens, these problems are largely the result of an organisation hamstrung by a conflicted legal status that inhibits its ability to exercise real decision-making authority, or normal complications that arise in any representative institution. If the Sámediggi is intended to realise Sámi political aspirations, its representative role should be emphasised. If that is the case, then notwithstanding some issues around administration, it appears that the Sámediggi satisfies this condition.

IV. CONCLUSION

The establishment of the Sámediggi in 1993 marked 'a radical break'[235] in Swedish politics. As this chapter has demonstrated, however, the ability of the Sámediggi to protect and promote Sámi interests is hindered by state attitudes that perceive Sámi as a sectoral interest group rather than an Indigenous people. This attitude is visible in the Sámediggi's conflicted legal status. As an elected government agency, Sámi have no guaranteed right to participate in the processes of decision-making, severely constrained autonomy on matters that directly affect them, and are entirely reliant on government funding that too often comes

[233] T Möller, 'The Parliamentary System' in J Pierre (ed), *The Oxford Handbook of Swedish Politics* (Oxford, Oxford University Press, 2015) 115, 127.

[234] Lawrence and Mörkenstam (n 18) 122.

[235] E Josefsen, U Mörkenstam and J Saglie, 'Sametingene–Institusjoner for Selvbestemmelse?' in E Josefsen, U Mörkenstam, R Nilsson and J Saglie, (eds), *Ett Folk, Ulike Valg: Sametingsvalg i Norge og Sverige* (Oslo, Gyldendal Akademisk, 2017) 24, 44.

with tight strings attached. Together, this structural position makes it difficult for the Sámediggi to ground itself within the Sámi community by identifying independent policy priorities and developing and implementing distinctive long-term plans. These challenges are even greater in an environment where attitudes towards the Sámediggi are overwhelmingly negative and characterised by criticism over its political instability and apparent poor administrative performance.

The concept of a Sámediggi had broad support from Sámi people, but concerns were initially raised about these very issues.[236] Nonetheless, the leadership of Sámi organisations believed that once 'established and operating, [the Parliament] could set its own agenda, thereby acquiring its legitimacy'.[237] Since 1993, however, Sámi agitation to enhance the autonomy and decision-making power of the Sámediggi, transforming it into an institution with real power, authority and legitimacy have largely fallen on deaf ears. The state's reluctance and resistance to imbue the Sámediggi with independent decision-making autonomy, and its demonstrated commitment to check decisions reached by the Parliament has clearly diminished its credibility. As Lennard Sillanpää has argued, while the existence of the Sámediggi suggests that the state comprehends and acknowledges Indigenous rights, in practice it tolerates those rights 'only so long as [they] can be integrated within the state administration',[238] exposing the limits of sectoral group politics.

The Sámediggi's experiences reveal several lessons for the design of Indigenous representative bodies. These will be explored in more detail in chapter seven, which focuses on the development of a contemporary representative body in Australia, but four points are worth noting here. First, even in a state built on corporatism, the opportunity to provide comment to relevant decision-makers has proven inadequate for Sámi to be heard in the processes of government. The Sámediggi's experience suggests that *voices* will only be realised if decision-makers are placed under an obligation to consult Indigenous representatives on issues that affect them. In the Sámediggi's case, this should be realised via political or legal agreements between the Parliament and national, county and municipal authorities that formalise discussion and enhance opportunities for informal contacts. Strengthening institutional opportunities for consultation cannot guarantee that state authorities will listen to or engage with Sámi interests, but it would entail a clear step up from existing practice, mitigating some of the current inequities, and potentially encouraging representatives to compromise and speak in one voice. Assuming it becomes an integral element of the ordinary operation of government, it could also build considerable moral force. As this shift would necessarily require increasing the Sámediggi's funding

[236] L Sillanpää, 'A Comparative Analysis of Indigenous Rights in Fennoscandia' (1997) 20 *Scandinavian Political Studies* 197, 207.

[237] ibid.

[238] Sillanpää (n 8) 167. Rauna Kuokkanen agrees, concluding that the Parliament is essentially an advisory body rather than a self-governing institution: Kuokkanen (n 97) 79.

and resources to accommodate additional work, it could also mark a distinct shift in state attitudes towards Sámi.

Second, while complete structural independence may not be necessary to ensure a domain of independent policy and decision-making power, or to ensure a representative body is recognised as legitimate by its constituents, the Sámediggi's status as a government agency is problematic in circumstances where the state has consistently evidenced its enthusiasm to rely on this status to check its autonomy. State interference robs the Parliament of authority and weakens trust and confidence among Sámi. Ultimately, this poses problems for the state. If Sámi ignore the Sámediggi, it will lose democratic legitimacy and its status as a referral body and government agency undertaking administrative responsibilities will be challenged. This may be a problem of all state-supported national Indigenous organisations with pressure group functions. As Sally Weaver argued many years ago, one solution is to support and enhance the autonomy of such bodies.[239] Only by fostering the political development of the Sámediggi – recognising a real domain of self-rule and permitting representatives to develop long-term policy that reflects Sámi values – will Sámi have confidence in the Parliament and will it become an effective instrument of and in governance. This will necessarily require the state rethinking its current approach.

Third, financial capacity is critical for an institution's ability to develop policy on issues that affect Indigenous peoples. While its status as a government agency has largely ensured financial sustainability, this position has ultimately proved damaging. The state's refusal to meaningfully engage with Sámi political aspirations has left the Sámediggi in a precarious position: the overwhelming majority of its funding is earmarked for administrative tasks, leaving its representative role not just underdeveloped but undeveloped. Only the President is employed full-time, and no representatives have staff to assist them in their duties. Without the financial capacity to fashion policy, strengthen party structures, or connect with constituents across Sápmi, the Sámediggi will remain embryonic. Creative solutions consistent with Sámi traditions and the Swedish constitutional framework should be explored. One suggestion involves transforming the Sámediggi into a non-territorial municipality, empowering Sámi to exercise the considerable authority granted to local government in the Swedish system – including the right to levy taxation.[240]

Fourth, the experience of the Sámediggi suggests that integrity issues may be used as a smokescreen for the state to interfere or challenge Indigenous institutions. Notwithstanding some teething issues connected to its institutional design and lack of resourcing, it appears that the Sámediggi is largely

[239] S Weaver, 'Australian Aboriginal Policy: Aboriginal Pressure Groups or Government Advisory Bodies? Part II' (1983) 54 *Oceania* 85.

[240] I thank Ulf Mörkenstam for this suggestion.

practising proper stewardship. Nonetheless, media and state attitudes towards the Parliament both emphasise problems and frame those problems as the fault of Sámi alone. As this dynamic suggests, securing a fair relationship between Indigenous peoples and the state(s) in which they reside requires more than just structural or institutional reform. To ground lasting change, an ethic of respect must permeate non-Indigenous – Indigenous relations. Only if this eventuates, will the state acknowledge that integrity issues can be resolved in a manner that does not require weakening Indigenous organisations.

7

Structural Reform and Empowerment in Australia: Voice Plus

I. INTRODUCTION

INDIGENOUS REPRESENTATIVE BODIES can empower Indigenous peoples with the capacity to have their voices heard in the processes of government. Depending on their precise powers and structure, they may provide a guaranteed opportunity for Indigenous voices to inform and influence decision-makers, as well as delineate a zone within which Indigenous peoples can exercise a degree of independent policy and decision-making authority. The experiences of the Aboriginal and Torres Strait Islander Commission (ATSIC) and the Swedish Sámediggi demonstrate, however, that these institutions are also beset by many tensions and challenges. Drawing on these two case studies, this chapter presents a detailed, complex picture outlining how an Indigenous representative body could meet Aboriginal and Torres Strait Islander peoples' aspirations for structural reform.

I begin by identifying the key challenge that Indigenous representative bodies must confront: managing an unreceptive government. The relationship between government and an Indigenous representative body is critical because these institutions do not have a determinative vote. Indigenous representatives' ability to influence legislation and policy relies on their capacity to convince decision-makers to genuinely listen. As ATSIC and the Sámediggi found, developing productive relationships with the state can be difficult, but it will be especially challenging when an administration is either indifferent or hostile towards the body.

Those case studies revealed that two factors are vital in endowing an Indigenous representative body with the greatest prospect of effectively managing this challenge and remaining influential and secure in the face of an unreceptive government: prudent structural design choices, and a complementary surrounding institutional framework. An Indigenous representative body regarded as legitimate by Indigenous communities and credible by government and the public at large will more likely be able to weather intermittent storms of constituent criticism and state indifference or hostility. Chapter four identified that an institution that satisfies Indigenous aspirations for *voices*, *power*, *ownership* and *integrity* is more likely to be regarded as legitimate and credible. The key is designing an institution to meet these criteria.

This is not simple. Close examination of ATSIC and the Sámediggi demonstrate that the criteria can conflict, potentially sparking their own tensions, while imbalances in political power between Indigenous peoples and government may force the adoption of more modest aims. Indigenous peoples and communities must make difficult choices over the design of an institution that represents them in the processes of government. Significantly, Indigenous peoples themselves must make those decisions.[1]

Careful consideration of an Indigenous representative body's design can build its legitimacy and credibility, enhancing the prospect that it can manage an indifferent or hostile government. It is unlikely to be sufficient, however. As ATSIC and the Sámediggi illustrate, Indigenous representative bodies are valuable but limited mechanisms. To give the body the best chance of success, it should be integrated within a broader institutional structure that empowers Aboriginal and Torres Strait Islander peoples and communities. This is consistent with the aspirations of Indigenous Australians. In the Uluru Statement from the Heart, delegates called for the establishment of a First Nations Voice and a Makarrata Commission to supervise a process of agreement-making and truth-telling.[2] In doing so, delegates recognised that the effectiveness of a representative body is reliant, in part, on its position within a broader institutional setting.

Aboriginal and Torres Strait Islander peoples must determine their own preferred framework. In this chapter, I draw on the Uluru Statement to outline one possible complementary model, characterised as Voice Plus. I identify emergent treaty processes in Victoria, the Northern Territory and Queensland,[3] as offering the potential – assuming Commonwealth support is forthcoming – to embed and finance self-governance arrangements in Indigenous communities. Provided clear links between local, self-governing communities and the national representative body are established, Voice Plus offers real hope for restructuring Australia's governance system to empower Aboriginal and Torres Strait Islander peoples with the capacity to have their voices heard and their interests considered in the processes of government.

II. MANAGING INDIFFERENCE OR HOSTILITY

An effective Indigenous representative body must realise two sometimes opposing goals. Representatives must demonstrate they are authentic and accountable to Indigenous communities by accurately articulating the scope and intensity of their constituents' interests and priorities to decision-makers in government.

[1] United Nations Declaration on the Rights of Indigenous Peoples, GA Res 61/295, UN GAOR, 61st sess, 107th plen mtg, Supp No 49, UN Doc A/RES/61/295 (13 September 2007) (UNDRIP) arts 3–5, 18.

[2] Uluru Statement from the Heart, Uluru, 26 May 2017 (Uluru Statement).

[3] G Williams and H Hobbs, *Treaty*, 2nd edn (Alexandria, Federation Press, 2020) ch 8.

At the same time, relying on their chief advantage, representatives must demonstrate their worth by securing amendment to legislative proposals and government policy to better reflect Indigenous views.[4] While Indigenous representatives do not need to influence every policy, Indigenous peoples must nonetheless perceive the institution as furthering their interests, perhaps by contributing to policy development in formal or informal ways over the short or long term. Indigenous parliamentarians and public servants have explained that managing the tension between authenticity and influence, between 'the need for internal legitimacy and external recognition',[5] is a recurring challenge,[6] but it is easier to handle with a sympathetic government. A receptive government may meaningfully engage with Indigenous representatives even if it ultimately resolves to adopt a different path. Where an Indigenous representative body is faced with state indifference or outright hostility, it can become very difficult to realise these twin demands.

ATSIC's experiences neatly illustrate this central challenge. Concern that the Commission was presenting advice in conflict with government priorities contributed to decisions by both Labor and coalition governments to establish alternative sources of advice within the public service and reduce its input and access to Cabinet, undermining the Commission's potential influence. At other times, efforts by the Commission to prioritise its position within government challenged its claim to authentically represent Aboriginal and Torres Strait Islander communities. Caught between demands for authenticity and influence, ATSIC never obtained widespread community support or the political strength that it entails. Without that support, government suffered little political cost in ignoring the Commission. Without genuine engagement by government, many Indigenous peoples regarded the Commission as ineffective. As an ineffective and unrepresentative institution, ATSIC was unable to prevent its abolition.

The potential for this tension to emerge was acknowledged and considered during ATSIC's development. In a letter to South Australian Senator John Coulter, Wilfred Gray, Chair of the ATSIC Taskforce, Secretary of the Department of Aboriginal Affairs, and subsequently inaugural CEO of the Commission, identified the central conflict with the proposal. It is worth quoting his letter in detail:

> The fundamental purpose of the legislation is to give Aboriginal interests access to the executive processes of Government. To do this, it is necessary to design an organisation that does more than merely reflect Aboriginal and Torres Strait Islander interests – a purely lobbying role that could be fulfilled by any or all of the various national Aboriginal organisations. Rather, ATSIC must be capable of providing Governments

[4] M Dillon, 'Institutional Structures in Indigenous Affairs' in P Sullivan (ed), *Shooting the Banker: Essays on ATSIC and Self-Determination* (Darwin, North Australian Research Unit, 1996) 89–103.

[5] Paul Nadasdy, *Sovereignty's Entailments: First Nation State Formation in the Yukon* (Toronto, University of Toronto Press, 2017) 85.

[6] See ch 2.

> with sound and comprehensive advice on all matters relating to Aboriginal Affairs in a highly professional and credible manner. … [I]t needs to be understood that to the extent that the Commission is unable to effectively fulfil the role, of providing professional advice to Government, Ministers will seek advice elsewhere.[7]

Gray noted that this arrangement would present a 'challenge to the leadership of the Aboriginal community'. To the extent that:

> [T]hey provide Governments with professional, objective advice, they will (i) obtain access to information not otherwise available (and certainly not available to lobby groups) and (ii) obtain the opportunity to influence from inside the public sector the development of Government policy as it affects Aboriginal people. If, however, the Aboriginal leadership is unable to recognise the reality that no Government will abrogate ultimate responsibility for governing, and demands the 'freedom' to operate purely as a lobby group inside Government, the Commission will be isolated by the bureaucracy and will lose credibility and influence with Government.[8]

Gray's letter is partial. He frames the challenge entirely as one for Indigenous peoples, discounting the fact that the way that decision-makers in government choose to approach and respond to advice affects the tenor of that advice. An indifferent or hostile government that determines not to meaningfully engage, for example, removes the opportunity for influence, leaving Indigenous representatives' little option but to emphasise potentially antagonistic views in order to demonstrate authenticity. Nonetheless, Gray's essential point remains correct. Examination of ATSIC and the Sámediggi has demonstrated that if decision-makers in government consider an institution unable or unwilling to provide 'professional' advice, government may marginalise the body. Yet, Indigenous representatives who seek to avoid this fate by expressing aspirations in a manner that encourages government to respond productively risk accusations that they have been 'co-opted' by the state.[9]

The tension between accountability and influence is not soluble because Indigenous representative bodies are fundamentally conflicted organisations. Their logic is premised on the view that operating within the state offers the best prospect of ensuring that Indigenous priorities are reflected in state decision-making. This can be true. Chapters five and six documented several examples where ATSIC and the Sámediggi contributed positively to policy development, effectively imbuing Indigenous views in the design and development of legislation. At their highest, Indigenous representative bodies are valuable institutional mechanisms. However, while these institutions will

[7] Letter from Wilfred Gray to John Coulter. Cited in Senate Select Committee on the Administration of Aboriginal Affairs, Parliament of Australia, 'Administration of Aboriginal Affairs' (1989) 16–17 [2.19].

[8] ibid (emphasis in original).

[9] T Alfred, *Peace, Power, Righteousness: An Indigenous Manifesto*, 2nd edn (Oxford, Oxford University Press, 2009) 97–104.

not – and need not – be successful in every policy discussion, problems emerge when they are rarely successful. At their lowest, more than simply a matter of disappointing expectations, the formal existence of an Indigenous representative body 'advising' government may operate as a fig leaf to validate unilateral state decision-making.[10] Where this occurs, Indigenous peoples may decide it is better for the body to be abolished entirely.

This tension may not be soluble, but it can be managed. The case studies suggest that two factors are critical in designing a contemporary Indigenous representative body that is best placed to effectively empower Aboriginal and Torres Strait Islander peoples, even in the face of a hostile or indifferent Commonwealth. First, prudent structural design choices should centre on developing an institution that is regarded as legitimate and credible.[11] This requires an institution that meets Indigenous aspirations for *voices*, *power*, *ownership* and *integrity*. Although institutional design cannot guarantee influence, an organisation that realises these criteria will carry significant moral weight, making it politically more difficult for government to ignore or marginalise. Second, regardless as to how legitimate or credible an Indigenous representative body is, it remains just one mechanism and its impact will therefore be limited. A diverse array of institutional structures and processes aimed at empowering marginalised communities can be developed in democratic states. Situating an Indigenous representative body in a broader, interlocking framework of complementary mechanisms will reinforce its legitimacy and credibility, and enhance its capacity to empower Indigenous Australians. The remainder of this chapter will explore these two factors.

III. INSTITUTIONAL DESIGN CHOICES

The case studies have demonstrated the importance of an institution's legitimacy and credibility. Legitimacy and credibility depend on several factors, including the character and political judgment of an organisation's leaders as well as state attitudes and approaches towards the body. Institutional design cannot ensure representatives exercise proper stewardship or that the state commits to meaningfully engage, but prudent structural design can enhance this prospect. Institutional design is therefore critical to build an organisation that may satisfy these two values. Eight issues drawn from the case studies should be considered in the design of an Indigenous representative body, though their resolution is ultimately a matter for the relevant communities.

[10] HC Coombs, *Aboriginal Autonomy: Issues and Strategies* (Cambridge, Cambridge University Press, 1994) 183–84.

[11] As recognised in Joint Select Committee on Constitutional Recognition Relating to Aboriginal and Torres Strait Islander Peoples, Parliament of Australia, 'Final Report' (November 2018) 75 [2.303] (Joint Select Committee Final Report).

The first issue is most significant. An Indigenous representative body must be designed by Indigenous peoples and, to the greatest extent possible, reflect their own understandings and approaches to political authority. An Indigenous-designed body will increase the likelihood that *ownership* is initially satisfied, setting the body up with the greatest chance of success. For this reason, the process of the body's development is an overriding element from which all others flow. It is not the only important design choice. Institutional design must also ensure that leaders are accountable, exercising their responsibilities with probity, for a framework that encourages good governance will contribute to *integrity* and enhance the organisation's credibility. Other issues should also be considered. To realise *voices*, the body should be plural and inclusive, encouraging and enabling the participation of all Indigenous peoples. It must also be financed appropriately, so that it may comment on issues it considers pertinent to any relevant decision-maker, at all levels of government, at a stage in the policy-development cycle where it is capable of influencing debate. Contemporary proposals for a First Nations Voice have prioritised its representative function. Without independent decision-making authority, an Indigenous representative body will not meet more significant gradations of *power*, but institutional design can attempt to invest the institution with moral and political force, enhancing forms of soft power. Institutional design should heighten the prospect that consultation occurs, and that consultation is meaningful, reflecting Indigenous peoples' status as a constituent normative order within the state. The process of the body's establishment can assist in this endeavour.

A. Development of the Body

Indigenous peoples and communities must regard the body as legitimate. Legitimacy can be enhanced by several features of institutional design explored in more detail below, including the body's representativeness and its capacity to realise outcomes. Here, drawing on the challenges faced by ATSIC and the Sámediggi, I discuss a more fundamental element of that design. As those case studies revealed, these two institutions struggled – and in the case of the Sámediggi, continue to struggle – to secure widespread support throughout their communities because of concerns over their development. As the 'effectiveness of [governance] institutions depends in substantial measure on the extent to which they are meaningfully rooted in their societies',[12] an Aboriginal and Torres Strait Islander representative body must be substantially designed by Aboriginal and Torres Strait Islander communities.[13]

[12] G White, 'And Now For Something Completely Northern: Institutions of Governance in the Territorial North' (2001) 35 *Journal of Canadian Studies* 80, 81.

[13] Technical Advisers, Submission No 206 to Joint Select Committee on Constitutional Recognition Relating to Aboriginal and Torres Strait Islander Peoples, 11 June 2018, 7.

To meet this requirement a two-stage consultation process could be conducted.[14] Under this approach, genuine consultation designed and led by Indigenous peoples would be undertaken with communities across the country. This stage would focus on developing and articulating key themes and principles underlying a representative body and could loosely be based on the Victorian or nationwide models discussed in chapters three and four. It is imperative that a second round of detailed consultations is then run to allow communities to understand and critique the specific proposal.[15] Consistent with the right to self-determination, this two-stage process would allow Indigenous peoples and communities to take a leading role in the design of the institution. Nonetheless, limitations will persist. This process cannot guarantee that the final Bill will reflect Indigenous preferences. While Parliament ought to legislate in accordance with Indigenous views it is ultimately Parliament's Bill.[16]

The same tension exists once the Bill is adopted. Even if the representative body initially reflects Indigenous wishes, it is impossible to state with any certainty that a future government will refrain from imposing its own design priorities. Australia's electoral system does not empower Aboriginal and Torres Strait Islander peoples to elect representatives of their choice, let alone for those representatives to persistently advocate for Indigenous interests.[17] Consequently, a future Parliament could radically alter the structure and powers of an Indigenous representative body.[18] This challenge could be managed legally or politically, but neither option conclusively resolves the problem. Legally, detailed provisions regarding the structure of the body could be entrenched in the Constitution via a referendum. This would protect the institution but would also make it very difficult to modify its design in accordance with Indigenous desires in the future, inhibiting Aboriginal and Torres Strait Islander peoples' right to determine for themselves the political structure that best meets their needs.[19] Imposing manner and form requirements on the legislation poses similar, though not as extreme, challenges.[20]

[14] The Indigenous members of the Referendum Council responsible for the regional dialogues, and the Technical Advisers who supported them favour a two-stage process: P Anderson, N Pearson, M Davis, S Brennan, G Appleby, D Lino and G McKinnon, Submission No 479 to Joint Select Committee on Constitutional Recognition Relating to Aboriginal and Torres Strait Islander Peoples, 3 November 2018, 13–15.

[15] A second round of consultations was not conducted in the development of ATSIC: Senate Select Committee on the Administration of Aboriginal Affairs, 'Administration of Aboriginal Affairs' (1989) 76 [4.23].

[16] The Final Report of the Joint Select Committee on Constitutional Recognition recommended a process of 'co-design': Joint Select Committee Final Report (n 11) 77–78 [2.314] Recommendation 1.

[17] See ch 2.

[18] Of course, the body itself would have a say in any future legislation to alter it, but a government committed to imposing its own preferences would likely ignore those views.

[19] UNDRIP (n 1) arts 3–5, 18.

[20] D Lino, *Constitutional Recognition: First Peoples and the Australian Settler State* (Annandale, Federation Press, 2018) 211–14. Assuming such restrictions are permissible.

Political processes are similarly unsatisfying. A convention may develop whereby both major parties commit to only amend the legislation governing the representative body following genuine consultation with Indigenous peoples and in accordance with their wishes. This outcome is attractive, but is unlikely to withstand a hostile government. Another option involves adapting the approach in Victoria. The Advancing the Treaty Process with Aboriginal Victorians Act 2018 (Vic), discussed in chapter four, requires the state Government 'recognise' an incorporated Aboriginal representative body.[21] This hook establishes a relationship between the body and the Government but ensures that questions of design will reflect Indigenous priorities. A constitutional provision could similarly require the Commonwealth to recognise a First Nations Voice and empower it with financial capacity and functions to be determined in negotiation with Indigenous communities and government. A constitutionally entrenched provision along these lines ensures the continued existence of a body and prevents the parliament from interfering with its design. It does, however, leave questions concerning the powers and resourcing of the body to consultation, and a hostile government may simply jettison any agreement.

B. Governance

Institutional design must ensure that Indigenous leaders undertake their responsibilities with probity. An organisation that fails to meet standards of *integrity* will not be regarded as credible and will be ineffective at realising its key role: influencing legislation and policy. Good governance is not simply a matter of unreflexively applying a set of accountability mechanisms, however. The appropriate mechanisms will depend upon the status and role of the body. For instance, ATSIC's combination of executive and advisory functions led many to suggest that Commissioners were conflicted when determining funding priorities. A contemporary institution with a similar combination of responsibilities should establish policies that ensure real or perceived conflicts of interest are avoided. Roles may need to be more clearly delineated,[22] and a Code of Conduct,[23] or independent Ethics Council could be established to advise on standards and guidelines.[24] A purely representative body, on the other hand, may not require a delineation of roles, though an independent supervisory council would remain valuable.

[21] Advancing the Treaty Process with Aboriginal Victorians Act 2018 (Vic) ss 9–11 (Victorian Treaty Act).

[22] L O'Donoghue, 'In Indigenous Affairs Nothing is New, Just Forgotten' (1997) 56 *Australian Journal of Public Administration* 5, 8.

[23] See, eg: Murdi Paaki Regional Assembly, 'Charter of Governance' (April 2006) 17.

[24] See, eg: National Congress of Australia's First Peoples Limited, Constitution (15 April 2010) s 1.3(a)(5); s 14A.

As an Indigenous body, governance mechanisms should primarily be determined by Indigenous communities, who are entitled to decide upon the framework that ensures their leaders are accountable. Nonetheless, because the institution is intended to play a formal role in policy development and will be publicly financed to realise its responsibilities, the state will insist on exercising some supervisory functions. That is appropriate, but it should not overstep what is required for good public administration and interfere with internal self-governance or inhibit the institution's capacity to meet the demands of its constituents.

One key integrity mechanism needs to be discussed. ATSIC's experience indicates that processes for removal of members should be clarified. A critical question is whether government should have the authority to remove members. While guarantees against state-initiated removal can enhance the body's independence, processes for removal may bolster the institution's legitimacy by ensuring that members who fail to uphold appropriate standards will be disqualified.[25] At the same time, such processes could also leave leaders vulnerable to politically motivated complaints. As the body will exercise public functions, government will likely demand a power to remove representatives. Recalling our key focus on *ownership*, however, I consider that it is preferable that this power be reserved to the body itself, with appeals heard by an independent, Indigenous Ethics Council. This approach is consistent with the principle of self-determination.[26] It also better reflects the status and role of the body. Since the body is a political institution, accountability mechanisms should primarily be political and mirror those of the legislature. This does not prevent the adoption of clear legal standards for removal (such as imprisonment or bankruptcy, for example), but ensures that members maintain ultimate responsibility for the credibility of the body.[27] Although ATSIC's leaders may not have acted appropriately in the Geoff Clark and Ray Robinson scandals, the Board's failings are now well recognised, suggesting that representatives in a contemporary institution would act swiftly to remove members who bring the body into disrepute. If they choose not to do so, the effectiveness of the body will be limited.

C. Representativeness

An Indigenous representative body will be more likely to be regarded as legitimate and credible if it accurately reflects Aboriginal and Torres Strait Islander

[25] G Appleby, 'An Indigenous Advisory Body: Some Questions of Design' (2015) 8(19) *Indigenous Law Bulletin* 3, 4.

[26] Though of course self-determination allows Indigenous communities to adopt a different method.

[27] This is not strictly consistent with the approach taken for the Federal Parliament where appeals are heard by the High Court constituted as the Court of Disputed Returns. However, it is similar in the sense that unless and until Parliament chooses to refer a matter to the Court of Disputed Returns, questions about whether a member is incapable of sitting in Parliament are matters for Parliament itself: Constitution ss 44, 45; Commonwealth Electoral Act 1918 (Cth) s 376; *Alley v Gillespie* (2018) 264 CLR 328.

peoples' voices in all their diversity. Indigenous Australians are heterogeneous, constituting many distinct nations and cultural groups spread across the country. Any institution designed to empower Indigenous peoples to be heard in the processes of government must therefore be structured in a manner that fosters 'local input into local matters',[28] and avoids the homogenising tendencies that silence disparate communities. As discussed in chapter four, this notion of representativeness is interlinked with concerns over *power* and *ownership*. A genuinely representative body 'rooted in the local'[29] and capable of channelling diverse voices to the national level will enhance the prospect that meaningful policy comment and advice is expressed to relevant decision-makers and has an impact on the ground in community, thereby encouraging people to participate. In other words, the effectiveness of an Indigenous representative body relies on its ability to empower communities as well as internally variegated groups.

Indigenous peoples and communities are best placed to identify a structure that meets their needs, but ATSIC's design is a useful starting point to consider how local communities can express their voices within a national organisation. Several issues, including ensuring two-way communication between local and national levels and identifying appropriate electorate boundaries will need to be resolved, however. On the former point, the 2003 Hannaford Review recommended abolishing the Commission's zone system and reconstituting the board, with the chair of each regional council serving on a new 35-member national body.[30] This proposal has merit. Abolishing a layer of governance would reduce complexities and more directly empower local communities. The latter challenge may be more difficult. Chapter five explained that the Commission's regional council system did not always reflect traditional community boundaries, causing difficulties in practice and suggesting that this specific representative basis may not be appropriate or desirable for all communities in a contemporary institution. Nonetheless, the Hannaford Review's emphasis on a more localised representative structure makes sense, and approaches that more closely track traditional conceptions of authority can be considered.

The Commission's representative structure was designed prior to the recognition of native title. Native title processes have promoted 'a greater level of organisation within Indigenous communities', enabling them to gauge a 'coherent sense' of identity and boundaries,[31] as well as creating 'an important

[28] Cape York Institute, Submission No 244 to Joint Select Committee on Constitutional Recognition Relating to Aboriginal and Torres Strait Islander Peoples, June 2018, 32. See further Joint Select Committee Final Report (n 11) 75 [2.302].

[29] Evidence to Joint Select Committee on Constitutional Recognition Relating to Aboriginal and Torres Strait Islander Peoples, Parliament of Australia, Kununurra, 11 June 2018, 10 (Ian Trust).

[30] J Hannaford, J Huggins and B Collins, 'In the Hands of the Regions – A New ATSIC' (Report of the Review of the Aboriginal and Torres Strait Islander Commission, 2003) 78–80.

[31] Evidence to Joint Select Committee on Constitutional Recognition Relating to Aboriginal and Torres Strait Islander Peoples, Parliament of Australia, Adelaide, 5 July 2018, 10 (Alexander Reilly).

economic and cultural foundation'.[32] A contemporary representative body could build on these developments. Under the Native Title Act 1993 (Cth) (NTA), native title rights and interests are held and managed in trust by Native Title Prescribed Bodies Corporate (PBCs). In drawing their authority from country – the basis of Indigenous Australians' identity – PBCs have 'cemented' traditional governance structures in a 'contemporary form'.[33] PBCs could therefore serve as a culturally appropriate representative structure from which representatives 'who speak for country' may be elected or appointed to a national body, ensuring traditional owners are heard at the Commonwealth level.[34]

Two complications arise. First, demonstrating connection to country is difficult or impossible for many communities dispossessed from their traditional lands. Alternative institutional arrangements are therefore crucial for groups unable to secure native title rights – and indeed for communities with native title who may choose not to engage via PBCs. Second, there are 181 PBCs around the country, meaning that some form of amalgamation that is justifiable to and makes sense for the relevant Indigenous communities will be necessary to ensure disparate voices are effectively represented. One option involves drawing on the boundaries of the 15 regional Native Title Representative Bodies (NTRBs). Under this approach, individual PBCs within a defined NTRB region could select a representative to a regional body. The chair of the regional body would then also serve on a 15-member national board.[35] This approach scaffolds upon existing institutions, but may not be appropriate in all cases. Some communities may prefer to associate through other community governance structures, such as the Murdi Paaki Regional Assembly or the Ngarrindjeri Regional Authority.[36] The key point is that each community should determine for itself its preferred arrangement. The entire structure must be flexible.[37]

A representative body should not only ensure that traditional owners are adequately represented. As I have argued, insufficient representation of internally variegated groups is a recurrent issue that has weakened the effectiveness,

[32] A Reilly, 'A Constitutional Framework for Indigenous Governance' (2006) 28 *Sydney Law Review* 403, 433–34.

[33] Evidence to Joint Select Committee on Constitutional Recognition Relating to Aboriginal and Torres Strait Islander Peoples, Parliament of Australia, Adelaide, 11 June 2018, 8 (Christy Hawker).

[34] W Mundine, 'Practical Recognition from the Mob's Perspective' (Uphold and Recognise, 2017) 13; Cape York Institute, 'A First Nations Voice in the Constitution: Design Issues' (Report to the Referendum Council, June 2017) 30, 34–35, 44.

[35] Evidence to Joint Select Committee on Constitutional Recognition Relating to Aboriginal and Torres Strait Islander Peoples, Parliament of Australia, Adelaide, 12 June 2018, 4–6 (Peter Yu).

[36] For information on these arrangements see Murdi Paaki Regional Assembly, 'Regional Plan' (2016) ch 1; Ngarrindjeri Regional Authority, 'Annual Report 2016' (2016).

[37] At some point flexibility in selection of members may undermine the coherence of the body, but this is a question for Indigenous Australians to consider for themselves. It is sufficient to note that many existing representative bodies are not all constituted on the same basis. Consider for example the United Kingdom and Canadian Parliaments, which combine democratic election to the lower house with executive appointment (and in the United Kingdom some hereditary positions) in the upper house.

legitimacy, credibility and sustainability of previous bodies. ATSIC especially struggled with this standard. Although institutional arrangements ensured that the distinct views of Torres Strait Islander peoples were heard, the Commission failed to ensure equitable representation of women or to integrate women's perspectives, distorting its policy design and decision-making. Significantly, while the Commission advocated against proposals to enshrine equal gender balance, community attitudes appear to have shifted. The National Congress of Australia's First Peoples guaranteed 'substantial gender equality' in leadership positions,[38] and the 2018 Joint Select Committee on Constitutional Recognition found strong support for equal gender representation in a proposed First Nations Voice,[39] albeit with deference to customary authority.[40] Recent scholarship on the connections between self-determination and gender justice affirm the value of ensuring equitable gender representation,[41] though communities may ultimately decide to adopt alternative approaches.

This is an important point. More than simply emphasising that *ownership* will be a critical consideration in the effectiveness and legitimacy of any contemporary body, it reveals that institutional design produces tensions that are not always reconcilable. In some cases, in some communities, equitable gender representation may not be appropriate. Attempts to negotiate this challenge by, for instance, providing for each representative unit to select a male and female candidate, will double the number of representatives, exacerbating the complications discussed above. Indigenous communities must take note of their priorities; sometimes they will be forced to choose between competing options.

In considering these issues, it is vital to be clear about the body's function. If the representative body is to faithfully express Indigenous views within the processes of government it should be an inclusive and pluralistic forum, enabling the free participation of all significant groups within Indigenous polities.[42] This means that mechanisms should exist to encourage all people to contribute, though of course Indigenous peoples and communities themselves are entitled to determine the precise structure and design of those mechanisms. Two groups are worth noting, but others exist. First, consideration should be given to how members of the Stolen Generations could articulate their voices and have their interests reflected within the body. This is particularly important if the chief representative unit is the PBC, as members of the Stolen Generations are disconnected from their traditional lands and may be unable to participate through this institutional form.

[38] National Congress of Australia's First Peoples Limited, 'Constitution' (15 April 2010), r 13.1(c).

[39] Joint Select Committee on Constitutional Recognition Relating to Aboriginal and Torres Strait Islander Peoples, Parliament of Australia, 'Interim Report' (2018) (Joint Select Committee Interim Report), 115 [7.18]; Cape York Institute, 'A First Nations Voice in the Constitution' (2017) 44.

[40] Joint Select Committee Interim Report (n 39) 31 [3.46].

[41] R Kuokkanen, *Restructuring Relations: Indigenous Self-Determination, Governance, and Gender* (Oxford, Oxford University Press, 2019) ch 4.

[42] Cape York Institute (n 34) 39.

Effort should also be undertaken to enable young people to participate. This could occur via a committee system. The Sámediggi, for example, appoints a Youth Council composed of five members aged between 14 and 30 years of age for a two-year term. Empowered to strengthen the influence of Sámi youth within the Parliament, the Council encourages their engagement in politics and serves as an advisory body to the Sámediggi's Board and committees.[43] Care should be taken in adapting this model, however. While members of the Youth Council report that they are 'satisfied' with the system, the council is largely underdeveloped. It is not directly heard by the Sámediggi's decision-making bodies and, because of inadequate funding, is unable to fulfil its responsibilities.[44] Evidence suggests that the council 'rarely gets called upon to participate in important sessions and meetings of the Parliament', and is 'not often asked to provide input concerning political documents or motions that are being considered by the Parliament'.[45] Complications must be resolved, but this example illustrates that comparative examination is a helpful guide to developing a genuinely representative national body in Australia.

Finally, an institution is most effective when it speaks authoritatively in one voice, but a representative body will never secure consensus on all issues. This raises challenges faced by both ATSIC and the Sámediggi: how to manage division so that it can deliver a coherent message. This is largely a question for the political judgment of representatives, but design can assist. Chapter four noted that institutional design in Nunavut may have contributed to minimising expressions of disagreement, while chapter six proposed another key factor. Close observers of the Sámediggi persuasively argue that division with the Parliament largely stems from its limited influence.[46] This suggests that the potential for division and disagreement within a contemporary institution may (though not necessarily will) be reduced if its members believe that government will meaningfully engage with their advice. Representatives may be incentivised to reach a consensus position if it enhances the likelihood of reform.

D. Funding

An Indigenous representative body must be financed appropriately to effectively realise its responsibilities.[47] The question of resourcing highlights the

[43] E Biaudet, 'Study on the Right to Participation of Indigenous Youth in the Nordic Countries in Decision-Making Processes' (UN Doc E/C.19/2013/8 (12 February 2013) 6 [18].

[44] ibid [20].

[45] ibid.

[46] A-M Fjellström, 'Partiernas Rekrytering och Nominering av Kandidater Inför Valet 2013' in S Dahlberg, U Mörkenstam and R Nilsson (eds), *Sametingsval: Väljare, Partier och Media* (Stockholm, Santérus Förlag, 2016) 103.

[47] Referendum Council, 'Final Report of the Referendum Council' (Commonwealth, 2017) 30–31; Technical Advisers (n 13) 8.

central tension facing all Indigenous organisations. An institution's legitimacy and credibility are enhanced by secure financing, which enables the body to determine and undertake its own priorities. At the same time, in the absence of independent own-source revenue, stable financing is reliant on government support. ATSIC and the Sámediggi's experiences reveal how this tension can manifest. Australian and Swedish governments have frequently utilised their financial leverage to check Indigenous representatives' capacity to determine their own priorities. Budgetary cuts, quarantining of expenditure and the transfer of unwanted administrative responsibilities, among other levers, forced the Commission (and continue to pressure the Sámediggi) to reallocate funding from their own projects to those designed or favoured by the state. In addition to robbing the notion of self-determination of any content,[48] these practices weaken each institution's legitimacy and credibility.

Adequate financing is particularly important in Australia. Representatives must be able to travel widely throughout their constituencies to understand community concerns, relay them to relevant decision-makers and feed those discussions back to community. The precise quantum of funding will depend on the breadth of the body's functions, including, for example, whether it provides advice to state, territory and local governments, or monitors Aboriginal affairs expenditure,[49] but it must be sufficient to meet several minimum responsibilities. The institution must be able to hire a secretariat, policy staff and lawyers to ensure representatives can develop their own policy positions and are well-briefed when providing advice to decision-makers or consulting with the executive or Parliamentarians.[50] Office-holders should also be remunerated appropriately to reflect the body's status and draw qualified and politically adept individuals to the role.

There are various ways that an organisation's financial capacity can be protected.[51] Parliamentary office-holders' salaries and scrutiny institutions' budgets are often safeguarded by political mechanisms. Senate Standing Orders, for instance, provide that committees 'shall be provided with all necessary staff, facilities and resources'.[52] Similarly, in the ACT, legislation empowers the Speaker of the Legislative Assembly to recommend an appropriation for offices of the Assembly to the Treasurer, following consultation. If the Treasurer subsequently decides on a lower quantum, he or she must present reasons to the Assembly.[53] By forcing government to publicly justify itself, a similar provision could help

[48] HC Coombs, 'The Role of the National Aboriginal Conference' (Australian Government Publishing Service. 1984) 65.

[49] See below pts III.F and III.G.

[50] Referendum Council (n 47) 30–31.

[51] See also ch 4. I thank Gabrielle Appleby for helpful discussion on this point.

[52] Senate, 'Standing Orders' (August 2018) OO 19(12), 25(17).

[53] Financial Management Act 1996 (ACT) ss 20–20AC.

'provide political and moral pressure to maintain appropriate levels of funding' to a contemporary Indigenous body.[54]

Political mechanisms can assist but the experiences of ATSIC and the Sámediggi suggest that stronger protections may be required to ensure financing is secure. One approach that Aboriginal and Torres Strait Islander peoples could consider involves adapting processes used for the New South Wales Aboriginal Land Council (NSWALC), or the Northern Territory Land Councils. The NSWALC is resourced by the interest generated from a capital fund amassed by a 15-year 7.5 per cent levy of land taxes across the state, while the Northern Territory Land Councils are provided with a percentage of royalties from mining on Aboriginal Land.[55] Each approach provides a degree of independence from government but adopts a distinct method to do so: in New South Wales, funding was secured via an additional tax; in the Northern Territory, resourcing is via foregone Commonwealth revenue. Nonetheless, while these approaches are valuable, they do not entirely resolve the issue. Both rely on an unstable income source, and a contemporary body would likely still rely on government to provide top-up funding to ensure it can satisfy its responsibilities.

E. Scope

The issues on which an Indigenous representative body is empowered to provide advice will also need to be considered. Contemporary discussion on a putative First Nations Voice has assumed that this would encompass legislation enacted under ss 51(xxvi) and 122 of the Australian Constitution,[56] but 'the exact breadth of this mandate' has not been decided.[57] This is a critical issue because although these two heads of power constitute the Commonwealth Parliament's major legislative authority in Indigenous affairs, many laws of general application have a differentiated impact on Indigenous peoples. Recognising this, scholars have suggested varying formulations to enlarge its scope while avoiding the apparent risk of 'vexatious' advice.[58] Shireen Morris, for instance, suggests that a First Nations Voice should be empowered to comment on laws that are 'directed at, or significantly or especially impacting, Indigenous peoples',[59] while Cheryl Saunders has contended that Parliament should consult when Indigenous interests 'are affected directly, but not in relation to matters of a general nature affecting society as a whole'.[60]

[54] G Appleby, Submission No 132 to Joint Select Committee on Constitutional Recognition of Aboriginal and Torres Strait Islander Peoples, 12 June 2015, 15.

[55] Aboriginal Land Rights (Northern Territory) Act 1976 (Cth) Pt 6.

[56] Referendum Council (n 2) 37; Technical Advisers (n 13) 7.

[57] Technical Advisers (n 13) 8.

[58] Uphold and Recognise, Hearing Indigenous Voices: Options for Discussion (2018) 7.

[59] S Morris, *A First Nations Voice in the Australian Constitution* (Oxford, Hart Publishing, 2020) ch 6.

[60] C Saunders, 'Indigenous Constitutional Recognition: The Concept of Consultation' (2015) 8(19) *Indigenous Law Bulletin* 19, 21.

These are useful interventions to the extent that they highlight that legislation that affects Indigenous Australians does not merely rest on these two provisions. Beyond that, however, I contend that they add unnecessary complications. Indigenous Australians should determine this issue for themselves, but a simpler approach, and one that will enhance the institution's capacity to speak on relevant matters, is to adopt the formulation employed by ATSIC and the Sámediggi. ATSIC was empowered to advise decision-makers on 'matters relating to Aboriginal and Torres Strait Islander affairs', while the Sámediggi is responsible for providing information on 'Sámi conditions'.[61] Consistent with the principles enunciated in the UN Declaration on the Rights of Indigenous Peoples (UNDRIP) and reflective of Indigenous aspirations explored in chapter three, this expansive approach allows a representative body to decide for itself which Bills or policy proposals it will focus attention on, including (as will be discussed below) issues debated by state and local governments. Concerns over the volume of advice proffered are unpersuasive. In practice, a representative body will prioritise its work.[62]

F. Decision-makers

Aboriginal and Torres Strait Islander peoples are entitled to have their voices heard in all decisions that affect them. An Indigenous representative body could contribute to the realisation of this right by formally engaging with state, territory and local governments,[63] as well as international actors. Examination of ATSIC and the Sámediggi emphasises the importance of enacting clear procedures for consultation and negotiation with all relevant decision-makers. Despite formalising links through memoranda of understanding, the Commission was frequently criticised as a centralised organisation that failed to take full advantages of its regional structure by engaging with subnational governments. The Sámediggi has also struggled under an inadequate consultative framework, inhibiting its capacity to ensure Sámi interests are considered on key matters. These weaknesses limited (and continue to limit in the Sámediggi's case) each institution's ability to influence decisions that affect their communities, damaging their legitimacy.

The issue is pronounced in Australia where the division of constitutional responsibilities creates a complicated legal framework for Indigenous issues. The Commonwealth Parliament enjoys only a concurrent power to legislate with respect to Indigenous affairs, and responsibility for many issues of concern

[61] Aboriginal and Torres Strait Islander Commission Act 1989 (Cth) s 7; Sámi Parliament Act (SFS 1992:1433) ch 2, s 1.

[62] Anderson, Pearson, Davis, Brennan, Appleby, Lino and McKinnon (n 14) 8–9; Joint Select Committee Final Report (n 11) 29–34 [2.107]–[2.126].

[63] Several regional dialogues considered this point: Technical Advisers (n 13) 8.

for Indigenous peoples lies with the states. Although the possibility of federal override and the Federal Government's financial leverage suggests that any representative body should primarily engage with the Commonwealth, it should be capable of participating in legislative and policy development at the state and territory level, as decisions made here may have a serious impact on Indigenous communities. Opportunities could also be provided to allow Indigenous representatives to engage with local governments.[64] While local government authority is not constitutionally protected, its exercise can affect Aboriginal and Torres Strait Islander peoples who are entitled to be heard in such decisions. Even in recent years, for example, councils have debated whether to adopt Indigenous names for cities,[65] and to move Australia Day celebrations.[66]

Several proposals to extend and strengthen ATSIC's relationship with state and local governments could be considered for a contemporary institution. Considering a First Nations Voice's role and rationale, it may be appropriate that the chair serve as a full member of the Ministerial Council on Aboriginal and Torres Strait Islander Affairs,[67] which brings together the Commonwealth and all state and territory ministers with a responsibility for Indigenous matters. The chair could also sit on (or be provided with observer status at) the National Federation Reform Council,[68] enhancing opportunities for both formal and informal discussion.

More direct links can also be considered. Representatives on the national body could concurrently serve on state and territory advisory councils, empowered with similar functions to the national body.[69] If desired, leaders of significant state and territory Indigenous organisations could also be designated as *ex officio* members. This approach enhances the national body's stature by clearly articulating its links with subnational governments and enables Indigenous

[64] This was discussed in the Cairns regional dialogue: Anderson, Pearson, Davis, Brennan, Appleby, Lino and McKinnon (n 14) 10.

[65] C Gooley, 'Tensions in Hobart City Council Rise over Mayor's use of New Aboriginal Name Gifted to City', *ABC News* (8 June 2018), available at www.abc.net.au/news/2018-06-08/tas-tensions-in-hobart-council-over-use-of-nipaluna/9851284.

[66] 'Third Melbourne Council's Vote to Ditch Australia Day Criticised as "Divisive"' *Guardian Australia* (14 September 2017), available at www.theguardian.com/australia-news/2017/sep/14/australia-day-celebrations-axed-by-third-melbourne-council.

[67] Council for Aboriginal Reconciliation, 'Going Forward: Social Justice for the First Australians' (1996) Recommendation 18.

[68] Reviews into ATSIC recommended the chair sit, or be granted observer status, on the Council of Australian Governments (COAG), like the President of the Local Government Association: Hannaford, Huggins and Collins, 'In the Hands of the Regions' (2003) Recommendation 44. See also Aboriginal and Torres Strait Islander Commission, 'Recognition, Rights and Reform: A Report to Government on Native Title Social Justice Measures' (1995) 45. In May 2020, Prime Minister Scott Morrison announced that COAG would be abolished and replaced with the National Federation Reform Council.

[69] This draws on the State Advisory Committees that were established under ATSIC: Aboriginal and Torres Strait Islander Commission Office of Evaluation and Audit, 'Putting the Pieces Together: Regional Plans, Data and Outcomes' (2003) 19.

Australians to play a major role in legislative and policy development at all levels of government. Depending on the views of Indigenous Australians, these state and territory advisory councils could be provided with legislated access to government and the public service as the primary or sole Indigenous advisory structure at the state/territory level.[70] Consistent with Australia's allocation of constitutional powers, that access will require complementary legislation enacted by each government.

Empowering the body to engage with all levels of government is vital in developing an institution capable of managing indifference or hostility. In the face of an unreceptive Commonwealth, representatives could leverage their relationship with sympathetic subnational governments to continue to advocate for Indigenous interests. Taking advantage of Australia's federal structure could therefore enhance the body's efficacy and strengthen its legitimacy among communities. More than simply providing Indigenous peoples with a seat at *every* table, formalised procedures for engagement with all governments could also enhance the likelihood that a productive and respectful dialogue develops between decision-makers and Indigenous representatives.

The Referendum Council regional dialogues revealed that many Aboriginal and Torres Strait Islander peoples also believe that the body should have the capacity to represent them internationally.[71] International advocacy proved vital for ATSIC in developing and maintaining transnational relationships with Indigenous peoples globally, as well as differentiating and distinguishing itself from the Australian Government, deepening its legitimacy within communities. International advocacy has also been key for the Sámediggi. Among other forums, the Sámediggi is a member of the Sámi Parliamentary Council, a non-government organisation empowered to safeguard Sámi interests and strengthen Sámi cooperation across borders, and presently taking a leading role in efforts to develop a Nordic Sámi Convention. Described as 'a modern treaty between the Finnish, Norwegian and Swedish state-forming people, on one hand, and the Saami people, indigenous to the three countries, on the other',[72] the draft Convention is the 'the first attempt anywhere to create a regional treaty specifically concerning indigenous peoples'.[73] Although the Sámi are not legally a party to the treaty, the agreement will not be ratified by the three states until and unless each Sámi Parliament approves it, ensuring that the Sámi retain a right of veto. Negotiations finally concluded in January 2017, but the Sámi

[70] J Hannaford, J Huggins and B Collins, 'Review of the Aboriginal and Torres Strait Islander Commission' (Discussion Paper, 2003) 59 [7.19].

[71] Technical Advisers (n 13) 8; Evidence to Joint Select Committee on Constitutional Recognition Relating to Aboriginal and Torres Strait Islander Peoples, Parliament of Australia, Dubbo, 2 July 2018, 16 (Des Jones).

[72] M Åhrén, 'The Saami Convention' (2007) 3 *Gáldu Čála – Journal of Indigenous Peoples Rights* 8, 12.

[73] J Anaya, 'The Situation of the Sámi People in the Sápmi Region of Norway, Sweden and Finland', UN Doc A/HRC/18/35/Add.2 (6 June 2011) 5 [11].

Parliaments are unlikely to approve the current draft.[74] Nevertheless, its development illustrates the significance of international and transnational advocacy. A contemporary Australian representative body should be entitled (and financed) to operate similarly.

G. Timing

A representative body must be able to provide advice at a time when its intervention has a real potential to influence proposals. The case studies did not identify this issue as a key concern for ATSIC or the Sámediggi,[75] but that does not discount its importance, nor the potential problems a contemporary institution could face. Both ATSIC and the Sámediggi were/are empowered to speak to the executive, while the putative First Nations Voice has primarily been characterised as a voice to the Parliament.[76] This distinction may be telling. Under Australia's system of governance, legislative and policy proposals are developed within the executive and then presented to Parliament. Once a Bill is introduced, government is often reluctant to change course.[77] Advice provided at this stage will therefore likely prove unable to produce substantive amendments but merely refine already defined policy proposals.

Acknowledging these challenges, some commentators have proposed setting aside time for detailed consideration by Parliament. In a 2008 concept paper, Eric Sidoti suggested that an Indigenous Parliamentary Committee, modelled on Senate committees, and composed of directly elected Indigenous members (though not members of Parliament) could be established. Sidoti envisages his Indigenous Parliamentary Committee as enjoying the same protections and powers as ordinary Senate Committees, staffed with a secretariat, and with the ability to inquire into general matters, consider proposed government expenditure, and report on relevant bills.[78] While Parliamentary Standing Orders prevent non-Members of Parliament from constituting committees,[79] the powers of a contemporary institution could be modelled on those of Senate committees, allowing the body greater scope and capacity to inquire into relevant matters.[80]

[74] M Åhrén, 'Legal Analysis of the 10 January 2017 Draft Proposed Nordic Sami Convention' (Letter to Tiina Sanela Aiko, President of the Sami Parliament in Finland, 28 March 2017).

[75] Though ATSIC's involvement in cabinet processes diminished over its life: ch 5.

[76] Referendum Council (n 2) 36. But see Anderson, Pearson, Davis, Brennan, Appleby, Lino and McKinnon (n 14) 6–7.

[77] G Williams, 'Constitutional Recognition by Way of an Indigenous Advisory Body?' (2015) 8(19) *Indigenous Law Bulletin* 12, 13.

[78] E Sidoti, 'Indigenous Political Representation: A Parliamentary Option' (Whitlam Institute, 21 January 2008). See also J Chesterman, 'National Policy-Making in Indigenous Affairs: Blueprint for an Indigenous Review Council' (2008) 67 *The Australian Journal of Public Administration* 419.

[79] Senate, 'Standing Orders' (August 2018) O 27.

[80] Appleby, 'An Indigenous Advisory Body' (2015) 4.

Sidoti's proposal is valuable but it will not entirely resolve this issue. Chapter two noted that the committee system can encourage forms of deliberative reasoning within Parliament, but it also observed that the existing committee system does not always realise this standard and that Parliamentary procedures may be inadequate. Parliament has its own rules and procedures, and there is not always time for lengthy consideration of issues. The Parliamentary Joint Committee on Human Rights, for instance, has routinely struggled to provide detailed reports on proposed legislation affecting Indigenous peoples in the period before legislation is enacted. Infamously, all five bills of the Northern Territory National Emergency Response were introduced and passed without amendment in one sitting day.[81] In these circumstances, a contemporary representative body, even with powers akin to parliamentary committees, would not have adequate time to consider and report on relevant legislation.[82] As the Parliament cannot consider advice that is not provided, its effectiveness would be constrained.

These challenges indicate that while advice should be provided to Parliament, advice must also be considered at the policy development and drafting stage. This can be realised relatively easily by adapting existing notification and comment provisions. For example, a provision modelled on s 17 of the Legislation Act 2003 (Cth) could require rule-makers to consult with the national body before making legislative instruments.[83] Similarly, the public service and relevant ministers could notify the body when developing legislation or policy that relates to Aboriginal and Torres Strait Islander affairs, inviting it to discuss and provide comment on proposals. Procedures like these formalise relationships between Indigenous representatives and government, empowering Indigenous peoples to have their voices heard at relevant stages of the policy development cycle. By embedding such processes, additional informal contacts between members of the executive and the body may arise, further helping to ground a productive dialogue based on mutual respect and thereby enhancing the prospect advice is considered seriously.

These examples are both reactive, reliant on the executive contacting the body. Consistent with the principles of self-determination and Indigenous aspirations explored in chapter three, a representative body should also be empowered to take a more proactive role. This could include designing its own legislative proposals or amendments to existing legislation, and as suggested in the Referendum Council regional dialogues, 'reviewing, monitoring and overseeing

[81] Commonwealth, 'Votes and Proceedings No 183', House of Representatives, 7 August 2007, 2009–2011, 2015–2022.

[82] Anne Twomey has proposed a non-justiciable provision that would require the Parliament to consider tabled advice. However, if advice is not tabled (because the legislation has been passed too quickly) Indigenous representatives would have no legal recourse: A Twomey, 'Putting Words to the Tune of Constitutional Recognition', *The Conversation* (20 May 2015), available at www.theconversation.com/putting-words-to-the-tune-of-indigenous-constitutional-recognition-42038.

[83] Cape York Institute (n 34) 48–49.

funding coming into communities; and auditing and evaluating service delivery in Aboriginal and Torres Strait Islander affairs'.[84] This will necessarily expand the body's remit, requiring a larger secretariat and budget, further emphasising the importance of financial capacity. It also highlights the necessity of building institutional relationships with other levels of government and public agencies. The power to undertake broader reviews into Indigenous affairs may see the institution complement existing scrutiny institutions, like the Australian Law Reform Commission and the Aboriginal and Torres Strait Islander Social Justice Commissioner.

H. Dialogue

A representative body will not have veto powers.[85] Consistent with Australia's constitutional framework, any recommendations provided by an Indigenous body will be advisory only. This raises a key challenge: how can institutional design promote or encourage respectful dialogue, let alone ensure that consultation occurs?

Some commentators have suggested that no procedures governing consultation should be established, presumably assuming that it will occur naturally. For instance, Damien Freeman, founding director of Uphold & Recognise, argues that a First Nations Voice's relationship with government should be left to 'successive ministries', allowing a convention on constructive engagement to evolve.[86] There is some value to this proposition. The flexibility that comes from informal, unwritten rules may enable consultation to develop in novel and productive ways, even beyond that set out in legislation. It is also arguable that a constitutional or legislative provision mandating consultation is inconsistent with embedding a dialogue of mutual respect. The experiences of ATSIC and the Sámediggi caution against this approach, however. Both institutions have found that without clear procedures for consultation, there is no guarantee that consultation will occur. In this light, it is sensible that an obligation to consider advice provided by the body be imposed on relevant decision-makers. This could either be a political requirement,[87] or a justiciable duty.[88]

[84] Technical Advisers (n 13) 8.

[85] Referendum Council (n 2) 36.

[86] Evidence to Joint Select Committee on Constitutional Recognition Relating to Aboriginal and Torres Strait Islander Peoples, Parliament of Australia, Canberra, 18 June 2018, 9 (Damien Freeman).

[87] A Twomey, 'An Indigenous Advisory Body: Addressing the Concerns About Justiciability and Parliamentary Sovereignty' (2015) 8(19) *Indigenous Law Bulletin* 6; Morris, *A First Nations Voice* (2020).

[88] M Davis and R Dixon, 'Constitutional Recognition through a (Justiciable) Duty to Consult? Towards Entrenched and Judicially Enforceable Norms of Indigenous Consultation' (2016) 27 *Public Law Review* 249.

Non-justiciable consultative obligations can be effective. Chapter six discussed a proposal to require the Swedish Government consult with the Sámediggi on matters relevant to Sámi people.[89] This proposal draws on an obligation that has existed in Norway since 2005. Section 2(2) of the Norwegian Sámi Act 1987 provides that public agencies and bodies 'should give the Sameting [Sámi Parliament] an opportunity to express an opinion before they make decisions on matters coming within the scope of the business of the Sameting'. In 2005, this general obligation was transformed into a comprehensive political agreement. The agreement applies to all matters 'that may affect Sámi interests directly',[90] which is defined as encompassing all material and immaterial forms of Sámi culture, including land ownership rights. The agreement also covers all forms of decision-making including legislation, regulations, administrative decisions, guidelines and governmental reports. Consultation must be 'genuine and effective' and may include consideration and debate by the Sámi Parliament.[91] It does not extend to a veto, but Cabinet documents must indicate where agreement has not been reached and the views of the Sameting must 'be reflected in the documents submitted'.[92]

The Special Rapporteur has praised the agreement as 'represent[ing] good practice',[93] and 'generally in line with the consultation provisions of International Labour Organisation Convention 169'.[94] Scholars have noted that it has empowered the Parliament with 'significantly greater influence and increased responsibility in negotiating laws and measures that are of importance for the Sámi community'.[95] For instance, the agreement was integral to the adoption of the landmark Finnmark Act 2005,[96] which recognised Sámi rights to land in the northernmost Finnmark County. The formal consultation procedure also strengthened the position of the Sameting in pushing for amendments to the Reindeer Husbandry Act 1978, which recognised the traditional siida, 'bringing Norwegian law into closer conformity with traditional Sámi land management'.[97] Reflecting on these events, Torvald Falch, Per Selle and Kristin Strømsnes argue that the Sameting is no longer merely an interest group or advisory body, 'but a fully informed formal participant in public decision-making processes', exercising 'a real opportunity to influence both the process and the outcome of matters on which there is consultation'.[98]

[89] Ministerial Report, 'Konsultation i Frågor som rör det Samiska Folket' (Ds 2017:43) 43, 46–47.

[90] Procedures for Consultation between the State Authorities and the Sámi Parliament [Norway], signed 11 May 2005, art 2.

[91] ibid art 6.

[92] ibid.

[93] Anaya, 'The Situation of the Sámi People' (2011) 7 [17].

[94] ibid 6 [16].

[95] T Falch, P Selle and K Strømsnes, 'The Sámi: 25 Years of Indigenous Authority in Norway' (2016) 15 *Ethnopolitics* 125, 134–35.

[96] Anaya (n 73) 7 [18].

[97] ibid [19].

[98] Falch, Selle and Strømsnes, 'The Sámi' (2016) 135.

Political obligations may enhance the likelihood that Indigenous interests are presented to relevant decision-makers, but they cannot guarantee that consultation will occur or that it will be adequate. Unfortunately, evidence in Norway suggests that the consultation agreement has a 'mixed' record.[99] Sameting representatives have expressed concern that the Government has 'at times entered into consultations having already decided on outcomes',[100] and there is a perception among Sámi politicians that while the consultation process 'works well in matters of little significance ... in the case of issues of major economic and political importance ... Sámi input is incorporated to a very limited degree'.[101] Even Falch, Selle and Strømsnes acknowledge that consultation has sometimes taken the form of 'suggestions and views on the implementation of government positions that have already been formed, and so have more the character of briefings and explanations than of meaningful discussion on choice of solutions'.[102] For these reasons, the Sámi Rights Committee has recommended the agreement be given legal force.[103]

The Norwegian experience suggests that a justiciable obligation may be more effective at ensuring that consultation occurs and meets a requisite standard. That is the approach in Canada, where the Supreme Court has held that the Crown has a duty to consult and where appropriate, accommodate First Nations interests when contemplating executive conduct that might adversely impact Aboriginal or Treaty rights.[104] Consultation is distinct from consent, but the Court's jurisprudence nonetheless empowers First Nations to hold government accountable for the genuineness of any consultation, thereby exercising 'some degree of decisional autonomy within the existing structures of Canadian democracy'.[105] The obligation to consult does not extend to the legislative sphere, however. In *Mikisew Cree First Nation v Canada*, a majority of the Court held that it is 'rarely appropriate for courts to scrutinise the law-making process' as doing so could 'require courts to improperly trespass onto the legislature's domain'.[106]

Legislative development and design is a complex process with multiple actors. Concern that courts should not impose procedural requirements that could

[99] Human Rights Council, 'Report of the Working Group on the Universal Periodic Review: Norway', UN Doc A/HRC/13/5 (4 January 2010) 5 [24].

[100] Anaya (n 73) 11 [39].

[101] A Stepien, A Petrétei and T Koivurova, 'Sámi Parliaments in Finland, Norway, and Sweden' in T Malloy, A Osipov and B Vizi (eds), *Managing Diversity through Non-Territorial Autonomy: Assessing Advantages, Deficiencies, and Risks* (Oxford, Oxford University Press, 2015) 117, 130.

[102] Falch, Selle and Strømsnes (n 95) 139.

[103] Sámi Rights Committee, 'Den Nye Sameretten' (NOU 2007:13).

[104] D Newman, *Revisiting the Duty to Consult: New Relationships with Aboriginal Peoples* (Saskatoon, Purich, 2014).

[105] R Stacey, 'Honour in Sovereignty: Can Crown Consultations with Indigenous Peoples Erase Canada's Sovereignty Deficit?' (2018) 68 *University of Toronto Law Journal* 405, 409–10.

[106] (2018) 2 SCR 765, 782 [2], 794 [35] (Wagner CJ, Karakatsanis and Gascon JJ); 828–33 [116]–[126] (Brown J); 843 [148] (Moldaver, Côté and Rowe JJ) (*Mikisew Cree First Nation*).

potentially delay or complicate that process is valid but insufficient to reject a requirement for consultation with Indigenous peoples in Australia. As Abella and Martin JJ (who dissented in part) noted in *Mikisew*, the judiciary already exercises supervisory review of the legislative process in determining whether legislation has been enacted pursuant to valid manner and form requirements.[107] Although these requirements are imposed by Parliament itself, they reveal that there is no absolute bar to judicial oversight. This position is strengthened by the fact that existing notification and comment procedures operating within the law-making process, like s 17 of the Legislation Act discussed above, could easily be adapted for this purpose.

Separation of powers issues can also be managed. Challenges could be limited to after legislation enters into force,[108] and directed to the adequacy of consultation rather than to the content or substance of the Act.[109] Similarly, while the body would be authorised to provide advice on any matter it chooses, the obligation to consult could be engaged only on matters that have a 'significant' or 'disproportionate' impact on Indigenous peoples.[110] Such a standard is consistent with obligations Australia has accepted in international law,[111] and would force an indifferent or hostile government to engage. Finally, assuming that constitutional challenges can be resolved,[112] the appropriate remedy could be declaratory. Declaratory relief would not invalidate the legislation but may set 'down guidance for the disposition of future cases involving similar principles of law'[113] and structure the interactions between government and the representative body by clarifying the 'obligations and rights of both parties'.[114]

A justiciable consultation obligation is not being considered for the putative First Nations Voice. Delegates favoured an institutional arrangement that would 'not interfere with parliamentary supremacy'.[115] Although this may lead to weaker legal protection, the decision should be respected as the most critical element of any institutional mechanism is that its design reflects the views of Indigenous Australians. Alternative measures aimed at promoting respectful conversation and encouraging government to meaningfully listen to the representative body should therefore be developed.

[107] ibid 820 [96]. See, eg: *Attorney-General (WA) v Marquet* (2003) 217 CLR 545.
[108] *Mikisew Cree First Nation* (n 106) 818 [92] (Abella and Martin JJ).
[109] Davis and Dixon, 'Constitutional Recognition' (2016) 260.
[110] ibid 262.
[111] UNDRIP (n 1) art 19. See further ch 2.
[112] *Momcilovic v The Queen* (2011) 245 CLR 1. In *Momcilovic*, the Court held that to be constitutionally valid, a declaration must have some effect on the legal rights and duties of the parties or assist in the resolution of the dispute between the parties. In the former, the declaration would be considered an incident of judicial power, while in the latter it would be incidental to the exercise of judicial power.
[113] ibid 65 [89] (French CJ).
[114] *Mikisew Cree First Nation* (n 106) 821 [98] (Abella and Martin JJ).
[115] Referendum Council (n 47) 38.

Non-justiciable consultative obligations are effective to the extent they engender a moral obligation or extract a political cost to ignoring Indigenous voices. While the Norwegian example suggests that a simple political agreement may fail to engender such an obligation, it could be imposed via the process of the body's establishment. In the Uluru Statement, Aboriginal and Torres Strait Islander delegates called for a First Nations Voice to be constitutionally enshrined. This desire is informed by the experiences of ATSIC and earlier national Indigenous representative bodies in Australia,[116] but it also reflects their view that the legitimacy and credibility of the institution may be enhanced by its legal form. The argument is that constitutional entrenchment will not only strengthen the institution's independence, but by conferring democratic legitimacy through a national referendum, will insert the body 'into the public life and imagination of the nation'.[117]

The form that constitutional recognition takes may carry 'symbolic weight'.[118] As a symbol that 'shape[s] the political community',[119] constitutional entrenchment could 'express Indigenous peoples' foundational importance to the polity',[120] potentially grounding a political convention that government follows the body's advice or publicly justifies its reasons for failing to do so.[121] As Dylan Lino has noted, 'the 1967 referendum and its preceding campaign altered Australian constitutional culture in ways that exceeded the spare, underdetermined constitutional amendments themselves'.[122] A grassroots popular campaign leading to successful constitutional reform could build considerable moral and political pressure, compelling government and the Parliament to develop and enact legislation establishing a representative body capable of meeting Indigenous aspirations. However, although the Uluru Statement may be a potential constitutional moment, Lino cautions that these developments are limited by political horizons. The 1967 referendum may have galvanised cultural change, but that culture relied on a receptive government taking power five years later and has not prevented subsequent governments from enacting discriminatory legislation.

The process of the body's establishment is important in building legitimacy and 'political respect',[123] potentially engendering a moral obligation on government to engage, but it cannot ensure a constructive dialogue develops. It is important then to develop mechanisms through which a political cost could be imposed on an unreceptive government. One approach involves enhancing

[116] Technical Advisers (n 13) 7. See further ch 5.
[117] F Davis, 'The Problem of Authority and the Proposal for an Indigenous Advisory Body' (2015) 8(19) *Indigenous Law Bulletin* 23, 24.
[118] Lino, *Constitutional Recognition* (2018) 116.
[119] ibid 102.
[120] ibid 117.
[121] Davis and Dixon (n 88) 258.
[122] Lino (n 20) 263.
[123] Anderson, Pearson, Davis, Brennan, Appleby, Lino and McKinnon (n 14) 5.

visibility within the process of conferral and receipt of advice, as this will allow the public to gauge the volume and standard of consultation.[124] Several options could be considered. The Cabinet secretariat could report annually on the body's involvement in the Cabinet process,[125] including by noting the number of draft Cabinet documents the body is consulted or provides comments on.[126] This measure could be complemented by adapting the obligation under the Human Rights (Parliamentary Scrutiny) Act 2011 (Cth) to require the minister introducing legislation to explain how Indigenous views have influenced the Bill,[127] or why those views have not been adopted.[128] Similarly, the chair could be provided with observer status, permitting them to speak to either house on bills affecting Indigenous interests, and deliver an annual report to the nation on Indigenous affairs.[129] Advice may also be tabled in Parliament, allowing the public to assess whether the advice materially affected proposed legislation.[130]

* * * * *

Institutional design is important but, as the delegates at the regional dialogues acknowledged, it is necessary to be realistic. Even with a justiciable obligation to consult and the mobilisation of a constitutional moment, government will not always listen.[131] On issues of central importance to government or the state, it is unlikely that any substantial amendments will be countenanced, irrespective of whether an Indigenous representative body is legitimate and credible. For this reason, the body should take advantage of Australia's federal structure by engaging with all levels of government. It should also be integrated within a broader complementary institutional framework.

IV. A COMPLEMENTARY FRAMEWORK

A First Nations Voice is necessary to empower Indigenous peoples with the capacity to have their interests considered in the processes of government, but it alone is unlikely to be sufficient. An Indigenous representative body could expand the range of interests debated at a national level and provide a forum for contestation, potentially contributing to broader cultural or political change in the long term. Without a determinative vote or obligation to be consulted however, Indigenous representatives may still be ignored. A representative body

124 Hannaford, Huggins and Collins (n 30) 50.
125 ibid, Recommendation 31.
126 ibid 50.
127 Chapter 4 noted that this system is not effective.
128 Chesterman, 'National Policy-Making in Indigenous Affairs' (2008) 424.
129 As discussed in ATSIC (n 68) 156.
130 Twomey, 'To the Tune of Constitutional Recognition' (2015).
131 Technical Advisers (n 13) 7.

may also struggle to fulfil all Indigenous aspirations. Significantly, proposals for a contemporary Indigenous representative body in Australia have not envisaged investing the institution with significant gradations of power. Yet, Aboriginal and Torres Strait Islander peoples do not merely aspire to speak to Parliament; they also desire a level of decision-making authority over internal and local affairs so that they may steer their own vessel.[132]

Aboriginal and Torres Strait Islander peoples are entitled to develop their own decision-making institutions.[133] Here, I outline one integrated, complementary structural framework that I describe as Voice Plus. Under Voice Plus, self-constituting Indigenous communities would exercise autonomy at the local level, while clear structural links between communities and the national representative body would be developed to ensure that local voices are present and considered in the processes of government. Voice Plus draws on Indigenous aspirations explored in chapter three in a manner consistent with Australia's public law system. In recognising that Aboriginal and Torres Strait Islander peoples are normatively distinct from other Australian citizens, it seeks to establish a legal carapace within which Indigenous communities can re-establish their own governance institutions through which they may exercise political authority in a culturally appropriate manner.

Voice Plus draws on the Uluru Statement's call for agreement-making. In recent years, several Australian governments have commenced treaty processes with Aboriginal and Torres Strait Islander peoples whose traditional lands fall within their borders.[134] These processes are in their preliminary stages, making it difficult to assess potential outcomes. However, a recent agreement between the Noongar people and the Western Australian Government, struck outside an explicit treaty process, suggests that comprehensive settlements can meet Aboriginal and Torres Strait Islander peoples' aspirations for autonomy in a manner consistent with Australia's governance system.[135] Similar settlements across the country could lead to a renewed relationship based on trust and respect that recognises Indigenous Australians' status as distinct political communities. Integrating self-governing communities within a national representative body could strengthen the legitimacy and credibility of both institutions.

A. The Importance of Decision-making Authority

Earlier chapters articulated Indigenous peoples' desire for decision-making power. Those aspirations drove ATSIC's development. Comprehensive reviews

[132] See chs 3 and 4.

[133] UNDRIP (n 1) art 5.

[134] Williams and Hobbs, *Treaty* (2020) ch 8.

[135] H Hobbs and G Williams, 'The Noongar Settlement: Australia's First Treaty' (2018) 40 *Sydney Law Review* 1.

into the National Aboriginal Consultative Committee and the National Aboriginal Conference found that both institutions failed to develop into institutions capable of exerting meaningful political influence largely because they were merely consultative forums.[136] ATSIC was specifically empowered with decision-making authority in order to allay this criticism. Institutional reform that does not recognise a degree of autonomy would therefore repeat the mistakes of early Indigenous representative bodies in Australia, which 'did not promote self-determination and did not meet [Indigenous] expectations'.[137] Without decision-making authority, structural reform will not meet Indigenous expectations for *power*.

The importance of empowering Indigenous peoples with some minimum level of autonomy cannot be discounted, but the challenges faced by ATSIC and the Sámediggi in satisfying the *power* criterion indicate that a national Indigenous representative body may not be the most appropriate mechanism to invest with decision-making authority. Two clear problems stand out. First, critiques of these institutions often centre on the combination of representative and executive functions, contending that they impose an 'inherently unstable' accountability framework.[138] Whether or not that is true, it is clear that ATSIC struggled to reconcile responsibility for public spending with the potential for real or apparent conflicts of interest. It may be politically sensible to separate these functions.

The national focus of these bodies has also proven problematic. Consider ATSIC again. While the Commission sought to ameliorate this emphasis by adopting a regional structure that centred on devolving administrative responsibilities and service delivery to local communities, the precise institutional form did not always realise this objective. In reality, the Commission was a highly centralised organisation, with local policies and projects requiring approval by a national board. Many contemporaneous assessments of the Commission questioned this arrangement, arguing that centralised decision-making and administration is neither 'appropriate … [n]or consistent' with Indigenous community and family structures,[139] and called for powers and functions to be devolved.[140] Advocates of the First Nations Voice have implicitly acknowledged

[136] LR Hiatt, 'Australian Committee of Inquiry into the Role of the National Aboriginal Consultative Committee' (Australian Government Publishing Service, 1976) viii; Coombs, 'National Aboriginal Conference' (1984) 14.

[137] Hannaford, Huggins and Collins (n 30) 73.

[138] J Cunningham and J Baeza, 'An "Experiment" in Indigenous Social Policy: The Rise and Fall of Australia's Aboriginal and Torres Strait Islander Commission (ATSIC)' (2005) 33 *Policy & Politics* 461, 467. Some regional dialogues expressed concern that empowering a First Nations Voice with service-delivery functions would 'create a conflict of interest': Anderson, Pearson, Davis, Brennan, Appleby, Lino and McKinnon (n 14) 10.

[139] G Foley, 'ATSIC: Flaws in the Machine' (15 November 1999) 12, available at www.kooriweb.org/foley/essays/pdf_essays/atsic.pdf.

[140] Dillon, 'Institutional Structures' (1996) 102; Hannaford, Huggins and Collins (n 30) 5.

these complications by prioritising the institution's representative role. This may be an appropriate step, but it does not mean decision-making authority should not form part of any package of structural reform.

B. Self-Governing Communities

These lessons must be borne in mind in designing stable and secure institutional mechanisms that meet Indigenous peoples' aspirations. One solution that draws on views expressed in the Referendum Council regional dialogues as well as generations of Indigenous advocacy involves a layering of complementary structures. Decision-making power could be exercised by self-constituting communities. Each community will determine its own appropriate basis, but it could be identified along lines of kinship, language, custom, or historical and ancestral connection to land.[141] These communities, either individually or regionally, could then select representatives to the national body which focuses exclusively on providing policy advice and a national voice on Indigenous issues. This integrated approach recognises that it is at local and regional levels 'that the foundations of genuine self-empowerment and self-determination are laid',[142] but also understands that investing Indigenous communities with 'accountability, empowerment and responsibility' requires a structure to channel their voices to the federal government.[143] By integrating these complementary mechanisms, the hope is that they will reaffirm and strengthen each other.[144]

Developments in Australian law are helpful in designing a contemporary structure that accomplishes this task effectively. As noted above, recognition of native title and the development of PBCs to hold in trust and manage traditional lands has established an important cultural and economic foundation that may serve as an appropriate unit to invest with (or, recognise inherent) decision-making authority. PBCs and regional NTRBs presently exercise a limited form of political autonomy. Among other functions, they express and protect the interests of traditional owners, conciliate disputes between Indigenous people, and hold in trust and distribute payments from mining operations under negotiated agreements.[145] Their authority is imperfect and legislation and case law has further constrained their potential by failing to recognise powers of self-government. Nonetheless, PBCs have created a carapace for Indigenous

[141] These examples differ from Michael Mansell's calls for a pan-Aboriginal state: M Mansell, *Treaty and Statehood: Aboriginal Self-Determination* (Annandale, Federation Press, 2016).

[142] Aboriginal and Torres Strait Islander Commission, 'Strengthening ATSIC: The 1997 Review of the ATSIC' Act (1998) 24.

[143] Cape York (n 34) 30.

[144] Referendum Council (n 47) 30: The 'Voice to Parliament should be designed so that it could support and promote a treaty-making process'.

[145] Native Title Act 1993 (Cth) s 55; Native Title (Prescribed Bodies Corporate) Regulations 1999 (Cth) reg 6.

autonomy that can be extended upon. Creative political solutions that imbue PBCs with enhanced decision-making authority can reinvigorate the promise of native title by 'consolidat[ing] Indigenous governance structures and provid[ing] a stronger economic and land base for communities to interact with government'.[146] Of course, as noted, PBCs only exist on areas with declared native title rights; alternative governance institutions will need to be established for communities unable to secure native title.

The sheer number and diversity of Indigenous communities across Australia raises a challenge to this approach. While many Indigenous communities may desire greater autonomy, some may be too few in number, have limited capacity, or hold insufficient resources to administer and finance self-governance arrangements. The Canadian Royal Commission on Aboriginal Peoples recognised this challenge, recommending that First Nations governance should focus on aggregate communities that share a 'sense of national identity' and 'constitute[] the predominant population in a certain territory', rather than 'small local communities'.[147] Indigenous Australians should determine for themselves the appropriate level at which governance is undertaken, but this is an important point to consider.

If Indigenous communities prefer to exercise power along kinship lines, problems of scale could be managed through the negotiation of inter-Indigenous agreements. Neighbouring communities, particularly those with limited resources or capacity, may choose to pool their resources and administration. Agreements of this nature could lead to what Diane Smith characterises as 'regionally dispersed, layered community governance', whereby individual self-governing communities aggregate and 'scale up' their authority and responsibility.[148] Local communities would retain authority and responsibility commensurate with their capacity and aspirations, while the regional or aggregated governance level would undertake broader functions. As Smith notes, this flexible approach has two clear benefits. In contrast to the problems experienced by ATSIC's regional councils, it enables communities themselves to identify their preferred form of collective entanglement, be it along geographic, cultural or other lines. Smith's layered model also promotes accountability by spreading workload and distributing powers across two layers of governance.[149]

This solution will not resolve all administrative challenges and difficulties may be pronounced if the governance model crosses state boundaries. Regional and community governance forms will therefore need a clear relationship with all relevant governments. At the Commonwealth level, the institution invested

[146] Reilly, 'Constitutional Framework' (2006) 422.

[147] Canada, Royal Commission on Aboriginal People, 'Volume 2: Restructuring the Relationship' (1996) 158.

[148] D Smith, 'Jurisdictional Devolution: Towards an Effective Model for Indigenous Community Self-Governance' (Centre for Aboriginal Economic Policy Research Discussion Paper No 233, 2002) 25.

[149] ibid 26.

with decision-making authority – be it a PBC or alternative governance institution – could be the representative unit from which members are drawn for the national advisory body.[150] PBCs within a delineated region (either a NTRB or other amalgamation determined by the relevant communities) may select one member to serve on the national board. That member would be responsible for ensuring Indigenous interests from the region are considered in the processes of government, but decision-making authority will be exercised only at the local level. Relationships would also need to be clearly structured at the state and territory level.[151] One approach responding to recommendations for reform to ATSIC would involve regional representatives serving concurrently on their relevant state or territory council. This council would not be empowered with decision-making authority but could operate as the primary, or sole, advisory body to the state Government and Parliament.

Recognising Indigenous peoples' right to exercise autonomy at a community level and integrating those communities with the national body may carry positive consequences for the representative body. In particular, it could encourage the body to conceive of itself as a federal, rather than solely national, organ. As I argued in chapter five, despite ATSIC's regional structure, it was often perceived as too focused on the national level, a problem that proved damaging during the Howard Government when the Commission's capacity to influence federal government policy dropped precipitously. A contemporary First Nations Voice should take advantage of Australia's federal framework by engaging with receptive subnational governments when faced with an unreceptive Commonwealth administration. Such an approach could ensure that the body remains effective at influencing state or territory government policy and legislation despite its inability to influence the Federal Government – and vice versa. Clear links between the national body and multiple local, self-governing communities may therefore not only enhance the authenticity and legitimacy of the body but may also promote efficacy, security, and stability in difficult times.

C. Treaty-making

The structure outlined above identifies a flexible, quasi-federal approach to empowering Indigenous peoples with decision-making authority. The emerging treaty processes between Aboriginal and Torres Strait Islander peoples and Australian governments could make it a reality.

There are many examples of contracts or agreements between Indigenous peoples and governments, both in Australia and around the world, but a treaty is particular type of legal agreement that satisfies three conditions.[152]

[150] See above pt III.C.
[151] See above pt III.F.
[152] Williams and Hobbs (n 3) 7–17; Mansell *Treaty and Statehood* (2016) 99–102.

First, a treaty recognises Indigenous peoples as a polity, distinct from other citizens of the state, based on their status as prior self-governing communities. Second, a treaty is reached by a fair process of negotiation conducted in good faith and in a manner respectful of each participant's standing as a polity. Negotiation is the appropriate process for resolving differences between Indigenous peoples and the state as it reduces the risk that important rights and interests will be ignored, brings all relevant information and perspectives to the decision-making process, and recognises that winner-take-all processes are unlikely to endure or produce good policy. While securing a fair negotiation process can be challenging, the UNDRIP articulates a standard predicated on respecting the status of Indigenous peoples as a polity.[153]

Third, a treaty requires that both sides accept a series of responsibilities so that the agreement can bind the parties in a relationship of mutual obligation. Indigenous peoples are expected to withdraw all current and future claims relating to historical and contemporary dispossession, but the state must also agree to certain conditions. While the content of any negotiated settlement will differ in accordance with the aspirations of each Indigenous political community, a treaty must recognise that Indigenous nations retain an inherent right to sovereignty. As an exercise of that right, a treaty empowers Indigenous peoples with some form of decision-making and control that amounts to a form of self-government exercised within the state. In 'articulat[ing] basic terms and conditions of social coexistence'[154] and settling 'the consensual distribution of powers',[155] treaties between Indigenous peoples and Australian governments could lead to institutional reform that empowers Aboriginal and Torres Strait Islander peoples with real decision-making authority.

Treaty is a longstanding aspiration of Indigenous Australians.[156] In 1979, the National Aboriginal Conference passed a resolution calling for a 'Makarrata' between 'the Aboriginal Nation and the Australian Government'.[157] Several years later, the Senate Standing Committee on Constitutional and Legal Affairs delivered a report on the idea of a treaty, recommending constitutional change in order to implement a 'compact'.[158] In 1988, Prime Minister Bob Hawke adopted the Barunga Statement, promising to negotiate a treaty to respect and recognise Aboriginal sovereignty within the term of the Parliament.[159] Although no

153 UNDRIP (n 1) arts 15(2), 17(2), 19, 30(2) 32(2), 36(2), 38.

154 P Macklem, 'The Constitutional Identity of Indigenous Peoples in Canada: Status Groups or Federal Actors?' in A Arato, J Cohen and A von Busekist (eds), *Forms of Pluralism and Democratic Constitutionalism* (New York, Columbia University Press, 2018) 117, 124.

155 RL Barsh and J Henderson, *The Road: Indian Tribes and Political Liberty* (Berkeley, University of California Press, 1980) 270.

156 Williams and Hobbs (n 3) ch 2.

157 National Aboriginal Conference, 'The Makarrata: Some Ways Forward' (Position Paper presented at World Council of Indigenous Peoples, Canberra, April 1981).

158 Senate Standing Committee on Constitutional and Legal Affairs, Parliament of Australia, 'Two Hundred Years Later …' (1983) xii, Recommendation 1.

159 B Hawke, 'Statement of the Prime Minister: Barunga Festival' (1988) 2(6) *Land Rights News* 22.

agreement eventuated, calls for a national treaty did not abate. In the 1990s and 2000s, both the Council for Aboriginal Reconciliation and ATSIC continued to push for a comprehensive negotiated settlement.[160] In the Uluru Statement from the Heart, Indigenous Australians reiterated these aspirations, calling for the establishment of a Makarrata Commission to 'supervise a process of agreement-making between governments and First Nations'.[161] While the Federal Government has ignored the push for a Makarrata Commission, over the last several years a number of Australian governments have committed to entering treaty negotiations with Aboriginal peoples.[162]

In February 2016, the Victorian Government announced its commitment to negotiate a treaty with Aboriginal Victorians. Following consultative forums across the state explored in chapter three, an Aboriginal representative body was inaugurated in December 2019. That body is now working in partnership with the State Government to develop a treaty negotiation framework.[163] In September 2016, the Northern Territory Chief Minister outlined his support for treaty. In June 2018, the Government signed a memorandum of understanding with the four Aboriginal Land Councils to progress treaty,[164] and in February the following year, Mick Dodson (Yawuru) was appointed Treaty Commissioner to lead consultations across the Territory. Most recently, in July 2019, the Queensland Government announced that it too would commence a conversation about a pathway to treaty.[165]

The South Australian Government has also taken steps along this path. In September 2017, the first negotiations in Australia between a government and an Indigenous nation explicitly understood as treaty discussions commenced between South Australia and the Ngarrindjeri nation.[166] However, a change of government in March 2018 led the state to formally abandon those steps.[167] The experience in South Australia reveals the fragility of these processes. They require an ongoing political commitment both to the negotiations themselves and to reaching a substantive and meaningful settlement. Nonetheless, assuming genuine negotiations commence, the recent comprehensive agreement between the Noongar people and the Western Australian Government suggests potential outcomes.

[160] Council for Aboriginal Reconciliation, 'Reconciliation: Australia's Challenge' (Final Report of the Council for Aboriginal Reconciliation, 2000) 106, Recommendation 6; H McGlade (ed), *Treaty: Let's Get it Right!* (Canberra, Australian Institute of Aboriginal and Torres Strait Islander Studies, 2003).

[161] Uluru Statement (n 2).

[162] Williams and Hobbs (n 3) ch 8.

[163] Victorian Treaty Act (n 21) ss 8–10. See further ch 4.

[164] Barunga Agreement, The Aboriginal Land Councils – Northern Territory, signed 8 June 2018 (Memorandum of Understanding).

[165] A Palaszczuk, J Trad and L Enoch, 'Historic Signing of "Tracks to Treaty" Commitment' (media statement, 14 July 2019).

[166] N Grimm, 'Ngarrindjeri Regional Authority and Aboriginal Affairs Minister Meet to Mark "Historic" Negotiation' *The Murray Valley Standard* (25 September 2017).

[167] M Owen, 'Aboriginal People Failed by "Expensive Gesture" Treaties' *The Australian* (11 June 2018).

The Noongar Settlement is the largest and 'most comprehensive' agreement to settle Aboriginal interests in land in Australian history.[168] Although the settlement was reached through the NTA rather than a formal treaty process, its size and scope qualifies it as Australia's first treaty.[169] It is in this sense that it offers lessons for future negotiations. Under the Settlement, the Noongar people have agreed to extinguish their native title rights and interests in exchange for title to 320,000 hectares of land and a total compensation package of $1.3 billion. Among other elements, this package includes certain rights to lands not transferred, capital transfer payments, and the establishment of six regional corporations and one Central Services Corporation, receiving $10 million per annum for 12 years. These corporations will undertake broadly similar responsibilities to PBCs, including managing traditional land and waters, developing regional plans, and engaging with government and third-party stakeholders to further Noongar interests and priorities. Their substantial funding and position within the broader comprehensive settlement package, however, highlights the more significant role they may play. These institutions formalise limited rights to self-governance, empowering Noongar to exercise substantive decision-making and control over certain matters.

Decision-making authority can be articulated in gradations. Chapter four noted that treaties negotiated in Canada and the United States have recognised a domain of autonomy within which First Nations and Native American Nations can exercise control and decision-making over internal and local affairs. In some cases, authority extends beyond powers of local government. The Nisga'a Final Agreement, for example, empowers the Nisga'a to constitute a court to adjudicate disputes.[170] The Noongar Settlement does not approach this scope of authority, but in circumstances where treaty processes are ongoing across Australia, its negotiation and entry into force may lead to more 'robust forms of Indigenous jurisdiction'.[171] Drawing from the UNDRIP, this could encompass the capacity of Indigenous nations to wield greater control over land and resources, as well as the authority to maintain, protect and develop their religious, spiritual and cultural traditions, and establish and control their own educational institutions.[172] Among other things, this could empower Indigenous communities to determine whether formal educational teaching within their territory is conducted in traditional languages or English, or a combination of both.

Other models exist. Some states recognise autonomous regions whereby territorially concentrated Indigenous political communities can govern themselves.

[168] Western Australia, *Parliamentary Debates*, Legislative Assembly, 25 November 2015, 8903 (Colin Barnett, Premier).

[169] Hobbs and Williams, 'The Noongar Settlement' (2018). But see: H McGlade, 'The McGlade Case: A Noongar History of Land, Social Justice and Activism' (2017) 43 *Australian Feminist Law Journal* 185, 210. Note that the treaty has been challenged by several Noongar people and has not yet come into effect.

[170] Nisga'a Final Agreement, signed 4 May 1999, (entered into force 11 May 2000) ch 12(30).

[171] Lino (n 20) 238.

[172] UNDRIP (n 1) arts 8, 10–15, 25–26.

In Nicaragua, for instance, the North Caribbean Coast Autonomous Region and the South Caribbean Coast Autonomous Region were established in 1987 and elected their first regional governments in 1990. Although the central government initially 'resisted granting any significant decision-making power or funds to the regional councils or governments',[173] a successful challenge in the Inter-American Court of Human Rights by the Awas Tingni to expropriation of their traditional lands without consent, propelled action.[174] A similar approach has been adopted in Canada and Denmark. In 1999, the territory of Nunavut was officially separated from the Northwest Territories, and in 2009 Greenland gained self-rule from Denmark. While both Nunavut and Greenland adopted a public (rather than ethnic) government, demographics mean that Inuit are a majority within the two polities. As such, within these territories, Inuit people exercise real autonomy in prescribed areas.[175] In Nunavut, this encompasses, inter alia, legislative powers over the administration of justice, sale of land and property rights, education, marriage and preservation of game,[176] while in Greenland it extends to authority over judicial affairs, policing, and natural resources.[177] Although these models may not be feasible in Australia, their jurisdictional scope emphasises the capacity of public law to recognise and accommodate substantive domains of Indigenous autonomy.

Australia's federal system makes treaty making somewhat challenging. As I have discussed, the allocation of constitutional responsibilities presents a complicated legal framework for Indigenous issues. Because the states have considerable authority over issues relating to Aboriginal and Torres Strait Islander peoples, including in health, education and housing, meaningful settlements that empower Indigenous communities with substantive decision-making authority in these areas will need to be negotiated with state governments. Simultaneously, because the federal government enjoys concurrent authority over Indigenous affairs and the permanent possibility of overriding state-based treaties,[178] the viability of enduring self-government arrangements relies on Commonwealth support. For this reason, it is legally preferable that negotiations be conducted concurrently with all levels of government, even though some Indigenous communities may be uneasy or hostile to the idea of negotiating domestic agreements with subnational entities.[179]

[173] A Larson and J Lewis-Mendoza 'Decentralisation and Devolution in Nicaragua's North Atlantic Autonomous Region: Natural Resources and Indigenous Peoples' Rights' (2012) 6 *International Journal of the Commons* 179, 183.

[174] *The Mayagna (Sumo) Awas Tingni Community v Nicaragua*, Inter-American Court of Human Rights (Ser. C) No 79 (Judgment on merits and reparations of 31 August 2001).

[175] See Kuokkanen, *Restructuring Relations* (2019).

[176] Nunavut Act SC 1993, c 28, s 23.

[177] Act on Greenland Self-Government (Act No 473, 2009) ch 2, sch II.

[178] Constitution, ss 51(xxvi), 109, 122.

[179] For discussion see H Hobbs and G Williams, 'Treaty-Making in the Australian Federation' (2019) 43 *Melbourne University Law Review* 178, 217–30.

Treaty-making may also respond to financial concerns. Will Sanders has argued that empowering Indigenous communities with a degree of autonomy (in this case, recognised via treaties) may facilitate the (re-)emergence of an Indigenous order of government.[180] One of the advantages of this approach relates to financial arrangements. As Sanders notes, all organisations 'designated as governments within the Australian federation have an assured ongoing funding base, both through revenue-raising powers of their own and through ongoing general revenue-sharing arrangements with other levels of government'.[181]

Although the prospect of Aboriginal and Torres Strait Islander communities levying tax on their lands may be remote, intergovernmental revenue-sharing agreements may result in significant capital. Indeed, self-governing Indigenous communities recognised through treaties could be considered within horizontal fiscal equalisation calculations by the Commonwealth Grants Commission. They could also receive specific purpose payments and grants on similar conditions as those provided to states, and Indigenous representatives could be included on intergovernmental bodies that make decisions over Indigenous expenditure.

Treaty-making relies on the state agreeing to substantive and meaningful outcomes. It also relies on the state meeting its obligations. Historic treaties signed between First Nations and colonial powers in Canada, the United States and Aotearoa New Zealand may legitimate the status and aspirations of the Indigenous nations who signed those agreements, but the terms sometimes betray an assimilative rationale and the state often failed to fulfil its end of the bargain. Contemporary treaty-making may not necessarily resolve these challenges.[182] The modern British Columbia treaty process, for instance, has attracted criticism for subverting Indigenous claims and translating Indigenous communities into municipalities with limited authority.[183] If treaties are to recognise Indigenous sovereignty, the state must not foreclose certain outcomes, but must enter negotiations in a spirit of equal partnership, based on mutual recognition and respect.

Assuming this standard is met, appropriately negotiated treaties could empower Indigenous nations and communities with the capacity to independently drive and develop policy and administration. In areas where native title has been recognised, settlements could scaffold upon existing inchoate recognition of Indigenous governance to empower communities with real decision-making authority. By contrast, in areas where native title has not been recognised, the Noongar Settlement demonstrates that new institutional expressions of

[180] W Sanders, 'Towards an Indigenous Order of Australian Government: Rethinking Self-Determination as Indigenous Affairs Policy' (Centre for Aboriginal Economic Policy Research Discussion Paper No 230, 2002). See further Reilly (n 32) 434.

[181] Sanders, 'Towards an Indigenous Order' (2002) 12.

[182] See H Hobbs and S Young, 'Modern Treaty Making and the Limits of the Law' (2020) 71 *University of Toronto Law Journal* (forthcoming).

[183] See ch 3.

self-governance, perhaps drawn from existing approaches in Australian law, can be established relatively easily. Provided clear links between self-governing communities and the representative body are established, this layered approach could meet Indigenous demands for *voices*, *power*, *ownership* and *integrity* and effectively empower Aboriginal and Torres Strait Islander peoples with the capacity to have their voices heard, and their interests considered, in the processes of Australian government.

V. CONCLUSION

It is impossible to state with certainty that an Indigenous representative body will empower Aboriginal and Torres Strait Islander peoples with the capacity to have their voices heard in the processes of Australian government, particularly in the face of an unreceptive administration. Nonetheless, this chapter has argued that there are two key factors necessary to provide a First Nations Voice with the best prospect of success. First, careful institutional design should aim at developing a body that meets Indigenous aspirations for *voices*, *power*, *ownership* and *integrity*. An institution that meets these criteria will be more likely to be regarded as legitimate and credible and will therefore carry considerable moral weight. However, as these criteria can conflict and political realities may force Indigenous communities to adopt more limited aims, an Indigenous representative body should be situated within a broader complementary framework. Drawing on the Uluru Statement from the Heart, I have articulated one approach that builds up from communities and upon existing institutions in a manner that 'formally recognis[es] and facilitate[es] Indigenous governance'.[184] Aboriginal and Torres Strait Islander peoples will determine their preferred approach, but in integrating self-governing communities with the national body, Voice Plus provides one model of structural reform that empowers Aboriginal and Torres Strait Islander peoples.

[184] Reilly (n 32) 434.

8

The Limits of Structural Reform

William Cooper passed away on 29 March 1941, just three years after he met with Prime Minister Joseph Lyons. In the months between his petition and his passing, Cooper continued to write to federal and state politicians and administrators, seeking 'what the White Man, in his heart, knows is bare justice'.[1] Believing that there 'is a spark of human kindness in nearly every heart',[2] Cooper's correspondence and public writings reveal his conviction that discriminatory legislation and practice stemmed 'more from ignorance than malevolence'.[3] The white population, he explained to Lyons, 'need only KNOW what my people have suffered and are suffering to bring the relief long sought and now overdue'.[4] The 'whole position in a nutshell', he wrote to John McEwen, the Minister for the Interior, is that 'the white man has not yet shown any capacity for "thinking black"'.[5] For legislators to consider 'the interests of the natives', and 'see the position through an aboriginal's eyes',[6] structural change would be required:

> This is where we need our member, able to watch legislation on the floor of the House, able to speak for the native and to represent native interests. We are of the opinion that if we had a good man devoted to our interests he could do more for our cause than "a majority" in Parliament. Though he would have no vote and be the stronger for that fact, he would be the most powerful factor in the House.[7]

Legal and political reforms have overtaken Cooper's specific concerns, but his underlying anxieties persist. As chapter one demonstrated, despite significant reform, Australia's system of governance does not empower Aboriginal and Torres Strait Islander peoples with the capacity to have their interests considered in the processes of government at Commonwealth level. Structural features

[1] Letter from William Cooper to John McEwen, 26 July 1938; cited in A Markus, *Blood from a Stone: William Cooper and the Australian Aborigines' League* (Crows Nest, Allen & Unwin, 1988) 96, 98.

[2] Letter from William Cooper to the Prime Minister, 31 March 1938; cited in Markus, *Blood from a Stone* (1988) 85, 85.

[3] Markus (n 1) 13.

[4] Cooper (n 2).

[5] Letter from William Cooper to John McEwen, 17 December 1938; cited in Markus (n 1) 101, 102.

[6] Cooper (n 1).

[7] ibid.

of the Australian Constitution, underlying philosophical norms and values that give meaning to its institutions, and political practice, combine to inhibit the ability of Indigenous peoples to have 'a fair say even on matters that impact on [them] most'.[8] This reality prompts the key question that has driven this book: can Australia's governance system be restructured to empower Indigenous peoples? As contemporary debate has coalesced around the idea of a First Nations Voice to the federal Parliament, I have focused on whether and how a national Indigenous representative body would be effective at accomplishing this task.

Reform must be built on the views of those it is intended to serve. For generations, Aboriginal and Torres Strait Islander peoples like William Cooper have called for specific, substantive, reform to the framework of Australian governance. In response, Australian governments have often ignored or purposively mischaracterised their goals. Chapter three cannot correct this persistent failing, but by focusing attention on the perspectives of Indigenous peoples it can assist in developing a clearer image of Indigenous aspirations for structural reform. What emerges is a detailed, complex and nuanced picture of Indigenous thought. As this chapter identified, Indigenous resistance is and always has been a struggle to reassert sovereignty in its peoplehood, political and cultural conceptions, and establish relationships with the state on this basis. Reform must be built on those aspirations.

Exploration of Indigenous political thought is a prerequisite for meaningful reform, but it remains necessary to articulate those views into a form comprehensible to the state. Chapter four undertook this task by distilling four public law criteria to assess institutional structures aimed at empowering Indigenous peoples in the processes of government. Described as *voices*, *power*, *ownership* and *integrity*, the criteria are grounded in and reflective of Indigenous peoples' understandings of sovereignty and desire to establish a fair relationship with the state(s) that claims their land. The criteria are:

(1) Indigenous peoples must be heard when decisions that affect them are being made.
(2) Indigenous peoples must have the authority and financial capacity to exercise independent policy and decision-making power over matters relating to internal or local affairs.
(3) Institutions or processes that empower Indigenous peoples must be regarded by Indigenous peoples as legitimate.
(4) Indigenous leaders must act according to the purposes and values for which they have been entrusted with authority, and must be accountable for their actions.

[8] Empowered Communities, 'Empowered Communities, Empowered Peoples: Design Report' (2015) 9.

Indigenous peoples are entitled to develop their own decision-making institutions and determine the terms on which they choose to participate within state processes.[9] The criteria are framed in broad terms to respect the right to self-determination and enable differently situated communities to adopt mechanisms that best meet their unique needs and aspirations. Drawing on Aboriginal and Torres Strait Islander peoples' desires expressed in the Uluru Statement from the Heart,[10] the final three substantive chapters explored Indigenous representative bodies in detail.

Chapter five analysed the Aboriginal and Torres Strait Islander Commission (ATSIC), a representative body that existed in Australia between 1990 and 2005. Built on the failures of previous Indigenous advisory bodies, the Commission empowered elected Indigenous Australians with the ability to speak directly to government, as well as design policy and make decisions over public expenditure. ATSIC's establishment was greeted with considerable optimism. Only a few short years later, however, the Commission was abolished with bipartisan support. As this chapter revealed, there are several contributing factors for ATSIC's demise, including poor institutional design choices, the behaviour of some its senior leaders, and government interference inhibiting its capacity to determine and execute its own priorities. Together, these factors ensured that the Commission struggled to maintain legitimacy and credibility.

ATSIC's experiences suggest that Indigenous representative bodies may face complications in practice. Chapter six tested this proposition by analysing the Sámediggi, a national representative body for the Sámi who live in Sweden. As an institution designed to empower Sámi people with the capacity to have their voices heard in the processes of Swedish government, the Sámediggi serves a similar role to ATSIC. Key distinctions between Sweden and Australia concerning political culture, legal traditions and the diversity and breadth of Indigenous communities allowed the strengths and weaknesses of Indigenous representative bodies to be accurately assessed. Unfortunately, this chapter found that although the Sámediggi has proven effective at times, it also struggles to ensure Sámi interests and views are meaningfully heard by relevant decision-makers. The Sámediggi may still be operating, but the same challenges and tensions faced by ATSIC reappear and many Sámi question its value.

Those challenges and tensions were explored further in chapter seven. There it was noted that Indigenous representative bodies occupy a difficult political and legal field. Operating within the liminal space between a source of advice to the state for legislation and policy development, and as an institution advocating for and accountable to Indigenous peoples, members of these bodies must be skilled politicians capable of determining when to make uneasy choices.

[9] United Nations Declaration on the Rights of Indigenous Peoples, GA Res 61/295, UN GAOR, 61st sess, 107th plen mtg, Supp No 49, UN Doc A/RES/61/295 (13 September 2007) arts 3–5, 18.

[10] Uluru Statement from the Heart, Uluru, 26 May 2017 (Uluru Statement).

Challenges exist for the state too. An Indigenous representative body can serve the state's interests by acting as a conduit and central authority for deliberation and consultation with diverse peoples spread across the continent. If that body lacks legitimacy however, whether because its constituents perceive that it is insufficiently attuned to or ineffective at realising their aspirations, support will fall and its value to the state will decline. It is in the state's interest that an Indigenous representative body be effective. Just how effective the state can allow, and just how far the body can push, will be an ongoing, though potentially productive, source of tension.

The case studies demonstrate that prudent structural design choices are critical in investing an Indigenous representative body with the greatest prospect of success. Drawing on their experiences, chapter seven outlined eight issues that should be considered in establishing a contemporary First Nations Voice that could meet Aboriginal and Torres Strait Islander peoples' aspirations within Australia's system of government. Three points are worth emphasising. First, Indigenous peoples themselves should drive the development and design of any body. Second, the body should take advantage of Australia's federal structure by engaging with receptive state and territory governments. More than simply ensuring that it remains effective and influential in difficult circumstances, clear links with all levels of Australian governance will enhance the prospect that the body survives attempts to marginalise or abolish it.

Third, in the absence of a justiciable obligation to consult or a veto power, Indigenous representative bodies may be able to empower Indigenous peoples to have their voices heard in the processes of government, but they cannot ensure it. As William Cooper might say, Indigenous leaders working within a national representative body may watch legislation on the floor of the House, they may speak for Aboriginal and Torres Strait Islander peoples, and they may represent their interests, but they will not have a determinative vote. Whether the institution would 'be the stronger for that fact' largely depends on a confluence of factors surrounding its legitimacy and credibility. Institutional design can enhance these conditions by promoting its authenticity and accountability to Indigenous communities (*ownership* and *integrity*), as well as ensuring that it has a real opportunity to influence legislation and policy development (*voices*) and exercise decision-making authority (*power*). However, institutional design cannot guarantee legitimacy and credibility. Ultimately, its influence and success will rely on the development of productive relationships with all levels of government.

As this suggests and as chapter seven explained, the broader institutional framework in which an Indigenous representative body operates is vital. Drawing on the Uluru Statement and Indigenous aspirations explored in chapter three, I set out one complementary framework. Characterised as Voice Plus, the model I explored is centred on self-governing Indigenous communities exercising decision-making authority and integrated within a national representative body. This layered, quasi-federal approach aims at establishing a governance framework in which each mechanism reaffirms and strengthens the other.

Aboriginal and Torres Strait Islander peoples and communities should determine their preferred model. Emerging treaty processes across Australia present Indigenous Australians with this opportunity. Assuming negotiations commence, Indigenous communities will consider their own distinct aspirations and negotiate a settlement outcome that responds to their unique ambitions and capacity. Whether treaty processes in Victoria, the Northern Territory, Queensland, and perhaps elsewhere, ultimately result in meaningful outcomes, however, depends on the state.

That the effectiveness of an Indigenous representative body relies on the state exposes the limits of structural reform. If a First Nations Voice is to be the 'missing cog in the check and balance machinery of Australia's federal Constitution',[11] attitudinal and relational changes within government and the public at large are necessary. Institutional design can put Indigenous peoples in the room where decisions are made, but government will only listen to those voices if an ethic of respect, 'engagement',[12] or 'kindness',[13] permeates non-Indigenous–Indigenous relations. Research on the politics of listening,[14] and the responsibility of non-Indigenous peoples to engage in the reconciliation process,[15] can develop answers as to how this ethic of respect can be engendered. The Uluru Statement call for a Makarrata Commission to supervise a process of treaty-making and place-based truth telling can also assist.

Makarrata is a Yolŋu word that means 'a coming together after a struggle'. At Uluru, delegates explained that it 'captures our aspirations for a fair and truthful relationship with the people of Australia'.[16] Efforts are still progressing to establish this Commission, but the recent Canadian Truth and Reconciliation Commission into Indian Residential Schools reveals the value of truth-telling processes. In June 2015, the Commission issued 94 'Calls to Action' aimed at redressing the legacy of residential schools and advancing the process of reconciliation. Among other points, they call on all governments to promote Indigenous languages, educate Canadians on their history, establish a national centre for truth and reconciliation, and recognise Indigenous peoples as 'full partners in Confederation'.[17] These are difficult, long-term reforms, but their worth is their

[11] S Morris, 'The Argument for a Constitutional Procedure for Parliament to Consult with Indigenous People when Making Laws for Indigenous Affairs' (2015) 26 *Public Law Review* 166, 167.

[12] W Connolly, 'The Liberal Image of the Nation' in D Ivison, P Patton and W Sanders (eds), *Political Theory and the Rights of Indigenous Peoples* (Cambridge, Cambridge University Press, 2000) 183, 191.

[13] M Asch, *On Being Here to Stay: Treaties and Aboriginal Rights in Canada* (Toronto, University of Toronto Press, 2014) 140.

[14] See, eg: L Bassel, *The Politics of Listening: Possibilities and Challenges for Democratic Life* (London, Palgrave Macmillan, 2017).

[15] See, eg: S Maddison, T Clark and R de Costa (eds), *The Limits of Settler Colonial Reconciliation: Non-Indigenous People and the Responsibility to Engage* (Singapore, Springer, 2016).

[16] Uluru Statement (n 10).

[17] Truth and Reconciliation Commission of Canada, 'Canada's Residential Schools: Reconciliation' (2015) vol 6, 223, Calls to Action 13–14, 62, 77, 45(iv).

focus on developing durable cultural change. Future research should examine how multiple, local, place-based truth-telling processes should be structured to catalyse and contribute to similar change in Australia.

Aboriginal and Torres Strait Islander peoples conceive the Makarrata Commission as also supervising a process of treaty-making. While the Commission has not yet been established, the existing moves towards treaties in Australia evince the value of this approach. If genuine, treaties offer the prospect of developing a plural and inclusive view of Australian identity that takes seriously Indigenous claims. In articulating relationships between peoples, treaties tell stories about the interaction between different normative communities that share the land, and the values and responsibilities that secure the bonds of association between and among those communities.[18] More than recognising a limited domain of autonomy and self-rule for Indigenous communities, treaties provide a language for both Indigenous and non-Indigenous citizens to converse.[19] When combined with meaningful truth-telling processes, treaties can help to develop an intercultural dialogue that engages frankly with distinctive worldviews and recognises Indigenous peoples as equal participants in the design of a shared future. Truth-telling and treaty-making may therefore hold the key to inculcating a culture of respect where governments listen and hear Indigenous voices – whether they are expressed from within a national representative body or not.

* * * * *

On 26 July 1938, William Cooper wrote once more to John McEwen. Succinctly explaining the rationale for his activism, Cooper noted: 'we aborigines feel we have a right to a place in Australia and we feel we are robbed of that place'.[20] Would an Indigenous representative body empower Aboriginal and Torres Strait Islander peoples with the capacity to have their voices heard in the processes of government? As I have argued, the answer largely comes down to the state. The most significant issue Indigenous peoples and the state must reach agreement on before establishing a representative body is its purpose. The tensions that challenge and potentially overwhelm these institutions are intimately connected to a disjuncture over their central roles and responsibilities. By this I do not mean whether they exercise a combination of representative and executive functions but, more fundamentally, how government conceives of the institution. Is an Indigenous representative body intended to genuinely reflect Aboriginal and

[18] H Hobbs, 'Constitutional Recognition and Reform: Developing an Inclusive Australian Citizenship through Treaty' (2018) 53 *Australian Journal of Political Science* 176, 185.

[19] J Webber, *Reimagining Canada: Language, Culture, Community, and the Canadian Constitution* (Montreal, McGill-Queen's University Press, 1994) 192–93.

[20] Cooper (n 1).

Torres Strait Islander peoples' aspirations and express their priorities within the processes of government, or is it intended to provide a forum for Indigenous peoples to debate issues at a national level and provide advice to government, without meaningfully amending the structures and dynamics of public administration? Almost every challenge faced by Indigenous representative bodies can be traced back to this question. The consequence is simple. A First Nations Voice can succeed, but only if it is allowed.

Bibliography

Åhrén, I, 'Small Nations of the North in Constitutional and International Law' (1995) 64 *Nordic Journal of International Law* 457

Åhrén, M, 'Indigenous Peoples' Culture, Customs and Traditions and Customary Law – The Saami People's Perspective' (2004) 21 *Arizona Journal of International and Comparative Law* 63

—— 'The Saami Convention' (2007) 3 *Gáldu Čála – Journal of Indigenous Peoples Rights* 8

—— *Indigenous Peoples' Status in the International Legal System* (Oxford, Oxford University Press, 2016)

Aboriginal Community Assembly, 'Final Statement and Recommendations to the Aboriginal Treaty Working Group' (December 2017)

Aboriginal and Torres Strait Islander Boundaries and Electoral System Review Panel, 'Review of Electoral Systems' (1997)

Aboriginal and Torres Strait Islander Commission, 'Recognition, Rights and Reform: A Report to Government on Native Title Social Justice Measures' (Commonwealth of Australia, 1995)

—— 'Review of Boundaries' (Report of the Panel Convened by the Minister for Aboriginal and Torres Strait Islander Affairs to Review Matters Relating to the Boundaries of ATSIC's Zones, Regions and Wards, February 1995)

—— 'Review of the Operation of the Aboriginal and Torres Strait Islander Commission Act 1989 (Cth)' (1993)

—— 'Strengthening ATSIC: The 1997 Review of the ATSIC Act' (1998)

—— Office of Evaluation and Audit, 'The Final Report of the Evaluation of the Effectiveness of ATSIC Programs in Meeting the Needs of Aboriginal Women and Torres Strait Islander Women' (1995)

—— Office of Evaluation and Audit, 'Putting the Pieces Together: Regional Plans, Data and Outcomes' (2003)

—— Elections Review Panel, 'Review of Electoral Systems: A Report to the Minister for Aboriginal and Torres Strait Islander Affairs' (1995)

Aboriginal and Torres Strait Islander Social Justice Commissioner, 'Social Justice Report 2005' (Human Rights and Equal Opportunity Commission, 2005)

—— 'Building a Sustainable National Indigenous Representative Body' (2008)

Aboriginal Treaty Working Group, 'Aboriginal Community Consultations on the Design of a Representative Body' (December 2016)

—— 'Aboriginal Community Consultations on the Design of a Representative Body – Phase 2' (June 2017)

Ah Kit, J, 'Reconciliation and Constitutional Issues: Participation in Government – Sovereignty or Subjugation?' (speech delivered to the Australian Reconciliation Convention, Melbourne, 26 May 1997)

Aldrich, J, 'Rational Choice and Turnout' (1993) 37 *American Journal of Political Science* 246

Alfred, T, 'Deconstructing the British Columbia Treaty Process' (2001) 3 *Balayi: Culture, Law and Colonialism* 37

—— 'Sovereignty' in P Deloria and N Salisbury (eds), *A Companion to American Indian History* (Blackwell, 2002) 460–74

—— *Wasáse: Indigenous Pathways of Action and Freedom* (Toronto, University of Toronto Press, 2005)

—— 'Sovereignty' in J Barker (ed), *Sovereignty Matters: Locations of Contestations and Possibility in Indigenous Struggles for Self-Determination* (Lincoln, University of Nebraska Press, 2005) 33–50

—— *Peace, Power Righteousness: An Indigenous Manifesto*, 2nd edn (Oxford, Oxford University Press, 2009)

—— 'Colonialism and State Dependency' (2009) 5 *Journal of Aboriginal Health* 42

Allen, E, 'Our Treaty, Our Inherent Right to Self-Government: An Overview of the Nisga'a Final Agreement' (2004) 11 *International Journal on Minority and Group Rights* 233

Altman, J, 'Practical Reconciliation and the New Mainstreaming: Will it Make a Difference to Indigenous Australians?' (2004) 23 *Dialogue* 35

Anaya, J, *Indigenous Peoples in International Law* (Oxford, Oxford University Press, 2004)

—— 'International Human Rights and Indigenous Peoples: The Move Towards the Multicultural State' (2004) 21 *Arizona Journal of International and Comparative Law* 13

—— 'The Right of Indigenous Peoples to Self-Determination in the Post-Declaration Era' in C Charters and R Stavenhagen (eds), *Making the Declaration Work: The United Nations Declaration on the Rights of Indigenous Peoples* (Copenhagen, International Work Group for Indigenous Affairs, 2009) 184–99

—— 'Situation of Human Rights and Fundamental Freedoms of Indigenous People', UN Doc A/65/264 (9 August 2010)

—— 'The Situation of the Sámi People in the Sápmi Region of Norway, Sweden and Finland', UN Doc A/HRC/18/35/Add.2 (6 June 2011)

—— 'Report of the Special Rapporteur on the Rights of Indigenous Peoples: Addendum: The Situation of Kanak People in New Caledonia, France', UN Doc A/HRC/18/35/Add.6 (14 September 2011)

Anderson, C and Hokowhitu, B, 'Whiteness: Naivety, Void and Control' (2007) 8 *Junctures* 39

Anderson, I, 'The End of Aboriginal Self-Determination' (2007) 39 *Futures* 137

Anderson, P, 'Our Hope for the Future: Voice. Treaty. Truth' (17th Vincent Lingiari Memorial Lecture, Darwin, 16 August 2017)

Anderson, P, Pearson, N, Davis, M, Brennan, S, Appleby, G, Lino, D and McKinnon, G, Submission No 479 to Joint Select Committee on Constitutional Recognition Relating to Aboriginal and Torres Strait Islander Peoples, 3 November 2018

Anthony, T, *Indigenous People, Crime and Punishment* (Abingdon, Routledge, 2013)

Anton, T, 'Policy-Making and Political Culture in Sweden' (1969) 4 *Scandinavian Political Studies* 88

Appleby, G, 'An Indigenous Advisory Body: Some Questions of Design' (2015) 8 *Indigenous Law Bulletin* 3

—— Submission No 132 to Joint Select Committee on Constitutional Recognition of Aboriginal and Torres Strait Islander Peoples, 12 June 2015)

Arcioni, E, 'Excluding Indigenous Australians from "The People": A Reconsideration of s 25 and 127 of the Constitution' (2014) 40 *Federal Law Review* 1

—— 'Tracing the Ethno-Cultural or Racial Identity of the Australian Constitutional People' (2015) 15 *Oxford University Commonwealth Law Journal* 173

Arcioni, E and Stone, A, 'The Small Brown Bird: Values and Aspirations in the Australian Constitution' (2016) 14 *International Journal of Constitutional Law* 60

Ardill, A, 'Australian Sovereignty, Indigenous Standpoint Theory and Feminist Standpoint Theory: First Peoples' Sovereignties Matter' (2013) 22 *Griffith Law Review* 315

Arthur, W, 'Indigenous Autonomy in Australia: Some Concepts, Issues and Examples' (Centre for Aboriginal Economic Policy Research, Discussion Paper No 220, 2001)

Asch, M, *On Being Here to Stay: Treaties and Aboriginal Rights in Canada* (Toronto, University of Toronto Press, 2014)

'Att Återta Mitt Språk: Åtgärder för att Stärka det Samiska Språket' (SOU 2006:19)

Attwood, B and Markus, A, *Thinking Black: William Cooper and the Australian Aborigines' League* (Canberra, Aboriginal Studies Press, 2004)

Austin, R, *Navajo Court and Navajo Common Law: A Tradition of Tribal Governance* (Minneapolis, University of Minnesota Press, 2009)

Australian Electoral Commission, Submission No 120 to Joint Standing Committee on Electoral Matters, 'Inquiry into and Report on All Aspects of the Conduct of the 2019 Federal Election and Matters Related Thereto' (20 September 2019)

Australian Law Reform Commission, 'Recognition of Aboriginal Customary Law' (Report No 31, 1986)

—— 'Connection to Country: Review of the Native Title Act 1993' (Cth) (Report No 126, 2015)

—— 'Incarceration Rates of Aboriginal and Torres Strait Islander Peoples' (Discussion Paper No 84, 2017)

—— 'Pathways to Justice – Inquiry into the Incarceration Rate of Aboriginal and Torres Strait Islander People' (Report No 133, 2018)

Australian National Audit Office, 'Australian Government Procurement Contract Reporting' (Report No 19, 2017)

—— 'Indigenous Advancement Strategy' (Report No 35, 2017)

Axelsson, P, '"In the National Registry, All People Are Equal": Sámi in Swedish Statistical Sources' in P Axelsson and P Sköld (eds), *Indigenous Peoples and Demography: The Complex Relation Between Identity and Demography* (New York, Berghan Books, 2011) 117–34

Baer, L-A, 'The Right of Self-Determination and the Case of the Sámi' in P Aiko and M Scheinin (eds), *Operationalising the Right of Indigenous Peoples to Self-Determination* (Turku, Institute for Human Rights, 2000) 223–31

Barker, J, 'For Whom Sovereignty Matters' in J Barker (ed), *Sovereignty Matters: Locations of Contestations and Possibility in Indigenous Struggles for Self-Determination* (Lincoln, University of Nebraska Press, 2005) 1–32

Banducci, S, Donovan, T and Karp, J, 'Minority Representation, Empowerment and Participation' (2004) 66 *The Journal of Politics* 534

Barsh, RL and Henderson J, *The Road: Indian Tribes and Political Liberty* (Berkeley, University of California Press, 1980)

Barton, A, 'Public Sector Accountability and Commercial-in-Confidence Outsourcing Contracts' (2006) 19 *Accounting, Auditing & Accountability Journal* 256

Bassel, L, *The Politics of Listening: Possibilities and Challenges for Democratic Life* (London, Palgrave Macmillan, 2017)

Beach, H, 'The New Swedish Sámi Policy – A Dismal Failure: Concerning the Swedish Government's Proposition 1992/93:32, *Samerna och Sámisk kultur m.m.* (Bill)' in E Gayim and K Myntti (eds), *Indigenous and Tribal Peoples' Rights – 1993 and After* (Rovaniemi, Northern Institute for Environmental and Minority Law, 1995) 109–29

Beetham, D, *The Legitimation of Power*, 2nd edn (London, Palgrave MacMillan, 2013)

Behrendt, L, *Aboriginal Dispute Resolution: A Step Towards Self-Determination and Community Autonomy* (Annandale, Federation Press, 1995)

—— *Achieving Social Justice: Indigenous Rights and Australia's Future* (Annandale, Federation Press, 2003)

—— 'Representative Structures – Lessons Learned from the ATSIC Era' (2009) 10 *Journal of Indigenous Policy* 35

Bennett, S, *White Politics and Black Australians* (Crows Nest, Allen & Unwin, 1999)

Benton, R, 'Perfecting the Partnership: Revitalising the Maori Language in New Zealand Education and Society 1987–2014' (2015) 28 *Language, Culture and Curriculum* 99

Beresford, Q, *Rob Riley: An Aboriginal Leader's Quest for Justice* (Canberra, Aboriginal Studies Press, 2006)

Bergh, J, Dahlberg, S, Mörkenstam, U and Saglie J, 'Participation in Indigenous Democracy: Voter Turnout in Sámi Parliamentary Elections in Norway and Sweden' (2018) 41 *Scandinavian Political Studies* 263

Betänkande av Gränsdragningskommissionen för renskötselområdet, 'Samernas Sedvanemarker' (SOU 2006:14)

Biaudet, E, *Study on the Right to Participation of Indigenous Youth in the Nordic Countries in Decision-Making Processes*, UN Doc E/C.19/2013/8 (12 February 2013)

Blagg, H, Crime, *Aboriginality and the Decolonisation of Justice*, 2nd edn (Annandale, Federation Press, 2016)

Bodansky, D, 'The Legitimacy of International Governance: A Coming Challenge for International Environmental Law?' (1999) 93 *American Journal of International Law* 596

Borrows, J, 'A Genealogy of Law: Inherent Sovereignty and First Nations Self-Government' (1992) 30 *Osgoode Hall Law Journal* 291

—— *Recovering Canada: The Resurgence of Indigenous Law* (Toronto, University of Toronto Press, 2002)

—— 'Stewardship and the First Nations Governance Act' (2003) 29 *Queen's Law Journal* 103

—— 'Practical Recolonisation' (2005) 28 *UNSW Law Journal* 614

—— *Canada's Indigenous Constitution* (Toronto, University of Toronto Press, 2010)

—— *Freedom and Indigenous Constitutionalism* (Toronto, University of Toronto Press, 2016)

Borrows, J and Tully, J, 'Introduction' in M Asch, J Borrows and J Tully (eds), *Resurgence and Reconciliation: Indigenous – Settler Relations and Earth Teachings* (Toronto, University of Toronto Press, 2018) 3–25

Brand, O, 'Conceptual Comparisons: Towards a Coherent Methodology of Comparative Legal Studies' (2007) 32 *Brooklyn Journal of International Law* 405

Brennan, F, 'ATSIC: Seeking a National Mouthpiece for Local Voices' (1990) 2 *Aboriginal Law Bulletin* 4

—— *One Land, One Nation: Mabo – Towards 2001* (Brisbane, University of Queensland Press, 2001)

Brennan, S, Gunn, B and Williams, G, '"Sovereignty" and its Relevance to Treaty-Making between Indigenous Peoples and Australian Governments' (2004) 26 *Sydney Law Review* 307

Brennan, S and Davis, M, 'First Peoples' in C Saunders and A Stone (eds), *The Oxford Handbook of the Australian Constitution* (Oxford, Oxford University Press, 2018) 27–55

Broderstad, EG, 'Political Autonomy and Integration of Authority: The Understanding of Saami Self-Determination' (2001) 8 *International Journal on Minority and Group Rights* 151

Brown, AJ, 'Putting Administrative Law Back into Integrity and Putting Integrity Back into Administrative Law' (2007) 53 *AIAL Forum* 32

—— 'What is a National Integrity System? From Temple Blueprint to Hip-Pocket Guide' in B Head, AJ Brown and C Connors (eds), *Promoting Integrity: Evaluating and Improving Public Institutions* (Farnham, Ashgate, 2008) 33–52

Brunton, R 'Low Turnout Undermines ATSIC' (1994) 46 *IPA Review* 8

Buchan, B, *Empire of Political Thought: Indigenous Australians and the Language of Colonial Government* (London, Pickering & Chatto, 2008)

Burton, L and Williams, G, 'The Integrity Function and ASIO's Extraordinary Questioning and Detention Powers' (2012) 38 *Monash University Law Review* 1

Canada, Royal Commission on Aboriginal People, 'Volume 2: Restructuring the Relationship' (1996)

Cape York Institute, 'A First Nations Voice in the Constitution: Design Issues' (Report to the Referendum Council, June 2017)

—— Submission No 244 to Joint Select Committee on Constitutional Recognition Relating to Aboriginal and Torres Strait Islander Peoples, June 2018

Cavanagh, J, 'Selected Policy Statements on Aboriginal Affairs 1973–1974' (Australian Government Publishing Service, 1974)

Chesterman, J, 'Chosen by the People? How Federal Parliamentary Seats might be Reserved for Indigenous Australians without Changing the Constitution' (2006) 34 *Federal Law Review* 261

—— 'National Policy-Making in Indigenous Affairs: Blueprint for an Indigenous Review Council' (2008) 67 *The Australian Journal of Public Administration* 419

Chesterman, J and Galligan, B, *Citizens Without Rights: Aborigines and Australian Citizenship* (Cambridge, Cambridge University Press, 1997)

Coburn, E, 'Alternatives: Theorising Colonialism and Indigenous Liberation: Contemporary Indigenous Scholarship from Lands Claimed by Canada' (2016) 97 *Studies in Political Economy* 285

Coe, P, 'The Struggle for Aboriginal Sovereignty' (1994) 13 *Social Alternatives* 1

—— 'ATSIC: Self-determination or Otherwise' (1994) 4 *Race & Class* 35

Coghill, K, 'Ministers in Office: Preparation and Performance' (Lecture delivered at the Department of the Senate Occasional Lecture Series, Parliament House, 29 September 2000)

Committee on the Elimination of Racial Discrimination, 'General Recommendation No 23: Indigenous Peoples', 51st sess, UN Doc. A/52/18, annex V (18 August 1997)

—— 'General Comment No 32: The Meaning and Scope of Special Measures in the International Covenant on the Elimination of Racial Discrimination', 75th sess, UN Doc CERD/C/GC/32 (24 September 2009)

Commonwealth, Royal Commission on Australian Government Administration, 'Report' (1976)

—— Royal Commission into Aboriginal Deaths in Custody, 'National Report' (1991)

—— 'Recognising Aboriginal and Torres Strait Islander Peoples in the Constitution: Report of the Expert Panel', January 2012

—— 'Commonwealth Aboriginal and Torres Strait Islander Employment Strategy' (Australian Public Service Commission, 2015)

Connolly, W, 'The Liberal Image of the Nation' in D Ivison, P Patton and W Sanders (eds), *Political Theory and the Rights of Indigenous Peoples* (Cambridge, Cambridge University Press, 2000) 183–98

Coombs, HC, 'The Role of the National Aboriginal Conference' (Australian Government Publishing Service, 1984)

—— *Aboriginal Autonomy: Issues and Strategies* (Cambridge, Cambridge University Press, 1994)

Coombs, HC and Robinson, CJ, 'Remembering the Roots: Lessons for ATSIC' in P Sullivan (ed), *Shooting the Banker* (Darwin, North Australian Research Unit, 1996) 1–16

Cornell, S and Kalt, JP, 'Two Approaches to the Development of Native Nations: One Works, the Other Doesn't' in M Jorgensen (ed), *Rebuilding Native Nations: Strategies for Governance and Development* (Tucson, University of Arizona Press, 2007) 3–33

Corntassel, J, 'Re-Envisioning Resurgence: Indigenous Pathways to Decolonisation and Sustainable Self-Determination' (2012) 1 *Decolonisation: Indigeneity, Education & Society* 86

Corntassel, J and Witmar II, R, *Forced Federalism: Contemporary Challenges to Indigenous Nationhood* (Norman, University of Oklahoma Press, 2008)

Coulthard, G, 'Subjects of Empire: Indigenous Peoples and the "Politics of Recognition" in Canada' (2007) 6 *Contemporary Political Theory* 437

—— *Red Skin White Masks: Rejecting the Colonial Politics of Recognition* (Minneapolis, University of Minnesota Press, 2014)

Council for Aboriginal Reconciliation, 'Going Forward: Social Justice for the First Australians' (1996)

—— 'Reconciliation: Australia's Challenge' (Final Report of the Council for Aboriginal Reconciliation, 2000)

Craft, J and Howlett, M, 'Policy Formation, Governance Shifts and Policy Influence: Location and Content in Policy Advisory Systems' (2012) 32 *Journal of Public Policy* 79

Crawford, J, 'Relations between Civil Servants and Ministers in Policy-Making' (1960) 19 *Australian Journal of Public Administration* 99

Cronin, D, 'Trapped by History: Democracy, Human Rights and Justice for Indigenous People in Australia' (2017) 23 *Australian Journal of Human Rights* 220

Cunningham, J and Baeza, J, 'An "Experiment" in Indigenous Social Policy: The Rise and Fall of Australia's Aboriginal and Torres Strait Islander Commission (ATSIC)' (2005) 33 *Policy & Politics* 461

Dacks, G, 'Nunavut: Aboriginal Self-Determination through Public Government' (Report for the Royal Commission on Aboriginal People, 1993)

Daes, EI, 'An Overview of the History of Indigenous Peoples: Self-Determination and the United Nation' (2008) 21 *Cambridge Review of International Affairs* 7

Dahlberg, S, 'Voter Turnout in Sweden' (Friedrich Ebert Stiftung, July 2016)

Dahlberg, S and Mörkenstam, U, 'Valdeltagande i valet till Sametinget 2013' in S Dahlberg U Mörkenstam and R Nilsson (eds), *Sametingsval: Väljare, Partier och Media* (Stockholm, Santérus Förlag, 2016) 129–54

Daintith, T and Ng, Y-F 'Executives' in Saunders, C and Stone, A (eds), *The Oxford Handbook of the Australian Constitution* (Oxford University Press, 2018) 587–616

Davis, F, 'The Problem of Authority and the Proposal for an Indigenous Advisory Body' (2015) 8 *Indigenous Law Bulletin* 23

Davis, M, 'A Culture of Disrespect: Indigenous Peoples and Australian Public Institutions' (2006) 8 *University of Technology Sydney Law Review* 137

—— 'The United Nations Declaration on the Rights of Indigenous Peoples' (2007) 6 *Indigenous Law Bulletin* 6

—— 'ATSIC and Indigenous Women: Lessons for the Future' (2008) 10 *Balayi: Culture, Law & Colonialism* 73

—— 'Indigenous Struggles in Standard-Setting: The United Nations Declaration on the Rights of Indigenous Peoples (2008) 9 *Melbourne Journal of International Law* 439

—— 'To Bind or not to Bind: The United Nations Declaration on the Rights of Indigenous Peoples Five Years On' (2012) 3 *Australian International Law Journal* 17

—— 'Aboriginal Women: The Right to Self-Determination' (2012) 16 *Australian Indigenous Law Review* 78

—— 'A Rightful Place: Correspondence' (2014) 56 *Quarterly Essay* 73–81

—— 'Listening but not Hearing: When Process Trumps Substance' 51 *Griffith Review* (2016) 73

—— 'Self-Determination and the Right to be Heard' in S Morris (ed), *A Rightful Place: A Road Map to Recognition* (Melbourne, Black Books, 2017) 119

—— 'The Long Road to Uluru: Walking Together: Truth Before Justice' (2018) 60 *Griffith Review* 13

Davis, M and Dixon, R, 'Constitutional Recognition through a (Justiciable) Duty to Consult? Towards Entrenched and Judicially Enforceable Norms of Indigenous Consultation' (2016) 27 *Public Law Review* 255

Davis, M and McGlade, H, 'International Human Rights Law and the Recognition of Aboriginal Customary Law' (Aboriginal Customary Laws Background Paper 10, Law Reform Commission of Western Australia, 2006) 381–428

Davis, M and Langton, M, 'Constitutional Reform in Australia' in P Macklem and D Sanderson (eds), *From Recognition to Reconciliation* (University of Toronto Press 2016) 449–73

—— (eds), *It's Our Country: Indigenous Arguments for Meaningful Constitutional Recognition and Reform* (Melbourne, Melbourne University Press, 2016)

de Costa, R, *A Higher Authority: Indigenous Transnationalism and Australia* (Sydney, UNSW Press, 2006)

Deloria, Jr, V, 'Self-Determination and the Concept of Sovereignty' in J Wunder (ed), *Native American Sovereignty* (New York, Routledge, 1999) 118–24

—— *We Talk, You Listen: New Tribes, New Turf* (Lincoln, University of Nebraska Press, 2007)

Dexter, B, 'Stanner: Reluctant Bureaucrat' in M Hinkson and J Beckett (eds), *An Appreciation of Difference: WEH Stanner and Aboriginal Australia* (Canberra, Aboriginal Studies Press, 2008) 76–86

—— *Pandora's Box: The Council for Aboriginal Affairs 1967–1976* (Brisbane, Keeaira Press, 2015)

Dillon, M, 'Institutional Structures in Indigenous Affairs' in P Sullivan (ed), *Shooting the Banker: Essays on ATSIC and Self-Determination* (Darwin, North Australian Research Unit, 1996) 89–104

Dixon, R, 'Amending Constitutional Identity' (2012) 33 *Cardozo Law Review* 1847

Dodson, M, 'Aboriginal and Torres Strait Islander People and Citizenship' (speech delivered to the Complex Notions of Civic Identity Conference, University of New South Wales, 20 August 1993)

—— 'Assimilation Versus Self-determination: No Contest' (North Australian Research Unit, Discussion Paper 1, 1996)

—— 'Mabo Lecture: Asserting our Sovereignty' in L Strelein (ed), *Dialogue about Land Justice: Papers from the National Native Title Conference* (Canberra, Aboriginal Studies Press, 2010) 13–18

Dodson, M and Strelein, L, 'Australia's Nation-Building: Renegotiating the Relationship Between Indigenous Peoples and The State' (2001) 24 *UNSW Law Journal* 826

Dodson, M and Smith, D, 'Governance for Sustainable Development: Strategic Issues and Principles for Indigenous Australian Communities' (Centre for Aboriginal Economic Policy Research, Discussion Paper No 250, 2003)

Dodson, P, 'Foreword' in S Maddison, *Black Politics: Inside the Complexity of Aboriginal Political Culture* (Crows Nest, Allen & Unwin, 2009) vii–x

—— 'Beyond the Mourning Gate: Dealing with Unfinished Business' in R Tokinson (ed), *The Wentworth Lectures: Honouring Fifty Years of Australian Indigenous Studies* (Aboriginal Studies Press, 2015) 192–203

Dodson, P and Cronin, D, 'An Australian Dialogue: Decolonising the Country' in S Maddison and M Brigg (eds), *Unsettling the Settler State: Creativity and Resistance in Indigenous Settler-State Governance* (Annandale, Federation Press, 2011) 189–205

Dudgeon, P, 'Indigenous Identity' in P Dudgeon, D Garvey and H Pickett (eds), *Working with Indigenous Australians: A Handbook for Psychologists* (Perth, Gunada Press, 2000) 43–51

Dziedzic, A and McMillan, M, 'Australian Indigenous Constitutions: Recognition and Renewal' (2016) 44 *Federal Law Review* 337

Ekonomistyrningsverket, 'Analys av Sametinget: Finansiering och intern styrning och kontroll' (2017)

Emerson, L, 'Diné Sovereign Action: Rejecting Colonial Sovereignty and Invoking Diné Peacemaking' in L Lee (ed), *Navajo Sovereignty: Understandings and Visions of the Diné People* (Tusscon, University of Arizona Press, 2017) 160–78

Emerton, P, 'Ideas' in C Saunders and A Stone (eds), *The Oxford Handbook of the Australian Constitution* (Oxford, Oxford University Press, 2018) 143–64

Empowered Communities, 'Empowered Communities, Empowered Peoples: Design Report' (2015)

'En reformerad grundlag' (SOU 2008:125)

Eriksson, J, *Partition and Redemption: A Machiavellian Analysis of Sámi and Basque Patriotism* (PhD thesis, Umea University, 1997)

Expert Mechanism on the Rights of Indigenous Peoples, 'Progress Report on the Study of Indigenous Peoples and the Right to Participate in Decision-Making', UN Doc A/HRC/15/35 (23 August 2010)

—— 'Final Study on Indigenous Peoples and the Right to Participate in Decision-Making', UN Doc A/HRC/EMRIP/2011/2 (26 May 2011)

FaHCSIA National Representative Body Unit, 'Report on the Outcomes of the First Phase of Consultation for a National Indigenous Representative Body (NIRB)' (December 2008)

Falch, T, Selle, P and Strømsnes, K, 'The Sámi: 25 Years of Indigenous Authority in Norway' (2016) 15 *Ethnopolitics* 125

Fallon Jr, R, 'Legitimacy and the Constitution' (2005) 118 *Harvard Law Review* 1789, 1795.

Fenley, J, 'The National Aboriginal Conference and the Makarrata: Sovereignty and Treaty Discussions, 1979–1981' (2011) 42 *Australian Historical Studies* 372

Fforde, C, Bamblett, L, Lovett, R, Gorringe, S and Fogarty, B, 'Discourse, Deficit and Identity: Aboriginality, the Race Paradigm and the Language of Representation in Contemporary Australia' (2013) 149 *Media International Australia* 162

Finlayson, J and Dale, A, 'Negotiating Indigenous Self-Determination at the Regional Level' in P Sullivan (ed), *Shooting the Banker: Essays on ATSIC and Self-Determination* (Darwin, North Australian Research Unit, 1996) 70–88

Fiske, J-A and Patrick, B, *Cis Dideen Kat, When the Plumes Rise: The Way of the Lake Babine Nation* (Vancouver, University of British Columbia Press, 2000)

Fjellström, A-M, Mörkenstam, U, Nilsson, R, and Knobloch, M, 'Sametingets formella ställning, valsystem och partier' in S Dahlberg, U Mörkenstam and R Nilsson (eds), *Sametingsval: Väljare, Partier och Media* (Stockholm, Santérus Förlag, 2016) 77–102

—— 'Partiernas rekrytering och nominering av kandidater inför valet 2013' in S Dahlberg, U Mörkenstam and R Nilsson (eds), *Sametingsval: Väljare, Partier och Media* (Stockholm, Santérus Förlag, 2016) 103–28

Fletcher, A, *Australia's Human Rights Scrutiny Regime: Democratic Masterstroke or Mere Window Dressing?* (Melbourne, Melbourne University Press, 2018)

Foster, C, 'Cabinet Government in the Twentieth Century' (2004) 67 *Modern Law Review* 753

Forsey, E, 'The Courts and the Conventions of the Constitution' (1984) 33 *University of New Brunswick Law Journal* 11

Fuchs, L, 'Understanding and Implementing Self-Determination for Indigenous Peoples: The Case of the Sami in Sweden' (MSc thesis, Linnaeus University, 2014)

Gallarotti, G, 'Soft Power: What It Is, Why It's Important and the Conditions for Its Effective Use' (2011) 4 *Journal of Political Power* 25

Galligan, B, 'Judicial Review in the Australian Federal System: Its Origins and Function' (1979) 10 *Federal Law Review* 367

Ganter, E, *Reluctant Representatives* (Canberra, ANU Press, 2017)

Gardiner-Garden, J and Simon-Davies, J, 'Commonwealth Indigenous-Specific Expenditure, 1968–2010' (Parliamentary Library of Australia, 16 September 2010)

Gaykamangu, JG, 'Ngarra Law: Aboriginal Customary Law from Arnhem Land' (2012) 2 *Northern Territory Law Journal* 236

Geddis, A and Ruru, J, 'Places as Persons: Creating a New Framework for Maori–Crown Relations' in J Varuhas and SW Stark (eds), *The Frontiers of Public Law* (Oxford, Hart Publishing, 2020) 255–74

Ghillar, MA, 'Euahlayi Nation Declares Independence and Asserts Pre-Existing and Continuing Statehood' (press release, 12 August 2013)

Gilbert, K, *Because a White Man'll Never Do It* (Sydney, Angus and Robertson, 1973)

—— *Living Black: Blacks Talk to Kevin Gilbert* (Sydney, Penguin, 1977)

Godlewska, C and Webber, J, 'The *Calder* decision, Aboriginal Title and the Nisga'a' in H Foster, H Raven and J Webber (eds), *Let Right be Done: Aboriginal Title, the Calder Case and the Future of Indigenous Rights* (Vancouver, University of British Columbia Press, 2007) 1–33

Goot, M, 'The Aboriginal Franchise and its Consequences' (2006) 52 *Australian Journal of Politics and History* 517

Gover, K, *Tribal Constitutionalism: States, Tribes and the Governance of Membership* (Oxford, Oxford University Press, 2010)

—— 'Settler–State Political Theory, "CANZUS" and the UN Declaration on the Rights of Indigenous Peoples' (2015) 26 *European Journal of International Law* 345

—— 'From the Heart: The Indigenous Challenge to Australian Public Law' in J Varuhas, and SW Stark (eds), *The Frontiers of Public Law* (Oxford, Hart Publishing, 2020) 205–26

Grant, S, 'The Australian Dream: Blood, History and Becoming' (2016) 64 *Quarterly Essay* 1

Green, J, 'Decolonisation and Recolonisation in Canada' in W Clement and L Vosko (eds), *Changing Canada: Political Economy as Transformation* (Montreal, McGill-Queen's University Press, 2003) 51–75

—— 'Indigenous Feminism: From Symposium to Book' in J Green (ed), *Making Space for Indigenous Feminism* (Winnipeg, Fernwood, 2007) 14–19

Grenfell, L and Moulds, S, 'The Role of Committees in Rights Protection in Federal and State Parliaments in Australia' (2018) 41 *UNSW Law Journal* 40

Griffith, C, 'Interview with Neville Bonner', *Land Rights Queensland* (April 1995)

Gronlund, K and Setala, M, 'Political Trust, Satisfaction and Voter Turnout' (2007) 5 *Comparative European Politics* 400

Gwaans, 'Gitxsan Eviction Notice to Sportsfishers, Forestry and CN Rail' (press release, 10 July 2014)

Hall, P, 'The Swedish Administrative Model' in J Pierre (ed), *The Oxford Handbook of Swedish Politics* (Oxford, Oxford University Press, 2015) 299–315

Hancock, I, *John Gorton: He Did It His Way* (Sydney, Hachette Australia, 2011)

Hannaford, J, Huggins, J and Collins, B, 'Review of the Aboriginal and Torres Strait Islander Commission' (discussion paper, 2003)

—— *In the Hands of the Regions – A New ATSIC* (Report of the Review of the Aboriginal and Torres Strait Islander Commission, 2003)

Harris, M, 'From Australian Courts to Aboriginal Courts in Australia – Bridging the Gap?' (2004) 16 *Current Issues in Criminal Justice* 26

Harty, S and Murphy, M, *In Defence of Multinational Citizenship* (Vancouver, University of British Columbia Press, 2005)

Hawke, B, 'Statement of the Prime Minister: Barunga Festival' (1988) 2 *Land Rights News* 22

Henderson, A, *Nunavut: Rethinking Political Culture* (Vancouver, University of British Columbia Press, 2007)

Henderson, J, 'Empowering Treaty Federalism' (1994) 58 *Saskatchewan Law Review* 241

—— 'Sui Generis and Treaty Citizenship' (2002) 6 *Citizenship Studies* 415

Hendriks, C and Kay, A, 'From "Opening Up" to Democratic Renewal: Deepening Public Engagement in Legislative Committees' (2019) 54 *Government and Opposition* 25

Henriksen, J, 'The Continuous Process of Recognition and Implementation of the Sámi People's Right to Self-Determination' (2008) 21 *Cambridge Review of International Affairs* 27

—— (ed), 'Sámi Self-Determination – Scope and Implementation' (2008) 2 *Gáldu Čála – Journal of Indigenous Peoples Rights* 1

Hiatt, LR, 'Australian Committee of Inquiry into the Role of the National Aboriginal Consultative Committee' (Australian Government Publishing Service, 1976)

Highfield, J, Interview with Tim Fisher, Deputy Prime Minister of Australia (radio interview, 4 September 1997)

Hill, L and Alport, K, 'Voting Attitudes and Behaviour Among Aboriginal Peoples: Reports from Anangu Women' (2010) 56 *Australian Journal of Politics and History* 242

Hobbs, H, 'Locating the Logic of Transitional Justice in Liberal Democracies: Native Title in Australia' (2016) 39 *UNSW Law Journal* 512

—— 'Democratic Theory and Constitutional Design: Hearing Persistent Electoral Minorities' (2017) 24 *International Journal on Minority and Group Rights* 341

—— 'Constitutional Recognition and Reform: Developing an Inclusive Australian Citizenship through Treaty' (2018) 53 *Australian Journal of Political Science* 176

—— 'Aboriginal and Torres Strait Islander Peoples and Multinational Federalism in Australia' (2018) 27 *Griffith Law Review* 307

—— 'The Road to Uluru: Constitutional Recognition and the UN *Declaration on the Rights of Indigenous Peoples*' (2020) *Australian Journal of Politics and History* (forthcoming).

Hobbs, H and Williams, G, 'The Noongar Settlement: Australia's First Treaty' (2018) 40 *Sydney Law Review* 1

—— 'Treaty-Making in the Australian Federation' (2019) 43 *Melbourne University Law Review* 178

Hobbs, H and Young, S, 'Modern Treaty Making and the Limits of the Law' (2021) 71 *University of Toronto Law Journal* (forthcoming)

Hobbs, NT, Andrén, H, Persson, J, Aronsson, M and Chapron, G, 'Native Predators Reduce Harvest of Reindeer by Sámi Pastoralists' (2012) 22 *Ecological Applications* 1640

Holmberg, S, 'Politiskt förtroende' in S Dahlberg, U Mörkenstam and R Nilsson (eds), *Sametingsval: Väljare, Partier och Media* (Stockholm, Santérus Förlag, 2016) 219–30

House of Representatives Standing Committee on Aboriginal Affairs, Parliament of Australia, 'Our Future Our Selves: Aboriginal and Torres Strait Islander Community Control, Management and Resources' (1990)

Howell, E, 'Black Power – By Any Means Necessary' in G Foley, A Schaap and E Howell (eds), *The Aboriginal Tent Embassy: Sovereignty, Black Power, Land Rights and the State* (Abingdon, Routledge 2016) 67–83

Howson, P, *The Howson Diaries: The Life of Politics* (Melbourne, Viking, 1984) 892

Huggins, J and Little, R, 'A Rightful Place at the Table' in S Morris (ed), *A Rightful Place: A Road Map to Recognition* (Melbourne, Black Books, 2017) 147–72

Hughes, R, Interview with Neville Bonner (Australian Biography Project, 13 January 1992)

Human Rights Committee, 'Consideration of Reports Submitted by States Parties under Article 40 of the Covenant: Norway', UN Doc CCPR/C/79/Add.27 (4 November 1993)

—— 'Consideration of Reports Submitted by State Parties under Article 40 of the Covenant: Sixth Periodic Report – Sweden', UN Doc CCPR/C/SWE/6 (5 December 2007)

—— 'Concluding Observations of the Human Rights Committee: Sweden', UN Doc CCPR/C/SWE/CO/6 (7 May 2009)

—— 'Concluding Observations on the Seventh Periodic Report of Sweden', UN Doc CCPR/C/SWE/CO/7 (28 April 2016)

Human Rights Council, 'Report of the Working Group on the Universal Periodic Review: Norway', UN Doc A/HRC/13/5 (4 January 2010)

Human Rights and Equal Opportunity Commission, 'Aboriginal and Torres Strait Islander Social Justice Commission: First Report' (Commonwealth, 1993)

Hunt, J, 'Between a Rock and a Hard Place: Self-Determination, Mainstreaming and Indigenous Community Governance' in J Hunt, D Smith, S Garling and W Sanders (eds), *Contested Governance: Culture, Power and Institutions in Indigenous Australia* (Canberra, ANU Press, 2008) 27–54

Hunter, N, 'A Place at the Constitutional Table' in M Davis and M Langton (eds), *It's Our Country: Indigenous Arguments for Meaningful Constitutional Recognition and Reform* (Melbourne, Melbourne University Press, 2016) 114–17

Imai, S, 'Indigenous Self-Determination and the State' in BJ Richardson, S Imai and K McNeil (eds), *Indigenous Peoples and the Law: Comparative and Critical Perspectives* (Oxford, Hart Publishing, 2009) 285–314

Independent Working Group on Constitutional Transformation, 'The Report of Matike Mai Aotearoa' (2016)

Indigenous Advisory Committee, 'Indigenous Advisory Committee Bulletin No 9 Meeting 33' (Canberra, 27–28 July 2017)

Ingold, T, 'The Transformation of the Siida' (1978) 43 *Ethnos* 146

Ivanitz, M, 'Straddling Two Worlds: ATSIC and the Management of Indigenous Policy' (Centre for Australian Public Sector Management, Research Paper No 6, 1998)

—— 'The Politics of Accountability: ATSIC, the Coalition Government and Public Sector Service Outcomes' (Centre for Australian Public Sector Management, Research Paper No 9, July 1999)

—— 'The Demise of ATSIC? Accountability and the Coalition Government' (2000) 59 *Australian Journal of Public Administration* 3

Jacobsson, B and Sundström, G, 'Governing the State' in J Pierre (ed), *The Oxford Handbook of Swedish Politics* (Oxford, Oxford University Press, 2015) 347–61

Jahreskog, B (ed), *The Sámi National Minority in Sweden* (Stockholm, Almqvist and Wiksell International, 1982)

Jennings, I, *Cabinet Government*, 3rd edn (Cambridge, Cambridge University Press, 1959)

Joint Select Committee on Constitutional Recognition of Aboriginal and Torres Strait Islander Peoples, 'Final Report' (June 2015)

Joint Select Committee on Constitutional Recognition Relating to Aboriginal and Torres Strait Islander Peoples, Parliament of Australia, 'Interim Report' (July 2018)

—— 'Final Report' (November 2018)

Joint Standing Committee on Electoral Matters, Parliament of Australia, 'Civics and Electoral Education' (2007)

—— Joint Standing Committee on Electoral Matters, 'The 2013 Federal Election: Report on the conduct of the 2013 election and matters related thereto' (April 2015)

—— 'Report on the conduct of the 2016 federal election and matters related thereto' (November 2018)

Jonas, W and Dick, D, 'Ensuring Meaningful Participation of Indigenous Peoples in Government Processes: The Implications of the Decline of ATSIC' (2004) 23 *Dialogue: Academy of the Social Sciences* 4

Jones, C, *New Treaty, New Tradition: Reconciling New Zealand and Māori Law* (Vancouver, University of British Columbia Press, 2016)

Jones, E, 'The Purse Strings and the Policy Process: Bureaucratic Shaping of Industry Policy Capacity after 1945' (2001) 60 *Australian Journal of Public Administration* 21

Josefsen, E, Mörkenstam, U and Saglie, J, 'Different Institutions within Similar States: The Norwegian and Swedish *Sámediggis*' (2015) 14 *Ethnopolitics* 32

—— 'Sametingene–Institusjoner for Selvbestemmelse?' in E Josefsen, U Mörkenstam, R Nilsson and J Saglie (eds), *Ett Folk, Ulike Valg: Sametingsvalg i Norge og Sverige* (Oslo, Gyldendal Akademisk, 2017) 24–55

Josefsen, E, Mörkenstam, U and Nilsson, R, 'The Nordic Sámediggis and the Limits of Indigenous Self-Determination' (2016) 1 *Gáldu Čála – Journal of Indigenous Peoples Rights* 1

Kam, C, *Party Discipline and Parliamentary Politics* (Cambridge, Cambridge University Press, 2009)

Kessler-Mata, K, *American Indians and the Trouble with Sovereignty: A Turn Toward Structural Self-Determination* (Cambridge, Cambridge University Press, 2017)

Kenworthy, L, 'Quantitative Indicators of Corporatism' (2003) 33 *International Journal of Sociology* 10

Kernaghan, K, 'Politics, Policy and Public Servants: Political Neutrality Revisited' (1976) 16 *Canadian Public Administration* 432

Kickingbird, K, Kickingbird, L, Chibitty, C and Berkey, C, *Indian Sovereignty* (Indian Legal Curriculum and Training Program of the Institute for the Development of Indian Law, 1977)

Killey, I, *Constitutional Conventions in Australia: An Introduction to the Unwritten Rules of Australia's Constitutions* (London, Anthem Press, 2014)

King, K, 'Language Revitalisation Processes and Prospects: Quichua in the Ecuadorian Andes' (1999) 13 *Language and Education* 17

Kirmayer, L and Valaskakis, G, 'Preface' in L Kirmayer and G Valaskakis (eds), *Healing Traditions: The Mental Health of Aboriginal People in Canada* (Vancouver, University of British Columbia Press, 2009) xiii–xxi

Korsmo, F, 'Swedish Policy and Saami Rights' (1993) 11 *The Northern Review* 32

van Krieken, R, 'Rethinking Cultural Genocide: Aboriginal Child Removal and Settler–Colonial State Formation' (2004) 75 *Oceania* 125

Kuokkanen, R, *Restructuring Relations: Indigenous Self-Determination, Governance and Gender* (Oxford, Oxford University Press, 2019)

Kvist, R, 'Swedish Sámi Policy 1548–1992' in L Heininen (ed), *The Changing Circumpolar North: Opportunities for Academic Development* (Rovaniemi, Arctic Centre Publications No 6, 1994) 28

Kwaymullina, A, 'Recognition, Referendums and Relationships: Indigenous Worldviews, Constitutional Change and the "Spirit" of 1967' in S Young, J Nielsen and J Patrick (eds), *Constitutional Recognition of First Peoples in Australia: Theories and Comparative Perspectives* (Annandale, Federation Press, 2016) 29–47

Kwaymullina, A and Kwaymullina, B, 'Learning to Read the Signs: Law in an Indigenous Reality' (2010) 34 *Journal of Australian Studies* 195

Kymlicka, W, *Finding Our Way: Rethinking Ethnocultural Relations in Canada* (Oxford, Oxford University Press, 1998)

—— 'Beyond the Indigenous/Minority Dichotomy?' in S Allen and A Xanthaki, *Reflections on the UN Declaration on the Rights of Indigenous Peoples* (Oxford, Hart Publishing, 2011) 183–208

Ladner, K and Simpson, L, 'This is an Honour Song' in L Simpson and K Ladner (eds), *This is an Honour Song: Twenty Years Since the Blockades* (Winnipeg, ARP, 2010) 1

Laing, R (ed), *Odgers' Australian Senate Practice: As Revised by Harry Evans*, 14th edn (Department of the Senate, 2016)

Langton, M, 'Finding a Resolution to Constitutional Recognition of Indigenous Australians' in M Davis and M Langton (eds), *It's Our Country: Indigenous Arguments for Meaningful Constitutional Recognition and Reform* (Melbourne, Melbourne University Press, 2016) 27

Langton, M, Mazel, O, Palmer, L, Shain, K and Tehan, M (eds), *Settling with Indigenous Peoples: Modern Treaty and Agreement Making* (Annandale, Federation Press, 2006)

Lantto, P, 'Borders, Citizenship and Change: The Case of the Sámi People, 1751–2008' (2010) 14 *Citizenship Studies* 543

Lantto, P and Mörkenstam, U, 'Sámi Rights and Sámi Challenges: The Modernisation Process and the Swedish Sámi Movement, 1886–2006' (2008) 22 *Scandinavian Journal of History* 26

—— 'Action, Organisation and Confrontation: Strategies of the Sámi Movement in Sweden during the Twentieth Century' in M Berg-Nordlie, J Saglie and A Sullivan (eds), *Indigenous Politics: Institutions, Representation, Mobilisation* (Colchester, ECPR Press, 2015) 131–59

LaRoque, E, *When the Other is Me: Native Resistance Discourse, 1850–1990* (Winnipeg, University of Manitoba Press, 2010)

Larson, A and Lewis-Mendoza, J, 'Decentralisation and Devolution in Nicaragua's North Atlantic Autonomous Region: Natural Resources and Indigenous Peoples' Rights' (2012) 6 *International Journal of the Commons* 179

Lawrence, R and Åhrén, M, 'Mining as Colonisation: The Need for Restorative Justice and Restitution of Traditional Sami Lands' in L Head, K Saltzman, G Setten and M Stenseke (eds), *Nature, Temporality and Environmental Management: Scandinavian and Australian Perspectives on Peoples and Landscapes* (New York, Routledge, 2016) 149–66

Lawrence, R and Mörkenstam, U, 'Indigenous Self-Determination Through a Government Agency? The Impossible Task of the Swedish Sámediggi' (2016) 23 *International Journal on Minority and Group Rights* 105

Law Reform Commission of Western Australian, 'Aboriginal Customary Laws: The Interaction of Western Australian Law with Aboriginal Law' (Report No 94, 2006)

Lidström, A, 'Swedish Local and Regional Government in a European Context' in J Pierre (ed), *The Oxford Handbook of Swedish Politics* (Oxford, Oxford University Press, 2015) 414–28

Lindvall, J and Sebring J, 'Policy Reform and the Decline of Corporatism in Sweden' (2005) 28 *West European Politics* 1057

Lino, D, 'Towards Indigenous-Settler Federalism' (2017) 29 *Public Law Review* 118

—— 'The Indigenous Franchise and Assimilation' (2017) 48 *Australian Historical Studies* 363

—— 'Indigenous Recognition' in R Dixon (ed), *Australian Constitutional Values* (Oxford, Hart Publishing, 2018) 243–63

—— *Constitutional Recognition: First Peoples and the Australian Settler State* (Annandale, Federation Press, 2018)

Lof, A, 'Locking in and Locking out: A Critical Analysis of the Governance of Reindeer Husbandry in Sweden' (2016) 10 *Critical Policy Studies* 426

Ludwick, H, 'Through Black Eyes' in M Davis and M Langton (eds), *It's Our Country: Indigenous Arguments for Meaningful Constitutional Recognition and Reform* (Melbourne, Melbourne University Press, 2016) 42–47

Maaka, R and Fleras, A, 'Engaging with Indigneity: Tino Rangatiratanga in Aotearoa' in D Ivison, P Patton and W Sanders (eds), *Political Theory and the Rights of Indigenous Peoples* (Cambridge, Cambridge University Press, 2000) 89–109

Macklem, P, *Indigenous Difference and the Constitution of Canada* (Toronto, University of Toronto Press, 2001)

—— 'The Constitutional Identity of Indigenous Peoples in Canada: Status Groups or Federal Actors?' in A Arato, J Cohen and A von Busekist (eds), *Forms of Pluralism and Democratic Constitutionalism* (New York, Columbia University Press, 2018) 117–48

Maddison, S, *Black Politics: Inside the Complexity of Aboriginal Political Culture* (Crows Nest, Allen & Unwin, 2009)

—— 'White Parliament, Black Politics: The Dilemmas of Indigenous Parliamentary Representation' (2010) 45 *Australian Journal of Political Science* 663

Maddison, S, Clark, T and de Costa, R (eds), *The Limits of Settler Colonial Reconciliation: Non-Indigenous People and the Responsibility to Engage* (Singapore, Springer, 2016)

Magga, OH, 'The Saami Parliament: Fulfilment of Self-Determination?' in J Erikkson and K Karppi (eds), *Conflict and Cooperation in the North* (Umeå, Umeå University Press, 2002) 299–311

Mansell, M, 'Aborigines and the Constitution' (1993) 2 *Human Rights Defender* 5

—— *Treaty and Statehood: Aboriginal Self-Determination* (Annandale, Federation Press, 2016)

Marchetti, E and Daly, K, 'Indigenous Sentencing Courts: Towards a Theoretical and Jurisprudential Model' (2007) 29 *Sydney Law Review* 415

Marika, 'An Arnhem Land Story' in R Tonkinson (ed), *The Wentworth Lectures: Honouring Fifty Years of Australian Indigenous Studies* (Canberra, Aboriginal Studies Press, 2015) 180–91

Markus, A, 'William Cooper and the 1937 Petition to the King' (1983) 7 *Aboriginal History* 46

—— *Blood from a Stone: William Cooper and the Australian Aborigines' League* (Crows Nest, Allen & Unwin, 1988)

Marsh, I and Miller, R, *Democratic Decline and Democratic Renewal: Political Change in Britain, Australia and New Zealand* (Cambridge, Cambridge University Press, 2012)

Martin, D and Finlayson, J, 'Linking Accountability and Self-determination in Aboriginal Organisations' (Centre for Aboriginal Economic Policy Research, Discussion Paper No 116, 1996)

Martinez, J, 'Problematising Aboriginal Nationalism' (1997) 21 *Aboriginal History* 133

Mashaw, JL, 'Accountability and Institutional Design: Some Thoughts on the Grammar of Governance' in MW Dowdle (ed), *Public Accountability: Designs, Dilemmas and Experiences* (Cambridge, Cambridge University Press, 2006) 115–56

Matulick, T, Palmer, A and Westgate, A, 'Engaging Indigenous people with the Australian Parliament through the Senate committee system' (Australia and New Zealand Association of Clerks at the Table Conference, Wellington, 19 January 2016)

McCallum, K, Waller, L and Dreher, T, 'Mediatisation, Marginalisation and Disruption in Australian Indigenous Affairs' (2016) 4 *Media and Communication* 30

McCue, J, 'New Modalities of Sovereignty: An Indigenous Perspective' (2007) 2 *Intercultural Human Rights Law Review* 19

McGlade, H, 'Native Title, 'Tides of History' and Our Continuing Claims for Justice – Sovereignty, Self Determination and Treaty' in H McGlade (ed), *Treaty: Let's Get It Right!* (Canberra, Aboriginal Studies Press, 2003) 118–36

—— (ed), *Treaty: Let's Get it Right!* (Canberra, Aboriginal Studies Press, 2003)

—— *Our Greatest Challenge: Aboriginal Children and Human Rights* (Canberra, Aboriginal Studies Press, 2012)

—— 'The McGlade Case: A Noongar History of Land, Social Justice and Activism' (2017) 43 *Australian Feminist Law Journal* 185

McIntyre, G, 'Aboriginal Customary Law: Can it be Recognised?' (Aboriginal Customary Laws Background Paper 9, Law Reform Commission of Western Australia, 2006) 341–80

McKeown, D and Lundie, R, 'Crossing the Floor in the Federal Parliament 1950 – August 2004' (Parliamentary Library Research Note, 10 October 2005)

McMillan, J, 'Ten Challenges for Administrative Justice' (2010) 61 *Australian Institute of Administrative Law Forum* 23

McMillan, M, 'Is Federalism Being Undermined in the Current Surge to 'Recognise' Indigenous Australians in (and into) the Commonwealth Constitution?' (2016) 8 *Indigenous Law Bulletin* 15

Michaels, R, 'The Functional Method of Comparative Law' in M Reimann and R Zimmerman (eds), *The Oxford Handbook of Comparative Law* (Oxford, Oxford University Press, 2006) 339–82

Miller, R, 'Tribal Cultural Self-Determination and the Makah Whaling Culture' in J Barker (ed), *Sovereignty Matters: Locations of Contestations and Possibility in Indigenous Struggles for Self-Determination* (Lincoln, University of Nebraska Press, 2005) 123–52

Mills, A, *Eagle Down is Our Law: Witsuwit'en Law, Feasts and Land Claims* (Vancouver, University of British Columbia Press, 2014)

—— 'Rooted Constitutionalism: Growing Political Community' in M Asch, J Borrows and J Tully, J, (eds), *Resurgence and Reconciliation: Indigenous – Settler Relations and Earth Teachings* (Toronto, University of Toronto Press, 2018) 133–74

Minde, H, 'Assimilation of the Sámi – Implementation and Consequences' (2003) 20 *Acta Borealia* 121

Montin, S, 'Municipalities, Regions and County Councils: Actors and Institutions' in J Pierre (ed), *The Oxford Handbook of Swedish Politics* (Oxford, Oxford University Press, 2015) 367–82

Monture-Angus, P, *Journeying Forward: Dreaming Aboriginal People's Independence* (Halifax, Fernwood, 1999)

Morales, S, 'Bridging the Incommensurable: Indigenous Legal Traditions and the Duty to Consult' in O Fitzgerald and R Schwartz (eds), *UNDRIP Implementation: Braiding International, Domestic and Indigenous Laws* (Vancouver, Centre for International Governance Innovation, 2017)

Morden, M, 'Parliament and the Representation of Indigenous Issues: The Canadian Case' (2018) 71 *Parliamentary Affairs* 124

Moreton-Robinson, A, *Talkin' Up to the White Woman: Aboriginal Women and Feminism* (Brisbane, University of Queensland Press, 2000)

—— 'Introduction: Resistance, Recovery and Revitalisation' in M Grossman (ed), *Blacklines: Contemporary Critical Writing by Indigenous Australians* (Melbourne, Melbourne University Press, 2003) 127–31

—— 'Writing off Indigenous Sovereignty: The Discourse of Security and Patriarchal White Sovereignty' in A Moreton-Robinson (ed), *Sovereign Subjects* (Crows Nest, Allen & Unwin, 2007) 86–102

—— *The White Possessive: Property, Power and Indigenous Sovereignty* (Minneapolis, University of Minnesota Press, 2015)

Morito, B, *An Ethic of Mutual Respect: The Covenant Chain and Aboriginal-Crown Relations* (Vancouver, University of British Columbia Press, 2012)

Morphy, F, 'Whose Governance, for Whose Good? The Laynhapuy Homelands Association and the Neo-Assimilationist Turn in Indigenous Policy' in J Hunt, D Smith, S Garling and W Sanders (eds), *Contested Governance: Culture, Power and Institutions in Indigenous Australia* (Canberra, ANU Press, 2008) 113–52

Morris, S, 'The Argument for a Constitutional Procedure for Parliament to Consult with Indigenous People when Making Laws for Indigenous Affairs' (2015) 26 *Public Law Review* 166

—— 'False Equality' in S Morris (ed), *A Rightful Place: A Road Map to Recognition* (Melbourne, Black Inc, 2017) 209–38

—— *A First Nations Voice in the Australian Constitution* (Oxford, Hart Publishing, 2020)

Möller, T, 'The Parliamentary System' in J Pierre (ed), *The Oxford Handbook of Swedish Politics* (Oxford, Oxford University Press, 2015) 115–29

Mörkenstam, U, 'Indigenous Peoples and the Right to Self-Determination: The Case of the Swedish Sámi People' (2005) 25 *The Canadian Journal of Native Studies* 433

—— 'The Constitution of the Swedish Sámi People: Swedish Sámi Policy and the Justification of the Inner Colonisation of Sweden' in J Tripathy and J Padmanabhan (eds), *Becoming Minority: How Discourses and Policies Produce Minorities in Europe and India* (New Delhi, Sage, 2014) 88–110

—— 'Recognition *as if* Sovereigns? A Procedural Understanding of Indigenous Self-Determination' (2015) 19 *Citizenship Studies* 634

—— 'Some Remarks on the Criteria to Register in the Sámi Electoral Roll in Sweden' in L Heinämäki, C Allard, S Kirchner, A Xanthaki, S Valkonen, U Mörkenstam, N Bankes, J Ruru, J Gilbert, P Selle, A Simpson and L Olsén (eds), *Actualizing Sámi Rights: International Comparative Research* (Finnish Prime Minister's Office, 4/2017) 361–66

Mörkenstam, U, Gottardis, A and Roth, A, 'The Swedish Sámi Parliament: A Challenged Recognition?' (ACCEPT Pluralism, 2012)

Muga, D, 'A Commentary on the Historical Transformation of the Sámi Communal Mode of Production' (1986) 14 *The Journal of Ethnic Studies* 111

Mulgan, R, 'Transparency and the Performance of Outsourced Government Services' (Australia and New Zealand School of Government, Occasional Paper No 5, 2015)

Muller, S '"Two-Ways": Bringing Indigenous and Non-Indigenous Knowledges Together' in J Weir (ed), *Country, Native Title and Ecology* (Canberra, ANU Press, 2012) 59–79

Mundine, W, 'Practical Recognition from the Mob's Perspective' (Uphold and Recognise, 2017)

—— 'Recognising the First Nations' in S Morris (ed), *A Rightful Place: A Road Map to Recognition* (Melbourne, Black Inc, 2017) 195–208

Murphy, M, 'Relational Self-Determination and Federal Reform' in Murphy, M (ed), *Canada: State of the Federation 2003 – Reconfiguring Aboriginal–State Relations* (Montreal, McGill-Queen's University Press 2003) 3–35

—— 'Representing Indigenous Self-Determination' (2008) 58 *University of Toronto Law Journal* 185

Müller-Wille, L, 'The Sámi Parliament in Finland: A Model for Ethnic Minority Management?' (1979) 3 *Études/Inuit/Studies* 63

Myers, F, *Pintupi Country, Pintupi Self: Sentiment, Place and Politics Among Western Desert Aborigines* (Berkeley, University of California Press, 1991)

Nadasdy, P, *Sovereignty's Entailments: First Nation State Formation in the Yukon* (Toronto, University of Toronto Press, 2017)

Nakata, M, Nakata, V, Keech, S and Bolt, R, 'Decolonial Goals and Pedagogies for Indigenous Students' (2012) 1 *Decolonisation: Indigeneity, Education & Society* 120

National Aboriginal Conference, 'The Makarrata: Some Ways Forward' (Position Paper presented at World Council of Indigenous Peoples, Canberra, April 1981)

—— 'Establishment, Role and Functions' (1983)

National Congress of Australia's First Peoples, 'National Congress of Australia's First Peoples Strive to Survive' (media release, 2 November 2016)

Newfong, J, 'The Aboriginal Embassy: Its Purpose and Aims' (1972) *Identity* 4

Newman, D, *Revisiting the Duty to Consult: New Relationships with Aboriginal Peoples* (Saskatoon, Purich, 2014)

New South Wales Legislative Council Standing Committee on Social Issues, 'Enhancing Aboriginal Political Representation: Inquiry into Dedicated Seats in the New South Wales Parliament' (1998)

Nikolakis, W and Nelson, H, 'Trust, Institutions and Indigenous Self-Governance: An Exploratory Study' (2019) 32 *Governance* 331

Nikul, K, *The Lappish Nation* (Bloomington, University of Indiana Press, 1977)

Ng, Y-F, *Ministerial Advisers in Australia: The Modern Legal Context* (Annandale, Federation Press, 2016)

Ngarrindjeri Regional Authority, *Ngarrindjeri Kurangk Le:wunanangk Management Plan No 1* (2016)

Niezen, R, *The Origins of Indigenism: Human Rights and the Politics of Identity* (Berkeley, University of California Press, 2003)

Nilsson, R, Dahlberg, S and Mörkenstam, U, 'Inledning' in S Dahlberg, U Mörkenstam and R Nilsson (eds), *Sametingsval: Väljare, Partier och Media* (Stockholm, Santérus Förlag, 2016) 27–44

Nilsson, R, Mörkenstam, U and Svensson, R, 'Politiska skiljelinjer vid val till Sametinget' in S Dahlberg, U Mörkenstam and R Nilsson (eds), *Sametingsval: Väljare, Partier och Media* (Stockholm, Santérus Förlag, 2016) 181–200

Nilsson, R, Jansson, M, Mörkenstam, U and Dahlberg, S, 'Kön och politik i sametingsvalet 2013' in S Dahlberg, U Mörkenstam and R Nilsson (eds), *Sametingsval: Väljare, Partier och Media* (Santérus Förlag, 2016) 201–18

Northern Territory Law Reform Committee, 'Report on Aboriginal Customary Law' (2003)

Nunavut Social Development Council, 'A Discussion Paper: Towards an Inuit Qaujimajatuqangit (IQ) Policy for Nunavut' (1998)

Nye Jr, J, 'Soft Power: The Means to Success in World Politics' (New York, PublicAffairs, 2004)

—— 'Public Diplomacy and Soft Power' (2008) 616 *The ANNALS of the American Academy of Political and Social Science* 94

O'Donoghue, L, *An Aboriginal and Islander Consultative Organisation* (Department of Aboriginal Affairs, 1986)

—— 'Keynote Address: Australian Government and Self-Determination' in C Fletcher (ed), *Aboriginal Self-Determination in Australia* (Canberra, Aboriginal Studies Press, 1994) 3–12

—— 'In Indigenous Affairs Nothing is New, Just Forgotten' (1997) 56 *Australian Journal of Public Administration* 5

O'Faircheallaigh, C and Gibson, G, 'Economic Risk and Mineral Taxation on Indigenous Lands' (2012) 37 *Resources Policy* 10

O'Shane, P, 'Aboriginal Political Movements: Some Observations' (13th Frank Archibald Memorial Lecture, University of New England, 14 October 1998)

OECD, 'Contracting Out Government Services: Best Practice Guidelines and Case Studies' (Public Management Occasional Papers No 20, 1997)

Office of the Commissioner for Public Employment, 'Northern Territory Public Sector Indigenous Employment and Career Development Strategy 2010–2012' (Northern Territory, 2010)

Office of the Director of Equal Opportunity in Public Employment, *Yarnin' Up: Aboriginal People's Careers in the NSW Public Sector* (Sydney, Office of the Director of Equal Opportunity in Public Employment, 2001)

Ontai, KKNP, 'A Spiritual Definition of Sovereignty from a Kanaka Maoli Perspective' in J Barker (ed), *Sovereignty Matters: Locations of Contestations and Possibility in Indigenous Struggles for Self-Determination* (Lincoln, University of Nebraska Press, 2005) 153–68

Okonkwo, C, *Decolonising Agonistics in Postcolonial Fiction* (London, Palgrave Macmillan, 1999)

Oskal, N, 'Political Inclusion of the Saami as Indigenous People in Norway' (2001) 8 *International Journal on Minority and Group Rights* 235

Page, E, *Policy without Politicians: Bureaucratic Influence in Comparative Perspective* (Oxford, Oxford University Press, 2012)

Parliamentary Joint Committee on Human Rights, '2016 Review of Stronger Futures Measures' (Commonwealth of Australia, 16 March 2016)

Pearson, N, 'Reconciliation: To Be or Not to Be – Nation, Self-Determination or Self-Government' (1993) 3 *Aboriginal Law Bulletin* 14

—— 'Remote Control: Ten Years of Struggle and Success in Indigenous Australia' *The Monthly* (No 111, May 2015) 28–37

—— 'In Pursuit of Regional, Reciprocal Responsibility Settlement for Cape York' (speech delivered at the National Native Title Conference, Port Douglas, 18 June 2015)

—— 'Betrayal' *The Monthly* (No 140, December 2017) 24–34

Perkins, C, *A Bastard Like Me* (Sydney, Ure Smith, 1975)

Permanent Forum on Indigenous Issues, 'Report of the International Workshop on Methodologies Regarding Free, Prior and Informed Consent and Indigenous Peoples' (New York, 17–19 January 2005), UN Doc E/C.19/2005/3

Peterson, N and Sanders, W, 'Introduction' in N Peterson and W Sanders (eds), *Citizenship and Indigenous Australians: Changing Conceptions and Possibilities* (Cambridge, Cambridge University Press, 1998) 1–32

Petersson, O, 'Rational Politics: Commissions of Inquiry and the Referral System in Sweden' in J Pierre (ed), *The Oxford Handbook of Swedish Politics* (Oxford, Oxford University Press, 2015) 650–62

Phillips, A, *The Politics of Presence* (Oxford, Oxford University Press, 1995)

Pikkarainen, H and Brodin, B, 'Discrimination of the Sámi – The Rights of the Sámi from a Discrimination Perspective' (Discrimination Ombudsman, 2008)

Pitkin, H, *The Concept of Representation* (Berkeley, University of California Press, 1967)

Pitty, R and Smith, S, 'The Indigenous Challenge to Westphalian Sovereignty' (2011) 46 *Australian Journal of Political Science* 121

Porter, R, 'The Meaning of Indigenous Nation Sovereignty' (2002) 34 *Arizona State Law Journal* 75

Powell, M, 'Rhetorics of Survivance: How American Indians Use Writing' (2002) 53 *College Composition and Communication* 396

Pratt, A, 'Make or Break? A Background to the ATSIC Changes and the ATSIC Review' (Parliamentary Library, Current Issues Brief No 29, 2003)

Prime Minister, Attorney-General, Minister for Indigenous Affairs, 'Response to Referendum Council's report on Constitutional Recognition' (media release, 26 October 2017)

Rajanayagam, S, 'Does Parliament Do Enough? Evaluating Statements of Compatibility under the *Human Rights (Parliamentary Scrutiny) Act 2011*' (2015) 38 *UNSW Law Journal* 1046

Read, P, *Charles Perkins: A Biography* (Melbourne, Viking, 1990)

Referendum Council, 'Broome Regional Dialogue Discusses Constitutional Reform' (media release, 13 February 2017)

—— 'First Nations Regional Dialogue in Dubbo' (media release, 17–19 February 2017)

Referendum Council, 'First Nations Regional Dialogue in Darwin' (media release, 22–24 February 2017)

—— 'First Nations Regional Dialogue in Perth' (media release, 3–5 March 2017)

—— 'First Nations Regional Dialogue in Sydney' (media release, 10–12 March 2017)

—— 'Constitutional Reform Must Lead to Real Change' (media release, 20 March 2017)

—— 'Delegates Determine Self-Determination is a Priority' (media release, 28 March 2017)

—— 'Constitutional Reform: Speaking the Same Language' (media release, 7 April 2017)

—— 'Structural Reform Will Improve State and Commonwealth Decision Making' (media release, 10 April 2017)

—— 'Final Report of the Referendum Council' (Commonwealth, 2017)

Reilly, A, 'Dedicated Seats in the Federal Parliament for Indigenous Australians: The Theoretical Case and its Practical Possibility' (2001) 2 *Balayi: Culture Law and Colonialism* 73

—— 'A Constitutional Framework for Indigenous Governance' (2006) 28 *Sydney Law Review* 403

Rigney, L-I, 'Epilogue: Can the Settler State Settle with Whom it Colonises? Reasons for Hope and Priorities for Action' in S Maddison and M Brigg (eds), *Unsettling the Settler State* (Annandale, Federation Press, 2011) 206–11

Riksrevisionen, 'Revisionsrapport Sametingets årsredovisning 2009' (2010)

Robbins, J, 'Indigenous Political Representation in Liberal–Democratic Countries: A Comparative Analysis' in M Berg-Nordlie, J Saglie and A Sullivan (eds), *Indigenous Politics: Institutions, Representation, Mobilisation* (Colchester, ECPR Press, 2015) 61–94

Roman, A, 'The Determinants of Public Administrators' Participation in Policy Formulation' (2017) 47 *American Review of Public Administration* 102

Roughan, N, 'From Authority to Authorities: Bridging the Social/Normative Divide' in R Cotterrell and M Del Mar (eds), *Authority in Transnational Legal Theory: Theorising Across Disciplines* (Cheltenham, Edward Elgar, 2016) 280–99

'Rovdjuren och deras förvaltning' (SOU 2007:89)

Rowley, C, *The Remote Aborigines: Aboriginal Policy and Practice – Volume III* (Canberra, ANU Press, 1971)

Rowse, T, *Remote Possibilities: The Aboriginal Domain and the Administrative Imagination* (Darwin, North Australia Research Unit, 1992)

—— 'The Political Identity of Regional Councillors' in P Sullivan (ed), *Shooting the Banker: Essays on ATSIC and Self-Determination* (Darwin, North Australian Research Unit, 1996) 42–69

—— '"Out of Hand" – The Battles of Neville Bonner' (1997) 21 *Journal of Australian Studies* 96

—— *Obliged to be Difficult: Nugget Coombs' Legacy in Indigenous Affairs* (Cambridge, Cambridge University Press, 2000)

—— 'The Indigenous Sector' in D Austin-Broos and G Macdonald (eds), *Culture, Economy and Governance in Aboriginal Australia* (Sydney, Sydney University Press, 2005) 213–30

Ruong, I, *Samerna i historien och nutiden* (Stockholm, Bonnier Fakta, 1982)

Ruru, J, 'A Treaty in Another Context: Creating Reimagined Treaty Relationships in Aotearoa New Zealand' in J Borrows and M Coyle (eds), *The Right Relationship: Reimagining the Implementation of Historical Treaties* (Toronto, University of Toronto Press, 2017) 305

Ruska, P and Clayton-Dixon, C, 'Words of the Struggle' (2015) 1 *Black Nations Rising* 10

Russell, M, Glover, D and Wollter, K, 'Does the Executive Dominate the Westminster Legislative Process? Six Reasons for Doubt' (2016) 69 *Parliamentary Affairs* 286

Sámediggi, 'The Sámi Parliament's Living Environment Program: Eallinbiras' (adopted by the Parliament 19 February 2009)

—— 'Árbediehtu: Policydokument för traditionell kunskap' (2010)

—— 'Samisk Språkhandbok för förvaltningsmyndigheter' (2010)

—— 'Minerals and Mines in Sápmi: The Viewpoint of the Swedish Sami Parliament' (adopted by the Plenary Assembly in Åre, Sweden, 20 May 2014)

—— 'Ändringar i bestämmelser om val till Sametinget' (2018)
Sámi Rights Commission, 'Samerätt och Sameting' (SOU 1989:41)
Sámi Rights Committee, 'Den Nye Sameretten' (NOU 2007:13)
Sabin, J, 'A Federation within a Federation? Devolution and Indigenous Government in the Northwest Territories' (Institute for Research on Public Policy, No 66, November 2017)
'Sametingets roll i det svenska folkstyret' (SOU 2002:77)
Sanders, W, 'Reconciling Public Accountability and Aboriginal Self-Determination/Self-Management: Is ATSIC Succeeding?' (1994) 53 *Australian Journal of Public Administration* 475
—— 'Reshaping Governance in Torres Strait: The Torres Strait Regional Authority and Beyond' (Centre for Aboriginal Economic Policy Research, Discussion Paper No 74, 1994)
—— 'Towards an Indigenous Order of Government: Rethinking Self-Determination as Indigenous Affairs Policy' (Centre for Aboriginal Economic Policy Research, Discussion Paper No 230, 2002)
—— 'The Tasmanian Electoral Roll Trial in the 2002 ATSIC Elections' (Centre for Aboriginal Economic Policy Research, Discussion Paper No 245, 2003)
—— 'Participation and Representation in the 2002 ATSIC Elections' (Centre for Aboriginal Economic Policy Research, Discussion Paper No 252, 2003)
—— 'ATSIC's Achievements and Strengths: Implications for Institutional Reform' (Centre for Aboriginal Economic Policy Research, 2004)
—— 'Being a Good Senior Manager in Indigenous Community Governance: Working with Public Purpose and Private Benefit' (2008) 67 *Australian Journal of Public Administration* 173
—— 'Changing Agendas in Australian Indigenous Policy: Federalism, Competing Principles and Generational Dynamics' (2013) 72 *Australian Journal of Public Administration* 156
—— 'Electoral Administration and Aboriginal Voting Power in the Northern Territory: Reality and Potential Viewed from the 2019 Federal Election' (Centre for Aboriginal Economic Policy Research, Working Paper No 132, 2019)
Sanders, W, Taylor, J and Ross, K, 'Participation and Representation in ATSIC Elections: A 10 Year Perspective' (2000) 35 *Australian Journal of Political Science* 493
Sandström, C and Widmark, C, 'Stakeholders' Perceptions of Consultations as Tools for Co-Management: A Case Study of the Forestry and Reindeer Herding Sectors in Northern Sweden' (2007) 10 *Forest Policy and Economics* 25
Santow, E, 'The Australian Human Rights Commission' in M Groves, J Boughey and D Meagher (eds), *The Legal Protection of Rights in Australia* (Oxford, Hart Publishing, 2019) 123–42
Saunders, C, 'Indigenous Constitutional Recognition 1: The Concept of Consultation' (2016) 8 *Indigenous Law Bulletin* 19
Sara, MN, 'Siida and Traditional Sámi Reindeer Herding Knowledge' (2009) 30 *The Northern Review* 153
Schwartz, M, *A Question of Power: The Geoff Clark Case* (Melbourne, Black Inc, 2008)
Scott, C, 'Indigenous Self-Determination and Decolonisation of the International Imagination: A Plea' (1996) 18 *Human Rights Quarterly* 814
Sellers, J and Lidström, A, 'Decentralisation, Local Government and the Welfare State' (2007) 20 *Governance* 609
Senate Finance and Public Administration Legislation Committee, Parliament of Australia, 'Estimates' (26 October 2018)
—— 'Commonwealth Indigenous Advancement Strategy Tendering Process' (March 2016)
Senate Select Committee on the Administration of Aboriginal Affairs, Parliament of Australia, 'Administration of Aboriginal Affairs' (1989)
—— 'After ATSIC – Life in the Mainstream?' (2005)
Senate Standing Committee on Constitutional and Legal Affairs, Parliament of Australia, 'Two Hundred Years Later …' (1983)
Senate Standing Committee for the Scrutiny of Bills, Parliament of Australia, 'Final Report – Inquiry into the Future Role and Direction of the Senate Scrutiny of Bills Committee' (May 2012)

Sidoti, E, 'Indigenous Political Representation: A Parliamentary Option' (Whitlam Institute, 21 January 2008)

Sillanpää, L, *Political and Administrative Responses to Sámi Self-Determination: A Comparative Study of Public Administrations in Fennoscandia on the Issue of Sámi Land Title as an Aboriginal Right* (Helsinki, Finnish Society of Science and Letters, 1994)

—— 'A Comparative Analysis of Indigenous Rights in Fennoscandia' (1997) 20 *Scandinavian Political Studies* 197

Simpson, A, 'Parliaments' in Saunders, C and Stone, A, (eds), *The Oxford Handbook of the Australian Constitution* (Oxford, Oxford University Press, 2018) 563–86

Simpson, A, 'On Ethnographic Refusal: Indigeneity, "Voice" and Colonial Citizenship' (2007) 9 *Junctures* 67

—— *Mohawk* Interruptus*: Political Life Across the Border of Settler States* (Durham, Duke University Press, 2014)

Simpson, L, *Dancing On Our Turtle's Back: Stories of Nishnaabeg Re-Creation, Resurgence and a New Emergence* (Winnipeg, ARP Books, 2011)

Simon, P, 'Collecting Ethnic Statistics in Europe: A Review' (2012) 35 *Ethnic and Racial Studies* 1366

Slowey, G, 'A Fine Balance? Aboriginal Peoples in the Canadian North and the Dilemma of Development' in Timpson, AM (ed), *First Nations, First Thoughts: The Impact of Indigenous Thought in Canada* (Vancouver, University of British Columbia Press, 2009) 229–47

Smets, K and van Ham, C, 'The Embarrassment of Riches? A Meta-Analysis of Individual-Level Research on Voter Turnout' (2013) 32 *Electoral Studies* 344

Smith, D, *The Fiscal Equalisation Model: Options for ATSIC: Future Funding Policy and Practice* (Centre for Aboriginal Economic Policy Research, Discussion Paper No 30, 1993)

—— 'From Cultural Diversity to Regionalism: The Political Culture of Difference in ATSIC' in P Sullivan (ed), *Shooting the Banker* (North Australian Research Unit, 1996) 17–41

—— 'Community Participation Agreements: A Model for Welfare Reform from Community-Based Research' (Centre for Aboriginal Economic Policy Research, Discussion Paper No 223, 2001)

—— 'Jurisdictional Devolution: Towards an Effective Model for Indigenous Community Self-Governance' (Centre for Aboriginal Economic Policy Research Discussion Paper No 233, 2002)

—— 'Researching Australian Indigenous Governance: A Methodological and Conceptual Framework' (Centre for Aboriginal Economic Policy Research Working Paper No 29, 2005)

—— *Organising Aboriginal Governance: Pathways to Self-Determination Success in the Northern Territory, Australia* (Final Report to the Aboriginal Governance and Management Program, Aboriginal Peak Organisations of the Northern Territory, March 2015)

Smith, LT, *Decolonizing Methodologies: Research and Indigenous Peoples* (Dunedin, University of Otago Press, 1999)

South Australian Treaty Commissioner, 'Talking Treaty: Summary of Engagements and Next Steps' (Office of the Treaty Commissioner, 2017)

Spigelman, J, 'The Integrity Branch of Government' (2004) 78 *Australian Law Journal* 724

Stacey, R, 'Honour in Sovereignty: Can Crown Consultations with Indigenous Peoples Erase Canada's Sovereignty Deficit?' (2018) 68 *University of Toronto Law Journal* 405

Statskontoret, 'Myndighetsanalys av Sametinget' (2010:15)

Stellios, J, *Zines's The High Court and the Constitution*, 6th edn (Annandale, Federation Press, 2015)

Stepien, A, Petrétei, A and Koivurova, T, 'Sami Parliaments in Finland, Norway and Sweden' in T Malloy, A Osipov and B Vizi (eds), *Managing Diversity through Non-Territorial Autonomy: Assessing Advantage, Deficiencies and Risks* (Oxford, Oxford University Press, 2015) 117–38

Strelein, L, 'Missed Meaning: The Language of Sovereignty in the Treaty Debate' (2002/03) 20 *Arena* 83

Suchman, M, 'Managing Legitimacy: Strategic and Institutional Approaches' (1995) 20 *Academy of Management Review* 571

Svara, J, 'The Politics-Administration Dichotomy Model as Aberration' (1998) 58 *Public Administration Review* 51

Svenska Sametingets Kommitté, 'Förslag till strategi för en implementering av det samiska folkets rätt till självbestämmande påden svenska sidan av Sápmi' (May 2004)

Svenska Samernas Riksförbund, 'Förändring av Sametingets Funktion och Organisation' (2012)

Tatz, C, (ed), *Black Viewpoints: The Aboriginal Experience* (Sydney, ANZ Book Company, 1975)

Technical Advisers, Submission No 206 to Joint Select Committee on Constitutional Recognition Relating to Aboriginal and Torres Strait Islander Peoples, 11 June 2018

Thomas, A, Jakubowicz, A and Norman, H, *Does the Media Fail Aboriginal Political Aspirations? 45 Years of News Media Reporting of Key Political Moments* (Canberra, Aboriginal Studies Press, 2020)

Tickner, R, *Taking a Stand: Land Rights to Reconciliation* (Crows Nest, Allen & Unwin, 2001)

Tierney, S, 'Federalism and the Plurinational Challenge' in A Lev (ed), *The Federal Idea: Public Law Between Governance and Political Life* (Oxford, Hart Publishing, 2017) 227–41

Tomas, N, 'Māori Concepts and Practices of *Rangatiratanga*: "Sovereignty"?' in J Evans, A Genovese, A Reilly and P Wolfe (eds), *Sovereignty: Frontiers of Possibility* (Honolulu, University of Hawai'i Press, 2013) 220–49

Topf, R, 'Electoral Participation' in H-D Klingemann and D Fuchs (eds), *Citizens and the State: Beliefs in Government* (Oxford, Oxford University Press, 1995) 27

Trask, H-K, *From A Native Daughter: Colonialism and Sovereignty in Hawai'i* (Honolulu, University of Hawai'i Press, 1999)

Truth and Reconciliation Commission of Canada, 'Canada's Residential Schools: Reconciliation' (2015)

Tuck, E and Yang, KW, 'Decolonisation is not a Metaphor' (2012) 1 *Decolonisation: Indigeneity, Education & Society* 1

Tully, J, 'Reconsidering the BC Treaty Process' in *Speaking Truth to Power: A Treaty Forum* (British Columbia Treaty Commission, 2000) 3

Turnbull, M and Shorten, B, 'Referendum Council' (media release, 7 December 2015)

Turner, D, *This Is Not a Peace Pipe: Towards a Critical Indigenous Philosophy* (Toronto, University of Toronto Press, 2006)

Turpel, ME, 'Aboriginal Peoples and the Canadian Charter of Rights and Freedoms: Contradictions and Challenges' (1989) 10 *Canadian Women's Studies* 149

Twomey, A, 'An Indigenous Advisory Body: Addressing the Concerns About Justiciability and Parliamentary Sovereignty' (2015) 8 *Indigenous Law Bulletin* 6

United Nations, *State of the World's Indigenous Peoples* (Department of Economic and Social Affairs, 2009)

Uphold and Recognise, *Hearing Indigenous Voices: Options for Discussion* (2018)

Vivian, A, Jorgensen, M, Reilly, A, McMillan, M, McRae, C and McMinn, J, 'Indigenous Self-Government in the Australian Federation' (2017) 20 *Australian Indigenous Law Review* 215

Vizenor, G, 'The Ruins of Representation: Shadow Survivance and the Literature of Dominance' (1993) 17 *American Indian Quarterly* 7

Veth, P and O'Connor, S, 'The Past 50,000 Years: An Archaeological View' in A Bashford and S Macintyre (eds), *The Cambridge History of Australia: Volume 1: Indigenous and Colonial Australia* (Cambridge, Cambridge University Press, 2013) 17–42

Wallace, G, 'Nowra Circle Sentencing – Seven Years Down the Track' (2010) 7 *Indigenous Law Bulletin* 13

Walsh, T, 'The Impact of *Coleman v Power* on the Policing, Defence and Sentencing of Public Nuisance Cases in Queensland' (2006) 30 *Melbourne University Law Review* 191

Warrior, RA, 'Intellectual Sovereignty and the Struggle for an American Indian Future' (1992) 8 *Wicazo Sa Review* 1

Watson, I, 'There is No Possibility of Rights without Law: So Until Then, Don't Thumb Print or Sign Anything!' (2000) 5(1) *Indigenous Law Bulletin* 4

—— 'Settled and Unsettled Spaces: Are we Free to Roam?' in A Moreton-Robinson (ed), *Sovereign Subjects: Indigenous Sovereignty Matters* (Crows Nest, Allen & Unwin, 2007) 15–32

—— 'The 2007 Declaration on the Rights of Indigenous Peoples: Indigenous Survival – Where to from Here?' (2011) 20 *Griffith Law Review* 507

—— *Aboriginal Peoples, Colonialism and International Law: Raw Law* (Abingdon, Routledge, 2014)

Watson, V, 'Axing ATSIC: Australian Liberalism and the "Government of Unfreedom"' (2005) 23 *Policy and Society* 57

Weaver, S, 'Australian Aboriginal Policy: Aboriginal Pressure Groups or Government Advisory Bodies? Part I' (1983) 54 *Oceania* 1

—— 'Australian Aboriginal Policy: Aboriginal Pressure Groups or Government Advisory Bodies? Part II' (1983) 54 *Oceania* 85

Webber, J, *Reimagining Canada: Language, Culture, Community and the Canadian Constitution* (Montreal, McGill-Queen's University Press, 1994)

—— 'Beyond Regret: Mabo's Implications for Australian Constitutionalism' in D Ivison, P Patton and W Sanders (eds), *Political Theory and the Rights of Indigenous Peoples* (Cambridge, Cambridge University Press, 2000) 60–88

Westbury, N and Sanders, W, 'Governance and Service Delivery for Remote Aboriginal Communities in the Northern Territory: Challenges and Opportunities' (Centre for Aboriginal Economic Policy Research, Working Paper No 6, 2000)

White, G, 'And Now For Something Completely Northern: Institutions of Governance in the Territorial North' (2001) 35 *Journal of Canadian Studies* 80

—— 'Traditional Aboriginal Values in a Westminster Parliament: The Legislative Assembly of Nunavut' (2006) 12 *The Journal of Legislative Studies* 8

White, G and Hicks, J, *Made in Nunavut: An Experiment in Decentralised Government* (Vancouver, University of British Columbia, 2015)

Whittaker, A, 'White Law, Blak Arbiters, Grey Legal Subjects: Deep Colonisation's Role and Impact in Defining Aboriginality at Law' (2017) 20 *Australian Indigenous Law Review* 4

Williams, B, 'Realism and Moralism in Political Theory' in B Williams, *In the Beginning was the Deed: Realism and Moralism in Political Argument* (Princeton, Princeton University Press, 2007) 1–17

Williams, G, 'Race and the Australian Constitution: From Federation to Reconciliation' (2000) 38 *Osgoode Hall Law Journal* 643

—— 'Constitutional Recognition by way of an Indigenous Advisory Body?' (2016) 8 *Indigenous Law Bulletin* 12

Williams, G and Hobbs, H, *Treaty*, 2nd edn (Alexandria, Federation Press, 2020)

Williams, G and Hume, D, *Human Rights under the Australian Constitution*, 2nd edn (Oxford, Oxford University Press, 2013)

Williams, G and Reynolds, D, 'The Operation and Impact of Australia's Parliamentary Scrutiny Regime for Human Rights' (2016) 41 *Monash University Law Review* 469

Williams Jr, R, *Linking Arms Together: American Indian Treaty Visions of Law and Peace, 1600–1800* (Oxford, Oxford University Press, 1997)

Wolfe, P, 'Nation and MiscegeNation: Discursive Continuity in the Post-*Mabo* Era' (1994) 36 *Social Analysis* 93

—— 'Settler Colonialism and the Elimination of the Native' (2006) 8 *Journal of Genocide Research* 387

Wooten, H, 'Self-determination after ATSIC' (2004) 23 *Dialogue: Academy of the Social Sciences* 16

Wright, BC and Fowler, PE (eds), *House of Representatives Practice*, 6th edn (Department of the House of Representatives, 2012)

Young, S, 'The Sioux's Suits: Global Law and the Dakota Access Pipeline' (2017) 6 *American Indian Law Journal* 173

Yunupingu, G, 'Introduction' in G Yunupingu (ed), *Our Land Is Our Life: Land Rights – Past, Present and Future* (Brisbane University of Queensland Press, 1997) xv–xviii

Index

Introductory Note

References such as '178–79' indicate (not necessarily continuous) discussion of a topic across a range of pages. Wherever possible in the case of topics with many references, these have either been divided into sub-topics or only the most significant discussions of the topic are listed. Because the entire work is about the 'Indigenous aspirations' and 'Australia', the use of these terms (and certain others which occur constantly throughout the book) as an entry point has been minimised. Information will be found under the corresponding detailed topics.

www.ingramcontent.com/pod-product-compliance
Lightning Source LLC
LaVergne TN
LVHW011749200926
848484LV00003B/661

9781509940141